The Discourse Trap and the US Military

The Discourse Trap and the US Military
From the War on Terror to the Surge

By Jeffrey H. Michaels

THE DISCOURSE TRAP AND THE US MILITARY
Copyright © Jeffrey H. Michaels, 2013.

All rights reserved.

First published in 2013 by PALGRAVE MACMILLAN®
in the United States—a division of St. Martin's Press LLC,
175 Fifth Avenue, New York, NY 10010.

Where this book is distributed in the UK, Europe and the rest of the world, this is by Palgrave Macmillan, a division of Macmillan Publishers Limited, registered in England, company number 785998, of Houndmills, Basingstoke, Hampshire RG21 6XS.

Palgrave Macmillan is the global academic imprint of the above companies and has companies and representatives throughout the world.

Palgrave® and Macmillan® are registered trademarks in the United States, the United Kingdom, Europe and other countries.

ISBN-13: 978-0230-37204-7

Library of Congress Cataloging-in-Publication Data

Michaels, Jeffrey H.
  The discourse trap and the US military: from the War on Terror to the surge / by Jeffrey H. Michaels.
      p. cm.
  ISBN 978–0–230–37204–7 (alk. paper)
  1. United States. Dept. of Defense—History—21st century. 2. United States—Armed Forces—Public relations—History—21st century.
3. Military planning—United States—History—21st century. 4. United States—Military policy—Decision making. 5. Military doctrine—United States—History—21st century. 6. Afghan War, 2001—United States.
7. Iraq War, 2003–2011—United States. 8. War on Terrorism, 2001–2009. 9. Discourse analysis, Narrative. I. Title.

UA23.6.M555 2013
355.601'4—dc23   2012039050

A catalogue record of the book is available from the British Library.

Design by Scribe Inc.

First edition: March 2013

10 9 8 7 6 5 4 3 2 1

Contents

Acknowledgments		vii
1	Introduction	1
2	Global War on Terrorism	17
3	Shock and Awe	81
4	Characterizing the Irregular Adversary in Iraq	107
5	The Surge: From Iraq to Afghanistan	147
6	Conclusion	167
Notes		175
Bibliography		221
Index		257

Acknowledgments

My original interest in the impact of discourse and terminology on the US Defense Department stemmed from my own experience working in the sub-basement of the Pentagon during the period 2004–5. However, it was only in the course of my doctoral research in the Department of War Studies at King's College London that I was able to move from the world of practice to the world of theory and explore the wider implications of the discursive entrapment I had witnessed firsthand. The completion of this book, based largely on my doctoral thesis "The Discourse Trap: Constitutive Effects of Terminology Development, Dissemination and Control in the US Defense Department 2001–2006," would not have been possible without the support of many individuals. First and foremost, I am greatly beholden to my supervisor, Professor Sir Lawrence Freedman, for his brilliant guidance, encouragement, generosity, friendship, and remarkable patience over the course of many years. I am also grateful for the critiques provided by my thesis examiners Theo Farrell and Stuart Croft. Numerous friends and colleagues were also kind enough to read and comment on my PhD manuscript and subsequent revisions. Special thanks must go to Marcus Faulkner, Matthew Ford, David Ucko, Joshua Geltzer, Samir Puri, Lowell Schwartz, Tim Sweijs, and Rudra Chaudhuri. Numerous officials and former colleagues in the Department of Defense who will remain nameless provided both source material and guidance and their assistance proved invaluable for my research. In addition, the support of Peter B. Martin in initially opening up many doors in Washington, DC, for me effectively started the chain reaction that eventually led to this book. On a more personal note, thanks are due to my parents, Alan and Kathy, as well as other members of my family, for their unwavering love and enduring support.

CHAPTER 1

Introduction

In *Makers of Modern Strategy*, John Shy and Thomas W. Collier make a brief mention of the importance of language in "revolutionary war," claiming that words are weapons. They state, "Language is used to isolate and confuse enemies, rally and motivate friends, and enlist the support of wavering bystanders." Rather than being merely a tool of war, they also argue that language can shape a war: "But the same language directs—or misdirects—military effort; the rhetoric of political conflict becomes the reality of strategic theory."[1] This observation is one of the primary ideas informing this study. It is my contention that the importance political and military systems attach to the creation, dissemination, and control of language in war extends beyond "revolutionary war" and instead is a key feature of conflict more generally. Once introduced into the political-military discourse, words can shape a battlefield and be battled over themselves. This terminological phenomenon has so far received scant academic attention and represents a gap in the existing war studies literature.

This book aims to bridge this gap by examining how the discourses devised for political or military reasons can have a much greater, and in many ways, different impact than was intended when the discourse was first introduced. It will argue that discourse plays an integral role in conflict, direct as well as indirect. Discourse can take on a life of its own, forcing political and military leaders and their associated institutions to fall victim to a "discourse trap." This phenomenon is defined as the action that is motivated or constrained primarily by the discursive constructs ostensibly created to serve the needs of policy makers. In some instances, political and military leaders may feel compelled to adopt policies and practices in order to justify or abide by their discourse. In other instances, the discourse, perhaps out of sheer repetition, creates a "self-fulfilling prophecy"—defined as "a false definition of the situation which makes the originally false conception come true"—and can seriously impair strategic and operational performance.[2] Nevertheless, it should be noted that, similar to Robert K. Merton's observation that "unforeseen consequences should not be identified with consequences which are necessarily undesirable," the effects of the "discourse trap" might be undesired but not always undesirable.[3]

This study will attempt to establish the existence of the discourse trap by providing a framework for identifying the phenomenon and its associated effects and demonstrating the ways in which it impacts the conduct and study of warfare and strategy. Specifically, the discourse trap will be examined through the prism of contemporary US military operations. The cases to be studied are "Global War on Terrorism," "Shock and Awe," "Characterizing the Irregular Adversary in Iraq," and the "Surge." This introduction chapter will begin by establishing a framework to clarify how the discourse trap functions, which will then allow subsequent investigation into how it impacted the US military. The relevance of discourse to war must also be firmly established, particularly as the literature on this subject is limited as a result of scholars' reliance on a traditionally narrow approach to the function of language.

Discourse and War

Why is the study of discourse relevant to the study of war? After all, in the rich war studies literature, very little attention has been devoted to this subject. In comparison to the study of the nature and character of war, military history, military capabilities, military sociology, and so forth, the study of discourse remains marginalized. At best, the study of discourse in war has been subordinated to other areas of enquiry, such as those aforementioned, rather than existing independently. One of the main reasons for this is that scholars tend to view the function of language in war in very limited terms. For most scholars, language is relevant mainly for the study of propaganda and public affairs. Thus, in order to mobilize and sustain support for a war, or to undermine an adversary, political and military systems employ certain types of language. However, as will be highlighted, such a conception of the function of language in war is too limited. Instead, by expanding this conception, numerous avenues of enquiry can emerge.

The term *discourse* is one that has acquired many different meanings and is often used by a single author in multiple ways.[4] To avoid confusion, for the purpose of this book, *discourse* simply refers to the language actors use to discuss certain issues and assign meanings to them. For instance, when referring to "counterterrorism discourse" in the context of the US Department of Defense (DoD), I am merely referring to the way defense officials talk and think about "counterterrorism" and what they mean by it. However, the very fact that defense officials are talking and thinking about an issue in terms of counterterrorism, as compared to "counterinsurgency," also necessitates viewing discourse from the perspective of the terminology employed by the actors being studied. This then raises the problem of the relationship between *discourse* and *terminology*. My argument is that the two are mutually constitutive. *Discourse* gives *terminology* its meaning, or to put it slightly differently, *terminology* only acquires meaning within *discourse*. Simultaneously, *terminology* provides the essential building block for *discourse*, since it is impossible to discuss an issue without employing a term to describe it. By way of illustration, to take the example of *counterterrorism* again, the term itself can have many different definitions assigned to it and also be used and understood in both positive and negative ways depending on who uses it and when. In this specific case, and as will be shown in Chapter 2, the way defense officials employed the term *counterterrorism* in the 1980s was very different from the way it was used after 9/11.

Yet the way in which a term is employed in discourse is one thing; that the term is used in the first place is quite another. The simple fact that officials are employing the term *counterterrorism*, as opposed to *counterinsurgency* or some other term, can have the effect of guiding the discourse in a particular direction. It is here that the possibility of a "trap" emerges, in which a discourse is perceived to be misguided yet is difficult to escape from. In the context of defense policy, officials may perceive that the term *counterterrorism* is inappropriate to employ, preferring instead *counterinsurgency*, which they feel more accurately reflects reality and the use of which would lead to a different set of actions potentially resulting in more favorable outcomes. However, for either intended (e.g., political objections) or unintended (e.g., the effect of socialization or indoctrination) reasons, officials may find themselves constrained by the discourse of *counterterrorism* and find it difficult if not impossible for a discourse of *counterinsurgency* to emerge. Attempting to change a discourse is made particularly difficult when it is competing against a "dominant" discourse, or a discourse that can be considered "mainstream" or "acceptable," especially if it has become institutionalized.

When considering how the discourse trap functions, it is important to note that any number of discourses could be the subject of investigation, and the field should not be limited to national security actors. Nevertheless, for the purpose of the present study, the discourses under examination, and specifically the terminology that contributes to these discourses, will be limited to the field of contemporary US defense policy. The terminology employed in this field derives in large part from both political actors (these include civilian defense policy makers such as Donald Rumsfeld, Paul Wolfowitz, and Douglas Feith) and bureaucratic actors (in this case, the uniformed military and career civil servants).

Whether intended or unintended, these actors are often the audience for the terminology they spawn, and the way in which they employ this language sets the terms of discourse in the defense policy-making process. This is particularly the case when the terminology is disseminated throughout the system and becomes institutionalized or becomes institutionalized and is then further disseminated. In the context of the Department of Defense (DoD), evidence of the institutionalization of terminology can be found in any number of areas, including official statements (congressional testimony, press statements), official documents (military plans, policy papers, doctrine, defense journals and magazines, military dictionaries, operational orders, intelligence reports), as part of the military education curriculum, and the titles or mission statements of bureaucratic offices. While the salience of a discourse can be observed when it becomes institutionalized, the consequence of its institutionalization confers legitimacy, which then results in the further entrenchment of the discourse. Over a period of time, a cumulative effect of discourse salience emerges. In other words, as officials repeat a discourse, it becomes legitimate, and potentially a dominant discourse. Once it attains dominance, criticism often becomes confined to operating within the discourse, rather than a critique of the discourse itself, since the legitimacy of the discourse has become internalized.[5]

Related to this is the problem of a marginalized discourse, in which certain topics are not seen to be of relevance and therefore are considered unworthy of significant attention. In bureaucratic terms, this often means a particular topic is not placed on policy makers' agendas because it does not seem important or urgent. To take one example, Peter Neumann and M. L. R. Smith demonstrate how "discourse failure," defined as "the constriction of the language and vocabulary used to identify, analyze, and accept that a significant threat existed," inhibited the United States in the 1990s from countering al-Qaeda. The practical effects of "discourse failure" on the intelligence process were severalfold: intelligence collectors devoted resources to irrelevant areas, analysts emphasized issues that seemed to be of higher priority, and policy makers dismissed reports concerning the evolving threat.[6]

It can be extremely difficult for political and military systems to make a paradigm shift due in large part to the discourse traps they have created for themselves. Yet it can be reasonably argued that the discourse is merely the product of a political or bureaucratic interest, and therefore when the interest changes, the discourse will change as well. Unfortunately, this argument presumes such a shift in discourse is automatic and painless, excluding the possibility that it may be difficult and have unintended consequences. In many cases, the specific circumstances that allowed a discourse to become dominant, and possibly institutionalized, may no longer be valid. However, escaping from the old discursive constructs in order to deal with new circumstances can be very difficult. In some cases, this requires adopting new terminology or giving new meanings to old terms. In other cases, it may mean delegitimizing an old discourse to legitimize a new one. Whether the motivations for doing so are structural or not, this process occurs and can have unintended consequences that can impede the transition between discourses and constrain action.

Of the terms examined in this study, the majority derive from politicians and not only permeate the political discourse but also filter into the bureaucratic discourse. Conversely, in a minority of cases, the terminology used within the bureaucracy percolates into the political discourse. Rather than being a unified entity, in which there is a consensus on the terminology employed, the government includes countless factional interests, whether political or bureaucratic, that employ certain terminology or give it a particular meaning, which runs counter to the terminology used or meanings applied by other factional interests. In each of these instances, the government, rather than the population, is the audience. It is important to recognize that this occurs whether intended or not. For instance, a political discourse intended for popular consumption can unwittingly enter the bureaucratic discourse and have unintended consequences.

Political actors are aware that the terminology used inside the bureaucracy can have negative political consequences if it enters the mainstream discourse, including the discourse of politicians from an opposition party. Recognizing this danger, political actors may seek to impose controls on the terminology employed within the bureaucracy. Bureaucratic actors may also recognize the danger of employing political language and choose to impose their own discursive constraints. Regardless of whether the actor is political or bureaucratic, there is a general recognition that employing terminology that is deemed inappropriate, for one reason or another, can have negative consequences and that to avoid these necessitates placing controls on the terminology used.

The negative consequences that can arise from policy makers' inappropriate use of terminology, specifically analogies and metaphors, have long been recognized in the literature on political psychology and decision making. A key finding of this literature that is of direct relevance here is that the language used by policy makers often constitutes their actions by providing a prism with which they view a particular situation as well as the means of dealing with it. As Ole Holsti notes, "even experts may well use . . . shortcuts to organize their attitudes. 'Domino theory,' 'lessons of Munich,' 'lessons of Vietnam' . . . are among the shortcuts that have served . . . to guide the thinking of more than a few policymakers and their expert advisers."[7] Yuen Foong Khong, who analyzed the analogies American policy makers brought to bear on the decision to intervene in Vietnam, provides one important illustration of cognitive psychology in wartime decision making. While recognizing the public advocacy aims of the analogies US policy makers used in order to justify their decisions to the citizenry, Khong's analysis clearly shows that the same analogies were used to frame the private debate among senior policy makers and had a causal impact on the information processing that preceded decisions and the choice of policy options. Within the bureaucracy, analogies were more than rhetoric or convenient figures of speech; they were devices for consensus building and facilitating decisions, though in many instances they were the subjects of intense and heated debate.[8] Similar to historical analogies, policy makers also rely on metaphors as a mental shortcut.[9] Metaphors with which a security problem is understood can shape the perceived nature of the problem and its solutions, focusing on the aspects that are highlighted and marginalizing or ignoring those that are downplayed or hidden in the metaphors' entailments.[10]

Assuming that bureaucratic politics is the underlying rationale for promoting one discourse at the expense of another, it is reasonable to expect policy makers to rely on mental shortcuts, such as employing an analogy, image, or metaphor that supports the policy they are trying to promote, and use others to denigrate policies they disagree with. In such cases there is a risk that the discourse being employed can constrain or misdirect action, especially as many of the terms employed are used in a subjective way for the purpose of marketing a policy. But even if cases exist where policy makers' motives are purely altruistic and there is no apparent bias in the selection of analogy, metaphor, and so on, there will still be unintended consequences. For example, the analogy itself may be inappropriate to the situation for one reason or other. Moreover, one policy maker's use of an analogy is likely to be very different from that of another policy maker, and so once introduced into the mainstream discourse, its original meaning is almost certain to be lost. In its relation to decision making, the discourse trap doesn't discriminate with regards to policy makers' motives. Whether altruistic in intention or not, policy makers will have to deal with the consequences of the discourses they employ.

The role of discourse in politics, especially the constraints discourse places on political systems broadly and politicians in particular, bears a remarkable similarity to the role played by "ideology." In fact, the two concepts overlap in many respects, regardless of the definition of *ideology* that is chosen. Among the mainstream definitions of *ideology*, two stand out. The first relates to ideology in the formal political sense (conservative, liberal, Marxist-Leninist, etc.). The second relates to false consciousness, or as Slavoj Žižek has referred to it, the "unknown knowns"; "the things we don't know that we know."[11] Similar to ideology, discourse can function at both the conscious and unconscious levels. Moreover, the language we employ can be impacted by our worldview, but it can also constitute our worldview. Attempting to discern the fine line between where ideology ends and discourse begins, or vice versa, is an impossible task and will not be attempted here. Suffice it to say, it is observable that the link between ideology and discourse exists, and therefore, when examining the constraints that discourse places on political action, one can draw from the literature on the role of ideological constraints.

This being the case, what are ideological constraints, and how do they influence behavior? In many political systems, to take a cynical view, the role of ideology may be limited to providing justification for policies that would otherwise be deemed unpopular or to being a tool for obtaining power, quietly discarded once power is obtained. However, political ideologies can often constrain policy makers, especially as they are usually a source of legitimacy. Politicians that come to power touting a political ideology probably do not want to be seen by their supporters as deviating from core principles. Consequently, politicians must expend great effort to ensure that the actions they take can be presented as being consistent with their officially stated principles. Likewise, politicians may feel they have no choice but to refrain from actions that might be pragmatically advantageous but are indefensible from an ideological perspective and therefore cannot be explained to their constituencies without a loss of credibility.

However, a problem arises here. As is well known, during the Cold War, for instance, the United States maintained relationships with "friendly" dictatorships and referred to these "allies" as "freedom-loving." Were US policy makers who made these positive references liars, or were they genuinely stating convictions? Put another way, if policy makers think and talk in certain ways, does this influence their actions, or can they keep separate the public justification from the power politics? It would probably be somewhat naïve to suggest that policy makers can remain completely unaffected by their habits of thought and speech and therefore indulge in unrestrained Machiavellian politics. There may be exceptions to this rule, but on the whole it is fair to assume policy makers are indeed affected by the ideological prisms and language they are socialized in. As such, the effect of political ideology, similar to the effect of political discourse, is to impose a general framework for the perception of reality. This framework can have the effect of setting limits on policy options, as well as defining goals, priorities, and the methods for achieving them.

William Isaac Thomas's theorem "If men define situations as real they are real in their consequences" has important implications for the study of war.[12] One of the principal arguments of this book is that the conduct of war is inseparable from the language of war. In other words, to understand war necessitates understanding the language. This understanding should not be limited to knowledge of how and why terms are consciously created, used, interpreted, misinterpreted, and controlled but also take into account the conscious and subconscious actions, reactions, and counteractions of actors involved in making war.

The critical impact of discourse, not only in framing conflicts, but also in determining the methods used to wage conflict, cannot be understated.

According to Riikka Kuusisto, "Official definitions of conflict situations, publicly declared motives, names given to the warring parties, and explanations concerning decisions made in the course of the hostilities—the rhetoric and discourses of war—play as important a role in the progression of events as do the physical acts of belligerency that accompany them . . . War rhetoric is an essential part of 'real war'; it takes hold of the theater, lays out the campaign, reports on the advances, and assesses the outcome."[13]

To take just one example of how this process works, one can examine how the names given to a conflict can impact the conflict itself. Apart from merely examining why the names were chosen in the first place, which in many instances necessitates examining political motivations, it is also essential to explore the way those names impact political and military systems' approaches to those conflicts at the strategic, operational, and tactical levels. As Carl von Clausewitz insisted, "the first, the supreme, the most far-reaching act of judgment that the statesman and Commander have to make is to establish . . . the kind of war on which they are embarking: neither mistaking it for, nor trying to turn it into, something that is alien to its nature. This is the first of all strategic questions and the most comprehensive."[14]

Among the many ways in which politicians and military leaders have fallen into the discourse trap is the adoption of inappropriate terminology to define the conflict they are about to enter or have already entered into. As noted, Clausewitz clearly highlighted the imperative for governments to accurately define the conflict. And yet numerous cases can be found where political and military systems continue to struggle with this task. While the continued existence of this problem might be explained away in terms of ignorance, the reality is that the way in which a conflict is defined has important political connotations, and therefore political imperatives often trump more objective characterizations.

Another aspect of the discourse trap that showcases the importance policy makers attach to the language they employ is the existence of those cases in which a taboo is placed on certain terms. In some cases, actors within political and military systems naturally refrain from using certain language; in others, there is a deliberate attempt to control or delegitimize it. To illustrate this point, it is worth briefly considering the case of the Clinton administration's response to the "genocide" in Rwanda. In 1994, American officials perceived use of the term *genocide* in relation to Rwanda would compel the Clinton administration to authorize military intervention. To avoid the unwanted prospect of military intervention, officials refrained from using the term publicly but eventually conceded to using "acts of genocide."[15] As this example demonstrates, the distinction between intervention and nonintervention was perceived to be dependent upon the use of a single word. Thus the word *genocide* was not to be uttered by any US officials. Given that the use of certain terminology may directly impact the range and nature of policies pursued, especially if there are important legal or public relations issues associated with the terminology, limiting a discourse can sometimes have the deliberate motive of taking a certain action, or avoiding taking it.

But can the attempt to control terminology create a new set of problems? This would appear to be the case, particularly in instances where political actors attempt to restrict the use of terminology within the bureaucracy. For example, if, due to political sensitivities, a problem cannot be labeled in terms that bureaucratic actors would normally apply, this may then limit the range of options available to a bureaucracy to deal with it, which in turn may cause the problem to persist or worsen. The time dimension is a crucial consideration, because the perceived short-term gain associated with advocating certain terms or restricting others may be offset by the long-term consequences. Indeed, the consequences may only become apparent months or years after the fact. In a purely political sense, the discourse adopted by a political administration may entrap successive administrations. The same principle holds true for bureaucratic actors.

Types of Discourse Traps

The discourse trap can take a number of forms given different circumstances. As such, it is necessary to understand how a discourse trap functions depending on such factors as the nature of the discourse, the nature of the audience, how the discourse is employed, and the time period in which its effects are felt. Therefore, this section will establish a typology for classifying the means by which a discourse trap can be understood.

At least three types of ways discourse traps can take effect are observable. These three types are not mutually exclusive and in some cases may overlap. They will henceforth be referred to as "blowback," "bandwagoning," and "marginalization." Although a combination of all three is unnecessary for a discourse trap to occur, the strength of the phenomenon, or its visibility, increases the more these effects are present. A brief explanation of each follows:

1. *Blowback:* There are two primary ways blowback can occur. In the first instance, the terminology employed by political or bureaucratic actors is used by opponents to undermine a particular policy. In this sense, the blowback represents a case of being condemned by your words. It is often out of fear of blowback that leaders attempt to place controls on or marginalize a particular discourse or a specific term. As noted earlier, these attempts at control and marginalization can create their own problems.

A second means of blowback can occur when a discourse is developed for purely instrumental reasons, possibly to serve a specific purpose for a limited duration, but then takes on a life of its own and deviates from its original purpose if not outright contradicts it.

2. *Bandwagoning:* In this type of discourse trap, political and bureaucratic actors perceive an advantage (politically, personally or bureaucratically) if they "bandwagon" on a popular discourse, perhaps fearing negative consequences of not doing so. To a degree, this reflects an instrumental means for political or bureaucratic actors to "market" themselves and "stay relevant." This type of trap functions in at least two ways. First, the original meaning and "ownership" of a discourse becomes lost the more actors associate themselves with it. For instance, actors may choose to assign it new meanings and use it in different contexts than had been previously used in. As the original meaning is lost, or results in a situation in which numerous actors attempt to assign competing meanings, there is a serious risk of confusion, miscommunication, and misapplication, if not outright confrontation. There is also the risk that as more meanings are attached to a discourse, the discourse itself gradually becomes devoid of substance. Second, the result of more actors adopting a discourse is its likelihood not only of being institutionalized but also of becoming a dominant discourse that becomes immune to criticism. Consequently, debates occur within a discourse, rather than about whether the discourse itself is relevant. In such an instance, policy makers may feel that a discourse, even if counterproductive, cannot be criticized and that changes can only be effected within the discourse, which thereby necessitates a de facto acceptance of the discourse, a circumstance that policy makers may perceive to be a policy constraint.

3. *Marginalization:* When a discourse becomes dominant, this may have the effect of marginalizing alternative discourses. In some cases, the marginalization of an alternative discourse may be unintentional, whereas in others it may be deliberate. In other words, when attempting to promote a certain discourse, information that either contradicts the discourse or advocates for an alternative discourse not in the interests of a political or bureaucratic interest group will be marginalized, possibly to include the formation of a counterdiscourse intended to undermine the dissident faction. The important point here is that the consequences of deliberately marginalizing a discourse should not necessarily be examined from a subjective point of view, or one that would suggest that an alternative discourse would promote better policies; rather it should be examined from the objective perspective that marginalizing an alternative discourse means it cannot become a part of the debate in the first place. It follows that for policy makers intent on

promoting their policies, the policy options they present must be framed within an "acceptable" discourse, as policy options that fall outside either are ruled out as being unacceptable or face an uphill struggle to be recognized as legitimate.

All these types of discourse trap, though divergent in many respects, have one feature in common. They all demonstrate that the discourses created to serve the needs of policy makers or bureaucrats can have the unintended consequence of constraining or misdirecting action.

Historical Precedents of Discursive Entrapment

Although this study focuses on the post-9/11 period, it is important to highlight right from the start that the discourse trap is an enduring problem with a long history and that many of the same problems that will be addressed in the case studies are also observable in similar situations decades earlier. Therefore, it is worthwhile to briefly highlight some of the ways in which the United States has suffered as a result of this phenomenon by examining several aspects of its Cold War policies, particularly in Vietnam. This section will discuss some of the problems that arose as a result of the official characterizations of the conflict, as well as how allies and adversaries featured in US political-military discourse.

To begin with, it is worth considering American conceptions of the "Soviet threat" after the Second World War. A number of scholars have argued that successive American administrations deliberately exaggerated the Soviet threat, and these conceptions that were designed to elicit public and congressional support often came to be accepted as important truths by those who advanced them or by their successors. To put it slightly differently, the rhetoric employed to sell the "threat" took on a life of its own and actually had a boomerang effect on the policies meant to counter that threat. This boomerang effect resulted in numerous practical problems, including distortion of policy makers' understanding of reality, distortion of national priorities leading to the misallocation of resources within the national security realm, creation of self-fulfilling prophecies (the very argument that US credibility is at stake actually puts it at stake), generation of needless conflicts among allies who did not share the same exaggerated perception of the threat, undermining the believability of US foreign policy and creating a credibility gap, and forcing policy makers to overlook mutual interests with the USSR, thereby accentuating the conflict.[16]

The impact of the "domino theory" on US policy, especially with regards policy toward Vietnam, provides one of the most important illustrations of how this negative process functioned. It is almost inconceivable to understand the motivation behind the US involvement in Vietnam without at least acknowledging the role played by the dominant discourse of the domino theory in US Cold War thinking. Regardless of whether the interest in Vietnam was geopolitical, economic, or some similar reason, depending on one's interpretation, the way in which this issue was framed in the discourse of US policy makers at the time is quite revealing. Even if US officials did not believe in the domino theory, its use as a rationale provided the atmosphere and the background within which these officials operated. As Leslie Gelb and Richard K. Betts observed, "Words and deeds were making Vietnam into a showcase—an Asian Berlin. Consequently it became a test case as well of US credibility . . . Each successive President, initially caught by his own beliefs, was further ensnared by his own rhetoric, and the basis for the beliefs went unchallenged."[17]

Similar to the discourse trap, Jack Snyder highlights that the blowback of propaganda, the "blurring of the line between fact and fiction . . . sincere beliefs and tactical argument," entraps political leaders not only in their own confusions but in the political context they helped create.[18] He recounts how the Eisenhower administration highlighted the discourse of falling dominoes primarily as a matter of political expediency rather than out of genuine belief. Unfortunately, conditioned by a decade of Cold War rhetoric, the next generation of policy makers not only were "true-believing Cold Warriors" but were also constrained in their policy options due to the anticommunist discourse then prevailing in which "losing Vietnam" was not an option.[19] It is interesting that, in reply to President Lyndon Johnson's 1964 query to the Central Intelligence Agency (CIA) about the consequences for Southeast Asia if South Vietnam fell, the answer was that "with the possible exception of Cambodia, it is likely that no nation in the area would quickly succumb to Communism." However, despite the CIA's doubts that called the domino theory into question, "the impact of those doubts on policymakers was nil."[20] The problem with the domino theory was that, regardless of whether or not it had any basis in fact, its use by officials for public relations purposes created credibility issues, and therefore any doubts about it could not be officially expressed. On the one hand, undermining one of the chief rationales for the war called into question the credibility of the officials that had been making these claims. On the other hand, the United States had created a credibility trap for itself as a nation. Having showcased Vietnam as the key domino, it was difficult for officials to contemplate policies that would reduce the American role out of fear it would weaken the resolve of US allies.

It should come as no surprise that in relation to Vietnam, US policy makers both manipulated reality and deceived themselves as a result of their manipulation. As already noted, this was particularly the case in relation to US allies who were officially labeled as part of the "free world" and "defending democracy." For instance, the way in which the United States characterized its South

Vietnamese allies in glowing terms is particularly instructive. American support to South Vietnamese president Ngo Dinh Diem was predicated to a large extent on the public relations efforts beginning in the mid-1950s to sell him to the US public. In 1961, Vice President Lyndon Johnson went so far as to characterize Diem as the "Winston Churchill of Southeast Asia." In reality, Diem was highly corrupt and had little popular support apart from the country's Catholic minority, and his goals were often at cross purposes with those of the United States. Diplomats often found it frustrating to work with Diem, but due to the fact that he had numerous American backers and that the actual nature of his regime contradicted the official narrative of a "democracy," it was difficult to be critical internally and impossible to be critical in public. It was only when Diem's excesses became too visible, especially during the 1963 "Buddhist crisis," that the United States supported a military coup against him.[21] Thereafter, the United States would still stick to the official narrative of South Vietnam as a "free" and "democratic" country, whereas in reality the country was run by a series of military juntas with a heavy emphasis on repression and no system of checks and balances or oversight. The official characterization of South Vietnam as a democracy, despite the fact that the reality was very different, had important consequences for the failure of US officials to understand the adversary. Indeed it was the lack of democracy that was almost certainly one of the main reasons the Viet Cong insurgency was so strong in the first place and why there was only limited support for the South Vietnamese government among its population.[22]

Once it was committed to Vietnam, one key aspect of the American discourse was how the conflict was characterized. As Jeffrey Record observed, "perhaps no other issue has more bedevilled discussion of the Vietnam War than that of what kind of war it was."[23] Record notes those who believed the war "was morally noble or at least militarily winnable" characterized the conflict as a case of "international aggression," whereas those who believed that the war was unwinnable, or that the United States had no business in Vietnam, labeled it as a "civil war among Vietnamese."[24] In 1965, Hans Morgenthau derided Washington's changing the character of the war in Vietnam by "unilateral declaration from a South Vietnamese civil war to a war of foreign aggression," as a "glaring instance of the tendency to conduct foreign and military policy . . . as exercises in public relations."[25] But why was it deemed necessary to change the characterization of the conflict? It is unlikely the circumstances on the ground had altered in any significant way. A more likely explanation is that in order to obtain public support for the military intervention, it was perceived as necessary to change the characterization of the conflict. But, as Record notes, the official discursive shift from "civil war" to a war of "foreign aggression" had negative consequences for US strategy: "By refusing to recognize or admit that the Vietnam War was from its inception primarily a civil war . . . policymakers assumed that North Vietnam, was, like the United States, waging a limited war, and therefore would be prepared to settle for something less than total victory . . . In so making this assumption, policymakers . . . excused themselves from confronting the harsh truth that civil wars are, for their indigenous participants, total wars."[26] By not grasping this crucial distinction, US policy makers underestimated the adversary's capacity to prevail while overestimating their own. Moreover, the US military strategy of gradual escalation was predicated on the war being limited and therefore unlikely to succeed in the "total war" actually being fought. Larry Cable argues Washington's misrepresentation of the conflict as a "partisan war" rather than "insurgency" had the operational consequence of focusing the bulk of military operations on North Vietnam rather than on counterinsurgency in South Vietnam.[27]

The characterizations of the "Viet Cong" adversary used within the US government were also the subject of heated debate. Among the problems bureaucrats had with these characterizations was that, depending on the terms used to categorize the adversary, the strength of the opposition could radically increase or decrease. This issue had enormous political ramifications as policy makers wanted to demonstrate that the United States was "winning" the war and that enemy strength was declining. The emphasis to demonstrate "progress" was especially evident in the debates between Military Assistance Command-Vietnam (MACV) and the CIA over Viet Cong order of battle (O/B) estimates. In 1967, Westmoreland's intelligence staff estimated enemy strength at 299,000. However, when a CIA analyst informed his superiors that his figures were double those produced by MACV, a battle erupted over O/B estimates, with MACV attempting to keep the enemy numbers to a minimum. One of the main points of contention was the category in which different types of adversaries were placed. By eliminating the "irregular" categories, such as the "Viet Cong Self-Defense Forces" and "Viet Cong Secret Self-Defense Forces," the enemy figure could be reduced by some 121,000–132,000 personnel from the CIA's count, despite this category being included in the body counts. At that time, body counts were employed as one of the measures to determine the "crossover" point, or the point where the enemy was unable to replace their losses, a key indicator then being used to interpret the success or failure of Westmoreland's attrition strategy.

As the controversy raged inside the intelligence community, numerous political and military officials highlighted the danger of higher O/B figures being released to the public. For instance, National Security Adviser Walt Rostow warned Johnson that "the danger is press will latch on to previous underestimate [of the enemy order of battle] and revive credibility gap talk" if the higher figures were released. Likewise, deputy MACV commander Lieutenant General Creighton Abrams noted that "we've been projecting an image of success" and warned that if a much higher order of battle figure were released, newsmen would draw "an erroneous and gloomy conclusion as to the meaning of the increase." In response to the push for the CIA's higher estimates, Robert Komer, who headed the Civil Operations and Rural Development Support program, told one senior CIA official, "You guys simply have to back off. Whatever the true O/B figure is, is beside the point." If a much larger figure should be published, said Komer, within hours "some dove in State will leak it to the press; that will create a public disaster and undo everything we've been trying to accomplish out here." Similarly, US Ambassador to Vietnam Ellsworth Bunker warned there would be a "devastating result if it should leak out . . . that despite all our successes in grinding down VC/NVA (Viet Cong/North Vietnamese Army) here," statistics showed that "they are really much stronger than ever."[28]

There are two aspects of this debate that are particularly noteworthy. First, the O/B debate illustrates how the Viet Cong could lose hundreds of thousands of personnel, not by actual loss in battle, but merely by applying different labels and redefining types of enemy forces in the estimative process. Second, and perhaps more important, these interagency battles over language—specifically the terms used to name and categorize the adversary—reflected a political and military leadership more interested in manipulating reality to maintain an illusion of success than in shifting to a more effective political or military strategy.[29]

As Hannah Arendt noted in relation to the Pentagon's efforts to sell the Vietnam War, "there always comes the point beyond which lying becomes counterproductive. This point is reached when the audience to which the lies are addressed is forced to disregard altogether the distinguishing line between truth and falsehood in order to be able to survive."[30] In Vietnam, the narratives designed to keep the public and allies "on board" both limited policy makers' courses of action and also created an atmosphere within the bureaucracy in which "good news" was welcomed and "bad news" was buried or ignored. Policy makers might know the truth, but their statements and policies were unable to reflect the truth. As the order of battle case highlights, the key issue here was not only that US officials were advocating for an intelligence estimate that bolstered the "success" image but, more important, this meant any discussion of strategy had to be based on an inaccurate appreciation of the situation. The false image of success was finally punctured as a result of the 1968 Tet Offensive, with American public support turning even further against the war.

Conclusion

Gaining an appreciation for the relevance of discourse to war requires a broader understanding of the function of language than is found in the current literature. This necessitates not only studying a wider range of terms and actors but also examining how those actors employ, understand, give meaning to, and are guided or restricted in their actions by the use of language. Returning to the Shy and Collier quotation cited at the beginning of this chapter, one of the primary motivations for this study is to test the idea that language can "misdirect" military effort by misshaping the reality of a conflict. Another important goal is to demonstrate the ways in which war and the discourse of war are mutually constitutive. As even a cursory examination of military history shows, there have been numerous instances where terminology was misused, misinterpreted, or developed purely for its marketing value and produced policies that had negative consequences for a state and its military institutions. In contrast to many academic works on public affairs and propaganda that delineate the composer of a message and the recipient (government/elites versus people, or government versus another government or foreign audience), the cupboard is relatively bare when it comes to literature in which the government is both the author and the audience.

As this introductory chapter has attempted to illustrate, there are numerous means by which a government can become entrapped in its own discourse. It should be highlighted that when a state falls victim to a discourse trap, it does not necessarily imply that it will be defeated in war. The effects of the discourse trap may be limited to impairing a state, and especially its military, from optimal operational effectiveness and can therefore be classed in the category of Clausewitzian "friction." However, although measuring the effects of the discourse trap on different organizations, in different states, and in different historical contexts will potentially be a subject for future research, the primary aim of this book will be limited to the presentation of empirical evidence for the purpose of establishing the phenomenon in the war studies field. As the forthcoming case studies will demonstrate, comprehending the way language was employed within the US military is a central, rather than a peripheral, factor in explaining why and how the system functioned in the way it did. Furthermore, the case studies will attempt to prove that in the case of the US defense department since 9/11, the political-military discourse motivated and constrained, rather than merely reflected, the way in which strategy was formulated and operations were conducted.

CHAPTER 2

Global War on Terrorism

In the aftermath of 9/11, *counterterrorism* rose to the forefront of the US defense discourse, far outpacing *information warfare, network-centric warfare,* the *Revolution in Military Affairs,* the *China threat, rogue states,* and other topics dominant in the 1990s. Moreover, since the start of the "Iraq insurgency," the discursive emphasis on "terrorism" has increasingly merged with the topic of "insurgency," with the "war on al-Qaeda" being viewed as a "global counterinsurgency" as much as a "global war on terror." Yet despite all the attention paid to the topic, there has been no effort devoted to understanding the manner in which the US government, but more particularly the defense department, has understood and given meaning to the "Global War on Terrorism" (GWOT), viewed it as a national policy priority, and conceptualized its role within it. Attempting to study the way in which US defense officials have comprehended the term *GWOT* is an extremely arduous task, particularly as there have been many contradictory official statements on its meaning. Nevertheless, understanding how the officials who were in the forefront of waging this war actually defined it is a prerequisite for contextualizing not only the military's role in the conflict but also how the conflict itself has been defined and prosecuted more generally.

Although al-Qaeda was responsible for 9/11, it was the US government that decided to launch the GWOT. As such, it was Washington, rather than al-Qaeda, that set the rules of the game. But what were the rules of the game? Who was the enemy and where was the enemy? Was al-Qaeda the only enemy? What about other officially designated terrorist groups and state sponsors of terrorism? Was this a Global War on Terror, or a war on global terror? Being classed as a "war," was the military guaranteed to play the lead role? What did officials believe constituted victory or defeat? What sorts of resources were to be devoted to the GWOT in relation to other national security threats? Where did it begin and where was it supposed to end? Indeed, was it supposed to end at all?

These questions are not theoretical. For the Department of Defense (DoD), answers to these questions were necessary to organize the bureaucracy for the conflict, plan and conduct operations, train and equip the forces to do so, and provide justification for the mission. Therefore, the ways in which the term *GWOT* was understood and used by the DoD as a guide to its activities is quite central to how the conflict unfolded. But is there one definition of *GWOT*? Just as numerous US government departments and agencies have alternative definitions of *terrorism*, have they also been using different definitions of *GWOT*? Does the DoD have its own definition? Could it be that the term *GWOT* has never been officially defined and that defense officials, when asked, are unable to provide a definition, or at least a similar definition? Even with the change from Bush to Obama, which also included changing the name of the conflict from "GWOT" to "Overseas Contingency Operations," why was it that the new administration followed fairly consistently along the same path as its predecessor? Although these questions will be addressed in greater detail in the following sections, it is worth noting in advance that the primary purpose of this chapter is to demonstrate how in the case of the term *GWOT*, as well as the post-9/11 primacy of a "counterterrorism" discourse more generally, the DoD has fallen into the discourse trap, with the existing literature paying almost no attention either to how it fell victim to this predicament or to the unintended consequences for the future of the US military.

It would be impossible to capture all aspects of the DoD in relation to the GWOT. Therefore this chapter will limit itself to examining a number of the more important features of the GWOT discourse that touch upon how the senior DoD leadership conceived of the "war" and its role in the Pentagon's planning, strategy, and budgeting, as well as the way in which it helped constitute military intervention. The first section will highlight a number of critiques of the term *GWOT* made by US officials in order to set the stage for the rest of the chapter. The next section will trace the evolution of the "war on terrorism" discourse inside the DoD beginning in the Reagan era for the purpose of showcasing the broadening conception of "counterterrorism" after 9/11. Following from this, the third section will attempt to demonstrate a number of ways in which the GWOT discourse has become institutionalized throughout the DoD. The final section will focus on the GWOT beyond Afghanistan and Iraq, with particular emphasis on how the GWOT discourse has been employed by the US combatant commands and helped constitute and sustain a number of global military interventions. In the course of this analysis, it will be shown how the discourse of a war on terrorism, as it was employed within the DoD, constituted a discourse trap and that numerous examples were present of blowback, bandwagoning, and marginalization.

Criticizing *GWOT*

The GWOT has been harshly critiqued from terminological and conceptual perspectives both inside as well as outside the defense department. Unfortunately, one of the principle limitations of these critiques is that they often assume the GWOT is an uncontested concept, rather than one that can have an infinite number of interpretations, especially within the bureaucracies charged with its formulation and execution. In other words, the GWOT is accepted as a given, with little or no consideration given to the term's etymology, meaning, appropriateness, or political and bureaucratic function. Among the GWOT critics, only a handful address these core issues. Interestingly, these critics have included many senior defense officials, such as Defense Secretary Donald Rumsfeld. This section will examine a number of the arguments raised by these critics about the fundamental and existential questions on the nature and character of the GWOT, based on the use and interpretations of the term itself. These arguments are not merely academic but have constituted a significant critical discourse inside the DoD as well. Within the DoD this critical discourse arose due to dissatisfaction with the perceived nature of the conflict and the role the US military was expected to play in it.

Although the DoD had engaged in "counterterrorism" for decades, the discourse of counterterrorism was transformed after 9/11. Whereas the US military had previously engaged in "defensive" antiterrorism as well as "offensive" retaliation, the discourse of counterterrorism was expanded to include *preemption, prevention, stability operations, humanitarian assistance*, and so on. Terrorism would shift from the periphery of the military's "threat" discourse, to the point where it became the dominant discourse. In stark contrast to past usage of the "war on terror" terminology within the DoD, in the aftermath of 9/11, it developed into a metanarrative that would take on a life of its own, to include constituting security "crises" where previously there had been little interest. In a number of cases, what had earlier been considered as a local "insurgency" that bore little or no relation to US national security suddenly became a "crisis" to be dealt with in the context of the GWOT. As "terrorism" emerged as the most critical security issue to be dealt with, the discourse of "counterterrorism" became a driving force in almost all aspects of DoD policy, operations, and organization. To give just one example, before 9/11, Rumsfeld pushed very hard to "transform" the DoD. This policy program of "transformation" was originally intended to better enable the DoD to fight another great power, such as China. After 9/11, the term *transformation* was increasingly used in the context of counterterrorism, because al-Qaeda, rather than China, had emerged as the dominant security challenge.[1]

There is another aspect of the GWOT rhetoric that raised questions about how this conflict has been understood within the US government. Even if the scope of the GWOT remained hazy, the labeling of Iraq as the war's "central front" had several implications for placing into context actions that were justified as being a part of the GWOT and raised strategic questions of resource allocation. It was only in September 2003, nearly two years after the "war on terror" began, and at a moment when President Bush was requesting an $87 billion "war on terror" supplemental appropriation from Congress, that Iraq was officially designated as the "central front in the war on terror," a designation has shaped subsequent DoD strategy.[2] Due to the large US military presence in Iraq and its associated financial cost, which at that time made the commitment associated with all other GWOT-related military interventions combined pale by comparison, the conflict there, almost by default, was required to be the central front. This association was compounded by the US military's merging of the GWOT and the Iraq war in its internal as well as public discourse.

It has been argued that among the most important consequences of labeling Iraq as the central front had been to deemphasize the relative importance of the military role in Afghanistan, a country that many critics of the Iraq war claimed to be the real central front of the GWOT. Related to the issue of resource allocation among the various "fronts" of the GWOT was the broader problem of how the GWOT related to other US national security priorities. In the aftermath of the 2001 fall of Kabul, concerns were raised within the DoD about the possibility that US forces would become overextended if the number of GWOT missions expanded exponentially, and no controls were put in place to limit these. Even before 9/11, the term *overstretch* had been applied to the US armed forces, although this would take on a whole new meaning in the GWOT context, including debates over a return to the draft.[3] Conrad Crane observed in 2002 that due to force limitations, "the spread of the war on terrorism should be limited or at least carefully controlled."[4] Moreover, Crane recommended that the Army not allow the demands of homeland security, force protection, and the war on terrorism to detract from other global missions and general deterrence.[5] However, the notion of a "limited" war on terror never gained a prominent place in the GWOT discourse. It could be argued the lack of firm definition about the character of the enemy, or the types of missions that could be justified as "counterterrorism," encouraged a broadening of the war. At the very least, numerous interest groups were able to use the all-encompassing GWOT terminology as a means of expanding the war beyond Afghanistan.

The internal criticism of the GWOT discourse existed among both defense policy makers and practitioners, and in many cases, represents a trap in which officials found themselves critical of the terminology, yet unable to escape it. An important case in point, for instance, was Rumsfeld's mostly unsuccessful attempt to shift the Pentagon discourse away from the concept of a "war on terror." Beginning in late September 2001, Rumsfeld noted the "war on terrorism" was "very, very different" from what people think of when using the word *war* or *campaign* and it was necessary to "fashion a new vocabulary and different constructs."[6] Over the course of the next five years, Rumsfeld repeatedly employed the term *war on terror*, despite his dislike for it. In his last press interview as defense secretary, Rumsfeld was asked what he would have done differently during his tenure. He answered, "I guess I don't think I would have called it the war on terror."[7] This answer is curious for a number of reasons. Of the infinite number of answers he could have provided, Rumsfeld chose to focus on a semantic issue. For Rumsfeld, semantics had strategic implications because they could create misleading frames of thought, which, in turn, would form a biased appreciation of the military's role in the GWOT. Rumsfeld noted the term *war on terror* is "a problem for me, and I've worked to try to reduce the extent to which it is used, and increase the extent to which we understand it more as a long war or a struggle or a conflict, not against terrorism but against a relatively small number, but terribly dangerous and lethal, violent extremists."[8] Among Rumsfeld's most important reasons for disliking the term was his view that "the word 'war' conjures up World War II more than it does the Cold War" and "creates a level of expectation of victory and an ending within the 30 or 60 minutes of a soap opera."[9] Chairman of the Joint Chiefs of Staff General Richard Myers also emphasized his dissatisfaction, stating he had objected to the use of the term *war on terrorism* because it causes people to think that the military is the solution, whereas the solution is "more diplomatic, more economic, more political, than it is military."[10] For a number of years, defense officials have also complained that use of the word *war* elevated al-Qaeda and other transnational terrorists, giving them legitimacy as an opposition force to the United States. They also believed it tended to alienate Muslim populations in other countries, who saw the GWOT as a war on Islam and felt they needed to support al-Qaeda as a matter of defending their faith.[11]

In addition to disliking the word *war*, Rumsfeld was also uncomfortable with describing the adversary as "terror," "terrorism," or "terrorists." Instead, he preferred the term *violent extremists* because terror is the "weapon of choice" but the adversaries are the "extremists themselves."[12] From the earliest days of formulating the DoD's GWOT policy, the definition of the adversary was a very contentious one.[13] Undersecretary of Defense for Policy Douglas Feith remarked that the threat defied "simple definition" and determining how broad the target set should be "was no easy matter."[14] The enemy could not simply be defined as a set of terrorist organizations together with states because to do so would necessitate "declaring war against all countries that gave safe havens, funds, ideological, or other types of support to terrorists" and would include "Afghanistan, Cuba, Iran, Iraq, Libya, North Korea, Pakistan, Saudi Arabia, Sudan, and Syria."[15] Moreover, a formal list of terrorist organizations would require continual revision. At one point, defense policy makers considered "identifying the enemy as an ideology" and using a term like *radical Islam* or *Islamic extremism*, but this was rejected.[16] Feith liked the term *war on terror* because it "avoided the problem of lists," gave the President flexibility, and "called attention to differences between us and our enemies."[17] Indeed, one of the most important advantages of coining the term *war on terror* was that it "allowed the Administration to defer naming the enemy."[18] However, not defining the adversary in clear terms meant the threat would be "unbounded" and therefore necessitate pursuing a counterterrorism policy that would be open-ended and ultimately unsustainable militarily.

Perhaps the most important competing discourse to the GWOT within the DoD was the emphasis placed on defining the adversary in terms of a "global insurgency" rather than "global terrorism." As one officer put it, "if the US fails to identify the war on terror as essentially a counterinsurgency effort, then geographic combatant commanders will never be able to accurately assess the proper ways, means, and ends necessary to determine a calculus for victory, nor will they be able to properly identify the enemy's center of gravity to assist them in that calculation."[19] In a May 2004 memo, Rumsfeld considered whether to redefine the GWOT as a "worldwide insurgency."[20] The memo advised his aides to "test what the results could be" if the war on terrorism was renamed.[21] Although it is unclear what response was generated by Rumsfeld's memo, assuming any response was generated at all, Rumsfeld would attempt on numerous occasions during the next two years to change the terminology.

The origins of the term and concept of *global insurgency* in the US defense community can be traced to at least the period shortly after 9/11, but its evolution inside the DoD took a number of years before its use became widespread.[22] Among a number of counterinsurgency (COIN) experts, the term gained popularity as a result of an article published in the *Journal of Strategic Studies* in 2005 by David Kilcullen.[23] Although Kilcullen began developing the concept of global insurgency in 2002, its exposure inside the DoD was limited prior to the article's publication. However, the term was in use by at least some senior DoD officials, including by Rumsfeld, prior to this publication.[24] In April 2005, Deputy Undersecretary of Defense for Intelligence and War-Fighting Support Lieutenant General William Boykin stated the GWOT should be recast as a "war on insurgency," since the United States was fighting a "global insurgency."[25] Likewise, Acting Deputy Assistant Secretary of Defense for Special Operations and Combating Terrorism James Roberts argued, "We must run a global counterinsurgency if we accept what the war on terror actually is."[26] It should be noted that the move to shift from *GWOT* to *global counterinsurgency* was supported not only among defense policy makers but also by the operational leadership. For instance, in June 2006, deputy commander of the Army's Tenth Special Forces Group, Lieutenant Colonel Rick Steiner, said that to deal with the problem of how best to defeat worldwide terrorist networks required viewing the GWOT as a global counterinsurgency. For Steiner, a global counterinsurgency was mainly about waging an information war rather than applying military force.[27] Similarly, a November 2004 draft Joint Operational Concept for Defeating Terrorist Organizations prepared by the US Special Operations Command stated, "The fundamental nature of this war is an insurgency."[28]

In contrast to the advocates of labeling the adversary as either "terrorists" or "global insurgents," another viewpoint stressed "de-militarizing" the GWOT by "recriminalizing" the adversary.[29] In 2006, Army Colonel Gary Cheek, the head of the Strategic Planning Division in the Office of the deputy director for the War on Terrorism on the Joint Staff, said what was needed was to recast terrorists as criminals. According to Cheek, "if we can change the name . . . that changes the dynamic of the conflict."[30] The goal of changing the terminology would be to "migrate this from a war to something other than a war."[31] He argued changing the terminology could also be beneficial with regards to US relations with allies and noted how "our European allies are more comfortable articulating issues of terrorism as criminal threats, rather than war."[32]

Throughout the Bush administration, despite all the cases where DoD officials criticized the GWOT terminology, there were no successes in abandoning or permanently replacing it with an alternative. Other terms that entered the DoD lexicon, such as *Long War* or *Global Counterinsurgency*, were used interchangeably with the GWOT, rather than acting as replacements for it. This inability to replace the terminology had at least two important consequences. First, the GWOT became an entrenched and institutionalized discourse that was viewed by many defense officials as strategically counterproductive, yet could not be challenged. Second, because the GWOT discourse was a "permanent" feature of the Pentagon, the challenge for defense planners intent on shifting the DoD away from a "counterterrorism" focus was made all the more difficult. As will be demonstrated in the following sections, one method employed by DoD officials to beat the GWOT was to join it. Consequently, the *GWOT* label was used to cover any number of activities that had not been previously considered "counterterrorism." As a result, the discourse entrenched itself in the system that much further. This constitutes one of the more important features of the GWOT discourse trap—namely, the meanings and interpretations attached to the terminology continuously evolved to the point where any attempts to diagnose and prescribe remedies to this policy program inevitably fell short. As will be highlighted late, even with the abandonment of the term *GWOT* by the Obama administration, the primacy of the broader counterterrorism discourse remained essentially unchanged.

Evolution of the GWOT Discourse

Global terrorism, and terrorism directed at the United States, did not start on 9/11; they are security challenges that have existed for decades. Moreover, the perceived threat of a catastrophic terrorist act being conducted inside America has also existed for decades.[33] Indeed, a number of scholars have criticized the *new* in "new terrorism," especially given the lack of historical perspective evident in much of the post-9/11 discourse on the subject.[34] Many critics of the "war on terror" have also been critical of the term's use by the Bush administration, yet have neglected any treatment of its pre-9/11 usage. But it is important to note that Bush was not the first US president to use this rhetoric. Nevertheless, the difference between Bush's use of the term and that of his predecessors has to do not so much with the rhetoric itself but the way in which the government, and especially the military, embraced this discourse. In order to understand this distinction, it is worth briefly reflecting on how the US military approached counterterrorism prior to 9/11, to include how it responded to similar "war on terror" rhetoric emanating from the White House.

There is, in fact, a great deal of continuity in both the perceived nature of the problem (i.e., state-sponsored and nonstate actor terrorism) and the terminology used to characterize the US response to the problem (i.e., declaring a "war on terrorism"). Perhaps the most important change in the way the DoD approached "counterterrorism" after 9/11 was not necessarily a change in the way it perceived the capabilities of terrorist groups, or for that matter a change in the terminology used to characterize its own response. The big shift after 9/11 was not the nature of terrorism but rather the nature of "counterterrorism." According to Timothy Hoyt, 9/11 "drove a paradigm shift in the use of military force against terrorism."[35] This shift was predicated on new definitions and new interpretations of what could be considered counterterrorism.

The launch of the "War on Terror" after 9/11 wasn't a new war. To suggest otherwise implies the DoD was not previously involved in counterterrorism, or to be more precise, had never viewed counterterrorism as war. Such an implication has no basis in reality. According to Richard Jackson, "there is little that is new or unique about the language of the 'war on terrorism'; it is simply the manner in which American governments have always spoken about and responded to severe crises—it is a reflex, ingrained over time and institutionalized through practice."[36] What transpired after 9/11 was in fact the DoD's third "War on Terrorism," albeit one that was very much different from the previous two. In addition to the DoD's involvement in "wars" on terrorism, which can be dated back to the Reagan administration, its broader "counterterrorism" activities extend back even further. For instance, the DoD initially assigned the "counterterrorism" mission to its special operations community. During the Carter administration, it created the Army's Delta Force to deal mainly with "hostage rescue."[37] Other counterterrorism-related tasks included force protection for overseas bases and the military's domestic response to a terrorist attack, both of which involved organizations within DoD apart from special operations. By tracing the genealogy of the DoD's "counterterrorism" discourse, this section will demonstrate how for many years "counterterrorism" was on the margins of the DoD discourse. However, after 9/11, due in large measure to the expanding definition of what constituted "counterterrorism" and the efforts of the various bureaucracies within the DoD to become associated with it, "counterterrorism" emerged as the dominant discourse.

The First War on Terrorism

The natural starting point for studying the Pentagon's approach to counterterrorism discourse as it relates to the "war on terrorism" after 9/11 is to focus on how it incorporated this discourse in the first "war on terrorism" during the Reagan administration. Even a cursory examination of US counterterrorism discourse prior to 9/11 illustrates this terminology had been in existence for nearly two decades. Indeed, it was the Reagan administration that first made extensive use of the word *war* in relation to *terrorism*.[38] Moreover, it was under Reagan that the policy of retaliation was introduced, representing a dramatic shift in US counterterrorism doctrine.[39]

A key divergence from the post-9/11 DoD response to this discourse arises here. The rhetoric of Reagan's "war on terrorism" was not matched by "warlike" responses from the Pentagon. This unwillingness to wholeheartedly embrace the "war on terror" discourse can probably be attributed to the Pentagon's primary emphasis remaining on the Cold War priorities of conventional and nuclear deterrence, whereas low-intensity conflict (which included counterterrorism) was viewed negatively within the senior ranks of the military. Most notably, Secretary of Defense Caspar Weinberger saw terrorism as a danger but not something that should be actively fought against. For Weinberger, terrorism was criminal activity, not warfare. Weinberger feared devoting resources for counterterrorism would take emphasis away from building up conventional forces to counter the "Soviet threat."[40] Indeed, throughout this period, the Cold War was considered to be a higher priority than a war on terrorism, albeit the two were often rhetorically linked by the Reagan administration.[41]

The dominance of the Cold War and the Vietnam legacy were arguably the two most important reasons the Pentagon was reluctant to take on responsibility for low-intensity conflict projects such as "counterterrorism." Many senior military officers believed the military's primary mission was to deter and fight major wars, and, as such, low-intensity conflict was considered a peripheral mission that would draw scarce resources away from more important matters.[42] Therefore, low-intensity conflict generally, and warfare against terrorism specifically, was something the US military was reluctant to engage in because of its low priority.[43]

In addition to the low priority attached to counterterrorism, and perhaps reinforcing this, was the view that terrorism was a form of criminal activity and that the military was an inappropriate instrument to counter it. After the 1983 Beirut bombing, Chairman of the Joint Chiefs of Staff General John Vessey stated, "It is beneath our dignity to retaliate against the terrorists who blew up the Marine barracks."[44] There were also a number of risks associated with counterterrorism operations that further entrenched the view that the use of military force was inappropriate. Targets for retaliation were difficult to identify, and therefore missions to attack such targets were undesirable because of their low probability of success.[45] In response to the 1983 bombing, Weinberger argued against military retaliation.[46] Responding to Secretary of State George Schultz's call for preemptive strikes against terrorists, Weinberger said that such "retaliation would be analogous to firing a gun in a crowded theater in the slim hope of hitting the guilty party."[47]

Throughout the Reagan presidency, the US military resisted attempts by some elements of the administration to raise the profile of counterterrorism.[48] It was only in the special operations community that "counterterrorism" was characterized as "war," and the mission was viewed as a vital one. For instance, in spring 1985, Joint Special Operations Agency head Major General Wesley Rice testified, "We are in a state of war with terrorists."[49] However, the role of special operations within the broader defense community was deliberately kept a minor one. It was only in 1987 that the position of assistant secretary of defense for special operations and low-intensity conflict and the Joint Special Operations Command were established, both of which faced years of bureaucratic resistance inside the Pentagon prior to their creation.[50]

During the course of the Reagan administration, there were many instances where the US military could have intervened in response to an act of terrorism, such as in response to the Beirut bombing. In the majority of these instances, different types of military responses were discussed, but the military leadership was often reluctant to risk a large-scale intervention.[51] The main exception to this was the 1986 retaliation against Libya following a terrorist attack on US servicemen in Germany. Operation El Dorado Canyon, involving air strikes against targets in Libya, was a type of military counterterrorist action that was unprecedented for the United States.⁵² It was also one that was not repeated for a number of years thereafter, despite numerous Libyan-sponsored terrorist attacks.⁵³

Throughout this period, the DoD was quite happy not to take a lead role in "counterterrorism." The war on terror was viewed mainly as a diplomatic and covert action problem, and the military's role was merely to provide support, usually in the form of special operations forces. There was never a comprehensive military plan developed to counter international terrorism, nor any clear indication of who the enemy was. Indeed, within the US government, competing definitions of *terrorism* sparked a bureaucratic feud between the Pentagon, CIA, and State Department during the 1981 preparation of Special National Intelligence Estimate 11/2–81.⁵⁴ A Defense Intelligence Agency assessment used a definition of *terrorism* that "took every kind of national liberation movement, every leftwing movement that used violence, and called them terrorists."⁵⁵ It was only in 1989 that the Pentagon issued its first comprehensive guide of 52 groups it considered terrorists. However, the DoD's designation of certain groups as terrorists sparked a feud with the State Department, whose characterizations were different.⁵⁶ Inside the Pentagon, the majority of these terrorist groups were regarded as little more than a nuisance, not worth the effort to be systematically combated. Even the Abu Nidal Organization, which in the 1980s was officially viewed by the DoD as the world's most dangerous terrorist group, was not subjected to any large-scale US military action, nor did US defense officials view it as a major threat.⁵⁷ Although the "war on terror" rhetoric would continue throughout the Reagan administration and into the George H. W. Bush administration, the perception that the threat of terrorism was gradually diminishing meant that even within the special operations community, the "war on terrorism" discourse subsided, and the "war on drugs" was viewed as providing a more relevant mission.⁵⁸

The Second War on Terrorism

From the end of the Reagan administration to well into the Clinton presidency, the term *war on terrorism* fell out of use. During this period the law enforcement rather than the "war" approach to counterterrorism prevailed.⁵⁹ For instance, the Pentagon played no part in the US government's response to the 1993 attack on the World Trade Center. Following the Khobar Towers attack in 1996, the DoD was charged with increasing defensive measures for its facilities and personnel, but no offensive action was deemed appropriate.

The experience of the 1980s and early 1990s had suggested to the military that if it were to have a role in counterterrorism, it would either be a large-scale but short-term conventional retaliation against a state sponsor of terrorism or a small-scale Special Forces mission. The 1986 attack in Libya and the 1993 attack on Iraq (in response to the attempted assassination of former president

George H. W. Bush), both involving limited retaliation with air power aimed at deterrence, were used as precedents by the US military when developing counterterrorism plans. Even though the details of the 1993 strike are somewhat murky, US officials still used that strike as a precedent in their internal discourse. When considering options for military action against al-Qaeda in June 1998, Central Command (CENTCOM) head General Anthony Zinni developed a plan that was modeled on the two previous times the United States had used force to respond to terrorism. CENTCOM planners proposed firing Tomahawk missiles against eight "terrorist camps" in Afghanistan, including Bin Laden's compound at Tarnak Farms. However, the idea of committing ground troops was not seriously considered.

In response to the bombings of two US embassies in Africa in August 1998, the chairman of the Joint Chiefs of Staff, General Hugh Shelton, directed Zinni to put this plan into effect, albeit with a few alterations. On August 20, US submarines launched 79 cruise missiles at targets in Afghanistan and Sudan. Operation Infinite Reach was the largest US military response to a terrorist attack since the 1986 raid on Libya. Clinton invoked the imagery and language of war by describing military retaliation as the "first shot of protracted war."[60] Indeed, throughout the government, the operation was billed as the beginning of a new "war on terrorism."[61] However, the Clinton administration's rhetoric on the subject did not necessarily translate into a change in US policy from a mainly law-enforcement approach toward a war strategy involving increased military intervention. A number of reasons can be found to explain this chasm between rhetoric and reality. From the military's perspective, two reasons stand out. First, the results of Operation Infinite Reach were disappointing in terms of the failure of the cruise missile attacks to kill any senior al-Qaeda operatives or to alter the behavior of al-Qaeda. Second, the military was reluctant to escalate the means of retaliation to include the deployment of US ground forces into Afghanistan and resisted pressure from the White House to do so.

In the aftermath of Operation Infinite Reach, General Shelton ordered plans for follow-up strikes, codenamed Operation Infinite Resolve. However, Undersecretary of Defense for Policy Walter Slocombe advised Defense Secretary William Cohen that the available targets were not promising and wrote that the lessons of Infinite Reach "only confirmed the importance of defining a clearly articulated rationale for military action."[62] The issues of cost-effectiveness and utility were also raised, including questioning whether it was worth using very expensive missiles to destroy what Shelton called "jungle gym" training camps.[63] Despite being shelved, planning for Infinite Resolve continued, including an examination of options for possible use of ground forces. Throughout 1999, options were added to the Infinite Resolve plan, such as the possible use of strike aircraft and special operations forces to target terrorist training camps and other targets associated with Bin Laden.⁶⁴ It can be observed that this planning was based on a very different conception of counterterrorism than that which would emerge after 9/11.

In addition to the Infinite Resolve planning, officials in the office of the assistant secretary of defense for special operations and low-intensity conflict developed a plan that called for a broad change in national strategy and in the institutional approach of the DoD to counterterrorism. Implying a potential need for large-scale operations across the whole spectrum of US military capabilities, it urged the department to become a lead agency in transforming national counterterrorism strategy. The authors of this plan expressed concern that the DoD's approach to counterterrorism was outdated, even though the terrorist threat had grown. Warning the future might bring "horrific attacks," they outlined an eight-part strategy "to be more proactive and aggressive."⁶⁵ The assistant secretary of defense for special operations and low-intensity conflict, Allen Holmes, forwarded a memo titled "Toward a More Aggressive Counterterrorism Posture" to Slocombe in September 1998. However, the memo was not regarded favorably and was never forwarded to Secretary Cohen for review.

Recognizing the extreme reluctance to employ US military forces on the ground in Afghanistan, the CIA was tasked in 2000 to prepare its own plan to strike al-Qaeda in that country. The plan called for supporting the Northern Alliance in a proxy war against the Taliban. Interestingly, there was no intent to actually have the Northern Alliance defeat the Taliban and take over the country. Rather, the plan called for the Northern Alliance to pressure the Taliban into ending its support for al Qaeda. One of the key assumptions underpinning the so-called Blue Sky paper that outlined the plan was that the United States should not repeat perceived Soviet mistakes, and therefore a large-scale US military intervention was to be avoided. Indeed, prior to 9/11, it was a standard assumption among American policy makers that the US military would never conduct large-scale operations in Afghanistan precisely because it would lead to defeat. It was this CIA plan that served as the initial basis for the US intervention in 2001, in which the CIA, rather than the military, took the lead by supporting the Northern Alliance.⁶⁶

Following the October 2000 attack on the *USS Cole* in Yemen, the Pentagon resisted retaliation and kept Operation Infinite Resolve on the shelf. The military was also against an idea proposed by National Counterterrorism Czar Richard Clarke of a protracted bombing campaign against al-Qaeda targets in Afghanistan. CENTCOM head General Zinni was afraid it would have a negative effect in Pakistan, as well as placing an additional burden on an overstretched military, particularly the requirement to indefinitely station an aircraft carrier off Pakistan's coast.⁶⁷

General Observations of Pre-9/11 Wars on Terrorism

The lack of military retaliation following the *USS Cole* attack was not unusual; in fact, it was the norm. By contrast, Operations Infinite Reach and El Dorado Canyon were exceptions to the rule. In the aftermath of attacks on US targets, the military had a choice to intervene or not to intervene, and in the overwhelming majority of cases, the military advised against taking action.[68] It is important to note here a key distinction between the pre-9/11 discourse of military retaliation and the discourse of preemption and prevention that would gain prominence after 9/11. During Clinton's "war on terror," similar to Reagan's, military action was mainly limited to retaliation, rather than a full gamut of "counterterrorism" activities, ranging from attacking state sponsors of terrorism and military occupation to humanitarian assistance missions and strategic influence campaigns.

As can be discerned from the historical record, the DoD's participation in "wars" against terrorism prior to 9/11 is almost unrecognizable when compared to post-9/11. It is worth making a brief note of a number of the more significant features of the DoD's earlier "wars" in order to set the stage for examining how great the change was after 9/11 and how a transformed discourse on "counterterrorism" would help constitute this shift.

Arguably the most important feature of the DoD's role in the first two wars on terrorism was that it consistently played a reluctant and limited part. *Counterterrorism* may not necessarily have been considered a dirty word, but at the very least, this was not an area to which the DoD was willing to devote significant resources or to make the centerpiece of their planning and doctrine. In terms of organization, Special Forces were designated as the primary instrument with which to wage counterterrorism, and only in two cases were conventional operations mounted. In these two exceptional cases, the operations were retaliatory in nature, of short duration, and did not involve intervention by US ground forces.

The fact that three US administrations have rhetorically declared "wars" on terrorism raises the question of how the first two wars ended. It could be argued these wars didn't necessarily end; lack of institutional interest meant the rhetoric gradually fell out of use. In other words, the unwillingness of the bureaucracy to make counterterrorism a top priority and institutionalize it as such, led to other security discourses taking precedence. Moreover, in neither of the first two wars was there any effort made on the part of either politicians or bureaucrats to define what was meant by the term. For instance, there were no military planning documents for a "war on terrorism," nor was there a special budget designated for funding military "counterterrorism" operations.

Among the reasons identified that the first two wars on terrorism received lackluster backing from the bureaucracy was the general perception that terrorism was merely one of many security challenges, and a minor one at that. Moreover, defensive "antiterrorism" prevailed over offensive "counterterrorism." This can be discerned from the considerable financial resources the Clinton administration devoted to "consequence management" and ensuring the DoD's ability to play an important role in the event of a major terrorist attack involving weapons of mass destruction (WMD) inside the United States. In addition to an allocation of material resources favoring domestic operations, the senior DoD leadership was unsure of what the military's role in counterterrorism actually was and was reluctant to back large-scale conventional operations for counterterrorism purposes. By keeping counterterrorism limited mainly to Special Forces missions, the mainstream DoD bureaucracy concentrated on conventional missions where the bulk of the military's resources could potentially be employed, such as fighting major theater wars.

Transformation of Counterterrorism Discourse in the Third War on Terrorism

As Michael Cox observed, in the aftermath of 9/11, America's "notion of enemies, its concept of its own interests, and its definition of strategy began to expand most dramatically."[69] This was certainly the case with its definition and interpretation of counterterrorism and the military's place in it. Arguably the greatest transformation consisted of Rumsfeld's dissatisfaction with previous DoD responses to terrorist incidents, resulting in the subsequent broadening of the definition of the military's role. In so doing, he ensured the third war on terrorism would be fundamentally different from the previous two.

When President Bush announced his intention to wage a "war on terror" during a speech to Congress on September 20, 2001, there was little indication that the US military would play a prominent role relative to other instruments of national power. According to Bush, "Americans are asking, 'How will we fight and win this war?' We will direct every resource at our command—every means of diplomacy, every tool of intelligence, every instrument of law enforcement, every financial influence and every necessary weapon of war—to the destruction and to the defeat of the global terror network . . . Our war on terror begins with Al-Qaeda, but it does not end there. It will not end until every terrorist group of global reach has been found, stopped and defeated."[70]

Apart from al-Qaeda, the only other two "terrorist" groups mentioned in the speech were the Egyptian Islamic Jihad and the Islamic Movement of Uzbekistan, although Bush noted, "There are thousands of these terrorists in more than 60 countries."[71] But what would the US military role be in helping "defeat" these groups? Was this a mission for the US military as a whole, or just the special operations community? Most important, would the US military be in a *supported* or *supporting* role? The answer to this last question was of great importance to Rumsfeld. In the weeks after 9/11, he was adamant the US military, vice the CIA (which the US military was initially *supporting* in Afghanistan), would take on the lead role.

Immediately after 9/11, Rumsfeld instructed the military to develop plans to counter various terrorist groups, although it is not entirely clear which groups, apart from al-Qaeda, were considered potential targets. For instance, neither the Egyptian Islamic Jihad nor the Islamic Movement of Uzbekistan featured prominently in the DoD discourse on terrorist groups, even though they had been mentioned in Bush's speech. In response to what he perceived as a lack of creativity, Rumsfeld circulated a memo on October 10, 2001, titled "What Will Be the Military Role in the War on Terrorism?" In this memo, Rumsfeld notes that "for a month DoD has produced next to no actionable suggestions as to how we can assist in applying the urgently needed pressure on terrorists other than cruise missile as bombs."[72] He linked this to a culture of risk aversion within the military and compared the DoD's perceived inaction with the actions of other government departments, such as the Departments of Justice, Treasury, and State.[73] However, as has already been noted, the military's traditional response to a terrorist incident, in the cases where it had responded at all, had been retaliation using cruise missiles and bombs. Moreover, in earlier cases, the military pushed back against attempts to employ ground forces. The "counterterrorism" proposals Rumsfeld received from military commanders in the month after 9/11 could therefore be described as the military's initial conception of its role in this war on terrorism, a conception that drew its inspiration from the military's accepted pre-9/11 role. This is a crucial point, because it highlights the fact that despite the tragic scale of 9/11, the military's first response was to define its role in terms of limited retaliation, rather than an unlimited response.[74] It also demonstrates the continuity of the military's hesitancy to treat the problem of "counterterrorism" as one requiring the participation of the entire DoD. Instead, the military participants would be limited to Special Forces and select air and naval strike assets.

The October 10 memo is also illustrative of Rumsfeld's dissatisfaction with the military's "old thinking" on counterterrorism. Interestingly, this memo followed several earlier memos issued by Rumsfeld and his policy advisers that had tried to define the war on terrorism in a way that would give the military a more prominent role. The origins of the "new thinking" on the military's role in counterterrorism can be traced to a brainstorming session that occurred on 9/11 itself among several senior DoD officials transiting back to the United States from Moscow via Germany. Among the senior officials present on this flight were Undersecretary of Defense for Policy Douglas Feith, head of the Joint Staff's Strategy and Plans office (J-5) Lieutenant General John Abizaid,

Assistant Secretary of Defense for International Security Affairs Peter Rodman, Pentagon Comptroller Dov Zakheim, and Deputy Assistant Secretary of Defense for Near East and South Asia Affairs William Luti.[75] Although President Bush had not yet uttered the words *war on terrorism*, Feith recalls a Bush statement immediately after the attack in which he said, "Terrorism against our nation will not stand."[76] Feith interpreted this statement as Bush talking about war and proceeded on this assumption when drafting the first memos detailing the military response to the attack.[77] The first memo was produced within hours of the attack and delivered to Rumsfeld. It argued the attack was "more than just a law enforcement matter" and that retaliation should be directed not just against the perpetrators but also against the "broader network of terrorists."[78] Interestingly, Feith's memo made use of the first historical analogy of the war. He compared the forthcoming US action against terrorism to the Royal Navy's suppression of the slave trade in the nineteenth century.[79]

During these initial discussions, questions were raised about what role the US military would play in the war, how to define the enemy, and how to define the war aim. The discussions were recorded and formed the basis for the first DoD concept paper for the war, published on September 14 and titled "War on Terrorism: Strategic Concept."[80] According to this paper, the United States must confront "the entire network of states, nonstate entities, and organizations that engage in or support terrorism against the United States and our interests, including the states that harbor terrorists. All those organizations and states constitute a threat, jointly and severally."[81] The paper listed al-Qaeda, the Taliban, and Iraq as "the immediate targets for initial action."[82] This paper would inform subsequent DoD discussions and memos regarding the war, perhaps the most important of which was Rumsfeld's guidance to the combatant commanders related to war planning. It also provided the basis for the DoD's position on the subject in interagency meetings, especially in the National Security Council.[83]

DoD policy makers discursively constructed the enemy in the monolithic terms of a broad terrorist network that included not only nonstate actors such as al-Qaeda but state sponsors of terrorism as well. Rumsfeld saw the problem of countering global terrorism as that of countering a network rather than one organization and told senior DoD leaders *not* to "overelevate the importance of Al-Qaeda."[84] Meanwhile, targeting Iraq featured prominently in the discourse of senior DoD leaders such as Rumsfeld and Deputy Defense Secretary Paul Wolfowitz.[85] By contrast, the State Department and CIA took the position that military action be limited to Afghanistan, whereas diplomatic and covert action could be employed against the al-Qaeda network elsewhere.[86]

On September 19, Rumsfeld wrote a message to the combatant commanders to "guide their development of war plans."[87] Titled "Some Thoughts for

CINCs as They Prepare Plans," this memo informed commanders that the scope of the military action should be broadened to a "field of action . . . much wider than Afghanistan."[88] This point was echoed in a September 20 memo that referred to the possibility of launching an initial military strike against "someplace like South America or Southeast Asia."[89] Interestingly, this memo also included a no-strike option in which the United States would gradually build up its forces in the Persian Gulf and Eastern Mediterranean, most likely in an effort to pressure perceived state sponsors of terrorism.[90] At this time, senior DoD officials believed that attacking targets in Afghanistan wouldn't "seriously obstruct terrorist operations."[91] This viewpoint was partially justified on the grounds that the United States lacked intelligence on Afghanistan, and the number of potential targets was limited, thus making a country such as Iraq a preferable alternative.[92] In another memo, dated September 23, Rumsfeld cited Colombia, the Philippines, Somalia, and Sudan as locations for limited military action.[93] As with many of the memos written during this period, the geography of the proposed US military actions varied widely.

The writing of these memos coincided with a broader strategic discussion among senior DoD officials about how to conceive of a "global war on terrorism." The results of these deliberations were formalized in two documents. The first document, a paper intended for the president, was titled "Strategic Thoughts" and was delivered on September 30. This paper argued the United States should focus on state sponsors of terrorism, including indirect military action against some and other measures short of war against others. Military action would be primarily limited to train-and-equip activities, information operations, humanitarian aid, logistics, and intelligence support. Direct action by American conventional forces was to be avoided.[94] General Abizaid commented favorably on this approach because it encouraged a "nuanced use of power and a way to avoid stumbling into a major conventional war."[95]

Another key feature of the "Strategic Thoughts" paper was its call for the administration *not* to focus on taking down al-Qaeda but to establish new regimes in a series of states by "aiding local peoples to rid themselves of terrorists and to free themselves of regimes that support terrorism."[96] This list of states included Iraq, Afghanistan, Lebanon, and Sudan. Rumsfeld's proposal called explicitly for indefinitely postponing US air strikes and the use of ground forces in Afghanistan, and instead targeting states that had supported anti-Israel forces such as Hezbollah and Hamas. It urged that the United States should "capitalize on our strong suit, which is not finding a few hundred terrorists in caves in Afghanistan, but in the vastness of our military and humanitarian resources, which can strengthen the opposition forces in terrorist-supporting states."[97]

The second document, drawn up by the Joint Staff (J-5) and the office of the undersecretary of defense for policy, was approved by Rumsfeld on October 3 and consisted of the first formal instructions issued to combatant commanders for the development of "campaign plans against terrorism."[98] This document was titled "Strategic Guidance for the Campaign against Terrorism."[99] At least four terrorist organizations, including al-Qaeda, were designated as targets, as were six states, including Afghanistan and Iraq. This document made it clear that US military aims in regard to those states would go well beyond any ties to terrorism. The document said that the DoD would seek to isolate and weaken those states and to "disrupt, damage or destroy" their military capacities.[100]

With the publication of the "Strategic Guidance" paper, the initial course for the DoD's participation in the GWOT was laid out. Based on the intent of this paper and previous guidance issued post-9/11, the GWOT was enshrined as a "war" involving a wide variety of military actions to occur outside the Middle East and Central Asia. It is unclear, though, the extent to which these documents had any bearing on military planning. According to one US defense academic, as of October 2001, the only guidance the Joint Staff was getting about how to prosecute the war was based on whatever they could interpret from Bush and Rumsfeld's speeches.[101] Such was the broad nature of the war's objectives, combined with a lack of direction and coordination from Washington, that each combatant commander came up with his own list of theater GWOT objectives and then pursued them with the resources at hand.[102] Over time, disappointment with this guidance would lead to new guidance and memos being distributed, most notably the National Military Strategic Plan for the War on Terrorism.[103] However, it is crucial to note that the very existence of DoD strategy documents laying out a conceptual framework for a "war on terrorism" represented a significant departure from previous practice.

Limiting the GWOT

With the late 2001 collapse of the Taliban regime in Afghanistan, there were a series of deliberations within the Bush administration about limiting the war on terrorism and prioritizing the economy. At that time, public opinion polls indicated that for the first time since 9/11, concern about the economic recession eclipsed that about the threat of terrorism. A number of political advisors argued the United States should declare victory in the war, using the analogy of President George H. W. Bush losing the 1992 election due to a lack of attention paid to the economy. By contrast, a number of Pentagon officials expressed the fear that Bush would abandon the war effort prematurely. One senior DoD official acknowledged worries among some of Rumsfeld's advisers that powerful voices in the administration were urging the president to declare victory and retreat to domestic issues.[104]

By the time the late 2001–early 2002 debate over limiting the scope of the war on terror occurred, a number of events had taken place that reduced the probability of such an eventuality. For example, as early as October 2001, Rumsfeld had already authorized planning for the eventual expansion of the GWOT to the Philippines, Georgia, and elsewhere. Moreover, in November, CENTCOM was ordered to begin planning for war with Iraq.[105] Although many in the Army were aware of how multiple operations would stretch the Army, there was never any idea of limiting operations to Afghanistan only, though it was not entirely certain the United States would go to war with Iraq.[106] Despite the planning then under way, the US military had not actually intervened outside Afghanistan. Had Washington chosen to limit future military intervention in the GWOT, this would have been the period in which it could still have done so.

In order to explain how the GWOT expanded beyond Afghanistan, especially given the hesitation of numerous senior officials, it is necessary to consider how the Bush administration perceived the political benefits accrued from waging a "war on terror" and keeping it at the forefront of the administration's public rhetoric.[107] On the other hand, justifying the *need* for a "war on terror" because of political imperatives falls short of explaining how the "war," and particularly DoD's approach to it, developed in the way it did. The "war on terror" initially became the "global war on terror" when Afghanistan became a target. In the purely semantic sense, adding the word *global* to the *war on terror* differentiated this "war" from previous ones. The global nature of this war was discursively stressed from the outset, and given the reported global presence of al-Qaeda, there were numerous opportunities for military intervention of one variety or another. Indeed, the very discursive act of highlighting the word *global* ensured the Bush administration would likely have been criticized had Afghanistan been the only campaign. In this sense, the administration fell into the discourse trap soon after 9/11, but it is highly unlikely they were aware of neither the unintended consequences their rhetoric would have on the ability to control the scope of the "war" nor its transformational impact on the DoD. In the years following Afghanistan, the GWOT continued to metastasize to the point that senior DoD officials became concerned it had gotten out of hand.

From GWOT *to* Long War

As Brian M. Linn noted, "today, as our armed forces fight a Global War on Terror, the commanders of the armed forces seem no more able than their civilian leaders to define the enemy, the objective, or the meaning of victory."[108] Linn's observation could also be expanded to the definition and naming of the war itself. As highlighted earlier, the term *GWOT* did not sit well with many members of the DoD, including Rumsfeld, who was "unhappy from the start" with the term.[109] In the aftermath of the invasion of Iraq, the DoD leadership considered alternative names for the GWOT for the purpose of framing the conflict in what they considered to be more appropriate terms. For instance, in May 2004, Rumsfeld and senior DoD officials discussed the topic of how to frame the war in order to figure out "how best to describe the struggle we are in."[110] In response to these discussions, Undersecretary of Defense for Intelligence Steve Cambone provided a detailed exposition of why he thought the "phrase 'global war on terror' suffers . . . from a number of shortcomings."[111] Rumsfeld followed up on this by writing a short paper titled "What Are We Fighting? Is It a Global War on Terror?" which he then sent to Bush. According to Rumsfeld, "I do believe that how we characterize it (referring to global war on terror), how we set it up, directly affects what we do about it and what our coalition does about it."[112] In the paper, Rumsfeld argued, "What we may be facing now is not simply a law enforcement problem, it is also not a global war against generic terrorists, but rather a war by a radical extremist strain of Islam . . . We should test the proposition whether it might be accurate and useful to define our problem a new way—to declare it as a 'civil war within Islam' and/or a 'global ideological insurgency'—and find ways to test what the analytical results would be depending on how we set up the problem."[113]

Rumsfeld's criticisms of *GWOT* can be broken down into three main arguments. First, Rumsfeld was concerned the emphasis on *war* conveyed an approach to the conflict that was dominated by the military. Second, he argued the enemy wasn't "terrorism" but "violent extremism." The distinction Rumsfeld made between *terrorism* and *violent extremism* was primarily about highlighting the ideological nature of the conflict. Finally, Rumsfeld was adamant the conflict would be a protracted one, perhaps akin to the Cold War, and did not want the public to have false expectations about a timely "victory." These three themes would be evident in the language chosen to replace *GWOT*. However, though the intention may have been to replace *GWOT*, the term had become too entrenched in the US government lexicon, and therefore any attempt to rename the conflict was doomed to merely add a new name. Consequently, rather than more accurately characterizing the conflict, the new names only added further confusion as to the nature of the war.

Beginning in spring 2005, Rumsfeld introduced the term *Global Struggle against Violent Extremism* (GSAVE) into the US government lexicon during a series of interviews and speeches, although he had used iterations of this term since at least the fall 2004 but without the same frequency.[114] On July 25, 2005, General Myers stated he had "objected to the use of the term 'war on terrorism' . . . because if you call it a war, then you think of people in uniform as being the solution."[115] Myers said the threat instead should be defined as "violent extremism," with the recognition that "terror is the method they use."[116]

Despite the new term's use by the two top DoD officials, there is no evidence to suggest the bureaucracy used the term or that the bureaucracy interpreted the shift in language as an official intention on the part of the leadership to replace *GWOT* with *GSAVE*.[117]

In response to public queries about whether the new terminology reflected a change in policy, Pentagon spokesman Lawrence Di Rita said the change in language "is not a shift in thinking, but a continuation of the immediate post-9/11 approach."[118] Di Rita emphasized the need to use "all the means of national power and influence to defeat this enemy" and to look beyond "the military actions in Afghanistan and Iraq."[119] However, within a matter of weeks of being introduced into the defense lexicon, the new language was not deemed politically appropriate, and the White House took steps to reemphasize the "war on terror" and distance itself from *GSAVE*. Rumsfeld backtracked, stating, "Some ask, are we still engaged in a war on terror? Let there be no mistake about it. It's a war. The president properly termed it that after Sept. 11."[120] Attempting to play down any perceived disagreement between Rumsfeld and Bush over the terminology, Di Rita noted, "The secretary doesn't feel this is push back . . . He feels it's an important clarification."[121] According to Joint Staff Director of Operations (J–3) Lieutenant General James T. Conway, there had been "philosophical discussions" with US allies over the use of the phrase *GWOT* but noted "the 'global war on terrorism' translates pretty well into the various languages . . . so I think that continues to make it a part of the discussion."[122] Despite the taboo on *GSAVE*, Rumsfeld used the phrase until he left office.[123]

The short life of *GSAVE* resulted in a brief setback for those advocates in the DoD who wanted to find an alternative to the existing GWOT terminology. However, during this period, another term was also gaining prominence inside the DoD. Since 2004, CENTCOM head General John Abizaid was using the term *long war* to describe the war on terrorism and to underscore the long-term challenge posed by al-Qaeda and other Islamist extremist groups.[124] General Myers eventually picked up the term as well and used it in his final news conference before leaving office in September 2005. That month, the Joint Staff (J-5) also employed the phrase *Long War* in strategy briefs that were provided to public audiences.[125] Furthermore, Rumsfeld sent a memo to all senior military commanders in which he suggested that they "use the material in the Global War on Terror briefs, such as John Abizaid's 'The Long War,' in your upcoming speeches and testimony."[126]

At a January 11, 2006, senior leaders conference (a periodic gathering of a group that includes the defense department's senior civilian leaders, the service chiefs, and the combatant commanders), Abizaid presented a briefing titled "The Long War." During this meeting the appropriateness of the term *long war* was discussed at length.[127] Following the meeting, the term's usage continued to spread throughout the DoD and was most prominently displayed in the opening declaration of the 2006 Quadrennial Defense Review (QDR). On the eve of the Pentagon's release of the QDR, which sets out plans for how the US military will address major security challenges, Rumsfeld delivered a speech at the National Press Club titled "The Long War."[128] The term also received White House approval, as demonstrated by President Bush's 2006 State of the Union speech in which he stated, "Our generation is in a long war against a determined enemy."[129]

Once inscribed in the QDR, the term *Long War* took on a life of its own, not least because it was used for public relations purposes by defense officials. In 2006, a Joint Staff briefing titled "Long War" was given five or six times a week within the Pentagon to various public audiences, and as many as sixty times around the country. The goal of the briefing was to help the American leadership and public understand the nature of the conflict, the enemy and its actions, and the US strategy and tactics for defeating them.[130]

Similar to many of the terms used by DoD officials and inscribed in DoD documents, such as *GWOT*, the term *Long War* was never officially defined, though many officials attempted to give meaning to it. According to General Abizaid, the Long War "has to do with the battle against Sunni-Islamic extremism, Iranian hegemony, the other threats to stability, and the need to protect the global economy in the Middle East."[131] Chairman of the Joint Chiefs of Staff General Peter Pace stated, "The Long War refers to the fact that in all the terrorist campaigns that we have known about, the terrorist campaign has lasted 10, 20, 30 years, and therefore there is no reason to believe that these terrorists would have a time span in their minds of anything less."[132] According to Major General Douglas Lute, CENTCOM Director of Operations, the Long War amounts to a "broader fight . . . against the extremist network."[133] Likewise, Principal Deputy Undersecretary of Defense for Policy Ryan Henry said, "When we refer to the long war, that is the war against terrorist extremists and the ideology that feeds it, and that is something that we do see going on for decades."[134] Assistant Chairman of the Joint Chiefs of Staff Lieutenant General Raymond Odierno said the Long War would last "for at least the next 20 years" and that "part of our focus" will deal with "the extremist networks that . . . threaten the United States and its allies."[135] Odierno identified the will of the American people to confront the terrorists and defeat them as the center of gravity in the "Long War."[136]

As the comments from these senior defense officials reveal, there was no standard view on the scope of the Long War. In addition to combating extremist networks and their associated ideology, preventing Iranian hegemony and protecting the Middle East economy are also considered part of the ten- to thirty-year conflict. However, depending on one's interpretation, the Long War can be defined in a far broader manner than this, to the extent that missions that weren't part of the GWOT could be designated as part of the Long War.[137] For instance, in the course of a DoD press briefing on the 2006 QDR, a slide headed "Long War" listed prolonged irregular conflict (Afghanistan and Iraq), wider irregular operations (Philippines, Horn of Africa, Georgia, Pan-Sahel, elsewhere), humanitarian (Tsunami, Pakistani earthquake) and anticipatory actions (Haiti, Liberia), and operations in support of civil authorities at home (9/11, Katrina).[138] By this definition, almost every operation conducted by the US military post-9/11 fell under the Long War heading.

At an October 6, 2006, brainstorming session that included the Joint Chiefs of Staff and senior "military intellectuals," known as the "Council of Colonels," the topic under discussion was determining the military's role in the Long War. It was recognized that one of the key problems of waging the Long War was ascertaining its purpose of the "war." At issue was whether the US goal was spreading democracy or stabilizing a country or region like the Middle East.[139] During another Council of Colonels meeting on October 13, Army Chief of Staff General Peter Schoomaker asked, "What is the Long War?"[140] The tone of these high-level strategy discussions indicates America's senior military officials did not actually know what the purpose and scope was of the "war" they were responsible for waging. The timing of these discussions is also revealing, since they occurred not only months after the Long War was announced but also years after the GWOT was announced and numerous strategy documents had been published, such as the National Military Strategic Plan for the War on Terrorism. Lack of clear guidance about the Long War was also evident in a complaint made by Rumsfeld to National Security Adviser Stephen Hadley that NSC meetings "are always on Iraq, Afghanistan, etc. . . . I continue to worry that we will never fully understand it ourselves, or organize to deal with it effectively, if we don't have NSC meetings on the Long War/Global War on Terror/the Struggle against Violent Extremists . . . The difficulty of continuing along this path is that we fail to get clear in our minds what needs to be done, and who ought to be doing it. And as a result, we fail to organize, train and equip to win the Long War."[141]

With the reproduction of the GWOT discourse over several years, and with the introduction of the Long War (as encapsulated in the 2006 QDR), a broad structure for developing the US military's strategy, planning, programming, and budgeting over the coming decades emerged, even though a number of fundamental issues, such as who precisely the enemy was, were left unresolved.[142] Unlike *GSAVE*, originally intended to replace *GWOT*, the introduction of *Long War* was not a replacement for *GWOT* but merely a corollary to it. Indeed, the Joint Staff briefings presented to both internal and external audiences on the topic are titled "Global War on Terrorism: The Long War."[143] Similar to

GWOT, the endless repetition and lack of clear definition of *Long War* caused a number of problems and controversies. One senior military officer reflected on concerns raised by CENTCOM, the Pentagon, and some allied governments about using the term. He noted the term "certainly has some negative baggage" as "no one wants to be involved in a long war."[144] Another critic observed, "The Long War . . . is a self-defeating narrative."[145] Though problems with this terminology were recognized by senior military leaders, attempts to restrict the use of this language were unsuccessful, most likely due to the reality that after years of constant usage, it had become a part of the mainstream military lexicon.[146]

Within weeks of coming into power, the Obama administration instructed the US bureaucracy to cease using the term *War on Terrorism* and instead to employ the term *Overseas Contingency Operations*. They also characterized it as a "war against al-Qaeda and its affiliates." Despite the name change, which might have signaled the administration was backing away from retaining the "War on Terrorism" construct as the main prism through which national security issues were viewed, in actual fact, very little changed, as indeed some in the administration had suggested it would. The key difference between the Bush and Obama administrations had to do with the central front of the war, rather than the war itself. Under Obama, the main emphasis of US military operations would gradually shift by 2010 from Iraq to Afghanistan. This shift was predicated on a strong rhetorical emphasis on countering al-Qaeda, with military operations in Afghanistan considered essential to ensure it did not become an al-Qaeda "safe haven" as it had been prior to 9/11. In other words, the essence of the war on terrorism discourse was fundamentally retained, with the "terror threat" remaining the top US national security priority. Moreover, apart from the change of central front, US counterterrorism operations around the world continued to expand rather than decline.

Institutionalizing GWOT

In the months and years after 9/11, counterterrorism emerged as the "overarching concept" defining US strategy, with significant resources allocated for this mission.[147] In some cases, existing military organizations that dealt with this issue (e.g., Special Forces) received a portion of the increased resources. In other cases, new organizations emerged within the DoD devoted specifically to the "counterterrorism" mission (e.g., the Defense Intelligence Agency's "Joint Intelligence Task Force-Counterterrorism," the Office of the Secretary of Defense's "Policy Counterterrorism Evaluation Group," the Defense Advanced Research Projects Agency's "Total Information Awareness" program [later renamed "Terrorism Information Awareness"], the Joint Staff's (J-5) "Office of the Deputy Director for the War on Terrorism," the US Navy's "N5WoT" and "Cell for

Submarine Counterterrorism Operations,"[148] etc.). The creation of these new bureaucracies further entrenched, and kept to the fore, the GWOT discourse within DoD.

Were the discursive institutionalization of the war on terror merely limited to the creation of new offices, the GWOT would have remained a top priority for the DoD but may have taken a very different path. When considering the amount of resources allocated to both the old and new counterterrorism bureaucracies in relation to the DoD's total budget for counterterrorism, it is quite evident that the vast majority of funds have been consumed not by these organizations but by the mainstream DoD itself (e.g., the military services, combatant commands, and other DoD agencies). The reason for this was mainly related to the discursive linkage between the GWOT and the "wars" in Afghanistan and Iraq. For instance, because Iraq had been officially designated the central front of the GWOT, any military units serving there, or remotely associated with the deployment there, were considered part of the GWOT.

This section will examine how the institutionalization of the GWOT in the DoD worked in practice by concentrating on four important areas: (1) strategy documents, (2) budget justifications, (3) the military services, specifically the US Navy, and (4) homeland defense. Although limiting the focus to these four areas neglects a number of other important aspects of the GWOT's institutionalization, such as the GWOT's role in US military culture (e.g., GWOT medals, GWOT service required for promotions, etc.), it nevertheless provides a useful means for highlighting the wide scope of the GWOT discourse trap.

Strategic Plans

Before embarking on a "war of choice," or even a "war of necessity," it is usually accepted practice for military leaders, in consultation with politicians, to devise a war plan in which their objectives, strategy, adversary, and victory standards are enunciated. The purpose for doing so is to ensure the correct means are used to achieve the desired ends, thereby increasing the chances the war will be a "winnable" one. In the case of the DoD and the GWOT, the war preceded the war plan. As highlighted in the previous section, in the weeks after 9/11, numerous memos were issued by Rumsfeld, including general guidance for the development of war plans by the combatant commanders. However, this guidance did not constitute a formal GWOT war plan. As will be shown, in 2002, a formal war plan for the GWOT was developed, known as the National Military Strategic Plan for the War on Terrorism (NMSP-WOT), but one year later, Rumsfeld criticized this plan and insisted a new one be developed. In 2006, the Joint Chiefs of Staff formally released a new and unclassified version of the revised NMSP-WOT, which it described as "the authoritative document to describe the nature of the war, the nature of the enemy, and the military strategy to face the enemy."[149] By tracing the genealogy of the NMSP-WOT, it is possible to highlight how the DoD had initially conceived of and approached the concept of waging a war on terrorism, or rather, how little strategic thinking went into this.

In order to gain an appreciation for the document itself, it is necessary first to identify who wrote it and when it was written. The original drafting of the NMSP-WOT was undertaken by the Office of the Deputy Director of the War on Terrorism, Joint Staff (J-5). This office, headed by a one-star general, was originally created in October 2001 as a planning cell responsible for reviewing GWOT plans submitted by the combatant commands.[150] In summer 2002, General Myers ordered an initial drafting of what became known as the NMSP-WOT. The purpose of the document was not to describe specific battle plans or prescribe future operations but instead to lay down the principles to guide commanders around the world who were responsible for that planning.[151] The drafting was coordinated with Rumsfeld as well as the National Security Council and White House. In October 2002, Myers approved the first version of the NMSP-WOT. This 150-page document was classified Top Secret, thereby limiting its distribution within the DoD.[152] The document's framework identified three basic stages in the GWOT. The first stage was to attack al-Qaeda. The second stage involved putting pressure on countries that supported terrorism. The third stage aimed to build a long-term, antiterrorist global environment to discredit terrorism worldwide.[153] It is important to note here the description of the adversary—namely, al-Qaeda and "terrorism worldwide"—as this would change significantly in later versions of the NMSP-WOT.

On October 16, 2003, Rumsfeld sent a memo to the top four senior officials in the Pentagon under the subject heading "Global War on Terrorism." In this memo, Rumsfeld asked a number of questions that highlighted the problems inherent in managing a war on terrorism. Although this memo received a good deal of notoriety for its inclusion of the phrase "long, hard slog" in reference to Afghanistan and Iraq, a number of other issues raised in the memo are directly relevant to understanding the dissatisfaction with the GWOT war planning that had previously occurred. According to the memo, "does the US need to fashion a broad, integrated plan to stop the next generation of terrorists? The US is putting relatively little effort into a long-range plan, but we are putting a great deal of effort into trying to stop terrorists."[154]

Rumsfeld also queried about a lack of metrics to determine whether or not the United States was "winning or losing" the GWOT: "Today, we lack metrics to know if we are winning or losing the global war on terror. Are we capturing, killing or deterring and dissuading more terrorists every day than the madrassas and the radical clerics are recruiting, training and deploying against us?"[155]

The memo provided the inspiration for the drafting of a new version of the NMSP-WOT that would "state some fundamental propositions about the war."[156] The revised NMSP-WOT was also intended to settle a number of disputes inside the military over exactly whom it was fighting, and with what means.[157] The two officials responsible for developing this document were Feith and Deputy Director for the War on Terrorism Brigadier General Robert Caslen. This document took 18 months to produce, having undergone over 40 revisions in a coordination process that included the Campaign Planning Committee, the Joint Staff, the Office of the Secretary of Defense, the military services, the combatant commands, the National Security Council, and other agencies. In March 2005, the final 25-page report, plus 13 annexes, was signed and became formal Pentagon policy.[158] This report was classified Secret, although an unclassified version was released in February 2006.[159] The distribution of an unclassified version was part of a DoD effort to improve collaboration with other federal agencies and foreign governments.[160] The draft NMSP-WOT would also be briefed to President Bush in May 2004, who subsequently ordered it to form the basis of National Security Presidential Directive-46/Homeland Security Presidential Directive-15, otherwise known as the "War on Terrorism Directive."[161]

Unlike the original 2002 version of the NMSP-WOT, the revised 2005 version represented the first official strategy document that not only examined the nature of the GWOT and provided a road map for prosecuting it but also established metrics to determine where and whether progress was being made. According to General Caslen, prior to the publication of the revised NMSP-WOT, "everybody had their own idea of what the enemy was. Therefore, everybody had their own idea of how to fight it. We had different ideas among the services, among the commands, among the different agencies."[162] Curiously, the 38-page unclassified version of the NMSP-WOT makes only a single reference to operations in Iraq and Afghanistan, thus highlighting the "global" nature of the war while simultaneously downplaying the "centrality" of the Iraq war.[163]

Rumsfeld's query about creating metrics for the GWOT, apart from highlighting the lack of attention the DoD devoted to this problem in the first two years of the GWOT, also raised the broader issue of how to define the adversary, how to define the nature of the conflict, and how to identify the best means to achieve "victory."[164] All these issues would figure prominently in the revised NMSP-WOT and would prompt a number of debates within the DoD about the appropriateness of various metrics, as well as how best to define the adversary.[165] One Pentagon office tasked with developing "measures of effectiveness" for the GWOT and whose work fed into the revised NMSP-WOT was the Office of the Deputy Undersecretary of Defense for Advanced Systems and Concepts (DUSD-ASC).[166] In response to Rumsfeld's October 2003 memo, this office ran a number of war games to examine alternative strategies for the GWOT. In September 2004, the DUSD-ASC's Defense Adaptive Red Team (DART), which ran these war games, concluded that the nature of the GWOT was essentially about countering a "global insurgency."[167] As such, the DART advocated a strategy that incorporated many of the same methods used to counter classic insurgencies. A number of other study groups also reached this conclusion.[168]

Among the most important and contentious issues to arise during the course of intradepartmental coordination of the draft NMSP-WOT was the description of the adversary. As noted, there were a number of advocates for labeling the adversary a "global insurgency." There was also a strong constituency for retaining the emphasis on "terrorism." A compromise was reached and the adversary was characterized as "violent extremists" (Rumsfeld's preferred term), with some two dozen specific groups to be targeted.[169] In the document, the term *Al-Qaeda Associated Movement*, or AQAM (composed of al-Qaeda and associated extremists), was used to label the main adversary, although the broader threat was identified as "extremist Sunni and Shia movements that exploit Islam for political ends" and form part of a "global web of enemy networks."[170] Interestingly, the NMSP-WOT makes no mention of other "adversaries" that had previously and subsequently been officially associated as part of the GWOT, such as the Fuerzas Armadas Revolucionarias de Colombia (FARC).

Another significant issue highlighted in the NMSP-WOT was the need to counter ideological support for terrorism. This issue had been of concern to the DoD leadership since the start of the GWOT but had not previously been given as high a priority as "direct action" missions.[171] The establishment in 2001 of the Office of Strategic Influence had set a precedent, albeit initially short lived, for giving the DoD the mission of trying to undermine the adversary's ideological appeal.[172] Identifying this requirement is important for at least two reasons. First, tasking the DoD for this responsibility represented an extension of the DoD's definition of *counterterrorism* and broadened the number of institutions within the DoD that could play a role. Second, the mission of undermining the ideological appeal of "terrorist" adversaries, which in practice primarily meant increasing positive perceptions of the United States, would allow different elements of the DoD to label their missions as related to the GWOT. As will be highlighted in the next section, missions designed to "win over" populations in countries such as the Philippines and Djibouti, as well as humanitarian missions, including the US military support to the victims of the 2004 tsunami, were regarded as contributing to the GWOT. The perceived importance of these missions relative to "victory" in the GWOT cannot be understated.[173] For instance, in the course of describing US participation in the tsunami relief, Principal Deputy Undersecretary of Defense for Policy Ryan

Henry stated, "Our principal victory in our overall war on terrorism was demonstrating to [Indonesians] that we want to be in partnership with them, an element for good in the world."[174]

While the NMSP-WOT provided the broad framework for understanding the DoD's approach to the conflict, operationalizing this strategy into a campaign plan format was a responsibility allocated to the Special Operations Command (SOCOM). In January 2003, Rumsfeld had designated SOCOM as the "supported command" in the GWOT, whereas the regional combatant commands were to be "supporting commands."[175] As a result of this designation, SOCOM's focus shifted almost entirely to "planning, directing, and fighting the GWOT."[176] Annex C of the NMSP-WOT directed SOCOM to draft a global campaign plan and to "synchronize" the counterterrorism plans of the five combatant commands.[177] The resulting "Department of Defense Global War on Terrorism Campaign Plan," also known as "Concept Plan (CONPLAN) 7500," was drafted at the Center for Special Operations under the direction of Lieutenant General Dell Dailey and included specific geographic input from the special operations components of the regional combatant commands.

CONPLAN 7500 covered a wide variety of overt and clandestine military activities, but its main focus was on countering AQAM, including more than a dozen groups spread around the globe. These groups included the Egyptian Islamic Jihad, Ansar al-Islam, Jemaah Islamiya, and the Salafist Group for Preaching and Combat in Saharan Africa.[178] Since its 2004 drafting of a "Joint Operational Concept for Defeating Terrorist Organizations," SOCOM had defined the adversary as a "global insurgency" and the nature of the conflict as "a struggle for popular perceptions of political legitimacy and control over Islamic civilization."[179] However, due to the primacy of CENTCOM, as a result of its lead role in Iraq and Afghanistan (where SOCOM *supports* CENTCOM), SOCOM was relegated to fight this "global war" outside these two theaters. This administrative reality meant that whereas the large-scale military operations in Iraq and Afghanistan received the bulk of attention, there was a considerable amount of small-scale and discrete Special Forces activity occurring elsewhere. It would only be years later, as the large-scale US military presence in Iraq and Afghanistan declined, that these previously neglected operations would receive more attention and, along with the increased use of armed drones, be discussed as a "new" approach to "counterterrorism."[180]

Tracing the genealogy of the NMSP-WOT provides a useful means to illustrate the problems associated with arriving at a DoD consensus about the nature of the war and how to describe the adversary. It is important to note that until the publication of the revised NMSP-WOT in 2005, the DoD's actions to prosecute the GWOT were still being guided by a war plan that had been identified by the leadership as inadequate, even though it was the same leadership that had produced that plan. Thus Rumsfeld's 2003 request to his officials to draft a new war plan reflected the concern of the DoD leadership that the war had taken on a life of its own, and therefore a need existed to give definition to the conflict. As can be discerned by comparing the dates of the strategy documents (e.g., NMSP-WOT and CONPLAN 7500) with those of the US military interventions (such as the Philippines and Africa), the war plans were being defined by the war itself, rather than the other way around. The plans would also be instrumental in institutionalizing the GWOT in DoD. As of 2012, no evidence has come to light regarding any revisions to the NMSP-WOT since 2006, suggesting that the United States lacks an updated version of this plan.

The US Navy and the GWOT

As a result of the 1986 Goldwater-Nichols Act, the military services' role in US defense policy was limited mainly to organizing, training and equipping the armed forces, whereas operational control was allocated to the regional combatant commands. Nevertheless, the services themselves continued to play an influential role in defense policy making given their responsibility for military education, doctrine development, procurement, and so on. Moreover, although they lacked operational control over their forces, the services still retained their own bureaucracies, such as planning, intelligence, and congressional liaison. Consequently, when attempting to ascertain the breadth of dissemination of the GWOT discourse within the DoD, it is important to examine how this discourse was institutionalized within the services.

The reason the Navy has been chosen here is that it provides an opportunity to demonstrate how the war on terrorism discourse was employed by a military service that had played a perceived marginal role in the GWOT relative to the other services. As the GWOT was mainly a land-centric "war," as highlighted in Iraq and Afghanistan, where the participation of the Army and Marine Corps were most prominent, the Navy had been criticized, both internally and externally, for not marketing its participation in the GWOT, thereby suffering a loss of influence. Due to its perceived need to maintain relevance, the Navy has had to incorporate the GWOT discourse and adapt its forces accordingly, perhaps more so than any other service. Therefore this section will highlight the US Navy from the perspective of a military service defining and institutionalizing its role in the GWOT.

With the collapse of the USSR, the US Navy increasingly viewed countering a rising Chinese navy as one of its primary post–Cold War missions.[181] The "China threat" discourse that permeated the Navy was directly linked to maintaining a force aimed at a peer competitor, or one that traditionally stressed platforms such as aircraft carriers and nuclear submarines. Similar to the Cold

War period, the Navy emphasized a "blue-water" force rather than a "brown-water" or "green-water" one. Moreover, counterterrorism occupied little or no place in the broader Navy discourse on sea or maritime power, and it is very difficult to find any evidence of the Navy designing its platforms or restructuring its force for "counterterrorism" purposes.[182]

Before 9/11, the Navy's counterterrorism function was primarily assigned to its special operations component, the Navy Seals, although it was Navy ships that launched Tomahawk cruise missiles against Afghanistan and Sudan in 1998. After the terrorist attack on the *USS Cole* in 2000, the Navy chose to review its antiterrorism procedures but did not identify any new capabilities or make doctrinal changes.[183] In the years after 9/11, supporting the GWOT would gradually emerge as the Navy's top priority, including significant changes in the Navy's doctrine, procurement, structure, funding, planning, and operations. This change can be classed into two periods: from 9/11 to early 2005, and the period thereafter.

From 2001 to early 2005, the Navy took relatively minor steps to make the service relevant to the GWOT. Shortly after 9/11, Chief of Naval Operations (CNO) Admiral Vern Clark directed the formation of two entities responsible for conceptualizing the Navy's role in the emerging "war on terrorism." The first, and more senior of the two, was informally known as the "War Council." This body consisted of a dozen four- and three-star admirals who would meet once a week with the CNO to discuss the Navy's role in the war.[184] The council was also responsible for preparing a five-year plan of the Navy's "wartime" requirements.[185] The second entity was the Naval Operations Group, otherwise known as "Deep Blue," attached to the Navy Staff's Plans, Policy, and Operations directorate. Modelled on the Air Force's "Checkmate," Deep Blue was responsible for providing "intellectual support" to the CNO and the Navy's regional component commanders on potential Navy efforts to tackle the GWOT at the strategic level.[186]

Apart from the limited role played by these advisory groups in developing Navy policy, there was little attention paid to shifting the broader focus of the Navy toward a "war on terrorism" orientation. During this period, the Navy was reluctant to institutionalize the GWOT and make it a top priority, despite its participation in Afghanistan, Iraq, and other theaters. For instance, as part of the GWOT, the Navy intensified its board and search operations and conducted maritime interdiction operations, ostensibly for counterterrorism purposes and "homeland defense." In addition, the Navy established a GWOT role by sponsoring and cooperating with other navies in "counterterrorism" exercises and missions, such as NATO's Operation Active Endeavour. However, the Navy had not altered its organization or structure, nor attempted to determine how the GWOT would define the future Navy. For example, the Navy's 2020 vision statement, "Sea Power 21," reflected the naval thinking of the 1990s and showed few traces of the emerging war on terrorism discourse. It was only in 2005 that the Navy leadership began to shift the service's long-term priorities toward the GWOT.[187] The timing for this shift is unclear but may have been related to highlighting the Navy's relevance in the run-up to the 2006 QDR.[188] In spring 2005, the CNO tasked the head of Deep Blue, Rear Admiral Michael Mahon, to lead the Navy's "Global War on Terrorism Working Group," an entity created to identify Navy capability gaps in the war on terrorism and to provide a prioritized list of sea service requirements.[189] Also in 2005, but separate from the Deep Blue study, the CNO directed the Naval Studies Board to establish the "Committee on the Role of Naval Forces in the Global War on Terror" to assess the capabilities and capability gaps of naval forces in prosecuting the GWOT.[190] Within the Navy Staff, a strategy office called N5–War on Terrorism (N5WoT) was created to work with the other services to increase Navy support to land operations in Iraq and Afghanistan. This office was also responsible for organizing and chairing a weekly "War on Terror Federation" meeting to "synchronize and align GWOT efforts across the Navy."[191]

A June 2005 memo from Director of Navy Staff (DNS) Vice Admiral Albert Church III to the Navy's senior leadership outlined the CNO's plans for expanding the service's commitment to the GWOT.[192] This guidance was followed by a July 6 memo from the DNS titled "Implementation of Chief of Naval Operations Guidance-Global War on Terrorism Capabilities." This memo directed several actions to expand the Navy's capabilities to prosecute the GWOT.[193] In October 2005, the new CNO, Admiral Mike Mullen, issued guidance calling for *more* initiatives geared toward boosting the Navy's capabilities to fight terrorist networks. Specifically, the guidance called for the Navy to "identify requirements to organize, train, maintain and equip a Navy Expeditionary Combat Command (NECC) to coordinate the activities of several Navy organizations performing [counterterrorism] activities."[194] The Navy also announced a number of other initiatives intended to "increase its capabilities for participating in the GWOT." These included establishing a multilateral maritime partnership ("1,000 ship Navy"), establishing sea bases called "Global Fleet Stations" in various regions of the world, developing "Global Maritime Intelligence Integration," and reestablishing the Navy's riverine force, as well as creating several new intelligence and civil affairs units.[195] Another key aspect of the Navy's GWOT discourse was the service's ability to conduct humanitarian missions, such as the tsunami relief effort. For the Navy, these activities contributed to "winning hearts and minds," which was discursively constructed as being an essential mission in the GWOT, and one the Navy was uniquely capable of performing.[196]

By January 2006, the Navy had stood up the NECC and was in the process of adding an expeditionary force. Senior Navy officials justified these actions as instrumental to expanding the Navy's GWOT role.[197] However, in its effort to become more GWOT-relevant, the Navy met resistance from the other services. For instance, Navy plans to stand up riverine and combat forces were criticized as supplanting some roles of the Army, Marine Corps, and Coast Guard.[198] The Navy's plans to develop a "naval infantry" component that could take part in GWOT operations met strong resistance from the Marine Corps, thereby forcing the CNO to redesignate this new capability as a "maritime security force."[199] The extent to which the Navy was really intent on transforming itself to deal with "irregular warfare" is difficult to gauge. On the one hand, there were numerous statements connecting the establishment of a riverine capability with counterterrorism. As the commanding officer of one of the riverine squadrons noted, its very creation "sends a message to terrorists that we're serious about the global war on terrorism."[200] Likewise, the commander of another squadron stated that "we will be the Navy's face in the global war on terrorism."[201] On the other hand, there has been some criticism, including within the Navy, that the service was merely trying to adopt policies to abide by its own discourse on the need to be more relevant, rather than truly "transform." As one Navy officer wrote in the service's official publication *Proceedings*, "the bottom line is that Big Navy is paying the riverine concept only the attention required to keep the service relevant."[202]

As the Navy increased its discursive association with the GWOT, long-standing tensions emerged in the Navy between procuring capabilities intended for China scenarios and capabilities intended for counterterrorism. Due to the Navy's public emphasis on GWOT, there was a significant de-emphasis in the discourse related to China. According to naval analyst Ronald O'Rourke, the Navy had focused on GWOT-related activities to garner more funding support. However, O'Rourke warned, "If you keep talking to policymakers about a Navy for the GWOT and for general maritime security operations, then that's what you might get."[203] Among the most significant changes to the Navy, especially after 2005, was its increasing discursive focus on developing "brown-water" and "green-water" capabilities for GWOT purposes, rather than the traditional "blue-water" capabilities intended to counter a perceived "China threat." This focus was partially facilitated by a merger of the discourse on "blue-water" capabilities with the discourse on capabilities intended to showcase a "brown-water" Navy. For instance, in March 2005, the Navy commander of submarine forces, Vice Admiral Chuck Munns, established a Cell for Submarine Counterterrorism Operations responsible for demonstrating the role of submarines in the GWOT.[204] According to the cell's deputy director, Commander David Kelly, "today, the submarine has a substantial role in supporting the GWOT . . . our submarine force has never been in higher demand than it is today, including in the heyday of the Cold War."[205] Likewise, Rear Admiral Mark Kenny, who headed the cell and would later head the Navy's Irregular Warfare Office, stated that submarines "are the Navy's premiere counterterrorism tool, no doubt about it."[206] Statements such as these reflect the extent to which the Navy had discursively adapted to the counterterrorism mission, whereas only a few years previously, this scarcely existed at all in the Navy's discourse, much less in that of the submarine force. Even when the submarine force had been conducting "counterterrorism" missions, such as in 1998, the Navy had not viewed it as necessary to discursively associate submarines with counterterrorism, at least not in such a blatant way as it did later on. In late 2006, the original office's mission was expanded to include the surface and aviation branches of the service, and the office was renamed the Center for Expeditionary Counterterrorism Operations. More recently, in 2008, the admiral who set up that original office, Rear Admiral Kenny, was invited to head up the newly created Irregular Warfare Office on the Navy Staff. This office was tasked with institutionalizing ongoing "irregular warfare" missions into Navy strategic planning.[207]

Before proceeding further, a brief mention should be made about what the Navy means when it refers to "irregular warfare." Since at least the aftermath of the 2006 QDR, in which the term *irregular warfare* was highlighted, the Navy has institutionalized it in the service's discourse, preferring it to other terms such as *counterterrorism* or *counterinsurgency*. However, the term has not been without controversy. One of the semantic problems associated with the term relates to the difference between regular and irregular warfare. As head of the Navy's Irregular Warfare Office Rear Admiral Philip Greene has noted, "what is often described as irregular warfare is actually part of the regular mission set for the Navy."[208] In practice, this semantic debate had more to do with the types of ships and missions each were associated with. Regular missions were often associated with carrier battle groups, whereas irregular missions involved much smaller ships as well as Navy special warfare units. But in recent years, the Navy gradually widened the definition of irregular warfare to such an extent that conceivably any Navy platform could be associated with it. Moreover, the term *irregular warfare* was viewed as being too limited, with the consequence that it was superseded by references to "confronting irregular challenges." In this regard, the Navy has also taken the lead in widening the definition of what missions are relevant. Thus any action the Navy takes that is remotely related to preventing conflict, such as building a school or digging a well in the Horn of Africa, falls within the category of "confronting irregular challenges."[209]

In the case of the Navy under Obama, there has continued to be considerable public criticism about its "marginal role" relative to the Army and Marine Corps, as well as the rising costs of its ships. According to Defense Secretary

Robert Gates, "at the end of the day, we have to ask whether the nation can really afford a Navy that relies on $3 to $6 billion destroyers, $7 billion submarines, and $11 billion carriers."[210] And beyond the rising cost of the Navy's ships, the overall number of ships was increasing as well. Under Obama, the Navy has requested 324 ships for the future rather than the 313 projected under Bush.[211] However, in addition to making a case for a stronger Navy to match an increasing Chinese naval "threat," the Navy has also countered criticism over the rising costs and numbers of its ships by demonstrating their "relevance" to current and projected "irregular" conflicts.[212] Similar to under the latter years of the Bush administration, the Navy's use of the term *irregular warfare* to cover many of its activities has been a very noticeable trend, particularly with regards labeling various platforms that had previously been built to fight conventional conflicts, as also being useful for irregular conflicts. Similarly, considerable efforts have been made to promote the idea of a more "expeditionary" Navy whose skills could be useful in conflicts such as Iraq. For example, highlighted in the 2010 QDR was a reference to the Navy adding a fourth riverine squadron to its force structure, despite the fact that the declining US force levels and changing mission in Iraq were to leave the original three squadrons with a much smaller role, and in the aftermath of the US military withdrawal from Iraq at the end of 2011, no role at all.[213] Nor would these units play any role in Afghanistan.

The Navy's rhetoric surrounding its "irregular warfare" role has been employed quite deliberately. It was not a coincidence that at the same time the 2010 QDR was released, CNO Admiral Gary Roughead also released a paper titled, "The US Navy's Vision for Confronting Irregular Challenges."[214] But despite the Navy's rhetorical emphasis on adapting the Navy to "irregular warfare," the nature of the service's finances tell a very different story. Rather than allocating money from its baseline budget to fund initiatives associated with "irregular warfare," the Navy is mainly using money allocated from "emergency supplementals." In 2010, the Navy had both a baseline budget of $161 billion as well as $18.5 billion in supplemental funding. Not only did the supplemental funding pay for direct operational expenses, but it also funded the 40,000-strong NECC, as well as 206 new aircraft of all kinds.[215] It should be remembered that the NECC was created specifically for the purpose of making the Navy relevant to the "war on terrorism." That the Navy has been unwilling to incorporate its most "relevant" institution into the mainstream defense budget raises questions as to how seriously the Navy considers this issue, or to put it slightly differently, it casts significant doubt on the Navy's willingness to place constraints on naval spending in more traditional areas.

This reluctance to reduce expenditure in the "mainstream" Navy can be seen in the increasing discursive association of almost all aspects of the service with "irregular warfare." In their discourse, many senior Navy officials have rejected the notion that the NECC is representative of the Navy's efforts to be relevant for irregular warfare, instead insisting that traditional platforms play a crucial role as well. In other words, the NECC did not represent the sum total of the Navy's irregular warfare assets. For instance, Vice Admiral Barry McCullough, the Deputy Chief of Naval Operations for Integration of Capabilities and Resources, said he was worried that the NECC's scope was too narrow and noted how aircraft carriers, destroyers, and amphibious ships are not only conventional platforms but are flexible enough to do any mission.[216] McCullough's discursive association of conventional platforms to take on irregular missions has been notable in other cases as well. For example, the development of unmanned undersea vehicles became discursively linked to irregular warfare rather than antisubmarine warfare.[217] Also, Ohio-class ballistic missile submarines have been converted to carry conventional Tomahawk cruise missile and Special Forces to conduct irregular warfare missions.[218]

Within the Navy there have been a few dissident voices about the utility of aircraft carriers for irregular warfare, with the focus instead on other ships that can operate closer to land. However, these dissidents have been wary about reducing the number of carriers in the fleet, arguing they should still be kept in case of a conventional war.[219] In other words, even the dissidents within the Navy limit their criticism to the type of ships that are employed in irregular warfare and avoid making the more general criticism that the Navy may not be the most appropriate means of dealing with this type of conflict and that resources could be devoted to more productive endeavors.

Regardless of the validity or lack thereof in the arguments put forward to justify retaining and even expanding the Navy in a period of economic hardship and competing priorities, what is undeniably absent from this discourse is any significant criticism of continuing to employ this instrument of national power, particularly compared with nonmilitary instruments. As noted earlier, the idea of employing large-scale military forces for the purpose of counterterrorism is a post-9/11 phenomenon. However, in the present environment, to challenge the orthodoxy of the necessity for disproportionately large investments in military hardware to deal with this security challenge is akin to heresy and hence this is absent from the discourse on the subject.

The Defense Budget and GWOT Emergency Supplementals

One of the key means to determine the way in which the DoD has understood and given meaning to the term *GWOT* is to examine the use of the GWOT discourse when obtaining funding from Congress. Similar to the early days of the Cold War, when the public mood in the United States was one of support for almost anything proposed in the name of national security, with

Congress automatically approving increases in the defense budget, the DoD has also benefited from a post-9/11 boom in defense spending.[220] However, the problem of choosing among the almost endless list of ways and means to improve national security necessitates competition within the bureaucracy. As President Eisenhower observed, "words like 'essential' and 'indispensable' and 'absolute minimum' become the common coin of the realm—and they are spent with wild abandon."[221] In this sense, it was probably inevitable that as the GWOT became the top national security priority, various interest groups would justify requests for funding as being necessary for counterterrorism.[222] Resulting from this bandwagon effect has been an increase in interdepartmental and intradepartmental competition, as well as further definitional broadening and entrenchment of *GWOT* within the bureaucracy.

Unlike in previous wars, such as World War II, the Bush administration chose to fund the GWOT primarily from emergency supplemental requests rather than incorporating the cost of the war into the baseline defense budget after the first year or so of the conflict. The Cold War was not paid for by annual or biannual emergency supplemental requests; instead it formed the basis of the regular defense budget. After 9/11, the defense budget would increase significantly, but this extra funding merely supplemented a separate GWOT funding mechanism. Among the problems of labeling funds as *emergency* is the lack of effective external oversight. By assigning emergency status for GWOT appropriations, the DoD sidestepped the detailed justification and reporting requirements of the regular budget process, which is scrutinized by both the budget and armed services committees in Congress. Likewise, given their emergency status, the amount of time available for oversight is limited.[223] Furthermore, whereas the annual defense budget is subject to ceilings imposed both by the White House's Office of Management and Budget and by the Congress, emergency supplemental appropriations fall outside these ceilings. Since 9/11, these emergency funds constituted a rising share of the DoD's total resources. Annual GWOT funding grew from $14 billion in Fiscal Year (FY) 2001, when US military operations in Afghanistan began, to $120 billion in FY 2006.[224] As of 2006, roughly 80 percent of the GWOT-appropriated money was related to Operation Iraqi Freedom, with Operations Enduring Freedom and Noble Eagle (homeland defense) making up the remaining majority.[225] By 2008, emergency funding had reached more than $180 billion. Overall, from 2001 through 2011, the United States had allocated about $1.2 trillion to the Pentagon for the GWOT/Overseas Contingency Operations (OCO).[226]

The necessity for rapidly rising expenditures has been attributed to the GWOT and marketed to Congress as such by defense officials. According to Stephen Kosiak, the increasing expenditures stem not just from military operations but also from "the Defense Department's decision to expand dramatically the notion of what can and should be funded through GWOT supplementals, rather than through the regular annual defense budget."[227] This expansion was made explicit in an October 2006 memo from Deputy Defense Secretary Gordon England to the military services.[228] The memo provided the military services new guidance in drawing up their requests for supplemental funding. The guidance stated a supplemental request could now include "incremental costs related to the longer war against terror (not just OEF/OIF)"[229] The phrase *longer war against terror* was not defined and could theoretically cover anything remotely associated with the current or future operations that constituted the "war."

As England's memo demonstrates, placing items in the GWOT budget was viewed as a means of facilitating funding for items or projects that might otherwise have been difficult to receive approval for in the regular defense budget. With this official guidance, the DoD "opened the floodgates" in terms of what the Services could ask to have funded through GWOT supplementals rather than the DoD's traditional definition of war costs as strictly related to "immediate" war needs.[230] Emergency funding was sought for the acquisition of equipment that had long lead times and was unrelated to the urgent demands of war.[231] Each of the GWOT supplementals submitted has also included some funding for programs and activities that are, at best, only indirectly related to the wars in Iraq and Afghanistan. The most obvious example of this was the inclusion of funding for the Army's modularity program in the FY 2005 and FY 2006 GWOT supplemental requests, despite the fact the Army would be pursuing this program whether or not the service was engaged in Iraq and Afghanistan.[232] There have also been numerous other "emergency" requests submitted by the Navy, Air Force, and Marines to fund systems still in development.[233] Likewise, supplemental funding was requested for the expansion of the Army and Marine Corps. These two services requested "emergency" funds to expand by 92,000 personnel due to overstretch sustained as a result of the GWOT.[234]

Associating funding requests with the GWOT extends beyond obtaining funding through emergency supplementals but was also a key feature of the regular defense budget process. Testimonials for most weapon and platform acquisition programs, whether or not begun before 9/11, alluded to the GWOT as the reason for their purchase.[235] Indeed, most of the military budget increases were used to develop and procure military hardware that had little or nothing to do with traditional counterterrorism, such as ballistic missile defense, the Air Force's F-22 air-to-air fighter, the Marine Corps's V-22 tilt-rotor aircraft, the Army's Comanche helicopter and Stryker combat vehicle, and the F-35 Joint Strike Fighter. Similarly, proponents of "transformation" cited terrorism as one of the reasons the armed forces must exploit information technology and networking principles.

The funding of the GWOT helped constitute the nature and character of the conflict itself through the discursive identification of the DoD policies, programs, and personnel associated with it. It had the twofold effect of giving the impression that the use of large-scale military forces were an appropriate means of defeating terrorism and that defeating terrorism was the main operational mission of the US military. Additionally, placing the Iraq conflict in the GWOT budget further reified that conflict as GWOT related.[236] A number of critics have noted that empowering the US military to take on tasks traditionally handled by the State Department, such as training foreign militaries, not only has led to an increasing militarization of US foreign policy but has diverted the DoD's attention from its core missions.[237] Defense officials have also used the GWOT association to facilitate the funding of various programs that were only loosely connected with ongoing operations and could otherwise be funded through the regular defense budget. This has sparked a competition within the DoD to discursively construct their programs as relevant to the GWOT, since such a construction was perceived to have a direct impact on appropriations. Among the most important consequences of this process was to limit effective oversight of defense expenditure and to ensure Congress's continued funding of the conflict by designating appropriations as emergency and essential for the GWOT (i.e., politically harmful not to vote for).[238]

As already noted, shortly after coming into office, the Obama administration discarded the term *GWOT* in favor of *Overseas Contingency Operations*. While it is still unclear where the precise impetus for this change derived, the new term was employed in a memo that noted it originated from the Office of Management and Budget.[239] Despite the change in terminology, the same funding mechanism applied as before. As such, emergency supplemental appropriations for OCO replaced those for the GWOT. And like before, defense officials sought to use the emergency supplementals as a way of evading caps on the base defense budget. This practice would continue as of 2012, despite attempts by the administration to bring supplemental appropriations into the defense budget. Moreover, defense officials have repeatedly argued that the long-term "reset" costs associated with the wars in Iraq and Afghanistan—in other words the costs to replace and repair equipment—should also be funded from emergency appropriations as opposed to the mainstream defense budget.[240] This means that, theoretically at least, even when the US mission in Afghanistan comes to an end, that "emergency" funding will still be necessary for many years thereafter simply to purchase and upgrade equipment that had previously been used there.

Defending the Homeland

For the DoD, the GWOT was a war composed of a multitude of fronts, including a home front. Throughout the US government, 9/11 sparked a significant interest in protecting the homeland and devoting substantial resources for this task. Before Operation Enduring Freedom, US military forces had already deployed inside the United States, beginning on September 14, 2001, as part of Operation Noble Eagle. This operation, which was the third costliest in the GWOT, after Iraq and Afghanistan, involved fighter planes flying combat air patrols over US territory for the purpose of preventing another 9/11-type attack. These patrols would continue for a number of years (later replaced by permanent strip alert status) and were viewed as an important element of the GWOT, despite the emergence of other bureaucracies (e.g., Department of Homeland Security) charged with homeland security generally and airport security in particular.[241] The US Army also took part in Noble Eagle, which included deploying soldiers to guard airports, nuclear power plants, dams, power-generation facilities, tunnels, bridges, rail stations, and emergency operations centers. In addition, the Army's ground-based air defense artillery units were deployed in the National Capital Region. In the process of taking on this increasing number of homeland missions, the DoD created new bureaucracies, developed doctrine and operational plans, mobilized tens of thousands of reservists and members of the National Guard, assigned the counterterrorism function to a number of units, conducted numerous exercises, and broadened the definition of what constituted homeland defense and security.

Within the DoD, 9/11 transformed the discourse related to the department's domestic operational roles and responsibilities. As part of the trend within the US government of focusing on the homeland, the DoD chose to bandwagon rather than be left out. This shift ran counter to the military's traditional reluctance to accept responsibility for domestic missions, which were viewed as distractions from fighting wars overseas. Due to the perceived degradation of combat skills and high operational tempo that would ensue from a sustained domestic commitment, there was considerable ambivalence within the US military, particularly within the active-duty component, toward devoting resources to this task relative to overseas commitments.[242] For instance, the Navy viewed homeland defense as a peripheral rather than a core mission and preferred a forward defense strategy.[243] This cultural norm within the DoD was reinforced by the legal limitations imposed upon the military by the Posse Comitatus Act, which bars military personnel from searching, seizing, or arresting people in the United States.

Several years prior to 9/11, the DoD examined the possibility of an expanded role in domestic "consequence management," particularly its ability to respond to a WMD attack. During this period, homeland counterterrorism was viewed primarily as an Army function, rather than one in which the Navy and Air Force would also play significant roles. To help alleviate the increasing concerns of policy makers regarding the possibility of a major terrorist attack in the United States, the Army, which served as the executive agent within the DoD for domestic operations, began the process of defining its roles, missions, responsibilities, and requirements in this area. However, definitional debates within the military about what constituted homeland defense hampered this process.[244] In May 1999, the Army's Training and Doctrine Command produced a White Paper titled "Supporting Homeland Defense," even though the DoD did not have an official definition of *homeland defense*. At that time, Army war games involving homeland defense were limited to fighting another state adversary (e.g., another state's special operations forces) rather than a nonstate adversary (e.g., al-Qaeda).

By the winter of 2000, the definitional debates were unresolved and were to be further complicated by a new development. In response to civil libertarian and bureaucratic concerns with the DoD's potential domestic role in the event of a major terrorist attack, Deputy Defense Secretary John Hamre introduced the concept of "homeland security." As such, the concept of homeland defense became synonymous with homeland security, and the two terms would be used interchangeably without the necessary definitional clarity.[245] However, upon becoming defense secretary in January 2001, Rumsfeld specifically referred to *homeland defense* rather than *homeland security*. His reason for doing so was that *defense* implies deterrence and/or response whereas *security* is more comprehensive. The distinction was important to avoid having the Pentagon become embroiled in an ill-defined mission as the lead agency.[246] After 9/11, when Bush administration officials conceived of creating a "Homeland Defense Security Office," the DoD pushed back against including the word *defense*, arguing that "protecting the internal security of the homeland would be confused with the war-making mission of the Department of Defense."[247] The importance attached to defining terminology and assigning responsibility was made explicit in the 2001 QDR, which stated, "DoD must institutionalise definitions of homeland security, homeland defense, and civil support and address command relationships and responsibilities within the Defense Department. This will allow the Defense Department to identify and assign homeland security roles and missions as well as examine resource implications."[248]

After 9/11, the homeland defense mission was gradually institutionalized within the DoD through the creation of a number of bureaucracies, all of which were justified in terms of the war on terrorism. The most important of these was the creation of US Northern Command (NORTHCOM), headed by a four-star officer.[249] The impetus behind NORTHCOM originated in the late 1990s when the idea of an "Americas Command" responsible for defense of the Western hemisphere was floated in senior defense circles but rejected due to civil liberties concerns and objections from US Southern Command (SOUTHCOM). Instead, the DoD merely set up a Joint Task Force for Civil Support headed by a one-star officer under US Joint Forces Command. Rumsfeld initially considered the "Americas Command" option but rejected it in favor of a combatant command responsible only for the defense of the United States, Canada, and Mexico.[250]

A number of other offices throughout the DoD were created to meet the new mission. Initially, the position of special assistant to the secretary of defense for homeland security was created, as was a task force on homeland security. This would later change to the Office of Homeland Defense.[251] In 2003, Congress gave approval for a senior defense policy maker to supervise all the DoD's homeland defense activities, and the position of assistant secretary of defense for homeland defense was created.[252] In order to meet increasing planning requirements, the Joint Staff (J-5) established a Homeland Security Directorate. Likewise, in early 2002, Air Force Chief of Staff General John Jumper established a Homeland Security Directorate headed by a one-star general within the Air Staff, responsible for determining roles and institutionalizing the new requirements of homeland security into the Air Force's operations.[253] The Army, which had traditionally handled domestic operations through the Army Staff's Director of Military Support, also created a "homeland security integrated concept team," led by a director of homeland security at the Army Training and Doctrine Command.[254] One of the few operational units assigned to NORTHCOM, Joint Task Force-6, responsible for handling military support to counternarcotics operations, had its mission statement amended after 9/11 to include counterterrorism.[255] Other areas of increased DoD emphasis were biothreats, nuclear detection, and air and maritime domain awareness.[256]

The increasing domestic role of the DoD was further institutionalized in a number of documents. As noted earlier, agreeing to a common DoD definition of homeland security proved problematic and impeded doctrine writing. A March 2002 memo from General Myers gave official approval of a definition for homeland security, although the exact role played by the military was deferred.[257] In early 2004, Rumsfeld directed the creation of a homeland defense strategy that would finally clarify the military's role.[258] The resulting "Strategy for Homeland Defense and Civil Support" was published in June 2005.[259] At the operational level, NORTHCOM developed the first ever war plans for guarding against and responding to terrorist attacks in the United States. The plans consisted of two main documents known as "Concept of Operations Plan (CONPLAN) 2002" and "CONPLAN 0500."[260]

The discourse of homeland defense and security not only was institutionalized with the creation of DoD bureaucracies and documents but continued to broaden in terms of capabilities required to deal with this issue. Three examples will suffice to demonstrate this point. First, due to concerns that the Mexican and Canadian borders could be used to infiltrate terrorists into the United States, the military increasingly was employed in border security duties.[261] For the Navy, this included taking on new missions traditionally handled by the Coast Guard, such as harbor defense and port security.[262] Second, the Pentagon increased its domestic surveillance activities, targeting both Islamist organizations and antiwar groups. For instance, the Army's 902nd Military Intelligence Group ended up conducting surveillance on groups, many of which were quite harmless, that were already being tracked by the Department of Homeland Security as well as the FBI.[263] Third, the discourse related to the need to protect US airspace was also transformed due to the perceived terrorist threat.[264] Whereas before 9/11, acquiring a national missile defense system was discussed in connection with rogue states, after 9/11 the discourse shifted to countering terrorists. The shift in adversary shifted the debate on missile defense capabilities as well. Rather than merely countering Intercontinental Ballistic Missiles (ICBMs), the definition of missile defense was expanded to include cruise missile attacks, Unmanned Aerial Vehicles (UAV) attacks, as well as terrorist attacks launched from the sea.[265] This definition was subsequently used to justify developing deployable air and cruise missile defenses, as well as other tactical air defense assets, not to mention building up "persistent surveillance and reconnaissance" of the US maritime approaches.[266]

While the DoD discourse on homeland defense and security took on a life of its own, virtually absent from the discussion was whether or not the ever-expanding military response was necessary, particularly given the increasing overseas demands placed on the military as a result of operations in Iraq and Afghanistan, not to mention the plethora of resources dedicated to civilian agencies charged with the same mission.[267] By institutionalizing the homeland defense mission and contributing to the discourse on the need for military defenses to protect the homeland from terrorist threats, the DoD not only deepened its commitment to the GWOT but also ensured the marginalization of the pre-9/11 "minimalist" approach to domestic counterterrorism.

Constructing the Global War

This section will examine the DoD's GWOT discourse as it relates to regions or "fronts" of the war other than Afghanistan and Iraq. In so doing, it will examine various groups that have been officially labeled terrorists and have been incorporated into the GWOT discourse of defense officials. Although US military operations in Afghanistan and Iraq have constituted the vast bulk of material resources devoted to the GWOT, a more holistic understanding of what the GWOT consists of is impossible without an examination of US defense policy toward other regions of the world. This is a crucial point. Many politicians and commentators have framed the GWOT around its two most important theaters, with the consequence that this outlook fundamentally misrepresents both the totality of the GWOT and its embrace by the bureaucracy, particularly at the regional combatant command level. For instance, for many years Iraq was often portrayed as the "second front" of the GWOT, even though the Philippines had been labeled as such beginning in 2002. Many defense officials have also described Pakistan as being on the "frontline" of the GWOT, perhaps without recognizing that this designation has also been applied to other countries, such as Colombia.

Four "theaters" of the GWOT will be examined in this section, each of which involved some type of US military intervention and all of which were initiated prior to the Iraq war and continued for years thereafter. Each of the cases will examine the discourses related to the US military intervention with specific reference to how the "terrorist threat" was viewed prior to the intervention and how the discourse on the nature and importance of that threat evolved over the course of the intervention. The primary reason these cases were chosen was to illustrate the broad scope of the DoD's approach to the GWOT that began before the 2003 Iraq War and has grown broader ever since. Rather than keeping the GWOT limited, the DoD embarked on numerous missions in 2002 that were placed under the rubric of the GWOT but in reality had little to do with countering al-Qaeda, despite being marketed as such. Therefore, in order to understand how the DoD's discourse on the GWOT evolved to characterize the breadth of activities that were to occur during the period under examination, it is necessary to examine the military operations that were conducted beginning in 2002, the majority of which not only continued into the Obama administration but are likely to constitute an ongoing aspect, if not the core aspect, of US counterterrorism for many years to come.

The Philippines

Prior to the US-led invasion of Afghanistan in October 2001, there were numerous high-level meetings where the possibility of expanding the GWOT beyond Central Asia was discussed. An abundance of potential candidates were considered, including Iraq, Somalia, Yemen, Sudan, Indonesia, and the Philippines.[268] As early as November 2001, the US Pacific Command (PACOM) deployed a Special Forces team to the southern Philippines for the purpose of conducting an initial assessment of the local conditions.[269] Although the ongoing conflict in

Afghanistan occupied the majority of policy makers' time, a decision was made during that autumn to open a "second front" of the GWOT in the Philippines. Plans to send US troops to the Philippines for counterterrorism purposes were most likely finalized during Philippine President Gloria Arroyo's late November 2001 visit to Washington, where she asked President Bush for military aid to help battle the Abu Sayyaf Group (ASG).[270]

The US intervention in the Philippines was the military's first expansion of the GWOT beyond Afghanistan. Moreover, its target was not al-Qaeda but the ASG, a "terrorist" group that, although loosely connected with al-Qaeda, had local rather than global ambitions and capabilities.[271] This distinction is an important one because it demonstrates how substantially the US government's discourse on conflict in South East Asia had changed. Before 9/11, the United States regarded acts of terror and violence in the region as local uprisings and insurgencies in which there were no interests of any consequence at stake and therefore essentially ignored them. The region itself was not considered a major center of transnational terrorism, unlike the Middle East.[272] By contrast, over the next few years, the US military's discourse related to "terrorist" enemies in the Philippines would expand beyond the ASG, to include additional groups such as the Moro Islamic Liberation Front and the communist New People's Army, neither of which had previously been considered significant threats to US interests or had warranted US military action to counter them.[273]

In the months after 9/11, a good deal of the discourse on the GWOT revolved around the "Bush Doctrine," in which states who sponsored or harbored terrorist groups could potentially be targets of US military action. It was less clear what US policy would be toward states that were both friendly toward Washington and already fighting "terrorists" inside their own borders. Would the United States merely supply financial resources and/or military training? Or would the United States actively participate in direct action against terrorists operating inside friendly states? As the Philippines case shows, the US military was to follow a fairly ambiguous path and approached the problem in terms of limited involvement in a local "counterinsurgency." Rather than engage in active combat against ASG, the United States chose to play a supportive role, allowing the Armed Forces of the Philippines (AFP) to take the lead.[274]

Beginning in the fall 2001, the "terrorist threat" in the Philippines gradually gained greater prominence within the wider GWOT discourse.[275] In November 2001, Rumsfeld linked both al-Qaeda and Iraq to terrorists in the Philippines. According to Rumsfeld, there was "a good deal of interaction between the terrorists in the Philippines and the Al-Qaeda and people in Iraq."[276] In early 2002, PACOM head Admiral Dennis Blair stated, "The focus of our activities is to make sure that Asia is not the last bastion of Al-Qaeda, but to make it as inhospitable for terrorists to come here as possible."[277] In addition to the religiously motivated ASG and Jemaah Islamiyah (JI) "terrorist groups" operating in or near the Philippines, in summer 2002, Washington declared the communist New People's Army in the Philippines to be a terrorist organization as well.[278] In the case of the Moro Islamic Liberation Front (MILF), both President Arroyo and President Bush sought to associate, amalgamate, and compress the MILF with the ASG and JI, constantly arguing that the MILF needed to "reject terror" and referring to its bases as "terrorist lairs" and "terrorist training camps."[279]

With the decision to enlarge the scope of the GWOT, Operation Enduring Freedom (OEF), though initially referring to US military operations in Afghanistan, was expanded to cover the Philippines as well, and the original OEF designation was officially changed to include this distinction. As such, the two separate theaters would be given the designations OEF-Afghanistan and OEF-Philippines, and both were categorized as the military's operational component of the GWOT. Whereas OEF-Afghanistan consisted of a military response to 9/11 necessitating an invasion of that country, the size and scope of OEF-Philippines was of a very different character altogether.[280] In contrast to Afghanistan, one of the unique aspects of the "second front" was the lack of overt military action. Instead, the US military intervention was mainly limited to conducting a preplanned annual exercise called "Balikatan" (shoulder-to-shoulder). Unlike the previous year's Balikatan exercise, which focused on humanitarian aid and civic assistance and lasted a matter of weeks, the 2002 exercise was reconfigured to train local forces to deal with terrorism for a duration of six months.[281] In the April–May 2001 Balikatan exercise, US forces conducted a number of humanitarian missions, such as building schools. In the 2002 exercise, the bulk of US forces would similarly engage in humanitarian projects, albeit for the purpose of winning local "hearts and minds" as part of the GWOT. The most important difference between the two exercises was that the 2002 version included some 160 US Special Forces personnel responsible for training and advising Philippine units fighting ASG.[282] However, Rumsfeld was adamant US troops in the Philippines were "not there in an active military role."[283] Likewise, General Myers testified that US forces "are really there to assist the Philippine government and the Philippine armed forces in their quest to rid their country of terrorist organizations. This is not an operation like you saw in Afghanistan."[284] Admiral Blair similarly noted the mission in the Philippines illustrated how in Asia, the US military would support friendly governments fighting terrorists, rather than take a more direct combat role as it had in Afghanistan.[285]

The "indirect approach" taken by Washington in the Philippines was the result of the restraints imposed upon the US military intervention by Manila. Beginning during her November 2001 Washington visit, Arroyo invited American troops to assist in the fight against ASG but ruled out any combat role for them.[286] US forces were not allowed to engage in actual combat due to the Philippines's constitution, which forbade foreign military forces from this activity. This limitation had an important effect on the language employed to characterize the mission. As a result of local public hostility toward a US military presence, Filipino officials insisted on calling the mission an "exercise" or "war game." By contrast, the US military referred to the mission as a "training operation" intended to "train, advise and assist" the AFP in hunting Islamic terrorists.[287] Nevertheless, for the DoD, this "training operation" was officially designated as part of Operation Enduring Freedom. A US military task force, known as Joint Task Force–510, was created to train and equip AFP troops deploying on Basilan Island, where ASG had a significant presence. At the same time, US and AFP engineers engaged in various civil projects, including building roads and bridges, for the purpose of driving a wedge between ASG and local sympathizers. However, due mainly to tactical blunders, the militant leaders were able to escape from Basilan and regroup.[288]

Despite the lack of success on Basilan, OEF-Philippines would continue beyond the six months allocated for Balikatan. As has already been mentioned, beginning in summer 2002, the US terrorism discourse shifted to include groups such as the NPA and MILF. To put this in perspective, it is worth noting that before 9/11, PACOM's interest in terrorism was mainly limited to ASG, following its August 2001 kidnapping of a US citizen.[289] Over the course of the next several years, PACOM commanders would testify to Congress that "Southeast Asia is the front line of the war on terror (in the Pacific Command AOR)"[290] and that "Southeast Asia is a crucial front in the War on Terror."[291] As such, OEF-Philippines would remain open-ended and continue to provide training, advice, and assistance to the AFP in order to "improve their capability and capacity to combat terror."[292]

Soon after the Balikatan exercise ended, JTF-510 was reorganized into the Joint Special Operations Task Force-Philippines (JSOTF-P), which continued advisory efforts with select Philippine units at the strategic, operational, and tactical levels.[293] US military operations remained limited to conducting training in counterinsurgency and counterterrorism tactics, advising Filipino units, and participating in civil-military operations.[294] According to Lieutenant-Colonel Eric Haider, who led the task force, OEF-Philippines was "a model for how the US can wage the war on terror in a country where we are not at war, and sustain it over the long term."[295] By 2006, PACOM's security assistance program with the Philippine armed forces was the largest in its area of responsibility (AOR).[296]

In addition to training and exercises, Washington pledged millions of dollars in military aid and advanced military equipment, from night-vision goggles to combat helicopters. The main intent of this aid was to improve AFP counterterrorism capabilities and self-sufficiency. Post-9/11 military assistance programs to the Philippines, including grants, loans, and equipment, increased tenfold compared to previous levels. In November 2001, total US military assistance amounted to $92 million following an emergency appropriation after 9/11. In May 2003, Washington announced another $65 million training program for the Filipino military. In October 2003, President Bush pledged an additional $340 million aid package for increased counterterrorism training and operations against the ASG and other al-Qaeda–linked groups in the southern Philippines. From 2004 to 2006, US military aid to the Philippines remained at similarly high levels.[297] In the years thereafter, military aid related to counterterrorism declined and as of 2012 amounted to an annual appropriation of $15 million. However, overall military aid to the Philippines would rise sharply in 2012 as a result of the increasing US interest in building partnerships in the Asia-Pacific.[298]

Despite the significant US expenditure of military and financial resources, it has been alleged that instead of using the increased resources to expand its counterterrorism capabilities, individuals and entities in Manila profited from the GWOT funding. In order to secure material benefits from the United States, Filipino leaders emphasized the "terrorism" issue in their dealings with Washington, including groups that had little or no connection to al-Qaeda, such as the New People's Army. This in turn led the United States to expand its original definition of the terrorism threat in the Philippines. Moreover, some experts contend not all militant Muslim groups (such as the MILF) are aligned with al-Qaeda, and it is important that US counterterrorism efforts in the region do not motivate these groups to join al-Qaeda.[299] As part of their terrorism discourse, Philippine leaders repeatedly stressed the poverty-terror link and continually argued that US money was needed to boost employment and poverty levels as part of the country's overall counterterrorism plan.[300] Consequently, the majority of US military activity in the Philippines labeled as counterterrorism involved humanitarian projects and civic assistance that helped boost local economies, rather than the "direct action" approach taken in Afghanistan.

In recent years, JSOTF-P continued assisting the Philippine military in its "counterterrorist" mission, although no substantial changes have occurred. While the groups being targeted may have declined in strength over the years, US interest in this conflict remained minimal. Not only did US force levels remain relatively consistent, at about six hundred personnel, but there was no notion of an exit strategy. Instead, rather than attempting to "solve" the "terrorism problem" in the Philippines, "managing" the problem became an end in itself. Alternatively, it could be argued that "managing" the problem did allow the United States to improve US-Philippine military-to-military relations and also allowed PACOM to demonstrate its relevance to the GWOT, both of which were probably the more important motives for maintaining the presence of JSOTF-P for more than a decade. Eventually, once the Obama administration came to power and emphasized a "pivot" to Asia, improving relations with the Philippines to counter a rising China began to take priority. Though the "counterterrorism" mission continued, it was the "China threat" that became dominant again in the US military discourse regarding its ties with the Philippines.[301]

Georgia

The inclusion of the former Soviet republic of Georgia into the GWOT represents an interesting case demonstrating how the Pentagon expanded its counterterrorism role into a geographic area that had received scant attention as a "terrorist haven" prior to 9/11 and then sustained this presence ever since. As has been shown, in the early deliberations among US politicians and defense officials, a number of countries to potentially conduct operations in had been listed, yet Georgia, perhaps not unsurprisingly, was missing from this list. This raises the question of what led Georgia to become the "third front" in the GWOT, prompting the US military to commit forces for the purpose of conducting a "train and equip" program in order to help the Georgian military fight al-Qaeda in the Pankisi Gorge. Answering this question necessitates a brief examination of the impediments to US defense engagement with Georgia before 9/11, Russia's use of "international terrorism" discourse to justify its own actions in Chechnya, Tbilisi's desire to increase its military ties with Washington as a means to balance Moscow's regional dominance, and the bureaucratic interest on the part of the US European Command (EUCOM) to contribute to the GWOT at a time when other combatant commands (such as CENTCOM and PACOM) were already playing visible roles in counterterrorism. In addition to demonstrating how these various factors contributed to Georgia's inclusion in the GWOT, it is also worth examining the nature of the DoD's involvement and the discourses employed to justify it, particularly as these highlight the gradual broadening of the Pentagon's conception of what sort of missions could be classed as counterterrorism.[302]

Administratively, Georgia falls within the EUCOM AOR. Prior to 9/11, EUCOM had attempted to pursue closer military-to-military contacts with a number of formerly Soviet countries, although these contacts had traditionally been limited to small-scale military exercises due to those countries' fears about provoking Moscow, as well as Washington's concerns about damaging the US-Russia relationship.[303] Moreover, the EUCOM "concept" to send US military advisers to Georgia (later to be given the name "Georgia Train and Equip"—GTEP), preceded 9/11 and was intended to assist the NATO-aspiring Tbilisi with its attempt to become more interoperable with NATO forces.[304] However, this plan was shelved due to the political sensitivities aforementioned. As will be shown, despite being labeled as a counterterrorism mission, the GTEP was not intended to counter al-Qaeda.

The terrorism discourse related to Georgia before 9/11 was almost entirely one-sided. In the course of its war in Chechnya, Moscow had labeled the Chechens as "terrorists" and "bandits," although most Western countries, particularly the United States, referred to the Chechen "fighters," "guerrillas," "separatists," and "resistance." In order to counter Western criticism that the Russian military's methods were lacking any sense of proportionality and that the war was "unjust," Moscow consistently used the rhetoric of counterterrorism to justify its actions. This included highlighting the connections between the Chechens and international terrorism, specifically the connections with al-Qaeda. Russian officials repeatedly described Chechnya as the "frontline against international terrorism."[305]

In addition to the problem of Chechnya proper, Moscow also consistently characterized the presence of some seven thousand Chechens living in the nearby Pankisi Gorge in Georgia as providing a "terrorist haven" and base for "Islamic extremists." However, the Georgian government adamantly refused to admit there was a presence of Chechen "fighters" on its territory. It is therefore worth noting that prior to 9/11, it was only Moscow that referred to a "terrorist problem" in Georgia, whereas Tbilisi and Washington did not. After 9/11, however, both the Georgian and American discourse shifted considerably. This shift began in earnest during a visit to Washington in October 2001 by Georgian President Eduard Shevardnadze. Following discussions with President Bush and Deputy Defense Secretary Wolfowitz, EUCOM's pre-9/11 military engagement plan, which had previously been shelved, was reexamined, and efforts were put forth to persuade Congress to fund it beginning in 2002.[306] This was followed by a visit to Tbilisi by Rumsfeld in December 2001 where discussions of expanded US military engagement occurred.[307]

In February 2002, the US chargé d'affairs in Georgia announced that Mujahedin fleeing from Afghanistan had relocated to the Pankisi Gorge and were in contact with a known associate of Osama Bin Laden.[308] That same month, the Pentagon announced a plan to deploy US soldiers to train Georgian troops to help fight the war against terrorism.[309] Rumsfeld described the effort as meant to enhance the Georgian armed forces' "antiterrorism capability."[310] In March 2002, EUCOM head General Joseph Ralston testified there were "Al-Qaeda terrorists there."[311] However, some other US defense officials were vague about the details of al-Qaeda connections in the region and framed the GTEP as helping improve Georgia's "security capability," which in turn would be helpful for the GWOT.[312] Moreover, the head of GTEP stated in May 2002 he was unaware of any al-Qaeda presence in the Pankisi Gorge.[313] The training provided to the Georgians consisted almost entirely of basic infantry skills for several Georgian Army battalions, rather than any advanced training in "counterterrorism" techniques.[314] Despite the training, there is no evidence the Georgian military subsequently conducted any operations in the Pankisi Gorge to target al-Qaeda.

Whether or not an al-Qaeda presence existed in the Pankisi Gorge, it is probably fair to conclude that such a presence was a relatively minor one, especially in comparison to other countries that had been identified prior to 9/11 as "Al-Qaeda havens."[315] As such, it is not inconceivable that bureaucratic and geopolitical imperatives were the primary motives for Washington's decision to make Georgia a centerpiece of the GWOT. For EUCOM, the GTEP provided the initial means for it to showcase its contribution to the GWOT (later this would be expanded to Africa).[316] Indeed, although the size of the US mission to Georgia was small enough to be commanded by a major, it was decided to increase the mission's profile by appointing a lieutenant-colonel.[317]

From a geopolitical perspective, the GTEP enabled the United States to establish a military "footprint" in the Caucasus, much to the consternation of Russia. Although the United States had previously been reluctant to militarily engage in the region, a combination of Washington's desire to expand the GWOT and Moscow's own discursive linkage of the Pankisi Gorge to international terrorism provided a means for EUCOM to establish itself in the Caucasus. Moreover, EUCOM's presence was further entrenched as the GWOT discourse changed. In 2005, GTEP begat the Georgia Sustainment and Stability Operations Program, and EUCOM's efforts changed from providing Georgia help to counter its domestic "terrorism problem" to assisting Tbilisi's capability to provide forces for Iraq.[318] As such, EUCOM's engagement with Georgia was able to continue under the GWOT rubric.[319] During the August 2008 Russia-Georgia war, the United States was obliged to return Georgian troops based in Iraq back to Georgia, which effectively brought Tbilisi's participation in that conflict to an end. However, in 2009, EUCOM began a "Georgia Deployment Program" to prepare Georgian troops for Afghanistan, thus providing relative continuity with the earlier program, albeit the size of the US presence in Georgia was now smaller than it was prior to 2008.[320]

South America

Before 9/11, the US military's interest in South America was relatively minor and confined mostly to the "War on Drugs"; its interest in terrorist activity there was virtually nonexistent. However, in the weeks and months after 9/11, the discourse on terrorism in South America would change considerably.[321] During a September 15, 2001, National Security Council meeting, Secretary of

State Colin Powell mentioned targeting other terrorist networks in addition to al-Qaeda but specifically wanted to *avoid* the Colombian FARC.[322] Given that the FARC is a "terrorist" group that has a Marxist-Leninist rather than Islamist ideology, it is quite possible Powell wanted the emerging GWOT to merely focus on one set of religiously inspired terrorist groups, rather than every terrorist group officially designated by the US government. However, in a September 20 memo to Rumsfeld, Feith suggested the possibility of attacking terrorists in South America, given the lack of options then available in Afghanistan.[323] But which terrorist groups operating in South America would have been potential targets? Two officials who worked for Feith as part of the Policy Counterterrorism Evaluation Group argued that an attack on the border of Paraguay, Argentina, and Brazil, where intelligence reports said Hezbollah had a presence, would have ripple effects on other terrorist operations. Although other advisers met this proposal with skepticism, the "tri-border" area would figure prominently in subsequent statements by defense officials when referring to the "terrorist threat" in South America.[324] As this section will demonstrate, US officials included within their South America-related GWOT discourse Middle East groups that other combatant commanders hesitated to categorize as part of the GWOT (e.g., Hezbollah), much less take action against, as well as programs that had previously been associated with the War on Drugs.

The role of SOUTHCOM in the GWOT has been popularly associated with the military prison camp at Guantanamo Bay. That this should be the case is quite understandable. Guantanamo Bay has been the only part of SOUTHCOM's AOR that contained a significant al-Qaeda presence, albeit incarcerated.[325] Elsewhere in the SOUTHCOM AOR, officials were reluctant to specify any al-Qaeda activity, although many officials have employed the rhetoric of "ungoverned spaces" when discussing *potential* al-Qaeda activity. According to this argument, due to the large amount of "ungoverned" and "undergoverned" space in South America, "terrorists" could potentially set up a base there.[326]

Within SOUTHCOM, the main emphasis on counterterrorism had very little to do with countering al-Qaeda. This lack of focus was evident in the 2002 National Security Strategy, which highlighted South America as a refuge for terrorist cells and refers to an "active strategy to help the Andean nations . . . defeat terrorist organizations."[327] Yet the only groups that were considered "terrorists" were not Islamist groups; rather they were groups such as the FARC. Nevertheless, several Middle East terrorist groups were highlighted as constituting a threat within the SOUTHCOM AOR. For example, in 2002, SOUTHCOM head General James T. Hill linked drug sales to support for "terrorist" organizations such as Hezbollah, Hamas, and Islamiyya al Gammat, which had support cells in Latin America. In 2003, Hill argued that on the Venezuelan Margarita Island, money laundering, arms deals, and drug trafficking were occurring and funding Hamas, Hezbollah, and Islamiyya al Gammat and noted suspicious activity by Venezuela's Arab population.[328] It should be noted that whereas SOUTHCOM may have contemplated taking an active role against groups such as Hezbollah and Hamas, the policy of CENTCOM was to ignore these groups, probably fearing US interests in the Middle East would have been jeopardized had it militarily confronted them. As a result of this conundrum, SOUTHCOM was limited merely to using strong rhetoric against these groups; there is no evidence any military intervention occurred.

The DoD leadership did not view SOUTHCOM favorably in the pre-9/11 period of the Bush administration (especially its emphasis on the "War on Drugs"), and the combatant command's future role and existence were called into question.[329] However, in the aftermath of 9/11, SOUTHCOM was able to carve out a niche for itself within the GWOT. In addition to its role in charge of Guantanamo Bay, SOUTHCOM shifted its discourse on the "War on Drugs" by placing it within the GWOT context. For instance, the head of US Army South (SOUTHCOM's Army component command) argued that Army South's past efforts to prosecute the drug war "really supports that (the GWOT) focus."[330] During the summer of 2002, Wolfowitz authored a memo for senior DoD officials in which he stated that the Pentagon was to focus its counternarcotics activities on programs that "contribute to the war on terrorism."[331] In November 2002, Bush signed National Security Presidential Directive–18 authorizing the US military to actively counter "terrorist" groups in Colombia as a part of the GWOT.[332] Within the DoD Comptroller's Office, counternarcotics programs in Colombia were placed under the GWOT supplemental budget requests to Congress.[333] DoD Comptroller Dov Zakheim insisted the counternarcotics budget request was "part of the global war on terrorism."[334] Likewise, in February 2003, the principal director for special operations and combating terrorism within the office of the assistant secretary of defense for special operations and low-intensity conflict, Tom Kuster, stated that the "fight against narcotics is now officially a subset of the fight against terrorism."[335] According to Kuster, money allocated for counternarcotics had a number of legal stipulations attached, and therefore a decision was made to expand the DoD definition of *counternarcotics*. Within the DoD, narcotics trafficking would be defined as a "direct contributor to terrorism" thereby allowing counternarcotics funding "to assist combating-terrorism operations around the world."[336]

Among the most significant discursive shifts in DoD language related to this region was the stress placed on use of the term *narco-terrorism* when discussing groups such as the FARC, whose primary interest to the US government prior to 9/11 had been drugs rather than terrorism.[337] By contrast, after 9/11, numerous official statements and testimony by DoD officials placed the

FARC on the GWOT "enemies list."[338] In 2003, General Hill stated, "The narco-terrorists in Colombia remain the largest and most well known threat in our region."[339] Similarly, Rumsfeld described Colombia as being "on the front line in the war on terrorism."[340] The United States sought to increase military funding for Colombia, which meant an explicit change in policy that in the past had allowed military aid for fighting "drug traffickers" but not "guerrillas." The Bush administration now argued both were terrorist groups and therefore no distinction should be made between them.[341] Likewise, General Hill testified to Congress that groups such as the FARC "are narco-terrorists rather than romantic guerrillas."[342] He also stated there is "no useful distinction between a narco-trafficker and his terrorist activity, hence the term narco-terrorist."[343] In 2002, Congress gave SOUTHCOM expanded authority to use counterdrug funds for counterterrorism missions in Colombia. This authority included expanding the US military advisory presence in Colombia. More important perhaps, the amount of US military aid to Colombia expanded considerably. By 2004, the United States supplied Bogota with over $680 million, placing it among the top five countries benefiting from US military aid. By comparison, in 2001, military aid totaled only $225 million. Colombia also became the fifth largest recipient of the DoD's Regional Defense Counterterrorism Fellowship Program, which is designed to train foreign militaries in counterterrorism techniques.

With the shift in the DoD's discourse toward South America focused increasingly on countering "terrorists" and "narco-terrorists," US defense engagement with the region's militaries was reoriented to encourage them to become more involved in intelligence gathering, law enforcement, and border patrol.[344] During meetings with his Latin American counterparts in 2002 and 2004, Rumsfeld repeatedly highlighted the terrorism issue and offered to help strengthen Latin American navies, improve systems for intelligence sharing, and strengthen regional peacekeeping cooperation. In October 2002, General Hill specifically suggested the armed forces of Argentina, Brazil, and Paraguay play a bigger role in combating terrorism.[345] In 2004, the vice chairman of the joint chiefs of staff, General Peter Pace, testified that US-sponsored multilateral exercises were promoting security in the tri-border area between Argentina, Brazil, and Paraguay. Moreover, he stated that US military aid was helping improve border control and denying safe havens to terrorist groups such as Hezbollah and Hamas.[346]

In addition to the propagation of the "terrorist threat" in the US government discourse, South American governments, particularly Colombia's, also used the terrorism discourse to ensure continued US military and financial support.[347] Apart from the various political and material motivations underlying the South America terrorism discourse, the way the discourse was constructed raised an interesting dilemma with regards to America's broader GWOT policy.

For instance, if the Colombian FARC was part of the GWOT, did this mean that the DoD would have to take direct or indirect action against other non-Islamist "terrorist" groups, including those that didn't pose a risk to the United States? At the very least, the example of the United States labeling its operations against the FARC as a part of the GWOT clearly demonstrates that the DoD's approach to the GWOT extended beyond Islamist "terrorist" groups.

Apart from US efforts to counter the FARC, the US discourse on Islamist and Iranian-backed terrorist activities in South America was repeatedly emphasized. In 2009, SOUTHCOM head Admiral James Stavridis observed, "We have been seeing in Colombia a direct connection between Hezbollah activity and narco-trafficking activity."[348] In April 2012, Defense Secretary Leon Panetta noted, "We always have a concern about . . . the IRGC (Iranian Revolutionary Guard Corps) and efforts by the IRGC to expand their influence, not only throughout the Middle East but also into this region (referring to South America) . . . In my book, that relates to expanding terrorism." Similarly, one month earlier, SOUTHCOM head General Douglas M. Fraser had stated, "We do see evidence of international terrorist groups benefiting from the intertwined systems of illicit trafficking and money laundering in our AOR."[349] Thus, even during the Obama administration, US military discourse on South America continued to emphasize terrorist activities, and these were often discursively linked to drugs.

Africa

Unlike the US military's approach to Afghanistan and Iraq, both involving regime change and large-scale occupations, the DoD took a very different approach in Africa, despite the prospect of major combat operations on that continent being discussed by senior defense officials after 9/11. Similar to the cases of the Philippines, Georgia, and Colombia, the US approach to counterterrorism in Africa would rely on an "indirect approach" primarily consisting of training, arming, and funding local forces. The reason for US intervention was framed within the broader GWOT discourse of "ungoverned spaces" potentially providing "safe havens" for al-Qaeda. Rather than focusing on individual countries, as in other parts of the world, the US military approached the terrorism issue in Africa from a regional perspective. As such, rather than merely focusing on a single country, such as Ethiopia, Mali, or Algeria, they would refer to the Horn of Africa, the Pan Sahel, and the Trans-Sahara.

Among the many influences on the DoD's GWOT-Africa discourse, it was the administrative separation of the continent into two combatant commands (CENTCOM and EUCOM) that would prove to be a crucial one. This section will seek to highlight the different combatant command discourses and approaches to the GWOT in Africa, as a means of demonstrating the importance of bureaucratic competition within the US military and its effects on counterterrorism discourse more generally. For example, both CENTCOM and EUCOM would attach their Africa operations to Operation Enduring Freedom, but for very different reasons. Similarly, the "Pan-Sahel Initiative," which was controlled by EUCOM, did not include countries in the eastern Sahel region, because these fell within CENTCOM's AOR.[350]

On September 19, 2001, Rumsfeld asked CENTCOM head General Tommy Franks to consider how the War on Terror could be expanded to Somalia.[351] Following the initiation of US military operations in Afghanistan, military officials warned that countries such as Somalia might be a destination for fleeing al-Qaeda fighters, thereby necessitating a US military presence in the region.[352] In October 2002, CENTCOM established the Combined Joint Task Force—Horn of Africa (CJTF-HOA) as a "Crisis Response Force" to combat terrorism in the region.[353] For this reason, US forces operating in the area were designated as supporting Operation Enduring Freedom.[354] The region itself was defined to consist of Kenya, Somalia, Ethiopia, Sudan, Eritrea, Djibouti, and Yemen, thus including one country not in Africa. Though the CJTF-HOA was initially headquartered aboard the *USS Mount Whitney*, it moved to Djibouti in 2003. The original mission of CJTF-HOA was to take "direct action" against al-Qaeda targets in the region, but gradually, due mainly to a lack of targets, this mission evolved to include training local forces, humanitarian assistance, and other "nonkinetic" activities.[355] With the change of mission, the counterterrorism discourse changed as well. Rather than engaging in kinetic operations, CJTF-HOA prided itself on a nonkinetic, long-term approach to counterterrorism in East Africa. Major General Timothy Ghormley, who headed CJTF-HOA from 2005 to 2006, remarked that the humanitarian and civil assistance projects carried out by CJTF-HOA were part of a "a generational fight for hearts and minds."[356] The discourse of "soft power" as a weapon in the GWOT would become especially prevalent with regards US military activity in Africa. That being said, there is also some evidence that the "soft power" activities of CJTF-HOA were either a "complement" to, or a "cover" for, clandestine operations undertaken by US Special Forces in the region.[357]

In late 2005, Deputy Assistant Secretary of Defense for Africa Theresa Whelan noted there had been a paradigm shift in how the Pentagon viewed threats and strategic interests. For Whelan, poor human security and poverty and the inability of most governments to control their territories contributed to an environment conducive to creating terrorist safe havens and recruiting bases. As in other geographic locales, US military intervention in the Horn of Africa was justified and sustained using the discourse of "ungoverned spaces."[358] CENTCOM head General Abizaid referred to the Horn of Africa as potentially providing "safe havens" and "ungovernable spaces" for terrorists fleeing from Afghanistan, Iraq, and Pakistan.[359] Major General Samuel Helland, who headed CJTF-HOA during 2004 and 2005, similarly remarked, "We find the terrorist networks here using the fact that there is a lot of ungoverned space in the Horn of Africa."[360]

Over time, the CJTF-HOA would expand to include the Comoros, the Seychelles, Tanzania, and Uganda. By contrast, there was no US military presence in Somalia, which military officials regarded as the most likely regional "terrorist haven."[361] Major General Helland identified a number of "terrorist networks" in the Horn of Africa, including the Eritrean Islamic Jihad, Al Itihad al-Islamiya, the Somali Mujahideen, and the Lord's Resistance Army. Interestingly, Helland stated he suspected these groups were "connected to the worldwide network (Al-Qaeda)."[362] Helland's identification of these groups and his statement linking them to al-Qaeda raises two important issues. By linking the groups to al-Qaeda, it appears as though the discourse of the "monolithic enemy" was being employed to characterize US military intervention in what had previously been considered local insurgencies of no interest to US national security.[363] More important, attempting to link al-Qaeda with the Lord's Resistance Army (LRA), which is a Christian rather than Islamist group, appears highly problematic. In addition, US military personnel stationed in Uganda whose mission was to help undermine the LRA were told it was a GWOT mission and were awarded a GWOT medal.[364] Similar to the case of the FARC, by associating the LRA as part of the GWOT and making the task of countering them a part of the CJTF-HOA's mission, the war's boundaries were not limited to targeting Muslim groups.

In contrast to the terrorism rhetoric used to describe the CJTF-HOA mission for American audiences, defense officials employed different terminology when speaking to local audiences. Rear Admiral Richard Hunt who headed the CJTF-HOA beginning in April 2006 noted that the key to a successful US strategy was never using the word *terrorism*. According to Hunt, the war on terror is seen by most Muslims in the region as a US war on Islam. Therefore it was necessary to refer to *extremism* rather than *terrorism*.[365] Moreover, CJTF-HOA commanders and spokesmen have consistently insisted they were "waging peace," not waging war.[366]

Similar to CENTCOM's activities in East Africa, US military intervention in West and North Africa, conducted by EUCOM, was discursively justified on the grounds of denying safe havens for terrorists and countering Islamist extremist groups. EUCOM commander General James Jones referred to the ungoverned areas of Africa as "terrorist breeding grounds." Deputy EUCOM commander General Charles F. Wald referred to the need to "drain the swamp." In March 2005, head of EUCOM operations Rear Admiral Hamlin Tallent testified, "Africa is an emerging haven for our enemies in the Global War on Terrorism."[367] Likewise, a EUCOM spokesman stated, "There are clear indications that Muslim extremists from the Middle East and Afghanistan have moved into these open spaces (referring to the Sahara)."[368] Indeed, a good deal of EUCOM's discourse related to the Sahara refers to the problem of "ungoverned spaces" that could potentially become a "new Afghanistan."[369] In addition, the 2006 QDR cites the presence of US combat aviation advisers in Niger as helping prevent "the underdeveloped eastern part of the country from becoming a safe haven for transnational terrorists."[370]

Within EUCOM's AOR in Africa, the Algerian Salafist Group for Prayer and Combat (GSPC) was perceived to constitute the most serious "terrorist threat." However, according to one study, the GSPC did not appear to be a terrorist group as much as an internal insurgency against the government. In addition, the study noted that the GSPC was trying to stay alive through shakedowns, roadblocks, and incursions to raise cash and other resources.[371] Yet, far from portraying the GSPC as an important but relatively isolated aspect of North African security, US policies after 9/11 contributed to maintaining the group's relevance, thus creating a self-fulfilling prophecy.[372] The importance attached to the GSPC "threat" was evident in the discourse of senior EUCOM officials. Special Operations Command-Europe (SOCEUR) head Major General Thomas Csrnko considered the GSPC the biggest threat to security in the region and cited the potential for terrorist camps in the Sahara comparable to those once run by al-Qaeda in Afghanistan.[373] Likewise, in 2005, a SOCEUR spokesman labeled the GSPC the number one threat to the Sahel region.[374] As early as 2002, EUCOM officials had attempted to gain authorization to conduct air strikes against groups that allegedly had ties to the GSPC, although these were rejected by the State Department who both questioned the "terrorist ties" of these groups and warned of the consequences of radicalizing "a bunch of desert tribesmen" whose activities were limited to fighting other desert tribes.[375]

Instead of embarking on "direct action" missions in the Sahara, the United States chose instead to initiate the Pan Sahel Initiative (PSI) in late 2002. The PSI sought to enhance regional cooperation with the Sahel nations of Mali, Mauritania, Niger, and Chad to combat terrorism, track the movements of people through the Sahel and Sahara, and protect the region's borders. However, it is worth noting that prior to 2002, there was no mention in any official US government document linking an international terrorism presence to these four countries, whereas numerous links had been identified in Algeria, Morocco, and Tunisia.[376]

As the lead government department in charge of counterterrorism in the region, the State Department directed PSI but leaned heavily on the "foreign internal defense" training provided by SOCEUR. The PSI budget initially consisted of a mere $7.75 million. According to the Pentagon's West Africa country director, Colonel Victor Nelson, the US military was responsible for training "six motorized infantry companies to monitor the borders in an area as large as the United States."[377] Despite its limitations, Nelson described PSI as "an important tool" in the war on terrorism because "if you squeeze the terrorists in Afghanistan, Pakistan, Iraq and other places, they are going to find new places to operate, and one of those places is the Sahel/Maghreb."[378] In 2005, the PSI was renamed the Trans-Sahara Counter Terrorism Program (TSCTP) and expanded to include Algeria, Morocco, Senegal, Nigeria, and Tunisia, with proposed funding of $500 million over seven years.[379] Operation Enduring Freedom-Trans Sahara (OEF-TS) emerged as TSCTP's SOCEUR-led military arm. It is unclear why the program was designated as a component of OEF. Similar to the case of OEF-Philippines, the practice of different geographical commands using the same operational name runs counter to traditional DoD practice. As these names are usually chosen by combatant commanders, it is possible the EUCOM leadership wished to directly associate the operation with the GWOT as a means to secure funding or enhance its stature.[380] The purpose of OEF-TS was to conduct "military-to-military engagements and exercises designed to strengthen the ability of regional governments to police the large expanses of remote terrain in the Trans-Sahara."[381] Though focused primarily on this training mission, SOCEUR forces are reported to have taken part in offensive operations.[382]

Both OEF-TS and CJTF-HOA encompassed a diverse set of missions, including humanitarian and security cooperation functions. Yet each existed primarily to combat Islamist extremism in its respective region under the GWOT. Critics of the DoD's GWOT initiatives in Africa have noted their counterproductive nature, due in large part to the inappropriate discourses that have been used to conceptualize and justify them. These initiatives have been based on a discursive practice of "aggregation," in which localized and disparate insurgencies have been amalgamated into a monolithic whole. In addition, the "terrorist threat" has usually been framed in the context of Africa's sizable Muslim population, its overwhelming poverty, and its numerous ungoverned spaces and failed states.[383] Consequently, worst-case scenarios have often trumped more moderate assessments of illicit activity and localized insurgency.[384] Critics also complained that the region was not a terrorist zone as some senior US military officers asserted but rather that heavy-handed military actions and financial support that reinforced authoritarian regimes in North and West Africa would fuel radicalism where it scarcely existed.[385] A number of former officials observed that EUCOM exaggerated the terrorism problem in the region, most likely due to its marginalization by CENTCOM. Furthermore, regional governments reportedly exaggerated the terrorism threat in order to attract US funding and military aid.[386]

In 2007, the GSPC changed its name to Al-Qaeda in the Islamic Maghreb (AQIM), a move that virtually ensured the United States would devote more resources to countering it. Similarly, the United States stepped up its activities to counter al Shabaab in Somalia, to include assisting both the Ethiopian and Kenyan governments to launch military operations against them.[387] During this period, all the US military operations in Africa came under the authority of the newly created Africa Command (AFRICOM), which became operational in 2008. Under Obama, US military involvement in Africa would expand considerably, though this involvement was mainly of a clandestine nature in which a combination of Special Forces, drones, and intelligence operations targeted a number of groups. These groups included AQIM, Al-Qaeda in the Arabian Peninsula (AQAP), al Shabaab, Boko Haram, and the Lord's Resistance Army. To target these groups, the United States expanded its presence or built new facilities in such countries as Kenya, Uganda, the Central African Republic, Ethiopia, Djibouti, Mauritania, the Seychelles, and Burkina Faso. Following the departure of US forces from Afghanistan, it is expected that AFRICOM will receive considerably more resources and that it will increase its "counterterrorism" activities over the long term.[388]

Conclusion

From 2001 to the present, the "war on terrorism" discourse became a guiding force, influencing all manner of US military activities. Strategy, budgets, procurement, military organization and culture, and so forth, were all influenced, to one degree or other, by this dominant discourse. As the discourse became institutionalized, it was then perpetuated through institutional memory. The language and institutions became coconstitutive of the reality of the "war." This phenomenon was unprecedented when compared to the earlier "wars on terrorism." Policies that were once considered beyond the pale from a strategic perspective became internalized as "essential." The national security debate shifted from one that considered the relative merits and drawbacks of employing different elements of national power when dealing with a problem to one that focused purely on the merits of using *all* elements of national power, regardless of their relative utility. Examining this discursive evolution is necessary to understand why the "war" developed in the way it did, and why the Obama administration continued to pursue and fund the "war" without reexamining any fundamental assumptions.

When examining US military intervention in the GWOT, it is crucial to recognize the importance of the discourse employed by defense officials to characterize and justify how these interventions contributed to the "global war." This is especially the case with the identification of adversaries. As the empirical evidence amply demonstrates, there have been numerous instances where the adversaries were only named after 9/11, rather than before it. In other words, groups that were not considered a threat to the United States before 9/11 were subsequently named by US defense officials as being imminently or potentially hostile, thereby requiring some form of military intervention. Similarly, as has been highlighted by the numerous references to "ungoverned spaces," intervention was justified and sustained on the grounds of preventing various regions around the globe from becoming "future Afghanistans." In the case of Colombia, the flagging War on Drugs was reclassed as the War on Terror, with "guerrilla" groups such as the FARC redesignated as "narco-terrorists." Thus, by a shift in terminology, rather than a shift in adversary behavior, the DoD was able to justify expanding the GWOT.

The GWOT itself represented a paradigm shift in the DoD's approach to counterterrorism. Traditionally, the DoD had been reluctant to involve itself in counterterrorism, not viewing it as fitting within its prevailing emphasis on "real war" with its primary focus on "major combat operations" against other states. This was true both during the Cold War and in its aftermath. Prior to 9/11, the DoD's role in counterterrorism consisted of limited retaliation, air strikes, hostage rescue, special operations missions, protection of bases and facilities, and "consequence management." By contrast, after 9/11, the Pentagon "transformed" itself, embraced counterterrorism as its primary mission, and would increasingly be defined by this mission.

This transformation can be explained in large part by the bandwagon effect of the GWOT discourse inside the Pentagon. Rather than being viewed as a dirty word, *counterterrorism* emerged as a bandwagon concept, with various bureaucracies inside DoD wanting to be associated with the GWOT. This in turn created a snowball effect in which the GWOT gradually expanded in size and scope and has been used as a label for activities that have very little to do with traditional notions of counterterrorism. Constituting this process was both a "choice of enemies" as well as a "relabeling of enemies," which in turn was linked to new designations of GWOT-crises that had to be managed. The lesser-known cases of US military intervention (those other than Iraq and Afghanistan) are well suited to demonstrate how language was employed to further a mix of political, bureaucratic, and geopolitical agendas. Once placed under the GWOT rubric, these interventions continued to expand in size and scope. Moreover, by lowering the bar as far as what was considered acceptable to be labeled as being GWOT related, the number and type of missions continued to expand. This process was also abetted by foreign governments eager to use the terrorism issue as a means of garnering support, which then created a blowback effect.

Similarly, this effect was compounded internally with an expanding definition of the means that could be applied in counterterrorism.

Among the consequences of the GWOT bandwagon effect has been the perpetuation of a "dominant discourse of counterterrorism." This phenomenon exerts its influence in at least three important ways. First, within the dominant discourse of counterterrorism are numerous—and often competing—definitions of what the GWOT should consist of, who the adversaries are, and what the most effective means are of countering them. The conflicting nature of these definitions leads to ambiguities and inefficiencies in strategy formulation and execution that merely prolong the war's duration and cost. An important aspect of blowback is observable in the case of Rumsfeld attempting to change the way the conflict was labeled, viewing the GWOT as an increasingly counterproductive discourse and seeing greater advantage to a discourse of a GSAVE, but being unable to do so once the GWOT had become the dominant discourse. Similarly, Obama was also constrained despite his administration's shift to *Overseas Contingency Operations*. Second, rather than a "counterterrorism" strategy being employed as one means of achieving national security goals, other US interests (e.g., military-to-military engagement for geopolitical reasons and humanitarian assistance) were discursively constructed as a means of achieving "counterterrorism" ends. Third, despite the fact that many DoD missions were peripheral to counterterrorism, the discursive linkage of the conventional capabilities needed to deal with these missions with those required to wage the GWOT has meant those capabilities were unavailable for non-GWOT related tasks. This had the long-term consequence of ensuring US defense policy remained focused on the GWOT while marginalizing other national security "challenges," such as a rising China. As important as the Asia "pivot" has been to the Obama administration, its main focus remained on Overseas Contingency Operations. Indeed, in the Defense Department's 2012 "strategic guidance," "counterterrorism" remained at the top of the priority list *followed* by references to "rebalancing" US military forces into the Asia-Pacific.[389]

CHAPTER 3

Shock and Awe

The term *Shock and Awe* has been popularly employed to describe US strategy during the initial stages of the 2003 Iraq War. Immediately prior to the commencement of hostilities in late March, the term was repeated constantly in the press. According to one count, more than six hundred news reports around the world referred to Shock and Awe during the first week of the war.[1] In the course of that week, Shock and Awe went from a theoretical concept that offered the prospect of a short and relatively painless war to one of popular derision and official distance. However, the term that emerged as a buzzword in 2003 was originally developed as a concept in a 1996 publication.[2] Its evolution within defense academia and among the senior Department of Defense (DoD) civilian and military leadership, its role in Iraq war planning, and usage by the media and antiwar critics provides an excellent case for testing the discourse trap, highlighting the importance of language in strategy development, as well as the consequences resulting from a lack of understanding among officials about the meaning behind the words they employ.

Examining the genealogy of Shock and Awe provides an important example of how the transformation of a military concept into a popular buzzword can have detrimental effects for the military. This case also demonstrates how a term associated with a controversial concept can gain a prominent position in the official discourse, and also the importance of personalities in getting a military system to adopt a particular term. The evolution of Shock and Awe raises questions about how a concept that was originally derided by orthodox civilian and military professionals working in the field of doctrine development and military education nevertheless managed to have a profound impact on the strategic discourse leading up to the war in Iraq. Whereas Shock and Awe never entered the mainstream Air Force discourse, one term that did was *effects-based operations*. While these terms have characteristics in common and can generally be classed within the broader Revolution in Military Affairs (RMA) discourse, they are far from synonymous. Regardless of the perceived similarities, the receptivity of the two terms by military audiences was very different. Whereas Effects-Based Operations emerged in the military discourse beginning in the early 1990s and remained prominent after 2003, Shock and Awe was marginalized in the military discourse prior to the period of Iraq War planning and then quickly vanished from the military lexicon after Baghdad's fall. The reasons Shock and Awe "gained its veritable 15 minutes of fame" and then became a taboo subject will be examined in the following sections.[3]

This chapter will begin with a focus on the origins and evolution of the term within defense academic, military, and political circles in the mid- to late 1990s, as well as its relevance to the broader RMA discourse to set the stage for its emergence as a concept that helped shape the planning for the Second Iraq War. The employment of the term by officials and the media prior to and during hostilities, and its use as a stereotype to criticize the military strategy both by antiwar protesters and war critics, will all be examined. The chapter will then conclude by focusing on the taboo placed on the term during the war and the taboo's relevance years later.

The Creation and Dissemination of *Shock and Awe*

Shock and Awe made its debut in late 1996 in a National Defense University (NDU) publication titled "Shock and Awe: Achieving Rapid Dominance." This publication was a product of Defense Group Inc., a Washington consulting firm. The principal authors were Dr. Harlan K. Ullman (a former Navy destroyer commander and NDU academic) and Dr. James P. Wade Jr. (a former Under Secretary of Defense). Four retired senior military officers—General Charles "Chuck" Horner (US Air Force, commander of Allied Air Forces during the First Gulf War), Admiral Leon Edney (US Navy, a former Supreme Allied Commander Atlantic), General Fred Franks (US Army, commander of US Army's VII Corps during the First Gulf War), and Admiral Jonathan Howe (US Navy, former Commander-in-Chief US Naval Forces Europe)—also took part in the study.[4] From 1995 to 1998, this ad hoc study group would eventually be enlarged to include a number of other senior retired military officers including General Gary Luck (US Army) and General Tom Morgan (US Marine Corps).[5] In the run-up to the Iraq War, Luck served as a mentor to Central Command (CENTCOM) head General Tommy Franks and advised on war planning.[6] A former and future Secretary of Defense, Donald Rumsfeld, would also be involved with the study group.[7] Many of the later critics of the concept would erroneously claim that Shock and Awe was based on the work of "egghead academics" rather than military professionals.[8] However, given the impressive nature of the military credentials of the study group members, Shock and Awe was hardly a concept developed in the ivory tower. Indeed, it was precisely because of their military credentials and personal connections within the military that Shock and Awe was able to survive the criticisms heaped on the concept from serving military officers.

In 1995, this study group began to develop the concept of Shock and Awe for the stated purpose of developing an "alternative strategic doctrine for designing and using military force."[9] During the course of the study group's deliberations, Ullman coined the term *Shock and Awe*, while retired General Franks coined the term *Rapid Dominance*.[10] The initial purpose of the group was to consider how a future Operation Desert Storm–style operation could be fought and won in far less time than the six weeks it took and with far fewer than the half million military personnel sent into the theater. Indeed, part of the motivation stemmed from a general dissatisfaction with the performance of US forces in the First Gulf War, at least insofar as the air campaign and logistics were concerned. The former commander in charge of the air campaign, General Horner, was particularly frustrated over not knowing where to "put the needle" in order to collapse the Iraqi forces' will to resist.[11] Despite thousands of air strikes and tens of thousands of weapons launched against Iraqi targets during Operations Desert Shield and Desert Storm, Horner was unable find the spot to topple the regime *prior* to the ground offensive that evicted Iraq from Kuwait in one hundred hours and destroyed much of the Iraqi army in the process. Thus the group tried to come to terms with understanding how a rapid and decisive victory could be achieved, especially in the event of another war with Iraq.[12]

In the 1996 NDU publication, Ullman and Wade asserted that the United States had achieved such "overwhelming military and technological superiority that the US defense establishment should now organize to strike with enough speed and destructive force to inflict Shock and Awe on its adversaries and thereby gain Rapid Dominance over them."[13] According to Ullman and Wade, revolutionary advances in US forces' ability to acquire and fuse information while denying the same to the enemy would enable American warfighters to achieve "dominant battlefield awareness," a condition that, when combined with rapid, destructive attacks, would impose "psychological dominance" over the adversary and "destroy, defeat, and neuter" his will to resist.[14]

Thus Shock and Awe was not so much a strategy as it was a psychological state, described by its authors as similar to that experienced by the Japanese in the aftermath of Hiroshima and Nagasaki. In the context of Rapid Dominance, the aim was to achieve a similar psychological state in the adversary, but using advanced high-tech conventional weapons rather than nuclear weapons. Achieving this aim would have to be accomplished not only using less horrific means of warfare but in roughly the same "rapid" period of time. However, the portrayal provided by the authors of applying a "strategy of shock" similar to the dropping of the atomic bombings did not account for many of the specific circumstances that contributed to the Japanese surrender but was limited to a general statement that it was only the "shock" from the bombings that caused the surrender.[15]

Following its publication by NDU, the outlines of Shock and Awe were presented to different offices at the Pentagon. In 1997, Ullman and Wade briefed members of the Air Staff on the concept, but according to one participant, it was not taken seriously. Indeed, the Air Force officers who were in the audience "nearly laughed them out of the room."[16] However, despite the lack of success at convincing the Air Force to buy into the concept and fund additional research, its authors refused to be dismayed and continued to seek ways and means of marketing Shock and Awe. They achieved a degree of success when the concept was featured at the September 9–10, 1998, National Defense University Joint Operations Symposium titled "21st Century Warfighting." Attending this symposium were Paul Wolfowitz (then Dean of the Johns Hopkins University School of Advanced International Studies, later deputy defense secretary) and Vice Admiral Arthur K. Cebrowski (then president of the Navy War College, later director of the office of force transformation).[17] One can only speculate on the degree to which the briefings and war games conducted at this symposium may have influenced the thinking of two individuals who would enjoy such prominence in Rumsfeld's Pentagon. However, regardless of the impact of the conference, Wolfowitz eventually became so enamored of the concept that he would later employ the term when discussing the Iraq war plan with CENTCOM commanders. However, the impact on Cebrowski is less clear. In 1999, Ullman wrote that Cebrowski "recognizes this interaction of shock and awe, and will and perception as well as anyone. In his own view of 'netcentric warfare,' he argues that the accumulation of rapidly applied, correct decisions will produce shock and awe and contribute to achieving decisive action."[18] By contrast, one of the senior officials in the Office of Force Transformation stated that Cebrowski was not a big supporter of Rapid Dominance, primarily out of concern for what happens after the fighting stops and the force you have available is too small.[19]

The high profile of the study group's members, such as General Horner, was also essential for spreading use of the term. Testifying at the "Hearing of the Military Procurement Subcommittee of the House National Security Committee" in 1996, General Horner cited "shock and awe" in reference to military modernization and the B-2 bomber.[20] In 1999, the author Tom Clancy, along with Horner, published the book *Every Man a Tiger*. Chapter 14 was titled "Shock and Awe." In it, Clancy and Horner note that "Shock and Awe" is otherwise known as "Rapid Dominance" and briefly describe the psychological effects imposed on the Iraqi military during the First Gulf War.[21] Likewise, both

General Gary Luck and Admiral Leon Edney wrote articles for military publications in which they highlighted the Shock and Awe concept.[22]

Despite the concept's endorsement by Horner and other former senior officials, the Air Force kept its distance from Shock and Awe. Apart from not funding development of the concept, the Air Force academic community chose not to embrace it as a theory of air power, with the result that it never featured in the mainstream of air power discourse in the way concepts such as Effects-Based Operations did. In response to the publication of the NDU study, Air Force Major Mark Conversino writing for the *Naval War College Review* in 1998 complained,

> Unfortunately, it is the reader who is "shocked." While the authors are all eminently qualified to expound on military affairs and strategy, the text is rambling, repetitious, and at times incoherent. The authors did not intend this to be a scholarly tome but expected their work to spark thought and debate. Yet a number of egregious errors call its credibility into question. The reader learns, for example, that "Operation Rolling Thunder III," executed in November and December 1972, brought Hanoi back to the bargaining table, that terrorists bombed the "Kolbah barracks" in Riyadh in June 1996, and that the Israelis struck Syria's nuclear reactors in 1982.[23]

In a stinging indictment, Conversino adds, "The evidence used to support the concept of Shock and Awe is uneven . . . I submit that neither my professors in graduate school nor my faculty colleagues at the Air Force Academy and the US Air Force School of Advanced Airpower Studies would have found the volume that I was asked to review to meet acceptable standards of evidence, organization, augmentation, and editing."[24]

Conversino was just one of many in the defense academic community to heap criticism on the concept. In a further denigration of Shock and Awe, one air power academic stated, "I received a copy of the book when I was a military professor at the School of Advanced Air and Space Studies. I considered assigning it to students as an example of bad theory, but after I read a few pages, I decided it was SO bad that it wasn't worth the time."[25] He also noted, "The logic on which Ullman and Wade build their theory is seriously flawed, and their interpretation of the empirical record is superficial and largely invalid . . . They throw an idea on the table with little or no evidence to support it and expect 'objective' and 'informed' readers to accept their view at face value."[26] He further adds, "I've never met a credible defense academic anywhere . . . who thought Shock and Awe was a meaningful strategy."[27]

The Rapid Dominance concept was also presented in the United Kingdom. As Ullman wrote in the *RUSI Journal* in fall 2003, "RUSI was partly responsible for the unveiling of Shock and Awe and the strategy of Rapid Dominance that accompanied the term."[28] In 1998, RUSI published a short book "Rapid Dominance: A Force for all Seasons" and the next year held a lecture given by Ullman in London. The RUSI publication differed significantly from its NDU predecessor in that its main emphasis was on the design and procurement of weapons for a Rapid Dominance Force, as opposed to the 1996 paper that focused on Rapid Dominance as a military concept for fighting future wars. The impact of the RUSI publication and lecture on the British military, and among British defense academics, appears to have been negligible. Whereas the concept of "effects-based operations" became part of the military lexicon and official doctrine in the United Kingdom, Rapid Dominance and Shock and Awe are nowhere to be found in any official publication or statement prior to the Iraq War.[29] That this should be the case is hardly surprising for two reasons. First, the Rapid Dominance Force proposed in the RUSI publication was never intended to be developed by any country other than the United States, although reference is made to "Allied contributions," which is presumably where the British military would fit in.[30] Second, the types of weapons systems a Rapid Dominance Force would need to be equipped with, including "Global artillery," "Hydrogen gas guns," "Electro-magnetic guns," and a "Liferay," would not be suitable for the British military and were highly unlikely to be given serious consideration or funding by the Ministry of Defence.[31] As it happened, the US defense department wasn't interested in these sorts of weapons either. Nevertheless, the RUSI connection to Shock and Awe helped give the concept some additional credibility and publicity.

In the preface to the 1998 RUSI publication, the authors express their gratitude to Andrew Marshall, "dean of American strategic thinkers and longtime director of the Office of Net Assessment (ONA) in the Office of the Secretary of Defense."[32] In 1997, Wade approached the ONA in an attempt to fund additional research. Limited funding was approved, and the study group expanded its membership.[33] Among those who would play a critical role in providing technological input was the former director of defense engineering and research, Dr. John Foster.[34] Foster was employed by the study group to look into the technology needed to produce psychological effects. These included weapons systems that could produce "dramatic visual effects" as well as "sound weapons."[35] For Marshall, Rapid Dominance represented a potential "capability for the President" to be able to "intervene with smaller forces."[36] The financial support provided by Marshall was essential to the development of the concept of Shock and Awe and its promotion among the senior Pentagon leadership. In 1999, a plan for further developing the Rapid Dominance concept was included in a report prepared for the ONA titled "Rapid Dominance: A Strategic Roadmap for Fielding and Testing an Experimental Rapid Dominance Force."[37] In comparison to the two previous publications, this internal study further explored the specific systems that would be required to impose Shock and Awe on an adversary but did not include any new additions to the basic concept of Rapid Dominance.[38]

When Rumsfeld was appointed Secretary of Defense in 2001, he assigned Marshall to conduct a review of the entire US military, both for his own familiarization as well as in preparation for the fall 2001 congressionally mandated Quadrennial Defense Review (QDR).[39] Though few details have been publicized, the review was considered by many senior military officers at the Pentagon, but particularly by the Army, as "a blueprint for transforming the military services along the Revolution in Military Affairs guidelines Marshall had been advocating for a number of years."[40] However, Marshall's review did not specifically incorporate Rapid Dominance or Shock and Awe in its recommendations, nor do the terms appear in the QDR.[41]

Among the reasons one would expect Shock and Awe to have been favorably received in Rumsfeld's Pentagon was that one of the earliest supporters of the concept in the late 1990s was none other than Rumsfeld himself. According to Ullman, "Rumsfeld was a rump member of the original Shock and Awe group, so he knew about the concept."[42] Shortly after the Kosovo war began in March 1999, Rumsfeld was interviewed by CNN about his views on the air campaign. According to Rumsfeld, "there is always a risk in gradualism. It pacifies the hesitant and the tentative. What it doesn't do is shock, and awe, and alter the calculations of the people you're dealing with."[43] Rumsfeld's preference for rapid application of force (vice gradual operations) producing instantaneous effects as the basis for strategy is made abundantly clear by his comment on the Kosovo conflict. It is also worth noting that Rumsfeld's comment came at a time when he was actively involved in advocating the Shock and Awe concept in the Washington corridors. Similarly, retired Admiral Leighton Smith, another member of the study group that helped create Shock and Awe, was openly critical of the Kosovo air campaign. In May 1999, during a Rapid Dominance conference at the National Defense University, Smith argued the allies should have won the war quickly and decisively by launching a Shock and Awe attack on Yugoslav President Slobodan Milosevic during the first day of the war.[44]

In September 1999, Rumsfeld served as cochairman of a panel that examined the concept in greater detail. This panel, which met at the National War College, consisted of about twenty people, most of whom were retired senior military officers, although former speaker of the house of representatives Newt Gingrich, also participated.[45] One month later, Rumsfeld joined three other former secretaries of defense (Harold Brown, Frank C. Carlucci, and James R. Schlesinger) in writing a letter commending the Rapid Dominance concept to Defense Secretary William Cohen.[46] In the letter, they said, "We are writing to you in support and endorsement of the concept of Rapid Dominance.

We believe that the concept of Rapid Dominance has sufficient merit to warrant further evaluation and experimentation."[47] In March 2000, Cohen wrote to Rumsfeld, thanking him "for your letter on the work being performed by Defense Group Inc. (DGI) on the concept of Rapid Dominance. We are of course interested in further developing our ability to strike promptly and induce 'Shock and Awe' in future adversaries."[48] Nevertheless, Cohen's letter merely represented a polite response rather than real endorsement, and he was not very interested in it.[49] By the time he was to assume his second tour as secretary of defense in January 2001, Rumsfeld was one of the few supporters of Shock and Awe and now in the position of ultimate authority in the defense department. During the handover from Cohen, Rumsfeld specifically mentioned the term in a memo in which he used it in connection with the QDR.[50]

Upon his return to the Pentagon, Rumsfeld brought with him a "transformation" agenda encapsulating many of the ideas found in Rapid Dominance. Beginning in early 2001, Rumsfeld convened 22 separate panels to explore different methods of transforming the military, although Shock and Awe did not play a central role in any of these.[51] However, so unpopular were his ideas of transformation among the military services, not to mention his efforts to implement them, especially in the Army (e.g., the cancellation of the Crusader artillery system), that by early September 2001, it was widely speculated that he would be the first member of the Bush cabinet to be fired.[52] According to Ullman, "despite high-level support (of Shock and Awe) among senior civilians, the bureaucratic realities were too strong. The option of Shock and Awe was too threatening to the conventional wisdom, and more important, to the current and planned conventional force structure."[53]

The initial stages of the War in Afghanistan, which included some air attacks on Taliban and al-Qaeda facilities, could in no sense be viewed as a Shock and Awe campaign, although several media commentators at the time did actually misuse the term to describe US strategy.[54] The fundamental problem with employing Shock and Awe in Afghanistan was that the ability to induce a psychological shock on either the Afghan population or the Taliban's fielded forces was minimal. As Robert Pape wrote afterward, "the first month of bombing, October 2001 . . . focused on command-and-control facilities and other leadership targets. But after that strategy failed to kill Mullah Omar or other critical enemy leaders, air power was turned against the Taliban's 25,000 or so troops in northern Afghanistan."[55] Consequently, the collapse of the Taliban regime came about after Northern Alliance forces, aided by US bombing and a small US ground component, physically conquered the country's territory. Thus the War in Afghanistan did not represent a Shock and Awe campaign, nor is there any evidence to suggest the concept featured in the Pentagon planning or that

CENTCOM planners were either aware of, or familiar with, the concept as of the autumn of 2001. It must be remembered that unlike the 2003 Iraq War, which would consist of 16 months of prior planning, the War in Afghanistan consisted primarily of "off the cuff" planning with relatively minimal interference by Rumsfeld (in contrast to the Iraq War plans). Nevertheless, the military campaign did encompass certain aspects of Shock and Awe, particularly the capability to respond rapidly to a far corner of the globe and accomplish a mission using a minimum-sized force. The perceived success of this approach sowed the intellectual seeds of the idea that a small US ground force supported by indigenous forces and US airpower, rather than reliance on heavy ground forces, could win wars, a theme that would be pushed, particularly by Rumsfeld and Wolfowitz, during the planning of the Iraq War.[56] In November 2001, Rumsfeld instructed General Franks to begin revising plans for a war in Iraq. In the ensuing months, Shock and Awe would emerge from its theoretical confines and make its debut in the world of practice.

War Planning

It was during the period of planning for the Iraq War (November 2001–March 2003) that the Shock and Awe concept would begin to directly shape policy, as well as evolving into a popular buzzword that would indirectly influence policy. Prior to November 2001, *Shock and Awe* was known only to a relatively small audience within the DoD, in comparison with many other terms associated with the RMA discourse, such as *network-centric warfare, effects-based operations*, and so forth. Yet within only a matter of months, it would be a term used in presidential briefings as well as by CENTCOM planners. This transformation from obscurity to prominence had much to do with the influence of senior DoD officials, such as Rumsfeld and Wolfowitz, who used the term to express their belief that a heavy ground force was unnecessary to defeat the Iraqi military and that because the Iraqi population hated Saddam Hussein, a quick Shock and Awe campaign would be all that was really needed to spur an internal revolt.[57] This was in no way meant to imply that US forces would not have to fight a conventional ground war but merely reflected a belief, which later turned out to be inaccurate and based on false assumptions, that the Iraqi population was eager to revolt against the Hussein regime, thus potentially obviating the need to deploy a large ground force. Interestingly, one of the unintended consequences of using a smaller ground force than military planners had originally believed essential was that air power assets were required to act as a force multiplier during the ground advance, with close air support missions receiving higher priority than strategic Shock and Awe missions.[58]

While Shock and Awe was being pushed from top down, military planners raised critical questions and expressed serious misgivings about applying the concept in an Iraqi context. For instance, would a heavy aerial bombardment "shock and awe" the Iraqis to the point where they would rise up against Saddam? Would the Iraqi military, particularly those elements like the Republican Guard that were loyal to Saddam, simply surrender in a matter of days? Translating the Shock and Awe concept into a war plan necessitated finding answers to these questions, but practical considerations ensured the theory would significantly differentiate from practice. Moreover, as *Shock and Awe* developed into a buzzword, military officials inevitably used the term in contexts for which it was not intended, and this also had an important impact on the planning process.

Before comparing the Shock and Awe concept with the reality of the war plan, it is first necessary to demonstrate that the term was used in the war plan itself and during the war planning process. The textual evidence can be found within the original CENTCOM war plan briefing slides, where Shock and Awe was referenced several times. For instance, on two slides the term is mentioned in relation to the Generated Start option (to be discussed later), including the need to leverage "Shock and Awe" with "information operations." In another slide, "Shock and Awe" is listed in reference to the five-day air campaign that was to precede ground operations. In the course of this five-day period, the label of "Shock and Awe" was used to describe the process of shaping the battle space through the deployment of special operations units in order to suppress Iraq's air defenses, support the Kurds, launch raids and other direct-action missions, establish a security zone, and conduct ground reconnaissance.[59] In other words, as stated in the war plan, Shock and Awe was not limited to strategic air operations but included a host of measures intended to throw the Iraqis off balance *prior* to the start of the ground war. Thus, according to the war plan, Shock and Awe was not about simultaneous operations; rather, it was about a sequence of operations. This distinction is important when attempting to gauge the validity of later claims that Shock and Awe was merely about simultaneous lines of operation. Given the five days of air operations and other Special Forces activities referenced in the documents, the war planners clearly did not interpret Shock and Awe as being a simultaneous assault by air and ground forces.

Compromise between theory and actual capabilities meant that the war plan that would eventually emerge (OPLAN 1003V) was a hybrid plan, and it was by no means a classic Shock and Awe strategy. Despite a number of press leaks about the war plan throughout the summer and autumn of 2002 that referenced the inclusion of Shock and Awe, the term did not become a buzzword until January 2003, following a press report detailing an unofficial briefing with an unnamed Pentagon official who claimed Shock and Awe was the basis of the war plan. Afterward, it soon became part of the public's lexicon, thus shaping the debate about going to war in Iraq. And yet, for reasons that are unclear, Defense Department officials were very careful not to use the term in official briefings, but neither did they deny that the concept was guiding the war planning when members of the Pentagon press corps raised questions about it. Indeed, it was the lack of official endorsement that helped spur the myth of Shock and Awe, leading a number of postwar commentators to believe that the widespread use of the term had more to do with psychological operations and military deception than with the concept upon which the war plan was based. For others, Shock and Awe represented Bush administration propaganda—a catchy slogan designed to sell a war. While there is little disagreement that Shock and Awe was a catchy slogan, there is no evidence that its public dissemination was deliberately concocted to mislead the Iraqi leadership or to win domestic public support for the war. By contrast, there is a great deal of evidence that Shock and Awe was internalized by defense policy makers and military planners when discussing US strategy, even if those officials had a poor grasp of what the term meant. It was only after it had disseminated among military audiences involved in the war planning that the term's dissemination would extend to the public realm.

At a November 21, 2001, White House meeting, President Bush directed Rumsfeld to initiate planning for an Iraq campaign. Six days later, Rumsfeld asked General Franks to begin planning for what would become Operation Iraqi Freedom.[60] As the planning process for Iraq got under way, Shock and Awe was still relatively unknown within the Defense Department. The Shock and Awe concept was no secret, but its wider dissemination within the US military had been stymied by lack of interest and official endorsement.

The planning process itself would be driven from the top down, with Rumsfeld consistently pressing Franks to produce a war plan with a shorter build-up timeline and smaller ground force. In early December 2001, after reviewing with Rumsfeld the war plan that had been produced several years earlier, OPLAN 1003-98, Franks was ordered to produce a new plan.[61] Sometime in December, Rumsfeld sent a note to Franks suggesting that the CENTCOM commander and his planners review the original Shock and Awe study.[62] Dr. James Wade, one of the coauthors of the study, forwarded Franks a summary of a report on the Rapid Dominance concept, as well as a six-page paper prepared by Horner titled "How and Where to Apply Shock and Awe."[63] This paper reportedly cited historical examples as far back as Genghis Khan.[64] In addition, retired General Gary Luck, one of the members of the Shock and Awe study group, would be assigned to Franks's staff to assist with the war planning.[65]

In the second week of January 2002 during an initial progress review at which Franks briefed Rumsfeld on a revised war plan—OPLAN 1003V "Generated Start"—Shock and Awe reemerged. During these discussions, Wolfowitz raised the idea of fracturing the regime in key areas before commencing ground operations.[66] The previous month, Wolfowitz had been briefed on a war plan produced by Ahmad Chalabi's Iraqi National Congress in conjunction with several senior ex–US military and intelligence officials and augmented and modified by a Pentagon planning group.[67] This plan was built on the "Afghan model," which included "bombing, a modest insertion of Special Forces, plus an uprising."[68] At the February 7, 2002, meeting of the National Security Council, Rumsfeld introduced Shock and Awe to President Bush. At this point it meant building up so much force and conducting various "spiking operations" and bombing that it might in itself spark regime change.[69] At a meeting with his component commanders at Ramstein Airbase in March, Franks also used the term *Shock and Awe* in relation to his vision of near-simultaneous air and ground attacks.[70]

Though *Shock and Awe* was a term being used with increasing frequency among the senior leadership in Washington, it took several months before it made its way into the lexicon of the CENTCOM planning staffs. Unfortunately, the evidence of the extent to which the concept of Shock and Awe was actually understood is somewhat contradictory. According to one Air Force officer attached to CENTCOM who contributed to the planning process for the Iraq air campaign, "Shock and Awe was a buzzword, but no one really knew what it actually meant . . . it became popular following a visit by Wolfowitz in March 2002 to CENTCOM HQ."[71] This officer recalled the term being used in discussions related to attacking Iraq's air defense network. By contrast, another CENTCOM planner noted, "Extensive efforts were made to study the concept and find relevant applications."[72] Nonetheless, whether it was used as a buzzword or actually understood as a concept, Shock and Awe had entered the discourse at CENTCOM and contributed to the planning process at the operational level.

Over the course of 2002, the war plan underwent several iterations.[73] Two general themes guided this process, both of which were directly relevant to the employment of Shock and Awe. The first was the belief that a small group of anti-Saddam fighters could take the lead in successfully bringing about a regime change if supported by the US military.[74] This view was especially prevalent among a number of senior officials within the Office of the Secretary of Defense who supported the formation of the "Free Iraqi Forces" led by Chalabi.[75] The second theme followed closely on the first. There was a belief that qualitative coalition advantages coupled with a selective application of force would reduce the number of ground troops required.[76] In practice, this idea appealed to the desire of some defense civilians for a smaller coalition force and a more rapid execution, both of which were underlying themes of Shock and Awe and also fitted in with the broader RMA discourse.[77] Both of these themes were likely instrumental in the October 2002 development of Operational Concept "Velocity." The idea behind this concept was an intense coalition strategic bombing campaign that would quickly force a regime collapse.[78] However, this concept was never formally adopted by CENTCOM as an operational plan.

When tracing the genealogy of Shock and Awe during the period of war planning, it is important to note the evolution of how the term was understood by the war planners, particularly the distinction between simultaneous and sequential lines of operation. It has been argued that initiating air and ground offensives simultaneously was an idea that grew from the focus on Shock and Awe.[79] According to the official US Marine Corps history of the war, "The vision that guided the planning was to win by creating 'shock and awe' through multiple lines of operation putting simultaneous pressure on the enemy—from the air, from conventional ground operations, and from various kinds of special operations, to include 'nonkinetic' operations and operations by proxies like the Kurds. For Marines, 'shock and awe' was something like the 'combined arms effect,' on a grand scale, of forcing the enemy into a series of dilemmas he could not resolve; if he turned to face one threat, he would make himself vulnerable to another threat."[80]

The concept of simultaneous lines of operations was first presented to CENTCOM component commanders by General Franks and Third Army head Lieutenant General Paul Mikolashek in February 2002. During this briefing, the term *Shock and Awe* was used to describe the concept.[81] Franks argued that the combined effects of both an air and land offensive, if launched simultaneously, might overwhelm Iraq. However, several component commanders rejected the concept, arguing it was necessary to begin military operations with an air assault, similar to Desert Storm, in which the beginning of the air war had preceded the ground war by 38 days.[82] Simultaneous lines of operations was a controversial concept because without a bombing campaign to "soften up" the Iraqi ground forces the coalition would launch its campaign against relatively fresh troops who had not been subjected to the practical and psychological hardships of enduring sustained attacks.[83] By March, Franks had been persuaded to include five days of preparatory bombing in the war plan.[84] It was this five-day period that would eventually be referred to by planners as Shock and Awe. Thus Shock and Awe originally referred to simultaneous lines of operations, then referred to sequential lines of operations, and would later revert back again to simultaneous lines of operations as the air campaign was scaled back.

The senior Iraq analyst working for the Directorate of Intelligence (J2) at CENTCOM during the war planning complained that part of the challenge of operationalizing Shock and Awe related to the ongoing coalition military pressure against Iraq.[85] In other words, how could a psychological state of "shock and awe" be induced?[86] According to this view, the Iraqis had suffered a defeat from coalition military power in 1991, followed by more than a decade of continuous daily contact with coalition military and intelligence efforts aimed at enforcing the containment policy. Given the high levels of continuous military pressure, the Iraqi military and populace were already familiar with the effect of coalition airpower, making it difficult to actually shock and awe them.

Creating shock and awe was made all the more difficult by the decision to intensify Operation Southern Watch (the monitoring of the Iraq no-fly zones) into what became officially known as Operation Southern Focus. In May 2002, Rumsfeld ordered Southern Focus, a more aggressive approach to monitoring the no-fly zones that included authorizing allied aircraft to attack Iraqi command and control centers as well as air defenses.[87] Southern Focus would have unintended consequences for the implementation of Shock and Awe and actually meant there would be no prospect of simultaneous lines of operations. Increased air operations under the auspices of Southern Focus had been continuing for weeks before the official start of the war. As such, the lines of operations were really sequential, with the targeting and destruction of a good portion of Iraq's air defense systems prior to the ground war.[88]

This increase in air activity, to say nothing of the publicity surrounding previous US air operations against Yugoslavia in 1999 and Afghanistan in 2001, meant that even new capabilities in the US inventory had been previewed, gradually allowing Iraq's military to adjust expectations and even attempt to develop countervailing tactics and equipment to defend the country.[89] For example, the precision levels achieved in the 1998 Operation Desert Fox by the first mass use of the Block III Tomahawk Land Attack Cruise Missile helped the Iraqis refine techniques for the rapid relocation of military, industrial, and government facilities in periods of heightened tension.[90] Similar to 1998, one of the arguments against overreliance on strategic airpower was that only a minimum practical effect would be achieved by attacking empty government ministries and Ba'ath party headquarters.[91] The sustained low-intensity bombing campaign that followed Desert Fox exposed the Iraqis to a number of emerging US capabilities, including Predator unmanned aerial vehicles and precision weapons such as the joint direct-attack munitions guided by global positioning system technology.[92]

Even the Iraqi civilians became inured to the harsh conditions of the interwar period in a way that would make Shock and Awe difficult to enact. For example, broad disruptions of Iraq's electrical power system, with its apparent practical and psychological effects on daily life and military activity, seemed on the surface like a potentially useful way to create shock and awe. But when CENTCOM planners considered the merits of deliberately attacking the Iraqi power system, many considerations were factored into the calculus—operational, legal, postconflict reconstruction—and one that led to the tactic's rejection was the expectation that denying power would have no dramatic effect on the Iraqis. After years of sanctions and a decaying power infrastructure, irregularity in power service was a routine part of Iraqi daily life. This factor eliminated any expectation that a severe shock could be induced through the disruption of electrical power.[93]

In addition, five-hundred high-value targets within the confines of Baghdad were off-limits to air strike.[94] Some of these targets were removed from the initial list because of overconfidence that the massive attack would lead to the immediate collapse of the regime and fears that attacking those targets would hamper postwar reconstruction.[95] Lieutenant Colonel David Hathaway, deputy chief of strategy at the Combined Air Operations Center at Prince Sultan Air Base in Saudi Arabia believed "there was a hope that there would be a complete and utter collapse of the regime early on. In order to let that come to fruition, air commanders initially held back those targets."[96] A number of the targets spared represented essential elements of Saddam's command and control system. For much of the 2003 war, Saddam's propaganda apparatus would remain untouched due to the decision to avoid targeting Iraq's television and radio broadcasting networks.[97] This decision was possibly based on the view that there was no harm in leaving so many lines of communication open, since most Iraqi field commanders fully understood the danger of passing along bad news to the senior leadership. However, in the war's early days, most Iraqi units likely interpreted the continued, uninterrupted broadcasts of the Baath regime as clear evidence that Saddam was still in control.[98] Other significant targets were off-limits to attack because of a pervasive fear of civilian casualties.[99] In the weeks leading up to the war, all 22 of the High Collateral Damage targets were pulled temporarily from the attack plan, and the air strikes were shifted from day to night. The sparing of such targets was a clear departure from Shock and Awe, yet one of the paradoxes of the concept is that "stunning the enemy with massive air strikes added substantially to the risk of unintended death and destruction."[100]

It is important to highlight that planning for the Iraq War was not only conducted by the United States; rather, it was planned in a coalition environment, in which the United Kingdom was intimately involved. Although CENTCOM planners were regularly using the term *Shock and Awe*, British planners deliberately sought to avoid using it, preferring the term *effects-based operations*.[101] As one British officer put it, "none of us ever approved of the phrase Shock and Awe because it painted totally the wrong picture, but it was the Pentagon's favorite slogan."[102] Interestingly, similar to most of the American planners, the British also appeared to have lacked any real knowledge about the concept. For instance, UK National Contingent Commander Air Marshall Brian Burridge thought the air power theorists John Boyd or John Warden coined the term.

However, he did correctly identify 1996 as the year it emerged, thereby indicating some familiarity with the concept. Burridge also thought Shock and Awe was a "sound bite which got rather regenerated in Washington and it may work for the internal US audience, but it was not very helpful elsewhere frankly."[103] During the course of planning, Burridge was adamantly opposed to beginning the war with "six days of shock and awe airstrikes in Baghdad" and told General Franks he believed it would actually have the effect of strengthening Iraqi resolve.[104] Due in part to British objections, the war plan was amended, and the air campaign was reduced to two days of bombardment before commencing ground operations.[105]

On the eve of war, the understanding of Shock and Awe among the military was minimal. For some, the term was only a catchphrase used in CENTCOM plans and orders merely to convey the intended effect of the "strategic" part of the air campaign to subordinate commanders.[106] There was also considerable skepticism expressed. As one officer put it in April 2002, "how can you have shock and awe and deploy such a massive ground force at the same time?"[107] Given that deploying a large land component could hardly be kept secret and would take many months to organize, the shock of strategic surprise was criticized as being farfetched. It was also feared that during this period, the Iraqis could choose to initiate military operations themselves.[108] In late January 2003, one senior official "called it a bunch of bull (referring to Shock and Awe), but confirmed it is the concept on which the war plan is based."[109] Nevertheless, most of the military (apart from the CENTCOM planners) were "pretty ignorant" of Shock and Awe until it hit the news in January 2003, after which time it became more of a catchphrase that officials throughout the military used in daily discourse rather than a military concept to which they would refer to and discuss intelligently. In many cases, officers inside the operational planning process were only using it because briefings from above used it.[110]

The lack of institutional understanding on the eve of war, especially within the Air Force, raises questions about the extent to which the Shock and Awe–style campaign that was being developed within the military bore any relation to the original concept. Apart from the political and military considerations that were taken into account when developing the plan, the limited theoretical understanding of the concept among military strategists may have meant that a real Shock and Awe campaign would have deviated considerably from the original concept in any event. For example, on March 19, 2003, Colonel Gary Crowder, plans director for strategy, concepts and doctrine at the air combat command, presented a briefing to the Pentagon press corps on "effects-based operations."[111] One of the briefing slides included a reference to Shock and Awe as an emerging operational concept, and one that US Joint Forces Command had been assigned to develop and further evaluate. When asked by a member of the press what the term meant, he responded, "I think it actually gets right back to some of the discussion on effects-based operations . . . I think the effects we are trying to create is to make it so apparent and so overwhelming at the very outset of military operations that the adversary quickly realizes that there is no alternative here other than to fight and die or give up."[112] In a later interview, when asked to describe his interpretation, Crowder stated he had no idea what Shock and Awe really entailed other than "hit 'em hard and fast to make fielded forces surrender."[113] He also thought the term was something that CENTCOM had made up.[114] Crowder's interpretation of Shock and Awe seems to have been generally representative of the lack of institutional understanding of the concept throughout the military system.

Despite *Shock and Awe* being increasingly used as a buzzword within the Defense Department and among the planning staffs during 2002, the media had yet to pick up on the term. The first report of Shock and Awe that gained significant attention was by CBS News correspondent David Martin, on January 24, 2003.[115] An unnamed Pentagon official told Martin that the strategy being devised would be based on Shock and Awe. With this mention of Shock and Awe, Harlan Ullman, who was then a senior advisor for the Center for Strategic and International Studies and a columnist for the *Washington Times*, became a figure constantly sought after by the press, and in the weeks preceding the war, he would give numerous interviews during which he would discuss his views on how Shock and Awe would be employed in Iraq. During one interview, Ullman said the purpose of Shock and Awe was to produce "a simultaneous effect, rather like the nuclear weapons at Hiroshima, not taking days or weeks but in minutes . . . You're sitting in Baghdad, and all of a sudden, you're the general and 30 of your division headquarters have been wiped out. You also take the city down. By that, I mean you get rid of their power, water. In two, three, four, five days they are physically, emotionally, and psychologically exhausted."[116]

This description of a classic Shock and Awe strategy contrasted greatly with the realities of the actual war plan that specifically avoided targeting the power and water supplies of Iraqi cities. Moreover, in another interview, Ullman stated, "You'll see simultaneous attacks of hundreds of warheads, maybe thousands, so that very suddenly, the Iraqi senior leadership, or much of it, will be eviscerated."[117] Again, the realities of intelligence weaknesses in locating high-value targets in real time meant that a significant departure from classic Shock and Awe was unavoidable.

Throughout February 2003, the term *Shock and Awe* was mentioned periodically, mostly from television talk show guests who disagreed with it. References escalated sharply after a March 4 press event featuring General Myers.[118] Myers said, "If asked to go into conflict in Iraq, what you'd like to do is have it be a short conflict . . . The best way to do that would be to have such a shock on the system that the Iraqi regime would have to assume early on the end was inevitable."[119] The following day, the *New York Times* ran an article under the headline "Top General Sees Plan to Shock Iraq into Surrendering." The article quoted military officials as saying "the plan calls for unleashing 3,000 precision guided bombs and missiles in the first 48 hours."[120] Headline grabbers such as this were associated with Shock and Awe and not only influenced popular perceptions about the scale and intensity of the initial air bombardment but left lasting impressions, especially among historians of the conflict, that Shock and Awe was all about strategic airpower.[121] Among the other unintended consequences of advertising Shock and Awe in advance of the war was that it likely reduced the psychological impact on the Iraqis it was meant to achieve in the first place.

War and Aftermath

The study of the strategy, operations, and tactics employed during the Iraq war have been, and are likely to be, analyzed in very great depth by professional military historians, and a further recounting of the history of the war here would be superfluous. Nevertheless, a brief recounting of some of the highlights of the war is necessary in order to ascertain the degree to which the military operation resembled a Shock and Awe campaign, to include the ability to actually cause shock-and-awe effects, as well as the degree to which the term itself became a point of contention.

As the Iraq war commenced, popular enthusiasm was high both for the term *Shock and Awe*, as well as the idea that the military power of the US campaign would be so overwhelming that the war would soon be over.[122] However, unlike the numerous erroneous expectations that were generated in the run-up to the war, the Iraqi regime was not shocked and awed into immediate surrender. Although top US defense officials did not explicitly say the strategy was based on the Shock and Awe concept, that impression was certainly conveyed in a number of unofficial statements, and they took no action to discourage this popular view.[123] For instance, Rumsfeld described the conflict as being one "of a force and a scope and a scale that has been beyond what has been seen before."[124] General Franks's first news conference after the conflict commenced referred to a campaign "characterized by shock," delivery of "decisive precision shock," and "the introduction of shock air forces."[125] Franks also talked about a "campaign unlike any other in history."[126] By not correcting false expectations, the Defense Department set the stage for popular misunderstanding of the term as well as the intense criticism that would follow the initial failure to bring about regime change in a matter of days.

After the first week of the war, which included the "heavy" bombardment of Baghdad on the night of March 21–22, Wade observed that the campaign "is going really well. It really is the 'Rapid Dominance' concept, too."[127] By contrast, Ullman was most critical of the popular linking of Shock and Awe to the actual strategy being employed:

> What they announced at the beginning of the war as Shock and Awe seems to me was largely PR . . . It did not bring the great Shock and Awe that we had envisaged . . . The public misunderstood our concept of Shock and Awe—and so perhaps did the Pentagon . . . Our concept calls for a 360-degree, nonstop campaign using all elements of power to coerce the enemy regime into succumbing rapidly and decisively . . . This has not happened in this war for two reasons: The opportunity to target Saddam accelerated the war's start before all the military elements were in place, and the decision to pause to see whether Saddam's generals would choose not to fight tempered the intensity of the initial onslaught. The Administration's version of Shock and Awe turned out to be a strategic air campaign and quick ground advance. This plan will soon defeat Saddam's regime, overwhelmingly, as it now appears, but it did not cause its immediate effect.[128]

At the same time, Ullman defended the March 19 attempted decapitation strike at the Dora Farms complex, which targeted Saddam Hussein, as a prime example of Shock and Awe: "The attack was advanced by several days in order to go after Saddam in an attempted decapitation strike. Had that strike worked, that would have been a textbook case of Shock and Awe . . . If you kill the emperor, the empire's up for grabs. And had we killed him, it would have been a classic application (of the theory): $50 million of ordnance, and we won the war."[129]

Though the initial emphasis of the air war was to target the Iraqi leadership and command and control, in order to bring about a quick collapse of the regime, this strategy failed.[130] During the night of March 21–22, the "full panoply of Coalition air power would rain down on Baghdad" contributing to a "spectacle of violent explosions that echoed throughout the capital."[131] This night of bombing was viewed by many commentators as the Shock and Awe–style campaign that they had been led to believe would bring about the fall of the regime. Moreover, many of the pilots conducting these missions would refer to "shock and awe targets," to make the contrast with close air support missions.[132] Fewer air strikes on strategic targets took place the following night, March 22–23, as well as during the remainder of the campaign. Coalition forces met increasing rather than decreasing levels of resistance from the Iraqi forces, especially beginning on March 25 as a fierce sandstorm (known as a *shamal*) engulfed advancing US forces. Throughout the three days of the *shamal*, the Iraqis concentrated their forces and began their deployments toward the advancing US Army's V Corps and the I Marine Expeditionary Force. After the *shamal*, as coalition forces closed in on Baghdad, the air campaign shifted its focus to supporting ground troops.[133] Two-thirds of coalition strike sorties now targeted the Republican Guard and irregular Fedayeen fighters.[134] By April 4, 85 percent of the coalition's air effort was focused on destroying Iraqi ground forces, particularly the Medina, Baghdad, and Hammurabi divisions, which were defending the Karbala gap and the approaches to Baghdad. Relatively few Iraqi troops seemed to have been killed, but strikes on their heavy armor apparently compelled most of them to keep away from the equipment, effectively disabling Iraqi resistance to the approaching US ground forces.[135]

As the conflict was being waged, US military personnel conducting operations employed the term *Shock and Awe*, albeit usually in reference to strategic military targets, rather than psychological ones. For instance, a number of pilots used the phrase "shock and awe targets" when referring to Iraq's command and control systems. According to Captain Darren Gray, an F-16CJ pilot attached to the 22nd Expeditionary Fighter Squadron, the lack of sophisticated Iraqi air defense indicated "they don't have any leadership, and that's the purpose of 'shock and awe.'"[136] The distinction between battlefield shock and awe and the shock and awe resulting from a bombing of strategic targets that would "shut the country down" is an important one, because the way the term was used by lower-level US commanders suggests an emphasis on the former, whereas higher-level policy makers and planners stressed the latter.

As in the First Gulf War, there are some indications that coalition forces achieved on the battlefield what Ullman and Wade would describe as "shock and awe."[137] The onslaught of a heavy aerial bombardment combined with ground forces far superior in technology and skill had devastating effects on Iraqi regular forces. Indeed, many Iraqi soldiers interviewed after the war exhibited symptoms of physical and psychological shock.[138] It is difficult to dispute claims that the coalition managed to impose some amount of shock and awe at the tactical level of war.[139] Even if they did not surrender, Iraqi regular forces "melted away" and therefore were of little help in the defense of Iraq. Nevertheless, Iraqi irregular forces, such as the Fedayeen, exhibited no significant indications they were in awe of coalition capabilities, despite suffering enormous losses in repeated attacks.[140] Nor did Saddam or the senior Ba'athist leadership appear to exhibit any symptoms of shock and awe. Instead, they remained defiant right up until coalition forces took Baghdad. Saddam appeared on television several times during the operation, looking confident and in command. Due to coalition concerns about collateral damage and Baghdad's use of mobile transmitters, Iraqi television was left on the air, allowing Saddam to shape domestic opinion in ways that helped forestall any popular uprising against him. That Saddam was able to appear on television at all, because of the command decision to leave the regime's "propaganda machine" functioning, contrasted with one of the primary objectives of Shock and Awe, which was to paralyze the adversary's ability to rally the willpower and determination of the population to continue fighting.[141]

Though coalition forces defeated all Iraqi forces that opposed them, there is no evidence to support claims that Baghdad's ability to command and control those forces had been severed. As Stephen Biddle testified to Congress, reporting the findings of a US Army War College study, "elements of four Iraqi divisions (the Hammurabi, Medina, Adnan and Nebuchadnezzar) redeployed across the V Corps axis of advance after D-day, and arrived in plenty of time to prepare their positions for combat. Some 10,000 paramilitary reinforcements were moved south from Baghdad to stiffen Iraqi defenses at Nasiriyah and Najaf once those cities became key battlefields. Perhaps most important, major concentrations of paramilitaries and Special Republican Guards were predeployed in Baghdad and other key cities long before Coalition forces reached them, and remained there until defeated by close combat in the urban centers."[142]

In every instance these Iraqi forces were decimated either en route or soon after contact with the coalition. But the fact that these forces were able to attempt such engagements suggests Iraq did not suffer from any degree of system-level shock or paralysis.[143] Many of the Iraqi field commanders may have made bad decisions, but many of these were directed from above.[144] Military incompetence paired with an inferior military system when matched against a high-tech force almost certainly had more to do with Iraq's military defeat than did any success of "shock and awe" effects against the regime.[145] Not only did the air attacks fail to get Saddam and his sons, but they failed to eliminate any of the Ba'athist regime's top leaders. It is arguable, of course, that the intense bombardment made it difficult for those leaders to function, but it did not substantially interrupt their ability to command and control their forces, nor did it cause either the Iraqi military or the Iraqi people to rise up against the regime.[146]

Though the notion that the term *Shock and Awe* was deliberately employed to increase support for the war is a contested one, there is no doubt the term was deliberately used by opponents of the war. As one article put it, "it is shock and awe that television and newspaper coverage of the war has adopted unanimously to describe the unprecedented heavy aerial bombardment unleashed on Baghdad, and other cities . . . and it is shock and awe that has also rapidly come to epitomize, among opponents of the conflict, all the indiscriminate, terror-inducing destructiveness they perceive in the Coalition military machine."[147] Both in the run-up to and during the war, *Shock and Awe* became a catchphrase for antiwar activists and war critics. Understanding the distinction between these two groups is important to understanding the significant difference in their interpretations of Shock and Awe. Antiwar activists can be categorized as those individuals who were against the war taking place at all. By contrast, war critics may have included in their ranks individuals who were against the war taking place but focused their main criticism on the conduct of the war, especially the military strategy that underpinned it.

Antiwar activists were quick to adopt Shock and Awe as the embodiment of the potential human catastrophe that would unfold if the coalition attacked Iraq. According to one commentary, Shock and Awe would have the potential of "making the aerial assault depicted in Picasso's Guernica look like a Monet watercolour."[148] Such comparisons led antiwar activists to label Ullman a modern-day "Dr. Strangelove."[149] Apart from the misrepresentation of Shock and Awe as a bombing campaign, with its inevitable "collateral damage," there was nevertheless an interest among some antiwar activists to read the NDU paper and make derisory comments about it.[150] Antiwar activists also tried to draw links between Shock and Awe and terrorism as one of their means of undermining support for the war. For instance, many activists referred to the Shock and Awe bombing of Baghdad as terrorism.[151] In many media outlets around the world, Shock and Awe was viewed mainly in negative terms.[152]

Given the failure of antiwar activists to generate enough political momentum to stop the war from occurring, the more enduring negative legacy of Shock and Awe came from the war critics. Prior to the start of the war, confidence in Rumsfeld's war plan (those parts that were leaked to the press) was undercut by criticism, especially from retired military officers.[153] Once the war began, this criticism would increase considerably and become a significant irritant for the DoD leadership. Some critics complained that Shock and Awe would be a rehash of the bombing campaigns that devastated Dresden and Hanoi but did little to effect the situation on the ground.[154] One of the most vocal critics of the war was former Army general Barry McCaffrey, who had served in the First Gulf War. The main thrust of McCaffrey's criticism was that the ground-forces component of the invading coalition force was too small. He attributed the emphasis on a light ground force to "Defense Department decision-makers with no battle experience."[155] According to McCaffrey, "these officials were prisoners of their own assumptions that the Iraqis would come apart under the Shock and Awe thunderstorm."[156] Criticisms regarding the lack of ground forces were also made by retired Lieutenant General Thomas G. Rhame and retired Major General William L. Nash.[157]

Along with McCaffrey, military commentator and former Army lieutenant-colonel Ralph Peters was also a vocal critic of the war strategy. Peters not only referred to Shock and Awe as a "farcical concept" and a "contractor's fantasy that rapidly became a decision-maker's embarrassment" but also labeled its creators as "deskbound theorists."[158] Whatever the merits of Peters's criticism of Shock and Awe as a "farcical concept," his reference to "deskbound theorists" was factually inaccurate given the wide range of military and combat experience shared by the members of the original study group.[159] Nevertheless, the view that civilian academics (especially those who were instrumental in advocating the war, such as Paul Wolfowitz) were using Iraq as a testing ground for fundamentally flawed political and military theories was one that quickly transferred into the criticism of the war strategy in general, and the concept of Shock and Awe in particular. Criticism of Shock and Awe also came from conservative commentators who complained that the Shock and Awe bombing was not shocking enough, particularly as too many targets had been deliberately avoided.[160]

Though Defense Department officials shied away from using the term in public, the media nevertheless associated Shock and Awe with the belief that the Iraqi military would collapse within a matter of days. Consequently, according to Deputy CENTCOM Commander Lieutenant General Michael DeLong, "when 'shock and awe' started, people were disappointed."[161] As Max Boot put it, there was a public expectation that the Iraqi regime "would collapse at the first whiff of gunpowder."[162] Once days turned into weeks (albeit only three weeks), and public confidence in the war plan began to decline, officials began to publicly distance themselves from Shock and Awe.[163] As Ullman would later note, "for the most part, Shock and Awe turned out to be a public relations disaster until cooler heads prevailed and the term quickly left the Pentagon lexicon."[164] By the end of the war's first week, the media mood had completely reversed from upbeat assessments of Shock and Awe to one of "dreary pronouncements about insufficient forces and overextended supply lines that could bog down the war for months."[165] At a Pentagon news briefing on March 25, 2003, Rumsfeld was asked, "Is it possible that you did raise expectations beyond reasonable levels by talking about a Shock and Awe campaign? I mean, wasn't the impression put out that, you know, 3,000 bombs are going to fall in the first 48 hours and the regime is going to collapse?" Rumsfeld replied, "Not by me, not by General Myers . . . Why would we have put in train the hundreds of thousands of people to do this task if we thought it was going to be over in five minutes?"[166]

Further denunciations by senior officials of Shock and Awe quickly followed. In an April 1, 2003, interview, Wolfowitz, when asked about Shock and Awe said, "I don't care for that phrase."[167] Lieutenant General Michael Moseley, the Combined Forces Air Component Commander, was of a similar opinion. At an April 5 press briefing, Moseley stated, "The term Shock and Awe has never been a term that I've used. I'm not sure where that came from."[168] Similarly, in early April, General Myers said, "I don't think I ever used the term Shock and Awe myself."[169] In July 2003, Franks told military historian Sir John Keegan that he "never cared for the use of the term Shock and Awe and, though no doubt the initial bombing of the government quarter did cause Shock and Awe, he had not seen that effect as the point of the air offensive."[170] These comments by senior civilian and military officials can be characterized as placing a taboo on Shock and Awe within the Pentagon, although there is no evidence that there were any official instructions given to subordinates not to use the term. Nevertheless, the very fact that senior civilian and military officials felt they needed to publicly distance themselves from Shock and Awe shows the importance they attached to avoiding any connection with the terminology.

Despite the fact that the actual military campaign was a far cry from a classic Shock and Awe campaign, the term gradually acquired a stigma of mock and derision. Wolfowitz's comment about "not caring for the phrase" is quite telling in that he was one of the promoters of the same phrase in the run-up to the war. In the aftermath of 2003, references to Shock and Awe by military officials declined markedly, and most of these were negative references related to the overemphasis on the conventional phase of operations to the detriment of postwar planning. For instance, in 2008, Defense Secretary Gates criticized the Shock and Awe concept, noting that it was an inappropriate means for the US to engage in future conflicts.[171] The Shock and Awe taboo can also be inferred by the lack of any public references to it by DoD officials in which it is characterized in positive terms, as well as the unwillingness of the defense academic community to pursue research into developing the concept further. This was not just due to the taboo on Shock and Awe per se but was also linked to the broader DoD discourse on the RMA and conventional operations being marginalized in favor of a discourse on counterinsurgency.

For the next several years, Effects-Based Operations (EBO) still retained a prominent place in the conventional operations discourse and was also later used in the counterinsurgency discourse, whereas Shock and Awe faded into obscurity, only to be employed as a criticism of the DoD leadership for its perceived failures to adequately prepare for the postconflict period in Iraq. Interestingly, though, due to the view that the transference of the term *effects-based operations* from the conventional discourse to that of irregular warfare was unhelpful (especially the way the Israelis employed it during the 2006 Lebanon war), the head of US Joint Forces Command (JFCOM) Lieutenant General J. N. Mattis complained, "It is my view that EBO has been misapplied and overextended to the point that it actually hinders rather than helps joint operations."[172] In 2008, Mattis ordered the term banned at JFCOM.[173] As the taboos placed on Shock and Awe and EBO demonstrate, the terminology that was once promoted for specific reasons eventually became counterproductive when the control over the meaning of those terms was lost.

Conclusion

The case of Shock and Awe provides important evidence of the mutually constitutive relationship between war and the language of war. Not only did the terminology have a direct bearing on the Iraq conflict, but the conflict also influenced the meaning of the terminology. As the Shock and Awe concept disseminated, initially inside the military, and eventually into the public realm, the term took on meanings that bore little relationship to that which was originally intended. This case also illustrates how terminology can take on a life of its own and negatively impact the individuals who were instrumental in introducing it into the military's discourse to begin with.

In response to the belief among a number of former senior defense officials that the 43 days of Operation Desert Storm reflected negatively on the capability of the US to defeat an enemy quickly, Shock and Awe emerged in 1996 as a concept intended to redefine the way the US military would organize and fight future wars. The designers and advocates of Shock and Awe contributed to an emerging American discourse of war whose characteristics included speed, precision, and limited liability. The belief in a Revolution in Military Affairs viewed the fighting and winning of wars as a matter of properly employed advanced military technology within the right organizational and doctrinal frameworks. Among the many negative attributes of this discourse that became particularly evident in the aftermath of Baghdad's fall was that this concept rarely extended beyond the winning of battles and campaigns to the tough work of turning military victory into strategic success. Hence it was more of a way of *battle* than an actual way of *war*.[174] In a number of respects, Shock and Awe was supposed to epitomize a new type of war—a nonnuclear equivalent of Hiroshima and Nagasaki that could rapidly bring an adversary to heel. However, such a strategy reflected such a poor grasp of the political, diplomatic, and cultural realities of modern war that when the time came to put the theory into practice, both politicians and military professionals showed themselves incapable of conducting a Shock and Awe campaign akin to what the authors of the concept had originally intended.

From the beginning of the Iraq War planning process in November 2001 to the start of the war in March 2003, the little-known and less-understood concept of Shock and Awe was gradually made known to the world. But just as no plan survives first contact with the enemy, the concept of Shock and Awe failed to survive its first contact with the reality of war. Apart from certain ideas of Shock and Awe that Rumsfeld, Wolfowitz, Myers, Franks, and other senior officials pushed for in the prewar planning, the question of whether a classic Shock and Awe campaign was employed by coalition forces must be answered in the negative.

In relation to discursive entrapment, numerous cases of bandwagoning on Shock and Awe were observable. Within the Pentagon, very few individuals were aware of the basic tenets of the concept, yet the term became part of the lexicon of the defense civilians, generals, and war planners responsible for organizing and conducting Operation Iraqi Freedom. Due to the media hype in the run-up to the war, false expectations among the public were propagated by using terms such as *Shock and Awe* that were indicative of a quick, simple, and relatively painless conflict. As Christopher Coker observed, "the Revolution in Military Affairs encouraged the US to go to war in the first place."[175] Coker notes that the United States "went in light to retain public support at home, to evade extensive political discussion of the conflict."[176] This aspect of the discourse highlights the negative consequences that resulted from the marginalization of an alternative discourse. Indeed, such was the prevailing belief about US conventional superiority and the idea the war would be a cakewalk, embodied in the discourse of Shock and Awe and the broader RMA, that the decision to go to war was facilitated, whereas had the war been framed in terms of a potentially costly long-term occupation, policy makers would likely have found it more difficult to gain support for the conflict. The negative effect of the dominant discourse on marginalizing the problems of postwar occupation was later highlighted by Defense Secretary Gates.

In terms of blowback, Shock and Awe not only was employed by advocates of the war but would also emerge as part of the discourse of antiwar activists and war critics. For instance, war critics would latch on to the term to indicate their displeasure that Hussein's regime did not collapse in the first two to three days of the conflict. Although Baghdad fell to the coalition in three weeks vice two to three days, Shock and Awe faded fast within the DoD. Further evidence of blowback can be found in the reaction of senior political and military leaders, who distanced themselves from the concept, going so far as to deny they had ever used the term. This delegitimizing of Shock and Awe meant that it was considered "essentially dead" at the Pentagon, despite the fact that a Shock and Awe strategy was never employed to begin with.[177]

CHAPTER 4

Characterizing the Irregular Adversary in Iraq

This chapter examines the terms used by US officials to characterize the irregular adversary in Iraq. It focuses on where they originate, how different actors and organizations have used them, and their impact on strategy and operations. By studying and deconstructing the official discourse, numerous inferences can be drawn regarding the perceptions, attitudes, and degree of comprehension within the Defense Department of who was responsible for the violence that followed the Hussein regime's collapse in April 2003. It can be argued that the inability or unwillingness within the bureaucracy to clearly and consistently identify the adversary was one of the primary impediments to the development of an effective strategy to achieve the desired end state of stability and security in Iraq. From even a modest inspection of official statements during the period under examination it can be inferred that there was never a clear and consistent characterization of the irregular adversary, no collective noun. To some extent, this lack of clarity and consistency is quite understandable given the polymorphous and evolutionary nature of the adversary. Nevertheless, despite the complexities inherent in understanding who the enemy was, many of the terms employed in the official discourse were used for their perceived positive political effect rather than their accuracy. Moreover, officials attempted to control terminology that was deemed accurate yet had perceived negative political implications.

This chapter is divided into three sections. The opening section will provide the background upon which the rest of the chapter is based by examining a set of terms the US military has used to characterize the irregular adversary. The following section focuses on the terminology battles over "insurgency," "guerrilla war," "sectarian violence" and "civil war" in order to show the interrelationship between "adversary characterizations" and "conflict characterizations." The final section more specifically examines the politicization of insurgency metrics.

Characterizing the Adversary

Numerous terms have been used to characterize the irregular adversary in Iraq, and to understand why, when, and how certain terms have been employed instead of others, necessitates reviewing their histories. Given the multitude of terms officially employed one must consider how these terms came into being, although due to time and space constraints, only a limited selection can be studied. In order to highlight the diversity of the adversary in Iraq, this section will examine the following categories: death squads, dead-enders and former regime elements, anti-Iraqi forces, terrorists and foreign fighters, and Shiite militias. Examining and listing the terms used, and the individuals and organizations that used them, puts into perspective the adversary's complexity, as well as the general lack of understanding of whom US officials believed they were fighting.

But there were also political imperatives that drove terminology development, as well as the restrictions placed on certain terms. As Lawrence Freedman observed, the United States "struggled to find language to describe those planting the bombs, in ways that sought to drain them of any legitimacy—as relics of the old regime, foreign adventurers, extremist opponents of democracy and Al-Qaeda agents. The labels fitted some but they played down the role of the US occupation in provoking violence."[1] The importance of this terminology was recognized at the highest levels in the Defense Department. As Rumsfeld noted to Wolfowitz, "the terminology we use is enormously important . . . We have to do a better job of using words that are well thought through and calculated to express exactly what we mean . . . I hope you will continue thinking through what words we use to describe the people who are causing us difficulties in Iraq."[2] Whatever the public affairs merits of employing terms that delegitimized the adversary, the same language was also internalized and hindered the prospect of more complex analyses of the adversary from emerging in the discourse of defense policy makers.

Death Squads

The use of the term *death squads* to describe the adversary in Iraq signifies the full-circle nature of the war's discourse given that the term was first employed in March 2003 to demonize the paramilitary force known as the "Fedayeen Saddam" and then reemerged two years later in the context of sectarian violence between Shiites and Sunnis. In its original context, the term *death squads* was usually prefixed in official statements by the word *terrorist* or *regime*. These references are an important point of departure for exploring the politicization of terminology associated with the conflict in Iraq as they represent the first characterizations of the irregular adversary.

The Fedayeen Saddam was a paramilitary force of up to forty thousand fighters operating independently of the regular Iraqi army that harassed coalition forces during the "major combat operations" phase of the war. Prior to the war, US intelligence agencies warned about the danger of the Fedayeen, but these warnings were either softened or ignored by political and military leaders.[3] Once war commenced, the Fedayeen Saddam had some limited success fighting a partisan-style war, especially against the stretched US supply lines.[4] Unlike the regular Iraqi army, which offered little resistance, the Fedayeen Saddam engaged in numerous attacks against coalition forces, many of which were conducted in a suicidal way.[5] It was in reference to the Fedayeen Saddam that on March 27 the commander of V Corps, Lieutenant General William Wallace, made the controversial remark "The enemy we're fighting is a bit different from the one we war-gamed against, because of these paramilitary forces."[6] Indeed, many officers in the field assessed the Fedayeen as a determined foe. Due to the perceived magnitude of the threat, Wallace wished to slow down the pace of the advance on Baghdad and instead devote additional resources to deal with the Fedayeen in the rear. Similarly, Coalition Forces Land Component Commander Lieutenant General David McKiernan concluded that his forces faced two centers of gravity: the Republican Guard, concentrated near Baghdad, and the Fedayeen. He decided to suspend the march on the capital for several days while continuing air strikes and engaging the Fedayeen. Franks and Rumsfeld opposed this decision, mainly because they viewed the Fedayeen as little more than a speed bump on the way to Baghdad.[7]

It is important to note that prior to March 27, the Pentagon was content with referring to the Fedayeen Saddam by their name, but that afterward, the language was changed. Following Wallace's comment, and due to the increasing realization that the military threat posed by the Fedayeen Saddam was undermining public confidence in the US military's ability to win a quick and easy victory, defense officials began applying terminology that demonized the Fedayeen and marginalized the military threat they posed.[8] Defense Department spokesperson Victoria Clarke stated that using the accepted terms of *irregular* or *paramilitary* to describe the Fedayeen Saddam had a positive connotation and therefore a new term was required. Rumsfeld referred to the Fedayeen Saddam as "death squads, enforcers" within the broader context that they "go into the cities and shoot people and threaten people."[9] While testifying at a Senate hearing, General Myers said that one possible definition is "regime death squads."[10] According to Myers, "it's tough to categorize them . . . A better description is probably regime death squads . . . They are putting guns to peoples' heads . . . to force them to fight."[11]

Demonizing references to the Fedayeen Saddam became a regular feature of Central Command (CENTCOM) press briefings.[12] Army Brigadier General

Vincent Brooks, CENTCOM's Deputy Director of Operations, told the press of ongoing operations to eliminate "terrorist death squads."[13] Brooks also told reporters that they operate "more akin to the behavior of global terrorists."[14] However, the references to "terrorist death squads" prompted enquiries about the legal status of the Fedayeen Saddam. In response to a query about their legal status given the negative characterization, Brooks stated, "We characterize them with terms that describe their behavior. It doesn't necessarily put them into any particular legal category."[15] Even among operational officers in theater, terminology was employed to demonize and marginalize the Fedayeen. Major General Gene Renuart, CENTCOM's Director of Operations, began referring to the Fedayeen as "almost terrorist-type forces."[16] Major General James Mattis, commander of the 1st Marine Division, said the Fedayeen "lack any kind of courage. They literally hide behind women and children, holding them in their houses as they fire . . . They really lack manhood. They are violating every sense of decency. They are as worthless an example of men as we have ever fought."[17] Major General Jim T. Amos referred to them as "cannibals," while Lieutenant General Wallace referred to them as "knuckleheads."[18] As these examples highlight, the Fedayeen Saddam were discursively constructed as being illegitimate and primarily a threat to Iraqi civilians, rather than as a legitimate force opposing US forces using guerrilla tactics.

After March 27, the Fedayeen would be officially renamed "regime death squads" by Pentagon edict, and this term would filter down throughout the military chain of command.[19] The term would be employed for internal purposes, including in operational orders and plans.[20] *Regime death squads* would also be used by many of the operational commanders to describe the Fedayeen, not just during the conflict, but also when reflecting on the conflict afterward.[21] By contrast, intelligence officials used the term *Republican Death Squads* to describe the amorphous collection of paramilitary forces, although it is unclear why the term *republican* was used in this context.[22]

Another aspect of using the label of *death squads*, which was a term previously used to describe organizations that were used to quell perceived *internal* dissent (especially in Central/South America), was that it downplayed what was actually the most effective Iraqi opposition to the invasion.[23] Among the consequences of downplaying the Fedayeen in the official discourse was to downplay the prospect that resistance to the invasion would continue after the fall of Baghdad. One Marine intelligence officer serving with Task Force Tarawa drafted a classified assessment comparing the Fedayeen attacks to the insurgencies in Nicaragua, El Salvador, and Colombia, pointing out similarities and differences. The assessment stressed that unless the coalition pursued the Fedayeen, their hit-and-run attacks would persist and hamper the stabilization of Iraq after the war.[24] Even though ignored, this assessment proved prophetic, as many of the Fedayeen continued their attacks following Baghdad's capture. A number of senior military leaders have argued that the most important consequence of downplaying the Fedayeen threat was the decision not to deploy the 1st Cavalry Division to assist with the occupation. Had the Fedayeen been taken seriously, more US forces would likely have been kept on hand to deal with the threat they continued to pose.[25]

Dead-Enders and Former Regime Elements

Following Baghdad's capture, the military's overemphasis of terms that implied that the main cause of the ongoing violence in Iraq was a desire of members of the former regime to return to power had important implications for US conduct of the war. Maintaining the linkages between the emerging "insurgency" and the former regime may have been useful as a tool for public relations, but the message itself represented an official lack of interest in explaining the complex adversary the United States faced. More important, it avoided the pertinent strategic recognition that an adversary motivated by nationalism and religion was an infinitely stronger foe than one fighting for a lost cause and that in a population with a high proportion of unemployed males, many could be persuaded to undertake attacks on US forces purely for monetary gain.[26]

In the period following the collapse of the Hussein regime, the US military focused its operations almost exclusively on groups and individuals associated with the Ba'ath party, because the logic was that by rooting them out the violence would cease.[27] As a result, large-scale military and intelligence operations, such as Operations Desert Scorpion and Peninsula Strike, were intended to round up the remaining members of the 55-card deck of most-wanted Iraqis, such as Saddam Hussein and his sons Uday and Qusay.[28] Even after the December 14, 2003, capture of Saddam Hussein, which should have heralded a significant blow to the insurgency, according to the logic of the dead-ender discourse, US officials continued to characterize the organized violence as primarily a Ba'athist phenomenon. The Bush administration, along with Coalition Provisional Authority (CPA) and Combined Joint Task Force-7 leaders, believed that Saddam's capture would be a significant turning point in the coalition's campaign in Iraq. Although the capture of Saddam probably ended any prospect of the Ba'athists returning to power, it did not end the Sunni Arab insurgency, nor did it lessen the Shia demands for dominance in any future government.[29]

As early as July 2003, Naval War College Professor Ahmed Hashim was highly critical of the official portrayal of the adversary since it overlooked a myriad of groups and ideologies responsible for the violence. He complained that although some "ex-supporters of Saddam's rule are involved, the opposition is not a monolith. At least a dozen groups are carrying out attacks for a variety of reasons." The complex adversary Hashim identified was not at all evident in the discourse of defense policy makers who preferred terms that downplayed, demonized, simplified, and mischaracterized the enemy's composition, goals, and resolve.[30] Among the terms used by senior officials at that time to label the adversary was *dead-enders*. Rumsfeld had originally used the term in November 2001 in reference to Taliban leader Mullah Omar, since he wasn't a "surrendering type."[31] During the initial invasion of Iraq, US officials used the term to describe Iraqis who resisted the coalition advance, particularly the Fedayeen Saddam. When coalition forces captured Baghdad and a few weeks later declared an end to "major combat operations," a significant number of senior Iraqi leaders remained at large. Resistance may have been disorganized and without effective command and control, but it continued nevertheless. Rumsfeld and other senior officials repeatedly used this derisory term to characterize those responsible for the ongoing resistance.

Whatever the perceived short-term benefits of using the term *dead-enders*, it would later be mockingly used to describe how Rumsfeld in particular had misjudged the nature of the enemy. As insurgent attacks increased and grew more sophisticated, it became more difficult politically to downplay the adversary as consisting merely of dead-enders, and the term gradually fell out of use.[32] In 2005, Senator John McCain would chastise senior military officials who were testifying before Congress that there seemed to be a credibility problem because the military had for so long been characterizing the enemy as "a few dead-enders" and yet in the course of a single year, coalition forces had killed or captured more than 15,000 of them.[33]

Dead-enders may have been the term of choice for Rumsfeld and other official spokespersons, but it wasn't considered a suitable term for internal bureaucratic use. Instead, the term *former regime loyalists* was coined and used to characterize the adversary in internal documents but was increasingly employed in the Department of Defense's (DoD) public discourse as well.[34] Due to the positive connotations of the word *loyalist*, this term eventually fell out of use to be replaced by *former regime elements*.[35] However, *former regime loyalists* did not disappear completely and was most prominently resurrected in the 2005 "National Strategy for Victory in Iraq."[36] As the word *loyalist* was the only part of the term that was contentious, it was replaced by the politically neutral word *elements*; thus *former regime loyalists* begat *former regime elements* (FRE). According to Lieutenant Colonel Wesley Odum, a V Corps plans officer, in the Summer 2003, "we lumped everyone together that was conducting attacks against the Coalition or a disruptive element that was causing insecurity and instability in the environment and labelled them as former regime elements."[37] Thus, within the internal military discourse, there was no attempt to disaggregate the adversary to gain a more accurate picture of whom it was they were fighting. Meantime, CENTCOM created the Joint Interagency Task Force-Former Regime Elements, headed by a one-star general, "to coordinate the hunt for members of Saddam's regime in and out of Iraq."[38] The view that the FRE were the main adversary of the US forces remained prominent in the discourse of defense officials for the next several years. A December 8, 2003, Defense Intelligence Agency (DIA) "Special Analysis Report" described the FRE as "primarily Sunnis who once served under Saddam, including the paramilitary force, the Fedayeen Saddam, the Iraqi Intelligence Service, the Special Security Organization, the Special Republican Guard, and former Baath Party leaders."[39] The report states that the FRE "are assessed to be behind the majority of attacks" and that they represented the "greatest threat of all anti-Coalition groups in the near term."[40] This emphasis on the FRE continued for some time and appears fairly consistent within the military bureaucracy. According to the Multinational Forces-Iraq (MNF-I) staff, as of July 2004, the "primary threat" to the accomplishment of US strategic objectives was the "former regime element insurgency."[41]

One critical aspect to the emphasis on the FRE was the de-emphasis on the nationalist and tribal nature of the "insurgency." Former Ba'athists probably directed the majority of organized attacks on coalition forces in the "Sunni Triangle," but they were not primarily motivated by a desire to bring back the former regime, in contrast to the statements made by Rumsfeld and other senior officials describing the motivations of "insurgents."[42] Though US intelligence officials recognized that the "insurgents" were driven primarily by "sheiks and Mosques, Islamic clerics, and nationalism," the mainstream DoD discourse still linked the majority of ongoing violence to the former regime.[43] Moreover, some "insurgent" groups sought dominance in a particular area for their tribe, or simply wanted their ethnic or sectarian group to have political control of Iraq when the dust settled. This latter goal was one of the most important motivating factors behind many Sunni groups and the militant Shia organizations.[44] It is unclear whether senior policy makers or military planners recognized the importance of these motivating factors, and there is little to or reference to them in the discourse of defense officials during this period.

In October 2004, Defense Intelligence Agency (DIA) analyst Derek Harvey presented Rumsfeld an analysis of an "organized, powerful, well-honed insurgency," whereas Rumsfeld still viewed the adversary as "thugs."[45] This assessment was later briefed to President Bush. It is important to note that even at this late date senior officials such as Rumsfeld still viewed the "insurgency" in minimalist terms, despite all the evidence to the contrary.[46] While commanders on the ground recognized the "insurgency" was receiving significant support from the population and wished to adopt strategies that would seek to reduce this support, the Bush administration argued the "insurgency" only included

Saddam loyalists and foreign jihadists and could be defeated by a combination of force and free elections.[47] In order to buttress this view, Rumsfeld insisted on defining the adversary in a particular way, such as in the case of the term *Sunni Arab rejectionist*. Senior officials arbitrarily redefined the category of Sunni Arab rejectionist to be consistent with the portrayal of the insurgency as small, isolated, and consisting largely of former members of Hussein's government. This approach contrasted sharply with an October 2004 intelligence assessment produced under the auspices of Multinational Corps-Iraq head Lieutenant General John Vines that was based on a very different set of assumptions about the "insurgency." The Vines assessment portrayed the "insurgency" as having an "enormous support base among Sunnis, because of a wide range of grievances, including unemployment, the arrest and killing of family members, and destruction of homes as well as opposition to foreign occupation."[48] Rumsfeld gradually accepted the fact that the "insurgency" had significant Sunni support but then began arguing that such support was motivated only by a desire to regain their old privileges. This definition of the threat predominated US political discourse and also featured in the administration's National Strategy for Victory in Iraq, which defined the "rejectionists" as those Sunni Arabs "who have not embraced the shift from Saddam Hussein's Iraq to a democratically governed state" and who opposed "a new Iraq in which they are no longer the privileged elite."[49]

Statements by senior officials during the two main battles for Fallujah (April and November 2004) also emphasized the participation of the "former regime elements" in the resistance.[50] CENTCOM Deputy Head of Operations Brigadier General Mark Kimmitt described the strategy of the dead-enders as "wanting to make Fallujah the last hold-out of Saddam."[51] It is possible that the demonizing characterizations of the enemy inherent in these terms may have blinded senior officials to the realities of the "insurgency" with regards the participants and their motivations. Kimmitt's reference to "the last hold-out of Saddam" was almost certainly an attempt to link the adversary in Fallujah with the "evil" former regime, thereby justifying the relatively large-scale military operations to retake the city. The message was curious because it failed to explain why Fallujah was "a last holdout of Saddam" given that Saddam had already been captured. In many respects the battle for Fallujah was misrepresented as a pivotal battle against the "insurgents" with a decisive defeat of the "former regime elements" signaling a crushing defeat for the "insurgency" nationwide.[52] This was a false representation that had the consequence of raising hopes that the end of the conflict was near. Large numbers of insurgents were killed in Fallujah, but in the aftermath of the November battle, the "insurgency" expanded rather than contracted.[53]

A number of analogies were employed by senior officials to describe the nature of the conflict and the adversary they faced, often choosing ones that linked the violence to the "former regime."[54] Prominent among these was the use of the Nazi analogy, an analogy used not only to describe Saddam Hussein's regime prior to the commencement of the war but also to characterize the irregular adversary after Baghdad's fall. There are several aspects of this analogy's usage that are noteworthy because they reflect on the political manipulation of a historical theme for the purpose of gaining public support, including the propagation of a discourse on the enemy's nature that sought to legitimize US actions while delegitimizing those of the adversary.

The political intent was most evident when both Rumsfeld and National Security Adviser Condoleeza Rice put out a coordinated message in their speeches to the Veterans of Foreign Wars in August 2003.[55] In comparing the difficulties of postconflict Iraq with postwar Germany, reference was made in both speeches to the "Werewolf" organization that was responsible for carrying out resistance against the Allied forces occupying Germany beginning in late 1944. Rumsfeld noted that "one group of these 'dead-enders' was known as 'Werewolves.'"[56] However, Rumsfeld also noted that despite their attempts at sabotage and assassination of German collaborators, the "Nazi dead-enders" comprised a "failed resistance."[57] Similarly, Rice's speech also referred to the postwar challenge of the Werewolves who attacked both "coalition forces and those locals cooperating with them, much like today's Baathist and Fedayeen remnants."[58] The terms that both Rumsfeld and Rice used in comparison to the Werewolves, such as "dead-enders" and "Baathist and Fedayeen remnants," on the one hand are illustrative of a lack of comprehension of who the adversary was as of late August 2003, but also indicated their optimism that Iraq would become a "success story" similar to Germany once the resistance from the previous regime was crushed. It was also probably an attempt both to compare the Second Iraq War as analogous to crushing an "evil dictatorship" and to offer a historical reference as a means to explain why resistance to the coalition continued after the end of major combat operations. Rice's inaccurate reference to "coalition forces" in the Second World War context rather than "allied forces" may have also represented more than a Freudian slip. One of the results of Rumsfeld's use of the Werewolf analogy was that General Abizaid assigned a senior officer to investigate whether or not this analogy was an accurate one. After consulting at least one academic expert on the subject, the senior officer reported to Abizaid that it wasn't an accurate analogy. As a result, it was never used at CENTCOM.[59]

Another proponent of the Nazi analogy was Deputy Defense Secretary Wolfowitz. When asked by a reporter in late July 2004 how he'd characterize the adversary in Iraq, Wolfowitz responded, "the terminology is important . . . for a long time we called them former regime loyalists. And that would be like calling former members of the Gestapo and the SS former regime loyalists . . . that word 'Baathist' really does come very close to being Nazi."[60] Wolfowitz also specifically referred to the Iraqi Intelligence Service (Mukhabarat) as "like the Gestapo."[61] His belief that the Iraqi intelligence services were the main force behind the resistance ran counter to the assessments of the US intelligence services, which by the summer 2004 had already determined that they were only a small part of a much wider problem.[62] This mischaracterization reflected on Wolfowitz's ignorance of the adversary, and also likely represented an attempt to demonize them.[63] Similarly, in Congressional testimony in January 2005, Wolfowitz played the "Nazi card" once again. He stated, "The secret security forces of the former regime—best analogized, I think, to the Gestapo and SS of the Nazi regime—are now allied with new terrorists drawn from across the region."[64]

Rumsfeld, Rice, and Wolfowitz were not alone in employing the Nazi analogy. Acting Army Chief of Staff General John Keane stated in late July 2003, "The Gestapo and Fedayeen are analogous to each other."[65] Keane's reference to the Gestapo suggests that it wasn't only civilian policy makers that were employing demonizing terminology. Perhaps the most egregious use of the Nazi theme was Rumsfeld's use of the analogy in a *Washington Post* op-ed in which he wrote, "Turning our backs on postwar Iraq today would be the modern equivalent of handing postwar Germany back to the Nazis."[66] By discursively constructing the adversary in Iraq as Nazis, Rumsfeld hoped to delegitimize opponents of the war. And yet there is also a good deal of evidence to suggest that policy makers such as Rumsfeld and Wolfowitz were not merely using the Nazi analogy as a public relations tool but that there was a constitutive relationship between this demonization and their discursive emphasis on the "former regime elements" when discussing Iraq behind closed doors.

Similar to the case of the Nazi analogy, another aspect of the irregular adversary discourse that stressed the role of the former regime as instigators of violence were the repeated references to the Iraqi Intelligence Services (Mukhabarat) of the Hussein regime. CPA head Paul Bremer recounts in his memoirs an intelligence briefing he received in August 2003 in which he was told of captured Mukhabarat orders dated prior to the invasion that laid out a strategy for organized resistance.[67] In a discussion he had with the CIA's Baghdad Chief of Station, Bremer was informed that the Mukhabarat's department responsible for special operations (M–14), and its head, Al-Halbusi al-Dulaymi, was considered to be a likely candidate responsible for organizing the ongoing violence.[68] Testifying before members of Congress in 2004, Wolfowitz cited a secret DIA report that stressed the role in the insurgency of M-14 personnel who specialized in kidnappings, hijackings, bombings, and assassinations. According to

Wolfowitz, "These people are in the field today . . . As that [DIA] report says, former Iraqi intelligence service operatives from M-14 have been involved in planning and conducting numerous improvised explosive devices, vehicle-born improvised explosive devices and radio-controlled improvised explosive devices for anticoalition attacks throughout Iraq."[69]

A DIA spokesman confirmed the existence of the document as well as the substance of what the deputy defense secretary told Congress about its findings. The DIA spokesman said former members of M-14 were playing a "significant" role in the "insurgency" and called them "probably the best-trained and most effective" members of the anticoalition force in Iraq.[70] In later interviews, Wolfowitz identified the M-14 division of the Iraqi intelligence service and the M-16 division, "which perfected new bombing techniques," as being the main culprits behind the violence.[71] Even as late as December 2005, Wolfowitz referred to the Mukhabarat along with other elements of the former regime as the insurgency's center of gravity, describing their goal as wanting to "bring back some version of the old dictatorship, maybe even bring back Saddam."[72] This was despite the fact that Saddam Hussein had been captured two years previously.

Anti-Iraqi Forces

The language used to characterize the adversary was not exclusively developed by civilian policy makers but also emerged from within the military itself. As the "Anti-Iraqi Forces" case will show, the motivation for developing new language can often be one of a commander's personal preference. For instance, a new commanding officer may not like the terminology employed by his or her predecessor and therefore will introduce new terminology. The very fact senior military officers have bothered at all to intervene in choosing the language they deem appropriate or inappropriate serves to highlight the importance they place in the language used by their subordinates. Among the other reasons language is chosen is due to its perceived public affairs value, rather than its accuracy. In this particular case, language was employed to downplay the presence of US forces in Iraq as a motivator of violence. This necessitated replacing a term that highlighted the coalition forces as the enemy's target and replacing it with one that emphasized Iraqis as the enemy's target.

Brigadier General Kimmitt first used the term *anti-Iraqi forces* at a press conference in December 2003. It was not subsequently used for official purposes until late March 2004 when I Marine Expeditionary Force (I MEF) was in the process of taking over control of Al-Anbar province from the Army's 82nd Airborne Division. This changeover of command was accompanied by a changeover in terminology. The term that was in use at the time was *anticoalition forces*, but this term was not considered acceptable by the Marine leadership. A public affairs officer attached to I MEF said that the organization's chief of staff, Colonel John Coleman, apparently on instructions from the commanding officer, Lieutenant General James T. Conway, instructed his staff officers to "come up with a better term to describe the enemy" than *anticoalition forces*.[73] The 1st Marine Division liaison officer, Lieutenant Colonel James Hartsell, offered up *anti-Iraqi forces* (AIF), which then became the standard terminology employed by I MEF.[74] The justification for the switch in terminology was that "it's more self-effacing for the Marines to say anti-Iraqi forces than to say anti-Coalition forces because it's not about us . . . It's about Iraq's future and progress."[75]

Within the course of the following month, *anti-Iraqi forces* worked its way into the lexicon of the higher headquarters echelon. For instance, at a press conference in late April 2004, CENTCOM Head of Operations Major General John Sattler referred to "those who have taken the town away from the Fallujan people what I refer to as anti-Iraqi forces."[76] Likewise, in the April 2004 battle of Fallujah, Major General Richard Natonski established as his forces' mission "to destroy anti-Iraqi forces in Fallujah to establish legitimate local control."[77] The usage of the term spread from one merely used at press conferences and by the Marines to one that was employed by all levels of command and different military services and became a standard term to be found in operational orders and intelligence reports. For instance, on April 16, 2004, 1st Armored Division commander Major General Martin Dempsey issued operational order 4-006, Operation Iron Sabre, which directed the division's brigades "to defeat Anti-Iraqi Forces (AIF) threatening stability and security."[78] Even a cursory examination of the Wikileaks "Iraq War Logs" reveals that the AIF designation was one of the terms most commonly employed by ground troops, particularly in their operations reports.[79] The term was also used in public affairs guidance for soldiers in their dealings with the media.[80] Even CENTCOM's Air Force component (CENTAF) would regularly refer to its missions against "anti-Iraqi forces" without giving further clarification about who was actually targeted during air strikes.[81]

By employing a term that stressed that the violence was directed mainly against Iraqis rather than coalition forces, policy makers and military officials attempted to legitimize the US presence and delegitimize the adversary. Despite the term's negligible value from an analytical perspective, *anti-Iraqi forces* was internalized within the US military discourse and was regularly employed in metrics designed to show progress. Even though the term was developed within the military, rather than by civilian policy makers, there was never any attempt by the latter to change this terminology, most likely as it complemented rather than detracted from their policy agenda.

Terrorists and Foreign Fighters

The Bush administration rationalized the Iraq War as part of the broader Global War on Terrorism both in terms of the initial invasion and over the course of the irregular conflict during which it was labeled the central front.[82] Five months after the fall of Baghdad, Rumsfeld stated that it was better to be fighting terrorists in Iraq than to be fighting them in the United States, a view that was repeated by other senior officials, including President Bush.[83] Constituting the central front rhetoric were the labels given to the adversary. Indeed, the stress placed on the "terrorist" nature of the adversary was a regular feature of official rhetoric.[84] Throughout the "postconflict" period, senior defense officials typically labeled the adversary as "terrorists." For instance, on July 24, 2003, Rumsfeld referred to the "terrorists' hopes of returning to power."[85] Wolfowitz stated he believed the United States was "still fighting terrorists and terrorist supporters in Iraq."[86] Likewise, US military officials in Baghdad and at Central Command "constantly dredged up Al-Qaeda" because it was the justification for the invasion.[87] At an August 20, 2003, National Security Council meeting, President Bush insisted that US communications strategy in Iraq highlight a theme that Iraqis should "not allow foreign fighters to come into Iraq" and a "sense of nationalism that will motivate Iraqis to cooperate with us to exclude the foreigners."[88]

In late November 2005, the Bush administration released the National Strategy for Victory in Iraq (NSV-I). It is important to highlight the NSV-I's byline—"Helping the Iraqi People to Defeat the Terrorists and Build an Inclusive Democratic State." Throughout the document, the goal of "defeating the terrorists" always precedes "neutralizing the insurgency," and Iraq is described as the "central front in the global war on terror." This discursive focus on "terrorism" was premised on the idea that the public's belief that Iraq was a part of the war on terror would strengthen support for a continued US presence and significantly increase casualty tolerance.[89]

The NSV-I showcases an important dimension of the discourse trap—namely, the consequences that result from political rhetoric becoming the reality of strategic theory. One of the main problems associated with US strategy in Iraq after April 2003 had been the lack of clear guidance as to the objectives of the ongoing "occupation." In other words, the desired end state was never clearly defined. In the lead-up to the war, Saddam Hussein's regime was linked with terrorism generally and al-Qaeda specifically. However tenuous those links may have actually been, they were nevertheless used as justification for regime change. Following the lack of hard evidence of weapons of mass destruction, combined with rising levels of violence, the terrorism issue was continually kept at the forefront of the Bush administration's rhetoric. References to the need to fight terrorists in Iraq rather than fight them in the US homeland was a typical rallying cry to maintain support for the occupation. Though a victory standard was never enunciated, the failure standard of Iraq becoming a safe haven for terrorists, similar to pre-9/11 Afghanistan, was touted as the primary justification to "stay the course."

The discursive emphasis on *terrorism* was also reproduced internally, but not necessarily due to political pressure. Officials are often socialized in the terminology used in the public discourse and can find it difficult, if not impossible, to speak in two languages. Given the complex nature of the adversary, US soldiers would often rely on the heuristic device of employing the terrorist terminology that was prominent in the mainstream discourse. It is important to note here that although US defense intelligence officials had identified a number of specific terrorist groups, it was the regular rhetorical practice for officials to amalgamate these groups into a monolithic al-Qaeda.[90] One Army intelligence officer noted that at the operational level, the term *al-Qaeda* was used as a generic term to label any fighter in Iraq regardless of affiliation, despite the fact that most of the individuals were Iraqis and not foreigners.[91] Inaccurate reporting at the field level was subsequently used in strategic analyses produced at the national level by the CIA and DIA. Defense intelligence analysts would automatically assign responsibility for attacks to al-Qaeda, despite lack of evidence of actual involvement, with the result that their analyses exaggerated the scale and importance of the threat.[92] Within the bureaucracy there were also more practical reasons for the emphasis on "foreign fighters." At the combatant command level, the role of foreign fighters and their support networks were underscored, because, for budgetary and prestige reasons, commanders wanted to associate military and intelligence operations outside of the CENTCOM area of responsibility as being conducted under the auspices of Operation Iraqi Freedom, thereby showing their commitment to this mission. This was especially true at the US European Command where significant resources were devoted to tracking foreign fighters from Europe and Africa who were infiltrating Iraq.[93]

Shortly after the fall of Baghdad, senior officers of the 4th Infantry Division who laid out guidance on detainee policy, including division head Major General Ray Odierno, reportedly commented that detainees were not enemy prisoners of war; rather, they were "terrorists" and were to be treated as such.[94] It has been argued that among the many reasons contributing to abuse of detainees in Iraq were the confusion regarding their legal status and the belief of the soldiers assigned to guard the detainees that they were guarding "dehumanized" terrorists. As Richard Jackson notes, "this language is the real origin of the (Abu Ghraib) prisoner abuse scandal . . . encouraging soldiers and prison guards to speak and think of their enemies as 'evil,' 'savages' and 'animals' led directly to the kinds of institutionalized mistreatment displayed in the Abu Ghraib photos."[95]

Thomas Ricks similarly argues that the strategic confusion about why the United States was in Iraq, particularly the insistence that the war was part of the counterattack against al-Qaeda–style terrorism, may have led some American soldiers to treat ordinary Iraqis as if they were terrorists, with the result that the methods the military used in the course of raids and other operations were excessively harsh.[96] Indeed, many of the interrogation techniques employed at Abu Ghraib had been copied from those used on terrorism suspects at Guantanamo Bay.[97] This harshness in turn led to increasing resentment of the US-led occupation and encouraged popular support among Iraqis for the "insurgency."

One of the means US forces used to demonize the "terrorist" element of the violence was to stress that they were mostly non-Iraqis.[98] For instance, Abu Mussab al-Zarqawi's Jordanian origins was a key theme of US information operations and was consistently featured in official statements related to terrorism in Iraq.[99] Another means of demonization was to link the vast majority of suicide attacks to al-Qaeda. Indeed, the name eventually assigned to Zarqawi's group, AQI, bore only a superficial relationship with the actual name of his group. As one senior intelligence officer observed, "Zarqawi operated through an organization known as Jamaat al-Tawhid w'al-Jihad (Unity and Jihad Group) which we called TWJ. Although Zarqawi had worked with al-Qaeda in the past, he did not formally pledge his allegiance to Bin Laden until October 2004. For several months, Zarqawi's organization was referred to as QJBR (Tanzim Qa'idat Al-Jihad in Bilad al-Rafidayn—Organization of Jihad's Base in the Country of the Two Rivers), but in the summer of 2005, the MNF-I began referring to QJBR and TWJ as al-Qaida in Iraq (AQI). That name has stuck."[100]

Military spokesmen often publicly cited the estimate that AQI was responsible for 90 percent of suicide attacks. While some of these statements specifically blamed AQI for 90 percent of these attacks, others laid the blame more generally on foreign fighters. It is unclear if military officials merely assumed that all members of AQI were of foreign nationality and neglected to investigate the possibility that AQI could have recruited Iraqis into their network.[101] According to Anthony Cordesman, the role of foreign fighters was intentionally exaggerated as a means of downplaying the role of Iraqi resentment, an attempt to make the government's counterinsurgency efforts seem more legitimate and to link Iraq to the war on terrorism.[102] However, Cordesman complained that too much US analysis was fixated on terms like *jihadist* in order to make the connection with Osama bin Laden, whereas his research supported the conclusion that the nationalist element was more important.[103] Among the unintended consequences of crediting AQI and Zarqawi with a far larger proportion of the violence in Iraq than they probably committed was that the US military inadvertently burnished Zarqawi's image in much of the Muslim world as a resistance hero, with the consequence of increasing rather than decreasing AQI recruitment.[104] In fact, shortly before Zarqawi's death in June 2006, senior defense officials, including Rumsfeld, saw a need to reduce the amount of reward money the United States was offering for Zarqawi in order to marginalize his importance. As Rumsfeld noted, the large sum of money then being offered as a reward "may have unintentionally elevated his status internationally."[105]

But were all terrorists of foreign origin, and were all foreign fighters actually terrorists? The connection between terrorists and foreign fighters was never clarified. This confusion was evident in the analyses produced by MNF-I's Combined Intelligence Operations Center, where senior officials would change the terminology used to characterize the "terrorists" every few months.[106] The participation of Arab volunteers fighting as irregulars in Iraq began during the conventional phase of the war, with as many as four thousand participating.[107] Although poorly trained and ill equipped, a substantial number of foreign fighters engaged in a "partisan war" against advancing coalition forces. After the end of conventional operations, some returned home while others remained and fought in the "insurgency."[108] Throughout the course of the conflict, US officials privately maintained that the most significant challenge to their stabilization efforts came from domestic Iraqi insurgents and not from foreign terrorists, despite a number of the more spectacular attacks having been organized or carried out by foreigners.[109] For instance, although Abizaid did not dismiss the threat posed by foreign fighters, he did not want the coalition to lose focus on the groups that formed the core of the Iraqi resistance. As Abizaid stated at the time, "while the foreign fighters in Iraq are definitely a problem that have to be dealt with, I still think that the primary problem we're dealing with is former regime elements of the ex-Baath party."[110] Nevertheless, despite their peripheral role, beginning in the early days of the conflict, US officials consistently stressed in public the role of foreign fighters as instigators of violence. For instance, during the November 2004 battle of Fallujah, the Defense Department provided its congressional liaison personnel with talking points that stressed the role of terrorists and foreign fighters in Fallujah.[111] And even in internal discussions, there was a strong emphasis on foreign fighters.[112] However, in the aftermath of the battle, US officers concluded that the overwhelming majority of fighters who battled the US forces were Iraqis.[113] The result of the rhetorical emphasis on foreign fighters was that military commanders were confused as to who they were fighting, which adversaries should be prioritized, and where best to direct limited resources.[114] For instance, it was not until the spring of 2005 that US commanders in Baghdad identified the "foreign fighters" and "extremists" as posing a greater threat than the "former regime elements" and subsequently repositioned some ground units and intelligence assets to fortify the border with Syria and block infiltration routes, as well as stepping up efforts to target these groups.[115]

The rhetorical emphasis on *terrorism* was also distinctly at odds with most ground-level military assessments as well as the strategic assessments of the intelligence community. These assessments recognized groups such as AQI contributed significantly to the violence but noted their numbers were small relative to the "insurgents," "militias," and other instigators of violence. In 2004, Abizaid ordered CENTCOM analysts to look for evidence that the insurgency was adopting extreme Islamist goals. However, the analysts concluded that ridding Iraq of US troops was the motivator for most of the "insurgency," not the formation of an Islamic state. According to one US Army study, "the vast majority of militants in Iraq have nothing to do with Al-Qaeda, and they are focused on Iraqi problems: security, distribution of power and money, and sectarianism. Those insurgents are a mix of Sunni nationalists, Ba'thists, Shia militias, and Islamist organizations. Mistaking any of these groups for Al-Qaeda is not simply wrong, it is dangerous."[116] Kalev Sepp similarly argued that the belief that foreign fighters were a major threat muddled strategic thinking in the early stages of the war, since it was used as an excuse to explain why US troops were facing violence when they were told they'd be treated as liberators. As a result, evidence that showed growing resistance within the Sunni community toward the occupation was disregarded. Also, since rising levels of violence were attributed to the foreign fighters, questions were raised within MNF-I whether more resources should be targeted toward these groups, rather than the "former regime elements," and commanders were unclear how big of a threat they posed.[117] As such, while the discourse on terrorists and foreign fighters may have had value in sustaining public support for the war, it also had negative repercussions when internalized by the military. Nevertheless, despite the conclusions reached by their own experts, senior political and military officials continued to refer publicly and privately to al-Qaeda–style extremism, while the problem of the US troop presence as a key motivator of violence remained a taboo subject.[118]

In May 2006, an official DoD report on Iraq provided to Congress stressed that "terrorists" and "foreign fighters," even with low numbers, constituted the most serious and immediate threat to Iraq.[119] This was because AQI, rather than being held responsible for the majority of violence, was instead deemed responsible for the mass casualty attacks that served as a "primary accelerant to the underlying sectarian conflict."[120] By March 2008, the "Sunni insurgency" as such had declined in size and scope, due in large measure to its switching sides in response to AQI excesses, as a result of which many of the former insurgents subsequently became the progovernment "Sons of Iraq." This meant that the two groups considered most dangerous were AQI and the Shiite militias, though there was considerable confusion about which one posed the greatest threat. As Rear Admiral Greg Smith, the MNF-I spokesman, noted in late March 2008, even though the United States was facing two distinct enemies— AQI and the "Iranian-trained and supplied special groups"—that "AQI is still Iraq's No. 1 enemy."[121] Interestingly, less than two weeks later, Petraeus testified that "unchecked the 'special groups' pose the greatest long-term threat to the viability of a democratic Iraq."[122] By 2011, the spokesman for US forces in Iraq, Major General Jeffrey Buchanan, stated that the largest threat to Iraq's security came from Iranian-backed militia groups. Buchanan noted that AQI still controlled between 800 to 1,000 fighters but that it was receiving little foreign support.[123] Indeed, according to a US military report one year earlier, AQI was "95 percent Iraqi."[124]

As US forces were set to withdraw from Iraq by the end of 2011, the resilience of AQI became a contested political issue. On the one hand, for the Obama administration to demonstrate America's relative "success" in Iraq, thereby allowing it to withdraw without having looked "defeated," the resilience of AQI, as well as violence more generally, needed to be downplayed. On the other hand, advocates for keeping a US military presence in Iraq beyond 2011 argued that because AQI was resilient, and also posed a threat to US interests, it was necessary to keep US forces engaged in the fight against it. By 2012, after the US forces had left, AQI attacks began increasing again. The new debate within the US government was not whether they should be countered by large numbers of American forces but if it would be possible to employ a counterterrorism strategy similar to the one being used to counter terrorist groups in Yemen, Pakistan, and other countries. However, in general, officials would stress that AQI had declined to the point where the Iraqi government could handle it with minimal outside assistance. Even so, the persistence of AQI continued to be an irritant to US policy makers, not only in relation to Iraq policy, but also for Syria policy as well. For instance, the Obama administration attempted to downplay the role of AQI in Syria, especially given the embarrassing situation in which both AQI and the US government were seeking the downfall of the Assad regime.[125]

The Shiite Militias

US officials consistently adopted a vague approach to classifying Shiite militias that fought against coalition forces, probably to avoid the risk of adding to home-front frustration by admitting that the Shiite majority was as wary of the occupation as the Sunnis were. Military officials privately insisted that portraying the "insurgency" in Iraq as a purely Sunni endeavour was wrong, since Shiite groups such as Moqtadr al-Sadr's Mahdi Army mounted many attacks on US forces. That the US authorities did not consider Shiite militias as part of the insurgency is evident from the terms they used to classify them, and to avoid classifying them with. References to a "mainly" or "primarily" Sunni insurgency left open the possibility of other non-Sunni groups participating but did not explicitly identify the Shiites as a source of armed opposition.[126] According to MNF-I's Strategy, Plans and Assessment Section head, Colonel William Hix, until the Mahdi Army's uprising in August 2004, "the definition of the insurgency had always been focused on the Sunni."[127] The downplaying of a Shiite insurgent threat can also be inferred by the numbers used as estimates for total insurgent strength as they were too small to have included the militia groups (according to various official estimates, the Mahdi Army alone consisted of some 15,000–60,000 members as of 2006 compared with official estimates placing overall insurgent strength at 20,000–30,000).[128] Moreover, neither the "National Strategy for Victory in Iraq" nor the DoD's quarterly "Measuring Stability and Security and Iraq" reports list the Shiite militia groups as a significant factor in the insurgency, listing them instead as a minor element of the Iraqi "rejectionist" category.[129] Additionally, not only was there a reluctance to downplay Shiite resistance, but there was also an attempt, initially at least, to downplay the role of Iranian support to the Shiite militias. According to one senior intelligence officer, the head of US military intelligence in Iraq, Brigadier General John Defreitas, told him that "Iran was not the problem in Iraq. The problem in Iraq was the Sunni insurgency. Every asset needed to be directed at that issue." This officer also noted that "two years later, Shiite militias associated with Iran were killing more US troops than Sunni insurgents were. But at the moment (referring to 2005), the senior military intelligence officer in Iraq was dismissing Iran as a threat."[130]

The downplaying of Shiite resistance was odd given that the Mahdi army had clashed with coalition forces since at least October 2003.[131] By the end of March 2004, significant elements of the Shia community rose in open rebellion against the coalition, culminating in heavy fighting in Najaf and Sadr City.[132] Shiites rather than Sunnis were also responsible for the majority of British casualties and had achieved a limited form of self-government in places such as Basra.[133]

For Washington, minimizing the Shiite element of the violence was officially justified on the grounds that the Shiites did not seek to overthrow the Iraqi government, probably because they already dominated the government. Moreover, the Shiite-dominated Iraqi government had considerable sympathy for the militias. Indeed, one of the primary problems affecting US military strategy was a threat definition that ran counter to the Iraqi government's.[134]

Whereas the United States viewed the Shiite militias as a threat, Iraq's Maliki government only wanted to concentrate on the "Sunni insurgency."[135] In a number of respects militias were a part of the government, and yet they were their own government. The militias included political wings that were in the government, such as Moqtadr al-Sadr's political party, known as the "Office of Martyr al-Sadr." Though they may have had no intention of overthrowing the government, militia groups actively clashed with coalition forces, which officially maintained their presence in the country at the behest of the Iraqi government. However, according to one Multi-National Corps-Iraq (MNC-I) official, merely fighting the "occupiers" did not officially merit getting into the "insurgent" category.[136] Likewise, within the DIA's Office of Iraq Analysis, "nobody referred to the Mahdi Army as insurgents."[137] CPA Order #91 outlined the categories into which militia groups were placed. A militia in existence during the Saddam era was considered "legal" as long as it didn't also fight the coalition. However, since the Mahdi Army did fight coalition forces, it was officially classified as "illegal." Hence the designation "illegal armed groups" as opposed to "insurgents."[138]

In late June 2006, MNF-I head General George Casey listed illegal armed groups as one of the four major security challenges in Iraq, along with meddling from Iran, the Sunni insurgency, and al-Qaeda in Iraq.[139] During Operation Together Forward in the summer and fall of 2006, US forces battled Shiite militia groups in Baghdad in order to counter rising levels of sectarian violence. Given the political implications associated with classifying the Mahdi Army as one of the principal targets of the operation, official spokesmen reverted back to the original CPA designation of "illegal armed groups" and refused to specify which ones in particular they were referring to. In their public statements, military officials redefined terms such as *militias* and *death squads*, both of which were associated with Shiites, in order to include Sunni insurgent groups. US commanders said their forces had rounded up dozens of "sectarian death squads" during the Baghdad sweeps but avoided specific descriptions of their sectarian or militia affiliations.[140] The taboo placed on identifying Shiite militias as a significant instigator of violence would continually confound US strategy. Because it was not addressed early on, this problem would gradually metastasize to the point where it became the coalition's primary concern.[141] It was only in the November 2006 "Measuring Stability and Security in Iraq" report that it was acknowledged the Mahdi Army had "replaced Al-Qaeda in Iraq as the most dangerous accelerant of potentially self-sustaining sectarian violence in Iraq."[142] In July 2007, General Odierno stated that Shiite militants had carried out 73 percent of the attacks that killed or wounded American troops in Baghdad. Odierno attributed this to the Iranians who were "surging support to the special groups."[143]

As noted earlier, by 2008 there was considerable debate about which was the more important adversary the United States faced: AQI or the Shiite militias. It is curious that the Shiites were considered a major danger after mid-2008, since official reports during this period highlighted that most of the Shiite militias that had previously attacked coalition forces had largely transitioned from violence to political action.[144] Although this debate had not been resolved by the end of 2011, when the remaining US forces departed, numerous US military officials continued to cite the Shiite militias as posing the greatest threat.[145] Concern about the Shiites was also directly related to broader fears about Iranian influence in Iraq. For instance, Major General Buchanan stated in 2011 that Iran was supporting Shiite militias and that the primary threat to the US forces came from three of these militias: the Promised Day Brigade, Ahl al-Haq, and Kataib Hezbollah.[146] Nevertheless, once the US military departed from Iraq, the primary American concern shifted to AQI, which was viewed as having regional ambitions that threatened US interests, whereas the Shiite militias were viewed as a mainly Iraqi problem.

Liberation versus Occupation

Before leaving this topic, it should be noted that an important issue to be considered is not only how the United States described its adversaries in Iraq but also how it described its own presence and how this description impacted on US military performance. The issue of "liberation" versus "occupation" was heavily debated within the US government prior to the war. Policy makers feared that being perceived as an "occupying power" would lead to delegitimized government, instability, and possible terrorist acts against US forces. As such, policy papers emphasized the need for an "occupation" but the desire to avoid the *appearance* of occupation. Therefore, defense policy makers, such as Douglas Feith, promoted "liberation" rather than "occupation" as the basic narrative of the administration's strategy in Iraq.[147] However, the after-action review of the Third Infantry Division's conduct of the conventional war notes that the emphasis on "liberation" rather than "occupation" led military commanders to operate in a hands-off way that allowed the chaos to increase in Baghdad after the Hussein regime collapsed. According to the report, "as a matter of law and fact, the United States is an occupying power in Iraq, even if we characterize ourselves as liberators . . . Because of the refusal to acknowledge occupier status, commanders did not initially take measures available to occupying powers, such as imposing curfews, directing civilians to return to work, and controlling the local governments and populace. The failure to act after we displaced the regime created a power vacuum, which others immediately tried to fill."[148]

As this example implies, military officials believed it was the discourse of liberation that was partially responsible for the initial chaos that then set off a series of actions and counteractions that created the occupation it was intended to avoid. However, this rhetoric was not only employed in the prewar period but also continued for years thereafter. The liberation rhetoric would continue to be employed by the Bush administration to maintain US public support for the occupation and to raise morale. Among the many unintended consequences of retaining the dominant discursive theme of liberation was to contribute to the taboo on the discourse that stressed the occupation was a source of violence.

Characterizing the Conflict

Identifying a war as a war, an insurgency as an insurgency, or a civil war as a civil war not only helps define the actors involved but also has numerous political, military, economic, and legal implications. The case of Iraq is not an original one as far as demonstrating the political and bureaucratic imperatives of correctly naming a conflict, especially an irregular one. In Malaya, the British government decided to avoid the terms *conflict* and *insurgency* and instead referred to the situation as an "emergency." The reasons for doing so were mainly economic. The terms of the insurance policies of Malayan colonials' tin and rubber plantations only covered losses of stocks and equipment through "riot and civil commotion" in an "emergency." Had Whitehall described the conflict in Malaya in terms that implied a state of war, or actions committed by "rebels" and "insurgents," London insurance companies were legally entitled to repudiate the policies, thereby risking financial instability. Consequently, for the first two years of the "emergency," the term *bandits*, rather than *guerrillas*, was employed by British officials to describe the enemy. Likewise, the term *Communist terrorists* was deliberately chosen to garner American support for the conflict by making the connection with the Cold War. Philip Deery notes that the effect of using euphemistic terminology impeded Whitehall's ability to take the emerging threat of a full-blown insurgency seriously and institute effective policies early on to counter it.[149]

In Iraq, the long delay in officially recognizing the conflict as an insurgency or guerrilla war hindered the process of taking effective countermeasures. This delay not only impacted on decision makers' ability to comprehend the nature of the conflict but also affected the bureaucracy's response. Similarly, the official stress on *sectarian violence* instead of *civil war*, which had more to do with domestic political considerations than academic ones, attempted to downplay this problem as an impediment to achieving the strategic end state of stability and security. This section will seek to highlight the importance senior officials placed on characterizing the type of conflict being fought in post-Hussein Iraq.

Whether or not the characterization of a conflict is derived from the actors involved, or vice versa, is a chicken-and-egg problem that is unlikely to evoke scholarly consensus. Nevertheless, it is almost impossible to understand the reasoning for one characterization without an understanding of the reasoning behind the other. Therefore, although this section focuses primarily on the description of the conflict, as opposed to the description of the actors, it does help contextualize the naming of adversaries.

Insurgency and Guerrilla War

A good deal of discourse related to the conflict's characterization during the period under review has been dominated by the term *insurgency*, with the conflict often being referred to as the "Iraq insurgency" and coalition troops being said to wage a "counterinsurgency" campaign. However, for a significant period after the start of the insurgency, there was a taboo placed on the term within the DoD. This taboo requires analysis in its own right, because it reflects a military system, particularly its leadership, that was unwilling to accept the reality of its predicament and chose to play language games and institute discursive controls rather than change to a strategy more in tune with the facts on the ground.

The question of whether the conflict in Iraq was an insurgency generated considerable debate both within the US government and in the wider public debate. The answer depended, in part, on one's definition of what constituted an insurgency, and several versions existed within the US government. The definition of insurgency according to the Defense Department's *Dictionary of Military and Associated Terms* was "an organized movement aimed at the overthrow of a constituted government through the use of subversion and armed conflict."[150] The semantic loophole in this definition—namely, the reference to "constituted government"—was exploited by Rumsfeld as a means of denying an insurgency was occurring. By contrast, the CIA defined insurgency as "a protracted political-military activity directed toward completely or partially controlling the resources of a country through the use of irregular military forces and illegal political organizations," and CIA analysts were reportedly using the term in their assessments beginning in June 2003.[151]

The reluctance by defense officials to characterize the ongoing violence in Iraq following the collapse of the Hussein regime as an insurgency, or those who were conducting attacks against coalition forces as insurgents, had significant repercussions on the ability of policy makers in Washington, DC, and field commanders to take appropriate countermeasures at precisely the time that such countermeasures could have been most effective at nipping the insurgency in the bud.[152] According to Army Lieutenant Colonel Isaiah Wilson III, "Redefining the war as a war of 'preventive counterinsurgency' in May of 2003 would have required the commensurate redesign and reallocation of resources of the war plan, from the major combat operation of Phase I-III, to the theater-wide ('theater-strategic') civil-military campaign required of a country-wide counterinsurgency . . . This kind of counterinsurgency war might have more effectively focused and integrated the good civil-military stabilization and reconstruction works . . . Instead, all these good tactical actions lacked a clear and coherent strategic purpose."[153]

Yet this reluctance to use the term *insurgency* continued throughout 2004 and 2005.[154] Political considerations were primarily responsible for determining what constituted insurgency and who could or could not be labeled an insurgent, because in both cases the definition used could radically increase or decrease the perceived magnitude of the problem.

Acting Army chief of staff General Jack Keane reportedly told Rumsfeld during a meeting of the Joint Chiefs of Staff in the summer of 2003 that the situation in Iraq was an insurgency and included the definition of the term. Afterward, General Myers told Keane to "be careful about that word (insurgency)."[155] According to Keane, the reason the term was rejected during that period was that Rumsfeld and General Tommy Franks thought resistance would be crushed within two to three months and "it wasn't worth all the rhetoric."[156] Within the Joint Staff, Myers instructed that use of the term be avoided.[157] Colonel Thomas X. Hammes criticized this reluctance to admit that an insurgency was forming, thereby allowing the insurgents a "long breathing space to get themselves organized."[158] Hammes recalled that in the spring of 2003 an officer had complained that senior political and military leaders "didn't even want to say the 'i' word . . . It was the specter of Vietnam. They did not want to say the 'insurgency' word because the next word you say is 'quagmire.' The next thing you say is 'the only war America has lost.'"[159] In another instance, an officer of the 3rd Armored Cavalry Regiment was specifically told by a visiting general in the summer of 2003, "This is not an insurgency."[160] Prior to the formation of the interim Iraqi government on June 28, 2004, Rumsfeld justified his resistance to the term because at that time Iraq did not yet have a sovereign government, and the official DoD definition of an insurgency specifically referred to a "constituted government."[161] Among some commanders, there was an evident frustration that senior leaders were unwilling to admit that an insurgency existed. Colonel H. R. McMaster argued that "militarily you've got to call it an insurgency because we have a counterinsurgency doctrine."[162]

For policy makers in Washington, DC, there was a strong aversion to using the word *insurgency*. In early July 2003, Rumsfeld queried a reference to insurgency in a CIA analysis of Iraq. In response to the query, Rumsfeld was informed that the Webster's dictionary definition would support the CIA interpretation but that the JCS dictionary (Joint Publication–1) might not as it emphasizes an "organized movement."¹⁶³ A couple of weeks later, Rumsfeld asked his military aide for the "complete Department of Defense Dictionary of Military and Associated Terms" and specifically for the definitions of "insurgency, guerrilla war, and belligerency."¹⁶⁴ In one instance in August 2003, the head of the CIA's Iraq Operations Group, John Maguire, presented evidence to policy makers of the growing insurgency, but that evidence was dismissed because the administration did not want to hear the word *insurgency* and would not allow it to be used in most meetings or in public statements.¹⁶⁵ The debate on whether to use the term *insurgency* reached a climax on November 11, 2003, at a meeting of the National Security Council.¹⁶⁶ During this meeting, Rumsfeld interrupted an intelligence briefing when CIA Near East Division head Rob Richer stated, "We are seeing the establishment of an insurgency in Iraq."¹⁶⁷ Rumsfeld objected to Richer's use of the word and asked for his definition of it. To justify use of the term *insurgency*, Richer referred to the sustained armed attacks and sabotage and the adversary's popular support and ability to act at will. Rumsfeld replied, "I may disagree with you."¹⁶⁸ President Bush followed Rumsfeld's lead, telling others who were present at the meeting, "I don't want anyone in the Cabinet to say it is an insurgency."¹⁶⁹ Interestingly, that same day, General Abizaid had sent Rumsfeld a memo in which he provided the definition of *counterinsurgency*, taken from the DoD dictionary. The memo read, "Sir, our doctrine states: 'Counterinsurgency—those military, paramilitary, political, economic, psychological and civic actions taken by a government to defeat insurgency.' . . . Clearly we must *integrate* elements of national power in any effort to defeat an insurgency."¹⁷⁰

This memo followed an earlier correspondence between Rumsfeld and Abizaid arguing over the definition of the conflict. In one of these memos, Rumsfeld cited a definition of *insurgency* used by Che Guevara, as a means of arguing the situation in Iraq was not an insurgency.¹⁷¹ This series of memos was illustrative of the increasing frustration within certain elements of the military against maintaining the terminology status quo. In this particular case, the theater commander wanted the Pentagon leadership to formally acknowledge the situation US forces in Iraq were facing was an insurgency, thereby requiring a counterinsurgency strategy to deal with it. And yet Rumsfeld dismissed Abizaid's opinion by refusing during the NSC meeting to admit there was an insurgency. Curiously, though, the next day Rumsfeld asked a deputy to inquire about a "classic insurgency . . . where the good guys have won—is it Malaysia or the Philippines? Let's find out and see what the lessons learned are."¹⁷² Moreover, nearly a month and a half after the November meeting, Rumsfeld wrote to Abizaid referring back to the latter's original memo on counterinsurgency. In it, Rumsfeld admitted, "You are right—it is interesting.

What do you propose?" thus suggesting that he had finally come to the conclusion that the United States was engaged in a counterinsurgency.[173]

Reluctance to use the term continued into 2004 and following the Coalition Provision Authority's (CPA) handover of power to the new Iraqi government. In early 2004, an Army Special Forces colonel attached to CPA head Bremer's office was reportedly insistent that "there is no insurgency here . . . there's a high level of domestic violence."[174] Moreover, it was not until January 2005 that intelligence officials attached to MNF-I's Combined Intelligence Operations Center, who were tasked with providing strategic assessments for the MNF-I commander, were allowed to use the term *insurgents* in their analyses. Instead, the term *civil unrest* had been used as an alternative to *insurgency*.[175] On the Joint Staff, the terms *uprising* and *resistance movement* were also banned.[176]

Among the reasons senior leaders rejected use of the term *insurgency* was that it conveyed a positive image of the insurgents themselves. In June 2004, Wolfowitz stated that the conflict was "not an insurgency in the sense of an uprising. It is a continuation of the war by people who never quit."[177] One month later, Wolfowitz specifically referred to disliking "that word insurgency" because "it conveys some sense of heroism to the people we are fighting."[178] Moreover, he stated, "I don't know of an insurgency."[179] In early 2005, Wolfowitz modified his stance by saying that there was no "nationalist insurgency" given that there was relatively high turnout in the Iraqi elections.[180] In November 2005, Rumsfeld again made specific reference to his dislike of the term *insurgent* and suggested the alternative "enemies of the legitimate Iraqi government."[181] Rumsfeld justified this by claiming, "They don't have a legitimate gripe" and therefore "don't merit the word 'insurgent.'"[182] However, no formal guidance was issued that would ban use of the term by DoD officials or to use *enemies of the legitimate Iraqi government* as a substitute.

Despite the successful performance exhibited by the US forces during the conventional phase of operations in March–April 2003, the US military was unprepared to fight a counterinsurgency war, resulting in numerous strategic and tactical blunders that would strengthen opposition to the occupation. In the aftermath of Vietnam and throughout the 1990s, the military remained wary of irregular wars and refused to make major changes in organization, doctrine, and training to accommodate them, preferring instead to concentrate on large-scale conventional wars.[183] Because the Army had discarded its institutional understanding of how to wage a counterinsurgency campaign, commanders were sent to do a mission for which they were unprepared and therefore had to improvise a response.[184] Although field commanders recognized early on that their existing doctrine was insufficient, the unwillingness to officially admit that an insurgency was under way in Iraq delayed the writing of a new field manual on counterinsurgency operations.[185] It was not until February 2004 that the head of the Army's Combined Arms Center, Lieutenant General William Wallace, ordered the writing of a new interim field manual.[186] Had the military started to write a counterinsurgency manual at an earlier date, it would by implication have contradicted the official public position of senior political and military leaders that US forces were not fighting an insurgency.

Upon taking over MNF-I in July 2004, General George Casey observed that many of the officials there were still thinking in terms of the "aftermath of a conventional war" rather than of a counterinsurgency. The earlier failures to clearly define the US mission in Iraq as counterinsurgency led Casey to choose the term "full spectrum counterinsurgency operations" as the mission statement in the Campaign Plan that was approved in August 2004.[187] According to Colonel Hix, this term was deliberately chosen to stress that "the Coalition was engaged in an insurgency and Coalition forces had to simultaneously conduct a range of operations to deal with that enemy."[188] It is important to note here that this operational-level official recognition of an insurgency occurred more than a year after many senior military officials believed it actually began. Kalev Sepp, who served as an adviser to Casey, also noted that under Sanchez, there was no attempt to develop any counterinsurgency expertise within his headquarters, most likely because he "did not think of the problems that they were facing and the violence that they were trying to fight as being related to an insurgency."[189]

Similar to the reluctance of senior US leaders to use the term *insurgency*, the guerrilla war terminology debate reflected the unwillingness to officially admit in the months after "major combat operations" had been declared finished that another war was just beginning. Admitting to the existence of a guerrilla war had negative political connotations, because it contradicted a number of the prewar claims, such as the insistence that US forces would be welcomed as liberators and not occupiers. Guerrillas are unable to operate effectively without some level of support from the local population, and to admit that the adversary was a guerrilla, as opposed to a dead-ender or terrorist, was to magnify the scale of the problem, since it implied a population sympathetic to the adversary.[190] Perhaps more important, the term itself evoked a degree of sympathy for the adversary from a public relations perspective, given that the guerrilla is traditionally viewed in romantic and sympathetic terms.[191] According to Rumsfeld, "the fact that so many of our folks are talking about the situation in Iraq as a 'guerrilla war,' with the word 'guerrilla' having a positive connotation in some people's minds, is unfortunate."[192]

The debate over the term *guerrilla war* began in earnest in June 2003 when senior political and military officials repeatedly denied they were facing one in Iraq. Wolfowitz argued that the situation did not resemble a guerrilla war because the adversary lacked the "two classical ingredients"—namely, the "sympathy of the population, and . . . any serious source of external support."[193]

On June 18, Major General Odierno told reporters, "This is not guerrilla warfare . . . It is not close to guerrilla warfare because it's not coordinated, it's not organized, and it's not led."[194] Odierno would later admit that his view of the adversary in June 2003 was that he was merely facing "remnants" rather than "insurgents" but that a month later he would have characterized the situation as guerrilla war.[195]

By the end of June, reporters repeatedly asked defense officials whether they were willing to admit they were in a war in Iraq.[196] For instance, on June 30, Rumsfeld was asked why he was reluctant to use the term *guerrilla war*. Responding that the reason he didn't use the phrase *guerrilla war* is because "there isn't one," Rumsfeld went on to say that the adversary functioned much more "like terrorists."[197] Even after being confronted with the DoD definition of the term, Rumsfeld refused to acknowledge that the situation was a guerrilla war.[198]

Dissatisfaction with the ban on *guerrilla war* provoked an act of perceived disobedience by General Abizaid. At a Pentagon press conference on July 16, Abizaid stated that coalition forces were facing a "classical guerrilla-type campaign . . . It's low-intensity conflict, in our doctrinal terms, but it's war, however you describe it."[199] After making this admission, Abizaid was asked to explain his use of the term, because defense officials had been hesitant to use it. Abizaid responded that there was a need to be "very clear" in describing the situation and accurately characterizing the adversary.[200] Abizaid's comments were immediately downplayed by the official Pentagon spokesperson standing next to him, who stated, "The discussion about what type of conflict this is . . . is almost beside the point."[201] In the aftermath of the press conference, Rumsfeld privately berated Abizaid, because Rumsfeld had to publicly explain why there was an open difference of terminology with his theater commander.[202] During a press conference two weeks later, when asked to explain the discrepancy, Rumsfeld maintained his view that the violence in Iraq did not constitute guerrilla war. He stated that he had consulted the DoD *Dictionary of Military and Associated Terms*, and that the term was not "perfectly appropriate" to characterize the situation.[203] Moreover, he stated that among the similar terms he looked up, such as *insurgency* and *unconventional war*, he could not find "a single bumper sticker phrase" that was appropriate.[204] It is debatable whether Rumsfeld either genuinely believed the United States was not involved in fighting a guerrilla war or felt that to make this admission, even in closed political and military circles, somehow reflected a personal failing that in turn could have jeopardized his bureaucratic position and authority. In either case, it is quite evident that Rumsfeld viewed the terminology as important and was determined to ensure the military avoided characterizing the conflict as an insurgency or guerrilla war, even overruling field commanders who believed otherwise.

Sectarian Violence and Civil War

In addition to the challenges posed by insurgents directing their attacks against coalition forces was the far worse prospect that rising levels of sectarian violence would propel Iraq into a state of civil war. A late-summer 2004 National Intelligence Estimate laid out three possible scenarios for the future of Iraq, the worst of which was the outbreak of civil war.[205] Civil war was the "worst-case" scenario from a political perspective because it represented a failure to achieve "stability and security" in Iraq despite official statements that the situation was improving rather than deteriorating.[206] From both a political and military perspective it also raised the question of what mission US forces would have under those circumstances and whether there was a need to increase the number of troops in the theater.[207] Furthermore, US forces lacked the doctrine and training to be effective in that kind of conflict environment. MNC-I head Lieutenant General Peter Chiarelli highlighted this deficiency when he stated, "In 33 years in the US Army, I never trained to stop a sectarian fight."[208] In the event of civil war, determining which side to support, and attempting to keep the violence limited to the confines of Iraq without spilling across borders, would also be significant concerns. Such a complex set of calculations necessitated that a civil war must not be allowed to occur, because politically it would symbolize the failure of the Bush administration's Iraq policy.[209] For that reason, the terminology over how to characterize the situation in Iraq moved beyond the debates over *insurgency* and *guerrilla warfare* into the more politically controversial *sectarian violence* and *civil war*. Rumsfeld himself would note in the autumn of 2006, "The situation in Iraq has been evolving, and US forces have adjusted, over time, from major combat operations to counterterrorism, to counterinsurgency, to dealing with death squads and sectarian violence."[210]

Due to the plethora of academic debates on the definition of *civil war*, a number of which had been used by politicians to justify their positions, it is impossible to argue in favor of one definition rather than another without betraying an obvious bias.[211] There were factions within both the "sectarian violence" and "civil war" camps. For example, advocates of proclaiming an Iraq civil war were split into at least two factions, such as those who believed it began in 2004 versus those who argued it began in 2006. It is important to note here that it is not my intention to make the case that an Iraqi civil war existed; rather it is to make the point that many defense officials did in fact believe that the situation in Iraq amounted to a civil war but were dissuaded from expressing their view. In actual fact, the DoD made a conscious effort to employ alternative narratives to counter claims of an Iraqi civil war.

Since 2003, *sectarian violence* had featured consistently alongside *insurgency* but was relatively contained. It wasn't until the February 22, 2006, bombing of the Shiite Al Askari Mosque in Samarra that what had been a lesser problem in comparison to the insurgency became the primary problem for the coalition forces to deal with. In the aftermath of the bombing, Shiite "death squads" attacked Sunni mosques, killed Sunni civilians, and murdered Sunni clerics. This sparked the formation of Sunni "death squads" who instigated further revenge killings, thereby causing a spiral of violence that threatened to plunge Iraq into civil war. It was reported more Iraqis were killed by Shiite "militias" than by Sunni "insurgents."[212] By March 2006, a number of senior US commanders said that containing the growing civil conflict was their primary concern and that it posed a greater threat to US efforts in the country than the insurgency; however, they consistently avoided referring to it as a civil war. DIA head Lieutenant General Michael Maples told a congressional hearing in February 2006 that although Iraq was not in a state of "civil war," "the underlying conditions for such a war are present."[213] Throughout the summer of 2006, senior officials continued to assert the potential for the conflict in Iraq becoming a civil war but stopped short of classifying it as such. In August 2006, Abizaid told a Senate Committee, "It is possible that Iraq could move toward civil war."[214] His remarks were echoed by General Peter Pace, who said, "We do have the possibility of that (the situation in Iraq) devolving into civil war."[215]

Iraqi Prime Minister Iyad Allawi's statement on the eve of the third anniversary of the invasion—"If this is not a civil war, then God knows what civil war is"—caused significant consternation in the Bush administration.[216] President Bush responded afterward, "We all recognized that there is . . . sectarian violence. But the way I look at the situation is the Iraqis looked and decided not to go into civil war."[217] This view was endorsed by other senior government officials and became the official line. At the White House, Press Secretary Tony Snow stated, "There is not a civil war going on."[218] Secretary of State Condoleeza Rice insisted that the Iraqis had "sectarian differences" but "it's not civil war."[219]

In Washington, the terminology debate had more to do with politics than achieving semantic accuracy. Critics of the Bush administration's Iraq policy used the term *civil war* to show that the military campaign in Iraq was failing.[220] To argue that Iraq was in a state of civil war was meant to imply that US forces should withdraw, whereas to argue that Iraq was experiencing sectarian violence meant that the country could spiral out of control but that it was the US military presence that was preventing it from doing so. The Senate Democratic leader Harry Reid argued that Bush's Iraq policy had "left Iraq on the precipice of all out civil war."[221] Similarly, the top Democrat on the Senate Foreign Relations Committee, Senator Joseph Biden noted, "A political solution is necessary to end the civil war in Iraq."[222] For a number of Democrats, the emphasis on civil war was meant to be indirectly critical of the Bush administration by raising the prospect that Iraq was falling apart but doing so in such a way that it did not risk the Republican countercharges of "cut and run." For the administration, the emphasis on sectarian violence held out the prospect that the situation could be contained and eventually reversed. Within Congress, Democratic senators, as well as some Republicans, repeatedly used the *civil war* term, especially when generals or other senior DoD officials were testifying.[223] By contrast, officials would respond that Iraq was not in a civil war but was experiencing sectarian violence.

In the aftermath of the February 2006 Samarra mosque bombing, a number of academics were quoted in the media claiming that Iraq was experiencing a civil war.[224] As these experts became increasingly vocal, a Pentagon official was assigned specifically to take issue with academics who argued that a civil war had begun.[225] Moreover, an alternative narrative was constructed and used by administration officials, including Rumsfeld, to downplay the issue. This alternative narrative utilized analogies, particularly the US Civil War analogy. Rumsfeld deployed the Civil War analogy in order to undermine the argument that the situation in Iraq had become a civil war. According to Rumsfeld, "it seems to me that it is not a classic civil war at this stage . . . it certainly isn't like our civil war."[226] By employing the analogy of the US Civil War—a war primarily characterized by large armies fighting a conventional war—Rumsfeld and other officials sought to utilize an inappropriate analogy to undermine their opponents.

In spite of the public denials of "civil war," many defense officials disagreed with this assessment. According to Cordesman, military and intelligence officers were privately saying that Iraq had been in a state of "low-level civil war with very slowly increasing intensity since the transfer of power in June 2004."[227] However, within the military and intelligence bureaucracy, there was a taboo on using the term *civil war*.[228] For example, on the Joint Staff, use of the term *civil war* was not permitted, and it did not appear in papers or briefings.[229] Emma Sky, an adviser to Lieutenant General Odierno, testified that in "'06/'07, we can't call it a civil war. I think by any definition . . . Iraq was in a civil war . . . they won't call it that, because it was politically too difficult to call it that, but people would start to say 'the sectarian violence.'"[230] She also noted, "Why can't we call a civil war a civil war, because it always meant you were applying . . . the wrong responses."[231] In November 2006, Colonel Thomas Greenwood complained to the Council of Colonels that "until we acknowledge that we are in the middle of a complex insurgency and a low-level civil war, our nation will not come to grips with the true character and nature of this conflict."[232] One intelligence officer noted that within the intelligence community, particularly the Defense Intelligence Agency, analysts were dissuaded from writing on the topic of civil war.[233]

Recognizing the conflict for what it was, or could potentially become, was more than a matter of semantics. Former Army Major General William L. Nash complained that the "failure to understand that the civil war is already taking place, just not necessarily at the maximum level, means that our countermeasures are inadequate and therefore dangerous to our long-term interest."[234] Colonel Bruce Reider similarly argued that labeling the conflict a civil war was not merely a matter of semantics: "Insurgency and civil war both require different strategic approaches for resolution. The complex nature of the conflict in Iraq necessitates a shift from a COIN-centric military strategy to an approach that addresses escalating sectarian violence and civil war as the main threats with the Sunni-based insurgency and counterterrorism operations against Al-Qaeda as supporting efforts."[235]

The sectarian violence / civil war debate also required having to use new terms to characterize the adversary. References to countering insurgents and terrorists gradually faded into the background since the priority of military operations had shifted. Operations intended to prevent sectarian violence from escalating, such as Together Forward, now targeted "death squads" and "illegal armed groups"; specific references to militia groups such as the Mahdi Army were usually avoided due to political sensitivities.[236] Political sensitivities also probably influenced the delay in the DoD officially recognizing the changing nature of the conflict. In the May 2006 version of the DoD's quarterly "Measuring Stability and Security in Iraq" report, "civil war" was mentioned as the goal of "anti-Iraqi forces" (listed as extremists and terrorists).[237] Three months later, the tone of the report had changed considerably. In the August 2006 version, the report stated, "Conditions that could lead to civil war exist in Iraq. Nevertheless the current violence is not civil war, and movement toward civil war can be prevented . . . since the last report the core conflict in Iraq changed into a struggle between Sunni and Shia."[238] The official recognition in August 2006 that the nature of the conflict had altered in comparison to what it had been three months earlier was a highly skeptical claim given rising levels of sectarian violence since February 2006. Rather, it was a belated recognition of a fact that had been obvious to many experts for some time. Interestingly, at that time, regardless of whether one characterized the conflict as sectarian violence or civil war, references to insurgency declined, as it was not seen as a relevant characterization anymore. And yet in the years that followed, beginning with the 2007 "surge," it was the US military's counterinsurgency approach that was credited with reducing the violence.

Insurgency Metrics

As US forces were still being attacked following the Hussein regime's collapse, analysts were tasked to track a number of metrics to assist policy makers in determining whether the insurgency was increasing or decreasing in strength. From a military perspective, insurgency estimates reflect on the amount of military and other national resources that are needed to counter it. For example, when asked how many troops were required to deal with the insurgency in Iraq, Rumsfeld remarked, "We need as many (Iraqi security forces) as are needed. If you have an insurgency that's this level you'll need X. If you have an insurgency that's that level you'll need X-plus. And if you have an insurgency that's quite low, you'll need X-minus."[239] Rumsfeld's pegging the number of Iraqi security forces needed to the total number of insurgents is just one example of how important senior policy makers may have perceived this issue, particularly since coalition strategy in Iraq was heavily dependent upon "standing up" Iraqi security forces and "standing down" coalition forces.

Regardless of their value from a *military* perspective, however, estimates of enemy strength can be a highly sensitive topic from a *political* perspective. If the strength of an insurgency is growing, this can reflect negatively on politicians' ability to sustain confidence that progress is being made. This in turn can also lead to questions about the quality of their leadership. Similar to the Vietnam order of battle controversy referred to in the introduction of this book, US policy makers during the Iraq War were also constrained by the perceived need to demonstrate progress. Indeed, just as their predecessors were obliged to highlight successes and hide failures, US policy makers during the Iraq war were cognizant of the negative reactions that could result from the disclosure of metrics and intelligence estimates that ran counter to official narratives about the progress being made.

In the case of metrics, for example, there were numerous contradictory remarks made by senior DoD officials on this subject. Since at least 2003, a weekly "Iraq Status Brief," later renamed the "Iraq Weekly Update," was produced by the Joint Staff and included numerous metrics by which to gauge progress.[240] In addition, in early 2005, Rumsfeld instructed the Joint Staff to set up an "Iraq Room" where metrics would be produced. Teams attached to the "Iraq Room" studied intelligence estimates on the number and types of insurgents, and their measurements appeared regularly in briefings to the Secretary of Defense.[241] Despite Rumsfeld's insistence on setting up an office for the sole purpose of developing metrics, he was also dismissive of metrics that supported the view that the insurgency was increasing in size and lethality. For instance, on February 7, 2005, Rumsfeld asked Cambone to "give me the best Intel estimate as to the size of the insurgency." Ten days later, Rumsfeld told the House

Armed Services Committee that he had trouble believing any of the estimates of the number of insurgents because it was so difficult to track them. Rumsfeld said that CIA and DIA had differing assessments at different times and that "I see these reports . . . Frankly, I don't have a lot of confidence in any of them."[242]

In another instance that occurred in the summer of 2005, following a visit to Iraq the former acting Army chief of staff reported that US forces had killed or captured some fifty thousand insurgents in the first eight months of the year.[243] In response to press queries about the accuracy of these figures, Pentagon spokesperson Larry Di Rita said, "Nobody's maintaining a count of the size of the insurgency or the numbers that we're capturing" because "it's not a metric that has a lot of meaning."[244] By contrast, there was a good deal of evidence to suggest that officials did take the metrics seriously. For example, General Pace would regularly ask intelligence officials for a figure of enemy strength that he could brief the president.[245]

As the irregular conflict evolved, US officials also used body counts as a measure of progress in their internal discourse, as well as for public relations purposes. Body counts were regularly used in various official press releases, although headlines such as "Coalition, Iraqi Troops Kill 15 Terrorists" underscored the inherent propaganda attributes of these figures and the unwillingness or inability to specify the categories into which the enemy dead would be placed.[246] During the course of the 2005 Tal Afar operation, the head of MNF-I's Office of Strategic Communications, Brigadier General Donald Alston, reported that the release of figures on enemies killed was done because the United States wanted to "provide more context" to operations but that there was "no intention of making this a practice."[247] In fact, this practice began at least a year before with the November 2004 battle of Fallujah where the Marine Corps estimated that between 1,200 and 1,600 insurgents had been killed in the fighting.[248] Body counts also featured regularly at National Security Council briefings, although it is unclear whether President Bush requested them or the military started briefing them without higher guidance.

Despite the use of body counts, officials publicly insisted they were *not* used because they were widely viewed as a dishonest and inaccurate measure of progress. In the summer of 2003, General Pace said that the Pentagon was not using body counts because this approach had had a negative effect on decision makers during the Vietnam War. This was an ironic situation because officials were afraid to admit they were using a system of metrics that they knew to be incorrect in the first place, and yet they continued using it nonetheless. General Abizaid reportedly made a similar point when, after publicly defending the estimate that there were only five thousand insurgents in Iraq, he privately told Bush that the coalition had killed at least three times that number and there was no indication the insurgency was weakening.[249] Despite all the problems with body counts, as of November 2006, and presumably thereafter, Bush continued to ask his field commanders for the numbers of enemy dead.[250]

Another significant impediment in the case of Iraq estimates was the lack of a clear definition of what constituted an insurgent. There are many different roles and levels of participation for individuals involved in an insurgency. Some insurgents may be hard-core fighters while others may be one-time actors.[251] In almost all cases, officials who cited estimates of insurgent strength failed to disclose whether the numbers they were referring to were active or part-time members. The majority of insurgencies depend on cadres that are part time and can blend back into the population. Although difficult to count, the number of part-timers is often higher than the number of active members of an insurgency.[252] Such ambiguities make it easier to politicize intelligence, since there are no objective criteria by which the goals, success or failure, and estimates of the enemy's strength can be accurately assessed.[253] Definitions, and hence data, are fluid and can be adjusted to suit the political and bureaucratic interests of all the participants in the process. One of the complicating factors in analysis of the Iraq insurgency was the status of Shiite militia groups that fought the coalition. Judging from official statements and statistics, the Shiites had never been classed as an independent category of "insurgents," although they had been occasionally downplayed as a subcategory of the "rejectionist" element of the insurgency. While there is no hard evidence to suggest that the failure to list the Shiite element as an independent category in the insurgency estimates was a deliberate attempt to keep the numbers low, their absence in the statistics raises serious questions whether US political and military officials understood the true nature and scale of the problems they were facing in Iraq.

It is unclear where in the intelligence bureaucracy the estimates of enemy strength in Iraq that were publicized originated, or what methodology and categories were used to make the analysis, particularly as officials referred to several methodologies. Within the intelligence community, DIA has primary responsibility for providing traditional military intelligence and order of battle analysis, although both the CIA and MNF-I intelligence staff duplicated this function. In contrast to traditional methodologies used in estimating the strength of a conventional enemy, which can involve comparing orders of battle and evaluating technical capabilities, estimates of insurgent strength are more prone to error.[254] In many cases insurgents are not organized into regular formations, making it difficult to assess their numerical strength accurately.[255] As T. E. Lawrence observed of the Arab rebellion in World War I, "No spies could count us . . . since even ourselves had not the smallest idea of our strength at any given moment."[256] Analysis of the Iraq insurgency was further complicated by the lack of hierarchy and the fact it consisted of many groups with a diverse set of motives.

Beyond the normal problems of doing an order of battle estimate of an insurgency, there were also political reasons that ensured higher insurgent numbers were frowned upon. It is unclear how determinations were made to increase or decrease the figures for the estimate of the insurgency's total size. As early as the fall of 2003, the Pentagon hosted regular briefings for think-tank experts in which it put insurgent strength at around 5,000.[257] The decision to raise the insurgency estimate from 5,000 in April 2004 to 15,000 in May 2004 (tripling the size of the insurgency) was never publicly explained, though some sort of correction was inevitably required following the high levels of violence that occurred in that month. As Cordesman noted, the figure of 5,000 insurgents "was never more than a wag and is now clearly ridiculous."[258] By October 2004 it was estimated there were between 8,000 and 12,000 hard-core insurgents, but the number would increase to 20,000 when active sympathizers or covert accomplices were included.[259]

One methodology Abizaid relied on to gauge the insurgency's strength was to link the size of the insurgency to its ability to disrupt the democratic process in Iraq. In March 2005, Abizaid cited intelligence estimates claiming that the insurgency had declined to only 3,500 fighters, or the maximum number fielded on Iraq's election day. Abizaid claimed that this figure represented the "whole force," thereby attempting to link a high election turnout with a decline in the insurgency's size.[260] In the aftermath of the elections, the level of violence intensified, and Abizaid returned to citing the figure of 20,000 insurgents. Another of the methods that was used to arrive at the figure of 20,000 was to deduce a figure based on a guesstimate of the percentage of insurgent strength relative to the size of Iraq's population. In June 2005, Abizaid stated that the number of Iraqis participating in the insurgency amounted to less than 0.1 percent of the country's population of 27 million and most likely did not exceed 20,000.[261]

According to a senior Baghdad-based military intelligence officer, the methodology used to estimate insurgent strength was based on calculations of how many individuals it took to lay an IED and to conduct a small arms attack. Based on this calculation, this officer argued that on any one day there were between 500 and 1,000 active insurgents, with the maximum figure around 2,000. Overall, he estimated there were no more than 12,000 to 20,000 insurgents.[262] Assuming these figures were accurate, the Iraq insurgency would be among the smallest in modern times, especially as insurgent movements have historically mobilized some 0.5 to 2 percent of the population.[263] Nevertheless, despite the fact that 23,500 insurgents were officially reported killed or detained in 2005, the insurgency's size officially remained at 20,000 into 2006.[264]

By 2007, military analysts had privately concluded that the size of the "Sunni Arab insurgency" consisted of 70,000 to 80,000 hard-line operators and part-time supporters.²⁶⁵ However, this analysis did not include any examination of the Shiite militias, nor was the figure of 70,000 to 80,000 referenced publicly. Despite being aware that the enemy's strength was much higher than the 20,000 to 30,000 figure cited publicly, operational commanders recognized that citing the higher figures, even within the bureaucracy, was "politically unacceptable" and therefore continued to repeat the lower figures.²⁶⁶ Putting aside the inherent deficiencies in analysis of insurgencies and recognizing that the DoD's figures were likely inaccurate, the fact that an artificial ceiling was placed on the irregular adversary's size indicates that officials were unable to escape from the discursive constructs they had previously created for themselves. Similar to the US experience in Vietnam, estimates of adversary strength that could undermine confidence in the war were not listened to, or were deliberately distorted, with the result that the official discourse of the war reflected political imperatives rather than a more accurate portrayal of reality.

Conclusion

In the case of the Iraq conflict, the comprehension of beginnings and endings was made all the more difficult given that the traditional formalities of warfare, such as a surrender ceremony or a peace treaty, were absent. Another factor that has made an understanding of this conflict difficult, was that the determination of the transition from conflict to postconflict, conventional war to irregular war, combat to "stabilization and support operations," conventional war to counterinsurgency, or counterinsurgency to civil war, has never been established by any of the main participants, except on the one occasion when President Bush announced the cessation of "major combat operations" on May 1, 2003. However, as General George Casey used the term in connection with US military operations in Fallujah in November 2004, clearly major combat operations were not over, despite the formal announcement that they were a year previously.²⁶⁷ This issue is not merely one of semantics but actually affects how policy makers and military professionals interpret the nature and character of a conflict, which in turn affects decision making and strategy. For instance, the perception that a conflict is in its final stages rather than its beginning ones can affect how many troops are deemed necessary to stay in a theater of operations. Moreover, prematurely ending a war can have severe political repercussions, particularly if the public mistakenly believes that victory has been achieved only to learn that victory has yet to be achieved.

The irregular war that simultaneously occurred with the conventional war prior to Baghdad's fall continued in the aftermath of the city's capture. Thus, whereas the conventional war ended, the guerrilla war continued, albeit in limited size and scope. In the aftermath of Baghdad's fall, and for a number of months thereafter, the enemy was characterized in the internal discourse as merely consisting of hold-outs from the previous regime, or the so-called dead-enders and noncompliant forces, as well as foreign fighters and criminals. However, this characterization confused the real nature of these groups, many of which had little or nothing to do with wanting to resurrect the former regime. Linking the ongoing resistance with remnants of the former regime marginalized an alternative discourse that recognized the growing importance of nationalism and sectarianism as primary motives behind the insurgency, as well as disenchantment with foreign occupation.

The many characterizations the United States has officially used to describe the irregular adversary have had important implications for politicians, civil servants, and military professionals, as well as for the general understanding, or misunderstanding, of the conflict's nature. As Emma Sky complained, "the enemy had been referred to as the enemy or anti-Iraqi forces or anti-Coalition forces. I mean, who were these people and why were they using violence?" By the time of the Iraq "surge," she noted it had become necessary to ban "use of the term FREs, FRL, all these different abbreviations, call them by their names, find out who they are and call them as such."[268]

How an adversary is characterized can also have an impact on determining the problem that needs to be solved and therefore affects the strategic emphasis of military operations. For instance, the constant references to a Sunni insurgency had a significant impact on the coalition's strategic threat perception. By focusing on Iraq's Sunni population as the only source of insurgency, an alternative discourse that recognized a Shiite threat was initially marginalized, despite Shiite militia groups regularly engaging in combat with coalition forces. Despite frequent fighting between Shiite militia groups and coalition forces since at least October 2003, the coalition chose to minimize the significant role played by the Shiites as part of the ongoing violence, and this is reflected in various terms used to characterize them and is further evidenced by intelligence estimates of adversary strength. The Mahdi Army was mainly viewed as an "illegal armed group" as opposed to an insurgent organization, although some official estimates had included it as a subsection of the "rejectionist" category of insurgents. Downplaying the role of the Shiites meant that the size and scope of the conflict was downplayed as well. Moreover, officials ignored estimates that showed the "insurgency" was several times the strength of publicly cited figures, preferring instead to continue repeating numbers their own analysts knew to be inaccurate.

Adversary characterizations have also been devised and manipulated for armed forces' morale and domestic political reasons. The role played by foreign fighters and terrorists was overemphasized in the official discourse even though they represented only a small fraction of the adversary's overall size. However, the bandwagoning that occurred in relation to this aspect of the adversary also resulted in blowback. The attention devoted to AQI head Abu Musab al-Zarqawi far outweighed his actual significance with the consequence that following his death in June 2006, a number of observers were under the mistaken impression that the AQI network would be permanently disrupted, violence in Iraq would decline, and the security situation would improve.

One of the more intriguing aspects of the terminology of this conflict was the degree of control senior US leaders felt they needed to maintain on managing the discourse. Rumsfeld in particular took terminology very seriously and personally intervened on numerous occasions to direct the war's discourse. Debates over which terms to use caused significant consternation among senior US political and military officials, particularly in the months following the fall of Baghdad when Rumsfeld chastised General John Abizaid for using the word *guerrilla*. It would seem that the language used in public by politicians and military officers can also impact a nation's civil-military relations and the extent to which military officers are willing to toe the party line by using the same terminology as their political masters. In Abizaid's case, terminology may very well have been a tool of dissent. In the case of *insurgency*, the evidence suggests that many military officials observed a blowback effect that resulted from attempts to place controls on use of the term. On the other hand, military officials were able to consistently avoid any public references to civil war, even though many privately believed the Iraq conflict *was* a civil war. Similar to the case of *insurgency*, officials also believed that the marginalizing of *civil war* resulted in negative consequences for the way the United States viewed and waged the conflict.

Each of the cases discussed in this chapter demonstrates the political and bureaucratic complexities inherent in naming adversaries and conflicts and their unintended consequences for military performance. Beyond the perceived importance policy makers placed on the need to manage the conflict's discourse are the effects this had on strategy. The confusion resulting from the conjuring and manipulation of the multitude of terms used to characterize the adversary and the nature of the conflict in Iraq resulted in a general state of ignorance and misperception among the officials responsible for supervising strategy and operations. For instance, attempts to control references to insurgency had the effect of delaying the US military's transition to waging a counterinsurgency, thereby giving US adversaries a "window of opportunity" to organize themselves.[269] In contrast to the belief that the US military's slow response to waging counterinsurgency was due to a "cultural" preference for conventional war and decisive battle, the discourse trap provides a better explanation of the military's behavior.[270] Although the culture argument can be used to explain why the military was slow to adapt to a counterinsurgency strategy after the conflict had been identified as an insurgency, or even to explain the military's changing definition of what constituted counterinsurgency, it does not explain why defense policy makers were unwilling to identify the conflict as an insurgency in the first place, despite many military leaders advocating that designation from early on in the conflict. As for intelligence estimates, both the enemy's size and its levels of support among the Iraqi populace were deliberately underestimated. Presumably, this manipulation was based on the need to consistently cite low enemy figures, since policy makers perceived this to be directly related to public support for the war. Had policy makers cited higher figures, it would have contradicted their rhetoric of victory and success. In this sense, policy makers and military officials were trapped in their own rhetoric. Among the unintended consequences of this for the military was that more realistic assessments of adversary strength could not be disseminated, even internally, and therefore US actions to defeat the insurgency were based on misleading intelligence.

CHAPTER 5

The Surge
From Iraq to Afghanistan

Since the beginning of 2007, the surge discourse has had a profound effect on the US military in relation to the wars in Iraq and Afghanistan. Prior to 2007, force levels in Iraq had remained relatively stable, at about 140,000 military personnel, and were expected to decline over time as Iraqi forces were stood up. For the better part of this earlier period, US commanders referred to what they were doing as counterinsurgency. However, with the perceived success of the "surge," the American discourse on the Iraq war and the military's appreciation of counterinsurgency would both be transformed. As violence in Iraq declined by late 2007 and was kept at a relatively low level over the next several years, albeit an insurgency continued to exist during this period and violence continues as of 2012, the example of the 2007–8 "surge" was repeatedly highlighted in internal discussions to demonstrate both that the mission in Iraq had been successful and that a similar outcome was possible for Afghanistan. In this way, the surge discourse helped constitute the Afghan conflict in that it shaped the context in which American decision makers understood what the prospects were if the United States increased its force levels in Afghanistan. By contrast, prior to the Iraq surge, these prospects were less, if at all, obvious to decision makers.

Understanding the success of the surge discourse in becoming a dominant discourse in relation to the wars in Iraq and Afghanistan, as well as counterinsurgency thinking more generally, necessitates tracing not only the evolution of the term itself but how it altered conceptions of success and vice versa. It is notable that while the Iraq surge is typically believed to have lasted the relatively short period from 2007 to 2008, the period lasting from the second half of 2008 through the end of 2011, when the remaining US troops withdrew, has received very little attention by the US military, not only in its own right, but also in relation to how successful or not the surge itself was. As this chapter will argue, in the process of becoming the dominant discourse, alternative critical discourses were marginalized, in large part because the "success" narrative aligned with both political and military preferences.

The specific meaning and interpretation of the surge has evolved considerably over time, with politicians and defense officials playing a key part in reinventing the term to suit the official needs of the day. Within the military, as well as the wider political discourse, fundamental questions arose in connection with the dominance of the surge discourse, such as what the surge consisted of, whether it was actually responsible for achieving success, whether it would be possible or advisable to replicate the surge in Afghanistan during the same time period and with the same number of forces, and so on. Attempts to answer these questions showcased not only the lack of overall consensus but also the highly charged nature of the debate. Depending on the answer, officials could be advocating a policy of increasing US forces, decreasing them, employing them in particular ways, not employing them in particular ways, restructuring the military to become more adept at counterinsurgency, or advocating against a military that was overly focused on counterinsurgency.

This chapter will begin by tracing the origins of the surge discourse, starting with its competition with the "drawdown" discourse. It will go on to discuss the way in which the Iraq surge was perceived to have resulted in a success and then examine how the narrative associated with it became institutionalized within the military. The next section will showcase how the success narrative initially caused problems from 2008 through mid-2009 in relation to the Afghan conflict and therefore had to be downplayed. However, when the political and military circumstances changed by mid-2009, the success narrative was then played up in order to make the case for a surge in Afghanistan. Once the Afghan surge occurred beginning in 2010, it was very much influenced, though not necessarily in a positive way, by the Iraq surge. This chapter will conclude by highlighting the problems that have arisen from this discursive entrapment and speculate on the future prospects of the surge in relation to the US military.

Drawdown or *Surge*

As the Iraq "insurgency" picked up in pace from 2003 to 2006, the Bush administration had continually rejected any significant increase in the number of US forces, despite the fact that military "force estimates" assumed that an increase in violence would need to be countered by an increase in US troop levels.[1] At this time, for military officials such as Multi-National Forces in Iraq (MNF-I) head General George Casey to have advocated for more troops was considered a nonstarter, if not outright insubordination. Instead, US policy discussions remained focused on "drawing down" US forces while simultaneously Iraqi forces were "stood up." Defense Secretary Rumsfeld, in particular, was a strong supporter of this policy. Two days before he was fired, Rumsfeld sent a memo to President Bush in which he advocated withdrawing US forces from "vulnerable positions," such as cities and patrolling, and moving US forces to a "Quick Reaction Force status" where they could support the Iraqis who were expected to take the military lead. Additionally, Rumsfeld also suggested recasting how the United States talked about its goals in Iraq in more "minimalist" terms.[2] In a December 8, 2006, memo to Bush, Rumsfeld, shortly before Robert Gates replaced him, laid out a proposal for the administration's Iraq policy. A fundamental feature of this proposal was that "coalition forces will reduce their presence and activities in major cities" and that "US forces will shift their main effort to the support of Iraqi Security Forces." He also noted, "No increase in the level of US forces can substitute for successful diplomacy in the region and . . . in getting the Iraqi Government to act." Accordingly, the MNF-I mission would be formally concluded by December 2007. Rumsfeld's only reference to a possible "surge" relates to helping Iraq "build more effective police, justice, and prison systems and/or to better protect their borders."[3]

About the same time of Rumsfeld's memo, the bipartisan Iraq Study Group released a report arguing for a shift in US strategy in which the "primary mission of US forces in Iraq should evolve to one of supporting the Iraqi army, which would take over primary responsibility for combat operations." During the course of their interviews with military officers several months prior to the report's release, the study group members discussed the possibility of adding more US troops but were told that additional troops were not needed and that their main aim was to get the Iraqis to assume more responsibility. For military leaders, increasing US forces might achieve a temporary decline in violence, but this was not considered a substitute for a political solution.[4] Nevertheless, there was a limited interest in the possibility of "surging" US troops. As the report notes, "we could . . . support a short-term redeployment or surge of American combat forces to stabilize Baghdad, or to speed up the training and equipping mission, if the US commander in Iraq determines that such steps would be effective."[5] That being said, this option was not given prominence in the report's recommendations that stressed a reduction of US forces to the point where "by the first quarter of 2008, subject to unexpected developments in the security situation on the ground, all combat brigades not necessary for force protection could be out of Iraq."[6]

While the mainstream political and military discourse was dominated by the idea of a reduction of US combat troops and an increase in support activities to the Iraqi military, discussion about the prospect of increasing US forces began to gather steam within certain elements of the US government dealing with Iraq policy, including the National Security Council and Joint Chiefs of Staff, as well as outside the government, specifically at the Washington, DC, think tank the American Enterprise Institute (AEI). The story of how the marginalized concept of "surging" additional US forces into Iraq became US government policy by the end of 2006 has been well covered elsewhere and does not need further explication here.[7] However, several points are worth highlighting in order to set the context for how the surge narrative eventually developed and would be labeled a success. First, the idea of a surge was considered a highly unpopular one and also contradicted the Bush administration's earlier attempts to demonstrate progress. Moreover, for the military, a troop surge was also thought an unlikely course of action due to its prior rejection by the politicians and potentially an undesirable one given the strains already being placed on overstretched US forces. Second, Petraeus was not directly involved in the initial AEI planning effort. Therefore the AEI idea of "surging" troops, which he later credited as inspiring the 2007–8 "surge," was not his.[8] Third, the AEI plans called for adding 50,000 troops to improve security in Baghdad and Anbar province, rather than the 30,000 that were eventually sent, much less the 21,500 that were initially announced.[9] As such, there was an important difference between the original AEI plan and the actual plan that was put into practice. At the time it was announced, critics of the "surge" referred to it instead as a "dribble."[10] Fourth, in contrast to the aim of the Rumsfeld memo and Iraq Study Group report regarding the timeline for "combat" troop levels to be withdrawn, which was for the withdrawal to be completed by the end of 2007 or early 2008, one of the results of the "surge" was for this timeline to be extended through 2010.[11] Finally, whereas the original notion of success had highlighted the idea of a decline in violence to allow for a political solution, this would later be amended to simply a decline in violence, with little concern about other political objectives.

The Iraq "Surge" and "Success"

In his January 10, 2007 speech announcing a troop "surge" in Iraq, Bush enunciated both the political and military goals to be accomplished. According to Bush, one of the key purposes of adding troops to Baghdad would be to "help the Iraqis break the current cycle of violence." Thus "reducing the violence in Baghdad" would help make "reconciliation possible" between Iraq's Sunni and Shia communities.[12] In terms of longer-term political goals, Bush stated, "Victory will not look like the ones our fathers and grandfathers achieved. There will be no surrender ceremony on the deck of a battleship . . . But victory in Iraq will bring something new in the Arab world: a functioning democracy that polices its territory, upholds the rule of law, respects fundamental human liberties, and answers to its people."¹³ As announced shortly after Bush's speech, the US military was going to surge an additional five combat brigades, or 21,500 troops into Iraq, specifically in Baghdad and Anbar Province. However, the figure 21,500 only referred to "combat troops"; when "support troops" were added, the figure rose to some 30,000 troops. When the latter figure was mentioned publicly in March 2007, many critics complained the surge had already failed because more troops were being requested, even though it was always the intention to send 30,000.¹⁴ Throughout the winter and spring of 2007, as violence in Iraq continued to soar, critics claimed the surge was not working, whereas defense officials noted the surge hadn't actually begun because the additional five brigades did not finish arriving until July and would then take time to fully deploy and become operational.¹⁵ It is noteworthy that following Bush's announcement of a surge, Democrats began using the term *escalation* instead to describe the new policy, in order to make the connection with Vietnam, though later when the "surge" appeared to be "succeeding," many Democrats would back away from their criticism.¹⁶ Indeed, by July 2008, when the last of the five surge brigades were removed from Iraq and the postsurge period began, criticism of the surge had virtually disappeared from US political discourse. Despite there being some debate about the success of the longer-term objectives of Bush's policy, there was much less debate about the decline in violence that occurred simultaneous to the surge. Whereas monthly fatalities had reached some 1,700 in May 2007, they subsequently fell to around 500 by December. From June 2008 to June 2011 the number of fatalities averaged around 200 per month, or about one-tenth of the rate for the last half of 2006.¹⁷

Instead, a new debate would emerge questioning whether or not it was the surge or some other factor that had resulted in declining levels of violence. This debate would occur throughout the defense community and quickly become associated with non-Iraq topics, such as the war in Afghanistan and reform of the US armed forces. Among the key questions debated were, Was it Petraeus and his approach to counterinsurgency that was responsible? Was it the Special Forces teams led by Lieutenant General Stanley McChrystal that were the key? Was it simply a matter of placing more troops into Baghdad and elsewhere, of removing them from large bases and having them "protect the population"? Could the surge have been conducted earlier, or were certain conditions present by 2007 that were not present beforehand? Were the Americans the key players in the first instance, or were the key changes made by the Iraqis themselves irrespective of the surge? Did the mere fact of the surge signal to the Iraqis that the United States was committed to continuing the conflict rather than drawing down and therefore served as an essential "morale booster"?

A revealing aspect of this debate has been interpreting what the surge did or did not consist of in the first place. For instance, in most of the narratives, *surge* refers only to the conventional ground component, the "surge brigades."[18] However, there was also an important air component. Similar to the relative absence of Special Forces "kill-capture" missions from the mainstream surge narrative, the lack of any serious attention to the air component reflects the dominance within the narrative of a soft power emphasis similar to that prescribed in US counterinsurgency doctrine. In reality, US air strikes increased nearly 500 percent between 2006 and 2007. While the ground forces "surged" by 30,000, the number of US planes, to include attack planes and B-1B bombers, were also increased significantly.[19] This lack of attention to the "hard power" aspects of the "surge" relative to "soft power" has raised fundamental questions about what factors were responsible for the lower levels of violence.[20]

In the mainstream narrative that emerged by 2008, the "success" of the "surge" was boiled down to a combination of increased troop levels and new "counterinsurgency" tactics associated with Petraeus and the new US Army-Marine Corps Counterinsurgency Field Manual (FM) 3-24. A key aspect of these new tactics was to shift from operating out of big bases to placing a military presence in population centers where they would engage in a "population-centric" counterinsurgency intended to win hearts and minds. The success of the "surge" has also been associated with the Anbar Awakening, in which the US military allied itself with and materially sponsored an array of mainly Sunni citizen patrols. The US military referred to these groups initially as Concerned Local Citizens and subsequently Sons of Iraq. In actual fact, both the employment of population-centric counterinsurgency tactics and the Anbar Awakening either began prior to or lasted beyond the period known as the surge, although in the mainstream narrative both have been discursively associated with it.

As a part of this narrative, a great deal of the "success" was attributed to General Petraeus. This attribution was based on a number of factors, but most notably, Petraeus was portrayed as the intellectual general who authored the new counterinsurgency field manual. Prior to his 2007 arrival in Iraq, Petraeus headed the team responsible for writing FM 3-24, a document that would acquire the informal name "the Petraeus Doctrine." The counterinsurgency tactics adopted by US troops in Iraq were also referred to as the Petraeus Doctrine, even though they bore only marginal resemblance to those listed in the field manual.[21] Petraeus's style was also significantly different from that of Casey, and he was considered a more inspiring, photogenic, and media-friendly general. Initially, in order to "sell" the "surge" to a reluctant Congress, the general's name was often invoked, particularly during Bush's speeches and press conferences.[22] Interestingly, though, during the September 10, 2007, congressional hearing on Iraq, referred to as the "Petraeus Report," the general placed the origins of the "surge" in December 2006, when he said Casey had requested the additional forces that would be referred to as the "surge brigades."[23] Furthermore, whereas the "surge" narrative would argue that Petraeus was the "first" US general to be conducting a "counterinsurgency" campaign, Casey's strategy was regarded as something "other than counterinsurgency." Petraeus would be credited with replacing Casey's "prior emphasis on large, fortified bases, mounted patrols, and transition to Iraqi security forces with a new pattern of smaller, dispersed bases, dismounted patrolling, and direct provision of US security for threatened Iraqi civilians."[24] However, many of the "new" counterinsurgency tactics employed by US military forces during this period were reportedly advocated by Casey's deputy, Lieutenant General Odierno, prior to Petraeus's arrival. Moreover, many of these tactics had been used earlier in the conflict, though they were probably not used as extensively as they were later.[25]

Another important debate related to the value of the surge and what it actually achieved relative to US aims. Proponents of the surge claimed that it was responsible for the declining levels of violence and that it prevented what many had previously claimed to be a civil war from expanding further. Curiously, the vast majority of discussion of counterinsurgency in Iraq ends with the surge in 2008, despite the fact that US forces only completed their withdrawal by the end of 2011. Thus the more than three subsequent years of a large US military presence is overlooked. In this sense, US military discourse related to the surge, both positive and negative, focuses on tactics and operations rather than on strategic issues. To the extent there is serious criticism of the surge, it exists within the framework of the surge, debating the merits and drawbacks of what occurred in 2007–8, without linking it to the eventual US military withdrawal or to wider policy goals. In other words, the surge discourse is based on a snapshot, rather than an examination of the war in a wider frame.[26]

Critics of the surge, while not doubting that the security situation in Iraq improved considerably by 2008, have nevertheless been concerned that inappropriate interpretations and lessons of why this occurred were being incorporated into US military thinking and serving as the basis both for its approach to the Afghan war and for the way in which it plans, organizes, and trains for counterinsurgency. These criticisms of what are perceived to be flawed interpretations include a number of themes, but four of them are particularly noteworthy. First, it has been argued that many of the "population-centric" tactics normally accredited to Petraeus had in fact been employed under Casey and that for the most part the only thing that changed was the scale rather than the content. Moreover, a number of officers complained that these tactics had not necessarily been successful prior to 2007. This then leads to the second criticism, that the timing of the surge was fundamental to understanding its success. As Steven Metz argues, "committing US military forces to population security prior to 2006 would not have worked because neither the Sunni Arabs nor the Shiites wanted it." By contrast, Metz notes that it was not until the end of 2006 that "nearly all Iraqis were . . . tired of violence. This was vital." As such the "timing of the strategic shift was as crucial as its content."[27] A third, and somewhat related criticism, is the idea that rather than placing the emphasis on what US forces did or did not do, the Americans were actually supporting a more important trend they had little control over—namely, the split that occurred between the more "moderate" Sunni insurgents and the extremist Al Qaeda in Iraq (AQI). In this view, the US never actually won the hearts and minds of Iraqis as a result of their new tactics. Instead, the Sunni insurgents were still opposed to the US occupation in principle, but their opposition to the United States was superseded by their feud with AQI, whose barbarous actions made the Sunnis turn on them, and this meant making a deal with the Americans for this purpose. In addition, the increasing violence between Sunnis and Shia was also said to have made a deal with the Americans an overriding priority for the Sunnis out of fear they would be ethnically cleansed if they did not do so. This being the case, one of the conclusions to be reached is that even with the surge there was never any reconciliation. Instead what occurred were "ceasefires," and it was the various groups involved, rather than the United States, that made the decision to end the violence for their own reasons.[28] The final criticism of the surge posits that US forces were not necessarily conducting a fairly bloodless "hearts and minds" counterinsurgency, in which protecting the population took priority. Instead, according to this view, what was occurring were a series of very bloody battles. Thus the numerous conventional battles occurring in Baghdad, the increased numbers of air strikes in urban areas, and the Special Forces kill-capture missions, which were all essential to the eventual decrease in violence, nevertheless represented a marked departure from the type of counterinsurgency described in FM 3-24 as well as that described in most of the success narratives. The implication of each of these aforementioned criticisms is that if the wrong lessons were learnt, this would then have a negative impact on future US military performance.

Institutionalizing the "Success Narrative"

By mid-2008 the success of the Iraq surge began to develop into a surge triumphalism within the broader American political-military discourse. The surge was not only held up as being mainly responsible for the improvements in security that led to declining levels of violence in Iraq but also increasingly became viewed as a template capable of being reproduced elsewhere. Once the narrative of the Iraq surge was associated with the idea of success, the tenets of FM 3-24 and population-centric counterinsurgency became more prominent within the US military. One commentator went so far as to note that "after the Baghdad surge, America's military leaders embraced COIN with the fervor of the converted. It became their defining ideology, just as free-market economics and Jeffersonian democracy were to the neoconservatives who had led the United States into Baghdad."[29] Counterinsurgency critic Colonel Gian Gentile similarly complained of the way the "surge" had become "dogma" within the US military. He noted that "Many army officers and Department of Defense thinkers seem to be able to think only about how to apply the perceived counterinsurgency lessons from Iraq to Afghanistan. A recent group of colonels asked the question 'how should the army execute a surge in Afghanistan,' instead of the more important questions of whether the army should use the surge counterinsurgency program there. A professor from a major Department of Defense university has gone so far as to call for the surge and its counterinsurgency techniques as the model for American strategy and policy throughout the entire Middle East."[30] This period also saw the rise to prominence of a "well-connected group of active and retired military officers, academics, think tank pundits, and commentators" who advocated on behalf of these ideas and helped entrench them in public policy discourse more generally. Many of these individuals were associated with Petraeus, particularly during the period in which he supervised the writing of FM 3-24. In popular jargon, this group was dubbed the "COINdinistas," and they would be at the forefront of pushing for an Iraq-style "surge" in Afghanistan.[31]

One important example of the way in which population-centric counterinsurgency had become institutionalized within the US Army can be found in its military education system. Two professors at the Army's Command and General Staff College noted that many officers "reference Iraq as the gold standard on how to fight a counterinsurgency. Most point to General David Petraeus, and the surge, as the basic elements in a new formula for counterinsurgency." In terms of the role and negative impact of a dominant discourse of "population-centric" counterinsurgency in the military education system, the two professors complained that "over half of the officers in our experience believe they have 'cracked the code' to waging a counterinsurgency and see no need to educate themselves beyond their present understanding." Among the reasons for this is that soldiers returning from deployments were being "force fed population-centric theories from their commanders and seldom given any other information needed to develop a deeper understanding of other theories, as well as the contextual parameters." This had the effect of creating a twofold problem in that it both "inhibited a true intellectual discussion on counterinsurgency theories" and also forced "many soldiers to remain silent on the issue, because they fear not being promoted if they differ from the prevailing trend."[32] Observing that employing the Iraq "solution" causes these officers to overlook the complexity of counterinsurgency warfare, they warned that "this failure of thinking leads to limited discussion or an outright disregard for any other thoughts or opinions that contradict their ideas . . . They believe they have discovered a magic counterinsurgency formula, when in reality they merely cherry-pick the same quotations and ideas that superiors have advocated. This creates a very narrow-minded counterinsurgent."[33]

Similarly, Gentile complained, "the unstated assumption is that a large American military presence in Afghanistan on the Iraq model will buy time for an eventual 'awakening' in Afghanistan as there was in Iraq. Our perceived success in Iraq has created a natural tendency to define all of our problems as insurgencies, since we now believe we have the tools to 'counter' such challenges."[34] An additional concern was that the Iraq "model" could be misapplied to cases other than Afghanistan in which the United States might potentially become involved in counterinsurgency, whereas alternative models would remain sidelined within the US military's discourse and doctrine, if not unknown altogether.

Playing Down an Afghan Surge

The surge triumphalism that emerged by mid-2008 occurred against the backdrop of the US presidential election, increasing levels of violence in Afghanistan, and, perhaps most important, the continued presence of some 140,000 troops in Iraq, which meant few troops were available to be sent elsewhere, even though large numbers would be necessary if the surge were to be repeated in Afghanistan. This latter point was recognized in early 2008 by John Nagl, one of the key proponents of an Afghan surge in 2009. Nagl noted in March 2008 that reversing the declining security situation in Afghanistan "would take an increase of more than 100,000 soldiers and Marines to give NATO commanders in Afghanistan the force ratios that General David Petraeus, the top US commander in Iraq, has enjoyed."[35]

Despite the success of the surge in Iraq, the idea of conducting a similar operation in Afghanistan was initially frowned upon by many senior defense officials. Among the key reasons they sought to downplay expectations of an Afghan surge, particularly in 2008 and early 2009, was that US forces were still heavily committed to Iraq. There was also a fear that the Iraq success was potentially reversible if the United States withdrew too quickly, and therefore it was necessary to keep large numbers of troops there for as long as possible. As will be shown, prior to mid-2009, in rejecting an Afghan surge similar to the Iraq surge, these officials came up with a number of arguments for why it would be a bad idea. However, by mid-2009, they would then reverse themselves, and without addressing their own critical arguments against a surge, subsequently argued in favor of an Afghan surge.

Prior to the Afghan surge that was announced by President Obama in December 2009, the security situation in Afghanistan continued to deteriorate despite the presence of an increasing number of foreign troops. In February 2009, Obama ordered 17,000 additional US troops to Afghanistan, and six weeks later he would dispatch a further 4,000. These new troops followed additional US forces that had previously been requested by the coalition commander in Afghanistan, General David McKiernan, at the end of the Bush administration. At this time, officials were adamantly opposed to a new surge in Afghanistan, and the reasons they gave are particularly noteworthy given the way events would unfold one year later. For instance, Gates employed the "Soviet analogy" to warn against an overreliance on foreign troops, cautioning that the Soviets "couldn't win in Afghanistan with 120,000 troops." Instead, Gates wanted to "put a lot more stress" on building up the Afghan security forces and said that it is "their country, their fight, their future."[36] Other US officials argued that Afghanistan's rugged geography and history of resistance to rule from Kabul should rule out an Iraq-style surge. As one senior military official noted, "it's a much different place, and to surge forces doesn't necessarily fit."[37] Undersecretary of Defense for Policy Eric Edelman observed that replicating the Iraq surge in Afghanistan was probably not possible. According to Edelman, "there are really rather large differences between the circumstances in Afghanistan and in Iraq . . . Even in the darkest days of '06, when we were facing very high levels of violence in Iraq, it always struck me that we . . . would be engaged in Afghanistan much longer than we would be in Iraq." Moreover, whereas Iraq had a centralized government structure in place, held significant oil reserves, and had a highly literate population but was confronted by a largely urban insurgency, Afghanistan was the fifth-poorest country in world, its population was mostly illiterate, it had no tradition of central government, and the insurgency was mainly a rural one that included a far more complex ethnic and tribal mix. While acknowledging that some lessons from Iraq could apply to Afghanistan, Edelman also added, "I would really counsel against sort of a one-size-fits-all [solution]."[38]

Arguments against an Iraq-style surge were also prevalent among commanders in Afghanistan, based mainly on the belief that a surge only referred to a short-term increase in forces. For instance, McKiernan stated, "I don't like to use the word 'surge' here because if we put these additional forces in here, it's going to be for the next few years . . . It's not a temporary increase of combat strength."[39] He also observed that "Afghanistan is not Iraq" and therefore what is needed is a "sustained commitment" that could last many years and would ultimately require a political solution, not a military one. McKiernan also doubted that the "Sons of Iraq" program could be replicated in Afghanistan to recruit tribes to oppose the Taliban.[40]

In late January 2009, prior to Obama making the decision to send 17,000 additional US combat troops to Afghanistan, the Pentagon's press secretary

Geoff Morrell was asked whether this new deployment, then being discussed, was viewed as a "surge" or a "sustained commitment." Morrell replied, "I don't believe anybody views this as a surge as we had in Iraq, and that—this has never been billed as that. But as you've also heard from the secretary . . . he is very cognizant of the danger of us being viewed as some sort of an occupying force in Afghanistan. Nobody wants that." When asked for further clarification, Morrell replied, "I think the implication of a surge is that you're doing it one time for a defined period of time."[41]

Perhaps the most interesting critic of an Afghan surge was none other than Petraeus himself. In a March 2009 speech, Petraeus rejected the idea that a military surge like the one in Iraq would work in Afghanistan on the grounds that there was not enough infrastructure in place to handle one and because it was imperative that Afghans not view the coalition forces as conquerors.[42] Several months later, despite these two conditions remaining the same, Petraeus began arguing in favor of a surge.

Making the Case for an "Afghan Surge"

Before proceeding to the autumn 2009 strategy debate that led to the Afghan "surge," a bit of background is necessary in order to place into perspective this decision. So long as Bush was president, Iraq remained the "central front" in the "war on terror." However, during his presidential campaign, Obama repeatedly made the argument that the Iraq War was a diversion from the war against al-Qaeda in Afghanistan and Pakistan. As already noted, Obama replaced the Global War on Terrorism (GWOT) with a "war against Al-Qaeda and its affiliates," the purpose of which was to "disrupt, dismantle and defeat Al-Qaeda." In Obama's rhetoric, the war in Iraq was cast as a "war of choice" whereas Afghanistan was a "war of necessity." Thus when Obama became president he decided to approve a longstanding request from McKiernan to add more troops. It has been suggested this decision was connected to Obama's earlier references to Afghanistan and that he "seemed to be boxed in by his campaign rhetoric." Therefore, any options other than adding more US troops were simply not conceivable.[43]

Apart from the geographic emphasis on Afghanistan, it was still unclear what new ideas Obama had about the role of military power in this war. Consequently, the ideas then prevailing in the mainstream discourse—that a large-scale counterinsurgency similar to the Iraq surge could be successful and that stability in Afghanistan would mean a defeat for al-Qaeda—increasingly dominated discussions of Afghan policy. Conversely, the prospect of an American defeat in Afghanistan was increasingly touted as resulting in an automatic victory for al-Qaeda. Hence proponents of using the Iraq model for Afghanistan framed their arguments in the context of the "war against al-Qaeda," with failure to adopt a large-scale counterinsurgency strategy being equated with defeat in Afghanistan.

By the summer of 2009, senior officials felt that the existing strategy was not working, and one of the "stars" of the Iraq "surge," General McChrystal, was chosen to replace McKiernan. Upon assuming command, McChrystal was ordered to produce a strategic assessment.[44] Though not referring specifically to Iraq, McChrystal's assessment, which was completed in August, stated, "Success demands a comprehensive counterinsurgency (COIN) campaign." This assessment was subsequently leaked and proved embarrassing for the Obama administration since it meant he could be open to political attacks for not taking the military's advice if he did not accept McChrystal's recommendations. Meantime, Obama had also become increasingly dissatisfied with the status quo trajectory of the conflict and therefore decided in September 2009 to commence a White House strategy review of US policy in Afghanistan and Pakistan in which arguments for and against a counterinsurgency strategy could be presented. The review itself would last from September through the end of November.

Set against the backdrop of the global financial crisis, and fearing that adding more troops would merely create a quagmire, a number of civilian and military officials began arguing against the idea that the Iraq model was applicable to Afghanistan. Led by Vice President Joe Biden, but also including military officials such as Lieutenant General Douglas Lute, a competing discourse emerged within the Obama administration. While accepting the importance of Afghanistan and the necessity to wage war on al-Qaeda, the competing discourse emphasized what would become known as a "counterterrorism" approach, in which the large-scale "counterinsurgency" operations to "protect" the Afghan population were replaced with more focused drone attacks and Special Forces raids aimed at both al-Qaeda and other irreconcilables. One of the key limitations of this alternative discourse was that it remained more of a civilian vision than an actual plan. By the time of the strategy meetings, military staffs had yet to perform calculations on force levels, budgets, and so forth, of the counterterrorism approach, though the very fact the military had not sought to operationalize this vision is an important indication in its own right that they believed that the preferred option for Afghanistan was to surge US forces based on the McChrystal request.

During the review, opponents of the more limited "counterterrorism" approach repeatedly employed the Iraq "surge" analogy.[45] One senior official noted that when Petraeus attended these meetings, he would "always brings up Iraq." One participant of these sessions commented, "Any time Iraq was mentioned it was like putting a hot rod under Petraeus. He would practically levitate."[46] Obama also asked Petraeus to assemble the lessons learned in the

Iraq surge that could be applied in Afghanistan.[47] Indeed, at one point, Obama reportedly said to Petraeus, "What I'm looking for is a surge."[48] The very fact that Iraq surge veterans Petraeus and McChrystal participated in this review, and were regarded as bringing "success" to a situation that had previously seemed beyond any hope, meant that, as one member of Obama's decision-making team observed, "they have a track record . . . I tend to give them the benefit of the doubt."[49]

In the course of the strategy review, there were a number of attempts by Petraeus to highlight ways in which the "surge" analogy was inappropriate. What is notable is that even while warning "What you need to do is throw away all the analogies," Petraeus continued to employ the Iraq analogy to bolster the case for an Afghan surge. For example, he pointed to the successes that occurred in Iraq by buying the support of former insurgents and the importance of moving troops out of large bases to better protect the population.[50] However, use of the surge analogy also had a negative impact on the discussions, from Petraeus's point of view at least, when it came to deployment timelines. When told that the deployment for an Afghan surge would take place over 21 months, whereas to deploy roughly the same number of troops for the Iraq surge took only 6 months, Obama reportedly said, "I don't know how we can describe this as a surge." When Petraeus told him that the plans for an Afghan surge were not modeled on Iraq, Obama replied, "Well, your presentation earlier was on Iraq."[51] Thus on the one hand, Petraeus was arguing that an enhanced troop density would allow the United States to "carry out strategies that can capitalize on the lessons that we did bring back from Iraq," such as experience in population protection, community outreach, and reconciliation of former members of the insurgency.[52] On the other hand, because of the poor roads and limited infrastructure in Afghanistan, the task of deploying troops would be considerably more difficult and time intensive than in Iraq. Despite the extended timeline that would be required simply to deploy the additional troops, Obama nevertheless wanted to retain the 18-month duration of the Iraq "surge" and announced that US forces would begin to withdraw in July 2011.

The Afghan "Surge"

Following its announcement on December 1, 2009, the Afghan surge encountered similar problems to the Iraq surge, most notably the fact that there was a long gap between the period new forces were ordered to go to Afghanistan and the time when they actually arrived. As such, commanders who encountered difficulties would blame the fact that the surge hadn't started, since all the forces had yet to arrive. During this period, the US conducted a large-scale operation in Marja and was also preparing large-scale operations in Kandahar.[53] In the case of Kandahar, the US operations there were analogized to those that occurred in Baghdad, with commanders turning to many of the same population-control tactics employed in the Iraqi capital. Furthermore, Chairman of the Joint Chiefs of Staff Admiral Michael Mullen said that Kandahar was as important to the overall war effort in Afghanistan as Baghdad was to the US surge in Iraq.[54]

While the Iraq surge provided one example of how to achieve success and remained a key theme in the military's overall discourse on Afghanistan, there was also an indigenous example that eventually emerged and was used to highlight how the tactics employed in Iraq could be successfully applied to Afghanistan. Since 2009, prior to Obama's December announcement, US forces based in the Nawa district of Helmand province had reportedly employed the "population-centric" tactics and force levels advocated in FM 3-24. The result was a significant drop in Taliban activity in the area, to such an extent, in fact, that Nawa was held up as the new "model" and a "proof of concept." McChrystal reportedly told his aides that Nawa had become his "number one Petri dish."[55] Unfortunately, given the disproportionately high force levels involved, the Nawa success could only be replicated in limited doses elsewhere.

At the time General McChrystal was fired in June 2010, the additional forces ordered the previous December were still several months away from arriving. Indeed, when Petraeus replaced McChrystal, the Afghan surge had not yet taken full effect. In order to explain the reasons the Afghan surge seemed to be having little impact, the issue of troop deployment timelines became an important excuse. Moreover, Petraeus was confident that just as the Iraq surge had initially been criticized, a similar transformation to a success was also possible in Afghanistan. For example, in his conversation with one journalist who complained about the ongoing high levels of violence, Petraeus noted that whereas there had only been 6 incidents in Iraq that day, there were roughly 220 a day in 2007. It was only in late September 2010 that Petraeus noted "only now do we have all the right inputs in place," even though it would be a further two months before the final component of the "surge" arrived in Afghanistan and all the "necessary resources" were in place.[56]

According to Ryan Crocker, the US ambassador in Iraq during the time of the surge, later appointed as ambassador in Afghanistan, "There are some interesting parallels. I think the surge strategy, if you will, in Afghanistan is modeled after the surge strategy in Iraq. I think it is absolutely essential. I think efforts such as the arming of concerned local citizens has parallels. But they are also fundamentally different places. Afghanistan, if anything, is even harder than Iraq was."[57] Despite recognizing the limitations of using the Iraq analogy in relation to Afghanistan, Petraeus and many other civilian and military officials referred to it constantly. For example, after his appointment as the new commander in Afghanistan, Petraeus described his strategy at a White House meeting and, while doing so, repeatedly referred to Iraq. One National Security Council staffer observed that he made more than two dozen references to Iraq in a single hour. The strategy itself, which he referred to as the "Anaconda strategy," was imported from his experience in Iraq, and the PowerPoint slide in which the strategy was laid out was nearly identical.[58] Moreover, one of Petraeus's favorite comments in Afghanistan, based on his Iraq experience, was that it was "all about getting the inputs right." In other words, there was one general set of counterinsurgency best practices to be applied universally, and the only question was about resourcing them.[59] Even before Petraeus took command in Afghanistan, he argued in favor of an "Anaconda strategy," noting that such strategies and tactics had helped in Iraq and could work again in Afghanistan. Nevertheless, Petraeus added the caveat that it was essential to take into account the cultural differences between the two conflicts. Specifically, Petraeus noted that whereas Iraq had a strong central authority, Afghanistan didn't. Also, rather than US troops moving into an Afghan village, as they might have done in Iraq, it was necessary instead to move on the edge of it.[60] Incidentally, Petraeus was not the only one who employed the Iraq analogy. One Canadian officer observed that "for the first few months after he arrived, almost every member of his new team in ISAF headquarters would drop the phrase, 'in Iraq we . . . ' into conversations" and complained that this was "a recipe for disaster in Afghanistan."[61]

Among the Iraq initiatives Petraeus tried to replicate in Afghanistan was the "Sons of Iraq" program in which the United States supported local defense forces. Yet such initiatives had also been tried before but had not met with any success. As one senior officer complained, "none of the conditions for the Sunni Awakening existed in Afghanistan."[62] Moreover, unlike the "Sons of Iraq," the Afghan units would not be composed of insurgents who had switched sides; rather, they would be unemployed villagers who were desperate for jobs.[63] Again, based on the Iraq analogy, it was assumed that such tactics could help counter the insurgency, and therefore a great deal of effort was put into standing these units up regardless of the distinctions between the two conflicts.[64]

As the 18-month period elapsed, two competing official views of the surge emerged. According to one Defense Department report, "the surge in US and coalition forces that arrived in Afghanistan throughout 2010 is responsible for much of the progress seen over the last six months."[65] A year later, one commentator observed that "by the spring 2011, top commanders believed they had a winning argument to forestall the drawdown. They pointed to Nawa, Garmser, Arghandab and Zhari to argue that the surge was working."[66] Petraeus similarly argued that the surge had been successful—defined as halting the Taliban's momentum—but that it was "fragile and reversible" if the United States failed to keep up the pressure.[67] As such, he advocated against drawing down

American forces, or, to the extent they did have to be withdrawn, he wished this could occur slowly. The alternative view of the surge was that while it had worked locally, particularly in southern Afghanistan where the bulk of troops had been deployed, it did not have a nationwide effect as originally envisaged. Moreover, the situation was perceived to have deteriorated rather than improved from what it had been in 2009. This was the dominant view in the US intelligence community, albeit the military attempted on numerous occasions to downplay their gloomier assessments.[68]

On June 22, 2011, Obama announced the withdrawal of the 33,000 US troops, thereby "fully recovering the surge I announced at West Point," with the remainder of US combat forces to be withdrawn by the end of 2014.[69] By making this announcement, Obama had effectively overruled Petraeus and other American generals who had wanted to retain those troops for a longer period.[70] Despite Petraeus's attempts to highlight the success of the Afghan surge, he wanted to retain the additional combat troops for a longer period. Indeed, similar to the Iraq surge, maintaining large numbers of troops over the next few years was deemed essential to ensuring the gains made in the course of the surge were irreversible. However, for the White House, many officials believed the surge had been a failure, but for political reasons, Obama's troop drawdown had to be cast in a favorable light. Therefore rather than admit that the surge was unsuccessful, the president's top advisers were obliged to publicly highlight that the "surge worked."[71]

Conclusion

As this chapter has attempted to demonstrate, the surge constitutes yet another discourse trap into which the US military has fallen, one that had an impact at the strategic, operational, and tactical levels of war. As of the time of writing, the 33,000 "surge" troops are in the midst of being withdrawn from Afghanistan. In some respects, it is notable that political-military discussions in 2011 of how many troops to withdraw from Afghanistan was based on the idea that the number to be withdrawn was precisely the number that had been added as part of Obama's December 2009 decision. Thus, by September 2012, immediately prior to the US presidential election, only those forces that were added to Afghanistan after December 2009 were to be withdrawn, whereas the number of forces that entered Afghanistan prior to this period would be withdrawn by 2015. In this case, military considerations were less relevant than being able to demonstrate for political reasons that the surge had ended. While the impact of this withdrawal, be it positive or negative, is yet to be determined, the correlation between the nature of the withdrawal and the discourse of the surge is clearly observable.

Since the time the discourse of a surge emerged in the American policy discussions on Iraq in late 2006, it has had a profound impact on the wars in Iraq and Afghanistan and more generally on the US military as a whole. However, the idea of sending more US troops to Iraq was not a new one when Bush decided to endorse it in late 2006; rather it had existed almost since the start of the "insurgency" in mid-2003 but had previously been rejected in favor of a "stand up, stand down" strategy. It was not until the political circumstances changed, and the idea became acceptable, at least to Bush, that the surge discourse was finally operationalized. But it was only when the surge was perceived as a success that the discourse became institutionalized and subsequently became a trap, at least insofar as it was then applied to Afghanistan. Indeed, it is worth considering how the surge discourse would have emerged had the Iraq surge not been perceived as a success. Put another way, had violence levels not declined, or had the surge been perceived as either having no effect or even resulting in higher levels of violence, it is almost certain the idea of surging US troops into Afghanistan would have had little or no support. Similarly, even within the success narrative, had the emphasis been placed on indigenous factors—namely, the impact of AQI excesses as the main reason Sunni "insurgents" decided to change sides—rather than the stress placed on exogenous factors, particularly the increase in US troop levels, changes to US tactics, and superior generalship, the applicability of the Iraq surge to Afghanistan may have had less appeal.

Curiously, similar to the Bush decision to "surge" in Iraq, applying the "surge" to Afghanistan was not an idea that transferred automatically. Until the political and military circumstances changed in 2009, so that military forces were becoming available and Obama was willing to consider increasing the number of forces deployed to Afghanistan, even surge advocates such as Petraeus had played down this prospect. Thus, on the one hand, while playing up the Iraq success, reasons had to be found why repeating the surge in Afghanistan was a bad idea. This trap applied to both the military and the politicians. For the military, especially Petraeus, conducting a surge in Afghanistan in 2008 would have meant massive reductions in the number of US forces still stationed in Iraq. Had these massive reductions occurred at that time, there was always a risk that the security gains could have been reversed, thereby undermining the success. For Obama, the success narrative, combined with his own rhetorical emphasis on Afghanistan as the necessary war, made it politically difficult to choose any course other than the one he eventually did. By the 2009 White House strategy review, the Iraq success narrative had become dominant not only within the military but also throughout the policy community and among the public more broadly. Consequently, advocates for policies other than a surge, most notably Biden's emphasis on a more limited counterterrorism approach, were fighting an uphill battle against the dominant discourse. By that time, the US military's attachment to and institutionalization of the surge discourse had the effect of crowding out alternative concepts in its approach to Afghanistan. Having found its winning formula, the key issue for the military became one of obtaining the resources to execute it, rather than questioning its applicability in the context of a different conflict.

Looking ahead toward the expected drawdown of US combat troops in Afghanistan by 2015, the potential exists for the military to blame perceived suboptimal outcomes on a lack of resources, which in turn will be attributed to limited political will, rather than flaws in the formula. On the other hand, for as long as it serves both political and military interests, the success of both the Iraq and Afghan surges is likely to be touted, as well as the counterinsurgency doctrine associated with it. This does not mean that another large-scale military intervention will therefore be likely in the near future. On the contrary, advocates for such interventions will have to compete with nonmilitary discourses that have begun to emerge, especially with regards to the need to fight less costly wars in the future. In other words, despite its success, neither Iraq nor Afghanistan will likely serve as a model anytime soon. As Gates warned Army cadets in February 2011, "in my opinion, any future defense secretary who advises the president to again send a big American land army into Asia or into the Middle East or Africa should have his head examined." Instead, he suggested that one of the benefits to be derived from the withdrawal of US forces from Afghanistan would be the "opportunity to conduct the kind of full-spectrum training—including mechanized combined arms exercises—that was neglected to meet the demands of the current wars."[72] In the event this occurs, an emphasis on conventional war may gradually marginalize the more recent stress placed on counterinsurgency, at least insofar as mainstream US military units are concerned.

Meanwhile, a separate discourse is also gradually emerging that may soon become the new dominant discourse in relation to the waging of "overseas contingency operations" against "terrorists." At the time of writing, with the military drawdown in Afghanistan, combined with war fatigue, the success of the Special Forces mission that killed Bin Laden, advances in drone technology, as well as the increasing strategic focus on Asia, the notion that an effective alternative exists to large-scale counterinsurgency is becoming increasingly dominant. This alternative would rely mainly on small-scale combinations of intelligence officers, Special Forces, and drones to target "terrorist networks." However, as noted in an earlier chapter, this approach to counterterrorism is not new. Instead, it has been the approach employed throughout the Global War on Terror, whereas it was only in Iraq and Afghanistan that large-scale conventional forces have borne the burden. Nevertheless, while the discourse on the relative "attractiveness" of employing drones and Special Forces may be more consistent with the nonmilitary discourse that stresses waging "cheap wars," it may also be the case that in the years ahead, a more critical discourse will emerge in which questions are raised about whether these "counterterrorism" techniques, which are hardly problem free, are making matters worse rather than better. As of late 2012, it is still too early to tell whether this critical discourse will eventually come to dominate US military policy, but the possibility certainly exists. Even so, just as earlier discourses took years to emerge, become institutionalized and dominant, and then fade away, so too will it almost certainly take years for a new critical discourse to emerge and displace the newly emerging dominant discourse.

CHAPTER 6

Conclusion

On July 27, 2009, the US Special Representative for Afghanistan and Pakistan, Richard C. Holbrooke, met with General McChrystal. In the course of this meeting, Holbrooke phoned Vietnam historian Stanley Karnow and then handed the phone to McChrystal. McChrystal asked Karnow what lessons were learned in Vietnam that could be applied to Afghanistan. Karnow replied, "We learned that we shouldn't have been there in the first place."[1] This anecdote is notable for three important reasons. First, the idea that Vietnam was analogous to Afghanistan and could offer lessons was assumed from the outset. Second, the view Karnow expressed might have warned against the strategy McChrystal would shortly thereafter argue in favor of—namely, to increase the US military presence in Afghanistan. Last, McChrystal's reaction to Karnow's warning was essentially to dismiss it, since presumably the strategic rationale for being in Afghanistan could not be questioned. Instead, his interest was limited to Vietnam lessons that could be applied at the operational and tactical level.

At the time of the autumn 2009 White House strategy review, senior US policy makers employed the Vietnam analogy on numerous occasions but also sought to avoid using it. The way in which this historical analogy was used, and which aspects of the analogy that were deemed relevant, also varied considerably depending on one's view of the present situation. For instance, at the start of one of these strategy meetings, Holbrooke compared the decision Obama would need to make about surging troops in Afghanistan with Lyndon Johnson and the Vietnam escalation. However, Obama cut Holbrooke off, not wanting to hear about Vietnam.[2] There was also a generational issue with regards to how Vietnam was viewed. Unlike Holbrooke, Obama and many of the younger members of the administration dismissed the analogy, officially at least. According to Obama, "you never step into the same river twice. And so Afghanistan is not Vietnam." Yet even while rejecting the analogy, Obama and other senior officials were reportedly reading books about Vietnam so that they wouldn't repeat the same mistakes. Two issues Obama noted in relation to the "lessons" of Vietnam were the "dangers of overreach and not having clear goals and not having strong support from the American people." Among other issues, these officials were also interested in the Johnson administration's decision making in relation to the 1965 escalation and the problem of how civilians dealt with the military.[3]

Throughout the strategy review, the way in which the Vietnam analogy was employed reflects a fundamental aspect of the discourse trap—namely, that there were limits to what was considered acceptable debate. In other words, the fundamental problem of Vietnam was well known, but this was not a topic that could be addressed in relation to Afghanistan, much less acknowledged as having validity. Indeed, this phenomenon is similar to other examples of the Vietnam analogy that have been highlighted in earlier chapters of this book, in which present-day officials understood the problems of Vietnam yet continued to repeat the same mistakes at the same time they were consciously aware and warning of them. While it is tempting to characterize this type of behavior in psychological terms, perhaps ascribing it to cognitive dissonance or masochism, the fact remains that in each of these cases officials were constrained in their action, usually because some alternative discursive construct took precedence, such as emphasizing "success" or "progress," or showing one's "toughness" out of fear of a loss of "credibility." Therefore, what in retrospect, if not at the time, might have been considered a more sensible strategy, was simply not considered acceptable to be discussed, with officials preferring self-censorship rather than speaking out of turn. It is these types of discursive constructs that can guide strategy in particular directions and place limits on certain types of actions.

This phenomenon should not be limited to the American system alone, much less only to states. Indeed, the same phenomenon is also observable with nonstate actors. For example, in the months preceding his death, Osama Bin Laden wrote a letter suggesting a name change for al-Qaeda. The reason for doing so was that Bin Laden felt the name *al-Qaeda*, which translates as "the base," was not religious enough, and he wanted to reinforce the message that the group was at war with the enemies of Islam. He was also concerned that the actions of affiliated groups had tarnished the al-Qaeda brand. In this letter, Bin Laden complained that although the formal title of his group was *al-Qaeda al-Jihad*, or "the base for jihad," the last part was often omitted. As possible alternatives, Bin Laden suggested changing the name to "Taifat al-Tawheed Wal-Jihad" (Monotheism and Jihad Group), or "Jama'at I'Adat al-Khilafat al-Rashida" (Restoration of the Caliphate Group).[4] Had Bin Laden lived, it is interesting to speculate whether or not he would have changed the name, but most likely he would have found that to do so risked considerable opposition from both his own subordinates and the affiliated groups. It is also interesting to speculate in the event the name was changed, whether the United States would then start referring to a "war on Taifat al-Tawheed Wal-Jihad" instead of a "war on al-Qaeda"? At the very least, one suspects this would cause some problems for policy makers in Washington.

It might seem odd to end this study with these recent US and non-US examples. However, all these cases highlight a key point about the discourse trap—namely, that similar examples can be offered from a range of domestic and foreign state and nonstate actors. While I am not necessarily arguing that the way in which the discourse trap affected the US military after 9/11 offers a universal theory for explaining the way political and military systems' approaches to war are driven by language and the range of acceptable debate, it is crucial to recognize the important role this plays in varying contexts.

In developing the concept of the discourse trap, I have tried to challenge the prevailing views of language within War Studies and move it from the margins of the field into the mainstream. Rather than being viewed mainly as a component of propaganda or public affairs, in which language is developed and employed in the waging of war, it is also important to view language as constituting war and being constituted by war. A key aspect to this distinction is the expansion of our conception of the audience for this language: the audience is not necessarily a foreign government or population, or a domestic constituency. Whether intended or unintended, the military itself may be the audience. For instance, many of the technical terms employed within a bureaucracy can constitute a language in its own right and are developed with only the bureaucratic audience in mind. On the other hand, even if intended for an external audience, political language can also be internalized. When examining military behavior, studying the language employed by defense officials in their internal discourse during wartime can offer a nonmaterial explanation of suboptimal military outcomes. As the case studies examined in this book demonstrate, comprehending the way language was employed, understood, and considered important within the Department of Defense (DoD) is a key component to explaining why and how the military system functioned in the way it did. In this final chapter, I will discuss several important conceptual conclusions that can be reached about the nature of the discourse trap. The chapter will then conclude by exploring possible ways of mitigating the effects of the discourse trap.

Conceptual Conclusions

In many fields, it is accepted that discourse can function as a structural constraint, although this is not a thoroughly examined notion in War Studies. This study has sought to expand the attention paid to the discourses employed by political and military systems in war. It is important to recognize that regardless of whether a discourse is viewed positively or negatively, it still constrains options by limiting the scope of actions available to policy makers to achieve a particular outcome. By studying how discourse acts as a constraint on policy—and in some cases, an enabler of policy—it may be possible for scholars to shed greater light on the centrality of discourse to war in a manner that has yet to be addressed in the academic literature.

For a number of scholars, discourse is everything. However, this study has tried to strike a balance between overemphasizing and underemphasizing the relevance of discourse to the field. Among many scholars of discourse, there is at least an appreciation for the importance of the nondiscursive (or material), and it is not the intention of this study to argue that nondiscursive aspects of war are unimportant. Rather, the intention is to demonstrate that just as defense policy makers are constrained by material capabilities, the nature of the political system they operate within, and so forth, they are also constrained by language. In contrast to theories of international relations and decision making that assume bureaucrats are immune from being socialized in the same rhetoric provided to outside audiences and therefore speak, think, and act in a distinctive "language of power," the empirical evidence presented in the case studies suggests this is not necessarily the case. Within bureaucracies, terminology can often take on a life of its own, acquiring meanings, audiences, and uses for which it was not intended.

As a number of cases provided in this study highlight, there are reasons certain terms are avoided within the bureaucracy, and there is often a history associated with the process in which these terms are delegitimized. In the course of this process, the advantages and disadvantages of using a term are deliberated on, and a decision is made to employ the term, avoid employing it, or find a compromise alternative. However, in many instances, the process of choosing terminology doesn't account for the unintended consequences that can occur, often because the short-term political benefits of employing certain language are perceived as more relevant than identifying the potential longer-term consequences.

Another aspect of the "discourse trap" that deserves critical investigation is those cases where the use of certain terminology has only limited or no consequences at all. For instance, upon labeling North Korea as one of the three countries in the "Axis of Evil," there was no military action taken in the way it was in Iraq or with other Global War on Terrorism (GWOT) military interventions. A number of explanations can be offered, but perhaps the most important one relative to the discourse trap is that neither the bureaucracy nor political elites had any serious interest in waging a war against North Korea. In order for a discourse trap to function, especially as it relates to defense policy, the discourse must be perceived as serious and legitimate and also serve the interests of both politicians and the bureaucracy. In terms of the GWOT, North Korea was never considered a serious priority, at least not one to be dealt with by military intervention, most likely because the US military had neither the interest nor the capabilities to fight a major war on the Korean peninsula given its substantial commitment of forces in Iraq and Afghanistan. It is highly unlikely US political elites had any significant interest in a war with North Korea either. A similar explanation might also be tested in the case of Iran, but this is best left for a future study.

Despite the popularity of terms such as *war on terror*, the language of war cannot be reduced to political language, or, to be more specific, the language used by politicians. It was not politicians who developed terms such as *effects-based operations* and *Revolution in Military Affairs*, yet these terms have enjoyed a prominent place in the American defense discourse. These terms and their associated concepts were invented by the military for internal consumption, albeit possibly to "sell" to an external audience (Congress). Only after they were developed internally did they take on new audiences (defense industry and politicians) and uses (marketing for military equipment). This study has therefore sought to highlight the relevance of military terminology, as well as political terminology, within the DoD's overall internal discourse.

The discourse trap also has a multinational dimension that is quite relevant for the study of war. In terms of gaining foreign support, one country may try to influence the discourse of another country, which can include highlighting certain terminology. During the Cold War, a number of countries emphasized their anticommunist credentials and/or highlighted the communist credentials of their opponents. In the case of the British in Malaya, the term *Communist terrorists* was developed by Whitehall for the purpose of gaining US support. Since most Americans had initially framed the conflict as one internal to the British Empire, and therefore one they were unwilling to support, British officials perceived it necessary to frame the conflict in Cold War terms, which the Americans viewed more favorably.[5] As has been noted in the case studies, in the aftermath of 9/11, many US allies have requested support in the name of counterterrorism, often by classifying their opponents as terrorists. Even though before 9/11 the United States considered many of these groups as local insurgents, after 9/11, officials started classifying them as terrorists.

In the next several years, as the United States withdraws from Afghanistan, it may well find itself trapped in its own rhetoric that served as justification for the sacrifices made since 9/11, although it could well be argued it has reached this point already, and will be forced to continue prosecuting a conflict that bears little objective relation to combating the "terror threat" that was the justification for the intervention in the first place. In the case of the discourses employed in contemporary US operations, the range of unintended consequences is quite extensive, but many of these will likely only become apparent after the conflicts end and the official records are opened. Nevertheless, preliminary evidence suggests there will be an abundance of cases to investigate, thereby further expanding upon the base of the discourse trap this study has sought to build.

The Way Ahead

This study has attempted to establish and raise awareness of the discourse trap in the War Studies field, in part for the purpose of informing policy and the study of policy. It has not been the purpose of this study to suggest there are any solutions to this problem. Thus far, it has been a descriptive study, rather than prescriptive. Nevertheless, having identified the discourse trap as a problem, policy makers who have an interest in the subject will probably be unwilling to accept a *fait accompli* and will seek ways of avoiding or mitigating the effects of this phenomenon. For the purpose of informing the public policy debate, and beginning to lay the groundwork for future research in this area, a few words should now be said regarding approaches to managing the discourse trap.

A number of observers have noted the negative effects that result when inappropriate terminology dominates the discourse on an issue and becomes immune to serious challenge. For instance, referring to the "unsubstantiated clichés" that dominated the US discourse on "transformation," Antulio J. Echevarria observed,

> Unfortunately, when phrases are repeated frequently enough, they begin to sound true. In policy circles, where haste often is by necessity the order of the day, that poor basis can suffice to justify any number of decisions. Clichés and catchwords are merely handy ways of capturing and conveying truths; they may reveal a lack of imagination on the part of the user, but they are hardly dangerous. Unsubstantiated clichés, however, are another matter. They can masquerade as truths and, unless exposed in time, ultimately prove costly and harmful to policy . . . Only by regularly challenging the many expressions we take for granted can we avoid wasting ever-scarce resources, and keep our military transformation on course.[6]

Coping with the discourse trap requires a similar approach to Echevarria's call for "regularly challenging the many expressions we take for granted." By being aware that language can have unintended consequences, and perhaps by taking greater care in selecting terminology, the effects of the "discourse trap" can be mitigated. As the example of the taboo on "insurgency" demonstrates, restricting terminology can also restrict action. Had US policy makers recognized the unintended consequences of imposing the taboo, they could at least have performed an expected utility analysis to determine whether the short-term benefits of the terminology taboo outweighed the long-term consequences of not officially recognizing the conflict for what it was and responding accordingly.

The impact of 9/11 on the DoD raises a fundamental point about escaping the discourse trap—namely, that changing a discourse may be determined by external factors such as political, geopolitical, economic, or military shifts. As mentioned earlier, the China threat discourse that pervaded the DoD prior to 9/11 was marginalized in favor of the GWOT discourse, although the former has not disappeared completely and now appears to be making a comeback as the US military withdraws from Afghanistan and is looking to the future. Change can also occur within a discourse. In the 2008 presidential election, although both candidates were caught within the GWOT discourse trap, there was an attempt by the Democrats to contest the content of the GWOT by arguing that Afghanistan was the central front in the war on terror, rather than Iraq. Regardless of whether Iraq or Afghanistan constituted the more important theater, the broader GWOT remained institutionalized as the central national security issue.

Ultimately, it is doubtful political and military systems can ever fully escape from the discourse trap. Such is the magnitude of discursive entrapments—which can range from the discourse of defense policy makers to the discourse of private soldiers and even further afield to legislators, the media, industry, and the public—that it is almost impossible either to control language or to grasp the consequences that result from its use. Enforcing discursive conformity on such a large organization as the DoD would appear to be a difficult endeavor. The difficulties notwithstanding, many attempts have been made to control the use of certain terminology, and some of these have been successful, as the case of *civil war* illustrated.

Even if it is not possible to escape from the discourse trap, the mere fact that the phenomenon's existence is recognized is probably the first step in finding ways of mitigating it. Admittedly, it is hardly preferable merely to wait for an external crisis, or deliberately to provoke one, in order for a shift in discourse to occur. Nor can it be assumed that one term is less harmful than the other and therefore all that needs to be done is to perform a calculation prior to choosing a term. Any methodology claiming to differentiate harmful terms from less harmful terms is bound to be suspect precisely because of the numerous variables that need to be taken into consideration. Thus if one had to choose between terms that signify the bland versus the emotive, the specific versus the general, there is little doubt each term would have its benefits and drawbacks. For political and military systems in particular, mitigating the discourse trap may necessitate greater discursive discipline when it comes to bandwagoning. The use of red teams that are given free range to say what other actors in an organization feel constrained in saying should also be encouraged. In most cases, though, these sorts of remedies are almost certainly to be insufficient. Instead, rather than attempting to find a solution, what is required is a perpetual awareness, to the extent this can be achieved, that discursive entrapment is a fact of life and that it needs to be taken into consideration along with numerous other factors that would normally be accounted for. Thus, paradoxically, mitigating the discourse trap requires that it should become a part of the mainstream discourse itself yet should not dominate discussion, lest it become its own trap and constrain action due to the fear that no matter what is said, negative consequences will result, and that therefore nothing should be said, much less done.

Notes

Chapter 1

1. John Shy and Thomas W. Collier, "Revolutionary War," in *Makers of Modern Strategy from Machiavelli to the Nuclear Age*, ed. Peter Paret et al. (Oxford: Clarendon Press, 1991), 821.
2. Robert Jervis, *Perception and Misperception in International Politics* (Princeton, NJ: Princeton University Press, 1976), 76–77.
3. Robert K. Merton, "The Unanticipated Consequences of Purposive Social Action," *American Sociological Review* 1 (1936): 894–904.
4. To take one example, for a discussion of the various uses of the term *discourse* within the work of Michel Foucault, see Sara Mills, *Michel Foucault* (London: Routledge, 2003), 53–66.
5. In terms of understanding the process of institutionalization and its legitimating effect on a discourse, the approach taken here imitates that which is used in relation to norms. See Andrew P. Cortell and James W. Davis Jr., "Understanding the Domestic Impact of International Norms: A Research Agenda," *International Studies Review* 2 (2000): 65–87.
6. Peter R. Neumann and M. L. R. Smith, "Missing the Plot? Intelligence and Discourse Failure," *Orbis* 49 (2005): 97–98.
7. Ole R. Holsti, *Public Opinion and American Foreign Policy* (Ann Arbor: University of Michigan Press, 2007), 55.
8. Yuen Foong Khong, *Analogies at War: Korea, Munich, Dien Bien Phu and the Vietnam Decisions of 1965* (Princeton, NJ: Princeton University Press, 1992).
9. Mark Schlesinger and Richard R. Lau, "The Meaning and Measure of Policy Metaphors," *American Political Science Review* 3 (2000): 611–26; Nancy Kanwisher, "Cognitive Heuristics and American Security Policy," *Journal of Conflict Resolution* 33 (1989): 652–75.
10. Keith Krause and Michael C. Williams, "Broadening the Agenda of Security Studies: Politics and Methods," *Mershon International Studies Review* 40 (1996): 215; Theodore R. Sarbin, "The Metaphor-to-Myth Transformation with Special Reference to the 'War on Terrorism,' Peace and Conflict," *Journal of Peace Psychology* 9 (2003): 149–57.
11. Slavoj Žižek, "What Rumsfeld Doesn't Know That He Knows about Abu Ghraib," *In These Times*, May 21, 2004.
12. William I. Thomas, *The Child in America* (New York: Alfred A. Knopf, 1928), 572.

13. Riikka Kuusisto, "Framing the Wars in the Gulf and in Bosnia: The Rhetorical Definitions of the Western leaders in Action," *Journal of Peace Research* 35 (1998): 603.
14. Michael Howard and Peter Paret, trans., *On War* (Norwalk, CT: Easton Press, 1991), 88–89.
15. Eric. A. Heinze, "The Rhetoric of Genocide in U.S. Foreign Policy: Rwanda and Darfur Compared," *Political Science Quarterly* 122 (2007): 359–84; "The Triumph of Evil: Transcript of Frontline Interview with Tony Marley, Political-Military Advisor for the US State Department from 1992–95," PBS, January 26, 1999; The Triumph of Evil: Transcript of Frontline Interview with Deputy Assistant Secretary for African Affairs James Woods at the Department of Defense from 1986–1994," PBS, January 26, 1999; Action memorandum from Assistant Secretary of State for African Affairs George E. Moose, Assistant Secretary of State for Democracy, Human Rights, and Labor John Shattuck, and Assistant Secretary of State, "Has Genocide Occurred in Rwanda?," May 21, 1994. Secret. http://www.gwu.edu/~nsarchiv/NSAEBB/NSAEBB53/index.html.
16. Robert H. Johnson, "Exaggerating America's Stakes in Third World Conflicts," *International Security* 10 (1985): 32–68; Thomas Trout, "Rhetoric Revisited: Political Legitimation and the Cold War," *International Studies Quarterly* 19 (1975): 251–84.
17. Leslie H. Gelb and Richard K. Betts, *The Irony of Vietnam: The System Worked* (Washington, DC: Brookings Institution, 1979), 242.
18. Snyder quoted in Peter J. Katzenstein, ed., *The Culture of National Security: Norms and Identity in World Politics* (New York: Columbia University Press, 1996), 27.
19. Jack Snyder, *Myths of Empire: Domestic Politics and International Ambition* (Ithaca, NY: Cornell University Press, Ithaca, 1991), 270–99.
20. Arendt, "Lying in Politics," 24–25; Harold P. Ford, "Unpopular Pessimism: Why CIA Analysts Were So Doubtful about Vietnam," *Studies in Intelligence* 1 (1997): 85–95; Gelb and Betts, *The Irony of Vietnam*, 190.
21. For more details, see Seth Jacobs, *Cold War Mandarin: Ngo Dinh Diem and the Origins of America's War in Vietnam 1950–1963* (New York: Rowman and Littlefield, 2006); Joseph G. Morgan, *The Vietnam Lobby: The American Friends of Vietnam 1955–1975* (Chapel Hill: The University of North Carolina Press, 1997); Jonathan Nashel, *Edward Lansdale's Cold War* (Boston: University of Massachusetts Press, 2005), 57–59.
22. Caroline Page, *US Official Propaganda during the Vietnam War, 1965–1973: The Limits of Persuasion* (London: Leicester University Press, 1996), 299, 303. D. Michael Shafer, "The Unlearned Lessons of Counter-insurgency," *Political Science Quarterly* 103 (1988): 57–80.
23. Jeffrey Record, *The Wrong War: Why We Lost in Vietnam* (Annapolis, MD: Naval Institute Press, 1998), 24.
24. Ibid.
25. Hans Morgenthau, "We Are Deluding Ourselves in Vietnam," *The New York Times Magazine*, April 18, 1965.
26. Record, *The Wrong War*, 28.

27. Larry Cable, *Unholy Grail: The US and the Wars in Vietnam 1965–1968* (London, Routledge, 1991), 5–6.
28. These quotes can be found in Harold P. Ford, *CIA and the Vietnam Policymakers: Three Episodes 1962–1968* (Washington, DC: CIA Center for the Study of Intelligence, 1998). For an insider account of the O/B controversy, see Sam Adams, *War of Numbers: An Intelligence Memoir* (South Royalton, VT: Steerforth Press, 1994).
29. Adams, *War of Numbers* (1994).
30. Hannah Arendt, *Crises of the Republic* (San Diego, CA: Harcourt Brace and Co., 1972), 7.

Chapter 2

1. Thomas P. Barnett, *The Pentagon's New Map: War and Peace in the 21st Century* (New York: Berkley Books, 2004), 104–6; Frederick W. Kagan, *Finding the Target: The Transformation of American Military Policy* (New York: Encounter Books, 2006), 310–22, 363–64; Andrew L. Ross, Michele A. Flournoy, Cindy Williams, and David Mosher, "What Do We Mean by 'Transformation?'" *Naval War College Review* 55 (2002): 27–42.
2. Maura Reynolds, "Bush to Seek $87 Billion for Effort in Iraq," *Los Angeles Times*, September 8, 2003.
3. Matthew J. Morgan, *The American Military after 9/11: Society, State and Empire* (New York: Palgrave Macmillan, 2008); Philip Gold, *The Coming Draft: The Crisis in Our Military and Why Selective Service Is Wrong for America* (New York: Balantine Books, 2006); Thom Shanker, "All Quiet on the Home Front, and Some Soldiers Are Asking Why," *The New York Times*, July 24, 2005.
4. Conrad Crane, "Facing the Hydra: Maintaining Strategic Balance while Pursuing a Global War against Terrorism," Monograph, *Strategic Studies Institute*, May 2002, 12.
5. Ibid., 17.
6. Donald H. Rumsfeld, "DoD News Briefing," September 20, 2001, http://www.defenselink.mil/transcripts/transcript.aspx?transcriptid=1901, accessed March 30, 2008.
7. "Interview with Secretary Donald Rumsfeld and Cal Thomas of Fox News Watch," News Transcript, Office of the Assistant Secretary of Defense (Public Affairs), December 7, 2006.
8. Ibid.
9. Ibid.
10. Myers cited in Eric Schmitt and Thom Shanker, "Washington Recasts Terror War as 'Struggle,'" *International Herald Tribune*, July 27, 2005.
11. Pamela Hess, "Terror War May Need Name Change," *United Press International*, September 5, 2006.
12. Rumsfeld, "Interview with Secretary Donald Rumsfeld and Cal Thomas of Fox News Watch."
13. Diane Jennings, "In Global Fight, Defining Enemies Not So Simple," *Dallas Morning News*, September 23, 2001.

14. Douglas J. Feith, *War and Decision: Inside the Pentagon at the Dawn of the War on Terrorism* (New York: Harper Collins, 2008), 9.
15. Ibid., 8.
16. Ibid., 50.
17. Ibid., 8.
18. Ibid., 9.
19. Grant R. Highland, "New Century, Old Problems: The Global Insurgency within Islam and the Nature of the War on Terror," Naval War College, February 3, 2003.
20. Memo cited in Ronald Wright, "From the Desk of Donald Rumsfeld," *Washington Post*, November 1, 2007.
21. Ibid.
22. Highland, "New Century, Old Problems."
23. George Packer, "Knowing the Enemy: Can Social Scientists Redefine the War on Terror," *The New Yorker*, December 18, 2006; David Kilcullen, "Countering Global Insurgency." *Journal of Strategic Studies* 28 (2005): 597–617.
24. Jim Garamone, "Life Is Not Predictable, Rumsfeld Tells New Army Officers," *American Forces Press Service*, May 29, 2004.
25. Boykin cited in Roxana Tiron, "Irregular Warfare: Counterinsurgency in Iraq Provides Template for Fighting Terrorism," *National Defense*, April 2005.
26. Roberts cited in Tiron, "Irregular Warfare."
27. Michael Sirak, "Meeting Demands of GWOT Still a Challenge, SOF Official Says," *C4I News*, July 6, 2006.
28. Joint Operational Concept cited in Thomas H. Johnson and James A. Russell, "A Hard Day's Night? The United States and the Global War on Terrorism," *Comparative Strategy* 24 (2005): 127–51.
29. All interviews were conducted in confidentiality and the names of interviewees are withheld by mutual agreement. Interview with senior US Army officer attached to the Office of the Deputy Director for the War on Terrorism, Joint Staff (J-5), March 29, 2008.
30. Cheek cited in Hess, "Terror War May Need Name Change."
31. Ibid.
32. Ibid.
33. Gavin Cameron, "Weapons of Mass Destruction Terrorism Research: Past and Future" in *An Introduction to Terrorism Research, in Research on Terrorism: Trends, Achievements and Failures*, ed. Andrew Silke (New York: Frank Cass, 2004), 72–90; Lawrence Freedman, *A Choice of Enemies: America Confronts the Middle East* (Doubleday Canada, 2008), 381–83.
34. Thomas R. Mockaitis, *The "New" Terrorism: Myths and Realities* (Stanford, CA: Stanford Security Studies, 2008); Isabelle Duyvesteyn, "How New Is the New Terrorism," *Studies in Conflict and Terrorism* 27 (2004): 439–54; Leonard Weinberg, Ami Pedahzur, and Sivan Hirsch-Hoefler, "The Challenges of Conceptualizing Terrorism," *Terrorism and Political Violence* 16 (2004): 777–94.
35. Timothy D. Hoyt, "Operational Limitations of Military Force in the Global War on Terrorism," Paper Prepared for the Annual Meeting of the American Political Science Association, September 2, 2004.

36. Richard Jackson, *Writing the War on Terrorism: Language, Politics, and Counter-Terrorism* (Manchester, UK: Manchester University Press, 2005), 156.
37. David C. Martin and John Walcott, *Best Laid Plans: The Inside Story of America's War against Terrorism* (New York: Harper and Row Publishers, 1988), 35–41.
38. Freedman, *A Choice of Enemies*, 4, 147–48; George P. Schultz, "Terrorism and the Modern World," Transcript of Secretary Shultz's Address, Department of State Bulletin, December 1, 1984; Richard C. Gross, "Weinberger on US Military Might against Adversaries," *United Press International*, January 14, 1986; Lou Cannon and David Hoffman, "US Officials Claim Unrest in Libya; Targets Said Chosen to Raise Discontent," *The Washington Post*, April 17, 1986; Norman D. Sandler, "Reagan: Terrorist 'Murder Inc.' at War against US," *United Press International*, July 8, 1985; Stuart Taylor Jr., "Reagan Sends Congress Four Bills Aimed at International Terrorism," *The New York Times*, April 27, 1984; Henry Trewhitt, "A New War—And New Risks," *US News and World Report*, April 28, 1986.
39. Richard Halloran, "Swift US Retribution for Terrorists Called Doubtful," *The New York Times*, February 3, 1981.
40. David C. Wills, *The First War on Terrorism: Counter-Terrorism Policy during the Reagan Administration* (Lanham, MD: Rowman and Littlefield Inc., 2003), 30.
41. Martin and Walcott, *Best Laid Plans*, 48–56.
42. Michael Getler, "Soviets and Terrorist Activity: World of Shadow and Shading," *The Washington Post*, February 7, 1981; Freedman, *A Choice of Enemies*, 379–80.
43. Wills, *The First War on Terrorism*, 42.
44. Vessey cited in ibid., 64.
45. Ibid., 42.
46. Tim Naftali, *Blind Spot: The Secret History of American Counterterrorism* (New York: Basic Books, 2005), 131–32.
47. Weinberger cited in Wills, *The First War on Terrorism*, 30.
48. Bryan Brumley, "Weinberger: Force Remains an Option to Fight Terrorism," *The Associated Press*, January 21, 1987; James Bennet, "Mission Improbable: War against Terrorism," *The Washington Monthly* 22 (1990): 22–32; Stephen Engelberg, "Washington Talk: The Bureaucracy; Tug and Pull over a Vacant Chart," *The New York Times*, December 31, 1987; Steven Emerson, "Bush's toothless war against terrorism," *US News & World Report*, October 31, 1988; Angus Deming, "How to Strike Back?" *Newsweek*, November 7, 1983; Walter Pincus, "Elite Secret US Unit Trains to Foil Terror," *The Washington Post*, February 7, 1982; Steven Emerson, "Stymied Warriors," *The New York Times*, November 13, 1988; Brad Knickerbocker, "A Cautious Battle against Terrorism," *The Christian Science Monitor*, December 12, 1984; David C. Morrison, "The 'Shadow War': The Air Attack on Libya," *The National Journal* 18 (1986): 1100–5.
49. Rice cited in Morrison, "The 'Shadow War,'" 1102.
50. Engelberg, "Washington Talk."
51. Michele L. Malvesti, "Explaining the United States' Decision to Strike Back at Terrorists," *Terrorism and Political Violence* 13 (2001): 85–100.
52. Morrison, "The 'Shadow War'"; Naftali, *Blind Spot*, 185.
53. Freedman, *A Choice of Enemies*, 175.

54. Bob Woodward, *Veil: The Secret Wars of the CIA 1981–1987* (New York: Simon and Schuster, 1990); Martin and Walcott, *Best Laid Plans*, 52–56. The full title for this document is "Soviet Support for International Terrorism and Revolutionary Violence."
55. Martin and Walcott, *Best Laid Plans*, 53.
56. Molly Moore, "Pentagon Publishes Profiles of International Terrorists; 'Know the Enemy,' Carlucci Says in Guide's Preface," *The Washington Post*, January 11, 1989; John Lichfield, "US Gives Freedom Fighters a Bad Name," *The Independent*, January 14, 1989.
57. Moore, "Pentagon Publishes Profiles of International Terrorists."
58. Douglas Waller, "Counter-Terrorism: Victim of Success?" *Newsweek*, July 5, 1993.
59. Brian Duffy, Richard J. Newman, David E. Kaplan, and Thomas Omestad, "The Price of Payback," *US News & World Report*, September 7, 1998.
60. Clinton cited in Yee-Kuang Heng, *War as Risk Management: Strategy and Conflict in an Age of Globalised Risks* (London: Routledge, Taylor and Francis Group, 2006), 92.
61. Thomas J. Badey, "US Counterterrorism: Change in Approach, Continuity in Policy," *Contemporary Security Strategy* 27 (2006): 308–24.
62. Cohen cited in *The 9/11 Commission Report, Final Report of the National Commission on Terrorist Attacks upon the United States* (New York: W. W. Norton, 2004), 121.
63. Shelton cited in ibid., 120.
64. Ibid., 120–21.
65. Ibid., 121.
66. George Tenet, *At the Center of the Storm: My Years at the CIA* (New York: Harper Collins Publishers, 2007), 130–31, 186; *The 9/11 Commission Report*, 197.
67. Richard A. Clarke, *Against All Enemies: Inside America's War on Terror* (Sydney: Free Press, 2004), 234.
68. Badey, "US Counterterrorism," 318–20.
69. Michael Cox, "From the Cold War to the War on Terror" in *The Globalization of World Politics: An Introduction to International Relations*, ed. John Baylis and Steve Smith (Oxford: Oxford University Press, 2005), 154.
70. George W. Bush, "Address to a Joint Session of Congress and the American People," September 20, 2001.
71. Ibid.
72. Memo from Rumsfeld to Myers and Pace, October 10, 2001, http://www.rumsfeld.com. Henceforth all Rumsfeld memos listed in the endnotes are derived from this source.
73. Feith, *War and Decision*, 55, 113–14.
74. See, for instance, Memo from Wolfowitz to Rumsfeld, "Using Special Forces on 'Our Side' of the Line," September 23, 2001. Interestingly, at this stage Wolfowitz referred to US involvement in Afghanistan as a covert operation involving only limited participation of US military forces.
75. Feith, *War and Decision*, 5.
76. Memo cited in ibid., 4.
77. Ibid., 3–5.
78. Memo cited in ibid., 4.

79. Ibid.
80. Ibid., 7–11, 570.
81. Ibid., 50.
82. Ibid., 51.
83. Bob Woodward, *Bush at War* (New York: Simon and Schuster, 2002).
84. Rumsfeld cited in Feith, *War and Decision*, 50.
85. Freedman, *A Choice of Enemies*, 7.
86. Feith, *War and Decision*; Jackson, *Writing the War on Terrorism*; Clarke, *Against All Enemies*.
87. Feith, *War and Decision*, 55.
88. Ibid.
89. Ibid., 66.
90. Ibid.
91. Ibid., 67.
92. Michael DeLong, *Inside CENTCOM: The Unvarnished Truth about the Wars in Afghanistan and Iraq* (Washington, DC: Regency Publishing, 2004), 35.
93. Memo from Rumsfeld to Bush, September 23, 2001.
94. Memo from Rumsfeld to Bush, "Strategic Thoughts," September 30, 2001.
95. Abzaid cited in Feith, *War and Decision*, 83.
96. Memo from Rumsfeld to Bush, "Strategic Thoughts."
97. Ibid.
98. Feith, *War and Decision*, 84.
99. Attachment to Memo from Rumsfeld, "Strategic Guidance for the Campaign against Terrorism," October 3, 2001.
100. Gareth Porter, "Document Recently Published about the Iraq War Decisions; Pentagon Targeted Iran for Regime Change after 9/11," *IPS*, May 6, 2008.
101. Email correspondence with senior US Army War College academic, April 16, 2008.
102. Ibid.
103. Feith, *War and Decision*, 652.
104. Richard L. Berke and Thom Shanker, "As Guns Still Blaze, Bush Aides Debate Shifting Focus to Butter," *The New York Times*, December 2, 2001; Paul West, "Keeping Focus on Fighting Terror; President Warns against Letdown amid Successes," *The Baltimore Sun*, January 30, 2002; Thomas B. Edsall, "GOP Touts War as Campaign Issue; Bush Adviser Infuriates Democrats with Strategy Outlined at RNC Meeting," *The Washington Post*, January 19, 2002; Richard L. Berke, "Political Memo; A High-Profile Speech Poses Knotty Challenges," *The New York Times*, January 28, 2002.
105. Freedman, *A Choice of Enemies*, 403.
106. Email correspondence with senior US Army War College academic, April 16, 2008.
107. Freedman, *A Choice of Enemies*, 386–87.
108. Brian McAllister Linn, *The Echo of Battle: The Army's Way of War* (Cambridge MA: Harvard University Press, 2007), 1.
109. Feith, *War and Decision*, 86–87.
110. Memo from Rumsfeld to Bush, "Framing the War," June 7, 2004.

111. Memo from Cambone to Rumsfeld, "Framing the War," May 25, 2004.
112. Memo from Rumsfeld to Bush, "Global War on Terror," June 18, 2004.
113. Rumsfeld paper, "What Are We Fighting? Is It a Global War on Terror?" June 18, 2004. This document can be accessed at http://www.rumsfeld.com.
114. Donald H. Rumsfeld, "Speech Delivered at Council on Foreign Relations," News Transcript, Office of the Assistant Secretary of Defense for Public Affairs, October 4, 2004; Donald H. Rumsfeld, "Speech to World Affairs Council," May 25, 2005.
115. Myers cited in Schmitt and Shanker, "Washington Recasts Terror War."
116. Ibid.
117. Susan B. Glasser, "Review May Shift Terror Policies: US Is Expected to Look beyond Al Qaida," *The Washington Post*, May 29, 2005; Richard W. Stevenson, "President Makes It Clear: Phrase Is 'War on Terror,'" *The New York Times*, August 4, 2005; Matthew David, "New Name for War on Terror," *BBC*, July 27, 2005.
118. Di Rita cited in Schmitt and Shanker, "Washington Recasts Terror War."
119. Ibid.
120. Di Rita cited in Stevenson, "President Makes It Clear."
121. Ibid.
122. Conway cited in Sandra Erwin, "Defense Department Rhetoric Reflects War Frustrations," *National Defense*, September 1, 2005.
123. Memo from Rumsfeld to Hadley, "Nature of the Long Struggle," August 4, 2006; Donald H. Rumsfeld, "Air Force War College," US Department of Defense Speeches, October 18, 2006; Donald H. Rumsfeld, "Landon Lecture," November 9, 2006, http://www.k-state.edu/media/newsreleases/landonlect/rumsfeldtext1106.html.
124. For some examples of Abizaid's references to *long war* during this period, see Bradley Graham and Josh White, "Abizaid Credited with Popularizing the Term 'Long War,'" *The Washington Post*, February 3, 2006; John Valceanu, "Abizaid: War on Terror Requires Patience, Perseverance," *American Forces Press Service*, February 17, 2005; Samantha Quigley, "War in Iraq Moving in the Right Direction, Says CENTCOM Leader," *American Forces Press Service*, September 26, 2004; Donna Miles, "Terror War Strategy Goes beyond Iraq and Afghanistan," *American Forces Press Service*, November 29, 2005.
125. Richard Schultz, "Global Insurgency and Counterinsurgency: United States Plans and Strategy for the 'Long War,'" Fletcher School, Tufts University, 2007; Ehsan M. Ahrari, "Why the Long War Can and Cannot be Compared to the Cold War," *Comparative Strategy* 26 (2007): 275–84.
126. Memo from Rumsfeld to Pace et al., "Public Affairs Effort," October 5, 2005.
127. Jason Sherman, "Abizaid Key in Persuading Senior Leaders to Adopt 'Long War' Label," *Inside the Pentagon*, February 2, 2006.
128. Josh White and Ann Scott Tyson, "Rumsfeld Offers Strategies for Current War: Pentagon to Release 20-Year Plan Today," *The Washington Post*, February 3, 2006.
129. George W. Bush, "State of the Union Address by President George W. Bush," January 31, 2006.
130. Pentagon, "Long War" Briefings. These briefings can be accessed at www.dtic.mil/ndia/2006psa_psts/schiss.pdf; www.msstate.edu/dept/isss/2006/Sullivan_Long_War_Brief_v2.pdf; www.itaa.org/upload/es/docs/Goldfein%20Presentation.pdf; and www.wilsoncenter.org/index.cfm?fuseaction=events.event_summary&event_id=172045.

131. Cited in "Quotes from AP Interview with Abizaid," *USA Today*, September 11, 2007.
132. Pace cited in Steven D. Smith, "Chairman Cites Continued Progress in Afghanistan, Iraq," *American Forces Press Service*, February 17, 2006.
133. Lute cited in Peter Spiegel, "All Agree Insurgents are Overwhelmingly Domestic, Sunni and Nationalist," *The Financial Times*, January 29, 2005.
134. Henry cited in Simon Tisdall and Ewen MacAskill, "America's Long War," *The Guardian*, February 15, 2006.
135. Odierno cited in Jim Garamone, "Military Culture Must Change to Fight 'Long War,'" *American Forces Press Service*, January 23, 2006.
136. Odierno cited in Jim Garamone, "Americans Must Understand US Is at War, General Says," *American Forces Press Service*, January 18, 2006.
137. Mark T. Berger and Douglas A. Borer, "The Long War: Insurgency, Counterinsurgency, and Collapsing States," *Third World Quarterly* 28 (2007): 197–215.
138. "DoD Capstone Capabilities Briefing: Quadrennial Defense Review Results," February 3, 2006, www.defenselink.mil/qdr/report/Pressbriefing3FebFINAL2.ppt.
139. Bob Woodward, *The War Within: A Secret White House History 2006–2008* (New York: Simon and Schuster, 2008), 167–68.
140. Schoomaker cited in Ibid., 173.
141. Memo from Rumsfeld to Hadley, "Nature of the Long Struggle," August 4, 2006.
142. US Congress. Senate. Committee on the Budget, "The Global War on Terror (GWOT): Costs, Cost Growth and Estimating Funding Requirements, Testimony of Steven M. Kosiak," February 6, 2007.
143. Brigadier General Mark Schissler, "Joint Staff Briefing," 2006, http://www.dtic.mil/ndia/2006psa_psts/schiss.pdf.
144. Graham and White, "Abizaid Credited."
145. Michael Vlahos, "The Long War: A Self-fulfilling Prophecy of Protracted Conflict and Defeat," *The National Interest*, September 5, 2006.
146. Thomas Barnett, "The Man between War and Peace," *Esquire*, April 1, 2008; Philip H. Gordon, "Can the War on Terror Be Won?" *Foreign Affairs* 86 (2007): 53–66; Robert F. Dorr, "GWOT or not? The term isn't important, but the facts are," *Army Times*, October 29, 2007; Demetri Sevastopulo, "Security Chief Decries 'War on Terror,'" *The Financial Times*, May 29, 2007.
147. Ian Roxborough, "Globalization, Unreason and the Dilemmas of American Military Strategy," *International Sociology* 17 (2002): 339–59.
148. Chris Johnson, "Navy Establishes Cell for Submarine Counter-terrorism Operations," *Inside the Navy*, April 3, 2006; Carl Hulse, "Threats and Responses: Plans and Criticisms; Pentagon Prepares a Futures Market on Terror Attacks," *The New York Times*, July 29, 2003; Francis Raven and Carolyn Kousky, "Name Game; Defense Department Renames Total Information Awareness, Does Little Else," *In These Times*, July 8, 2003.
149. David von Drehle, "Rumsfeld's Transformation: There's Been a Small Change in Plan," *The Washington Post*, February 12, 2006.
150. Interview with senior US Army officer attached to the Office of the Deputy Director for the War on Terrorism, Joint Staff (J-5), March 29, 2008.
151. Eric Schmitt, "Pentagon Draws Up a 20-to-30-Year Anti-Terror Plan," *The New York Times*, January 17, 2003.

152. William M. Arkin, "Rumsfeld's New War Plan," *The Washington Post*, January 25, 2006.
153. Schmitt, "Pentagon Draws Up."
154. Donald H. Rumsfeld, "Defense Department News Briefing," October 16, 2003.
155. Ibid.; More than a year earlier, Rumsfeld had requested a "scorecard for the global war on terrorism," noting that Bush had asked for this six months previously. See memo from Rumsfeld to Feith "Scorecard," June 20, 2002.
156. Feith cited in Linda Robinson, "Plan of Attack," *US News & World Report*, August 1, 2005.
157. von Drehle, "Rumsfeld's Transformation."
158. Jason Sherman, "President Issues 'War on Terror' Directive to Improve Government Coordination," *Inside Defense*, March 13, 2006; Robinson, "Plan of Attack."
159. "National Military Strategic Plan for the War on Terrorism," Department of Defense, 2006, http://www.strategicstudiesinstitute.army.mil/pdffiles/gwot.pdf; Sebastian Sprenger, "Edelman Sets Up Advisory Panel to Foster OSD-Joint Staff Cooperation," *Inside the Army*, November 21, 2005.
160. Sherman, "President Issues Directive."
161. Feith, *War and Decision*, 512.
162. Caslen cited in Robinson, "Plan of Attack."
163. In 2008, the NMSP-WOT was superseded by the Joint Strategic Capabilities Plan. See US Joint Chiefs of Staff, Joint Publication 3-26, Counter-Terrorism I-2, November 13, 2009.
164. Peter W. Singer, "The War on Terrorism: The Big Picture," *Parameters* 34 (2004): 141–48.
165. "Military Operations Research Society Workshop Report—The Global War on Terrorism: Analytical Support, Tools, and Metrics of Assessment 30 November–2 December" US Naval War College, August 11, 2005; Daniel Byman, "Scoring the war on terrorism," *The National Interest* 72 (2003): 75–85; Edward Mickolus, "How Do We Know We're Winning the War against Terrorists? Issues in Measurement," *Studies in Conflict & Terrorism* 25 (2002): 151–60; Raphael Perl, "Combating Terrorism: The Challenge of Measuring Effectiveness," *Congressional Research Service*, March 12, 2007.
166. Christian Lowe, "Department of Measures: The Pentagon Tries to Come Up with a Metric for Success in the War on Terror," *The Daily Standard*, August 23, 2005; Feith, *War and Decision*, 512.
167. Lowe, "Department of Measures"; "The Role and Status of DoD Red Teaming Activities," Defense Science Board Task Force, Office of the Under Secretary of Defense for Acquisition, Technology, and Logistics, September 2003, http://www.acq.osd.mil/dsb/reports/redteam.pdf, last accessed June 6, 2008.
168. See, for instance, "Military Operations Research Society Workshop Report, August 11, 2005."
169. Interview with senior US Army officer attached to the Office of the Deputy Director for the War on Terrorism, Joint Staff (J-5), March 29, 2008; NMSP-WOT (2006).
170. NMSP-WOT (2006).
171. Rumsfeld memo cited in Feith, *War and Decision*, 564–65.

172. Ibid., 172–77.
173. Ahrari, "Why the Long War."
174. Henry cited in John T. Correll, "Verbatim," *Air Force Magazine* 89.2 (February 2006).
175. Matthew Johnson, "The Growing Relevance of Special Operations Forces in US Military Strategy," *Comparative Strategy* 25 (2006): 273–96; Senate Armed Services Committee, "Senate Report 108-046—National Defense Authorization Act for Fiscal Year 2004 Report, Committee Reports for the 108th Congress," May 12, 2003.
176. Johnson, "The Growing Relevance of Special Operations Forces in US Military Strategy."
177. Robinson, "Plan of Attack."
178. US Congress. House of Representatives. Armed Services Committee. Subcommittee on Terrorism, Unconventional Threats, and Capabilities, "SOCOM's Missions And Roles—Testimony of Michael G. Vickers," June 29, 2006; Ann Scott Tyson, "Rumsfeld OKs Expansive Plans for Terror Fight," *The Washington Post*, April 23, 2006; Sean Naylor, "More Than Door-Kickers; Special Ops Forces Are Misused as Man-Hunters, Critics Say," *Armed Forces Journal*, March 1, 2006; Harold Kennedy, "SOCOM creates new hub for fighting war on terror," *National Defense*, February 1, 2004.
179. "Joint Operational Concept for Defeating Terrorist Organizations" cited in Thomas H., Johnson and James A. Russell. "A Hard Day's Night? The United States and the Global War on Terrorism." *Comparative Strategy* 24 (2005): 136.
180. Scott Shane, Mark Mazzetti, and Robert F. Worth, "A Secret Assault on Terror Widens on Two Continents," *The New York Times*, August 15, 2010, A1.
181. Peter Swartz, "U.S. Navy Capstone Strategies & Concepts (1970–2007) with Insights for the U.S. Navy of 2008 & Beyond," Center for Naval Analyses, 2007, http://www.jhuapl.edu/maritimestrategy/historic/swartz/Swartz_8-23-07.pdf; Micool Brooke, "US Navy Ready if Taiwan Crisis Explodes, Admiral Says," *The Associated Press*, August 13, 1999; Thomas E. Ricks, "For Pentagon, Asia Moving to Forefront: Shift Has Implications for Strategy, Forces, Weapons," *The Washington Post*, May 26, 2000.
182. John B. Hattendorf, "US Naval Strategy in the 1990s—Selected Documents," Newport Papers #27 (September 2006), Naval War College, Newport, RI; Art Pine, "A Navy in Search of a Course," *The National Journal*, December 2, 2006.
183. Raphael Perl and Ronald O'Rourke, "Terrorist Attack on USS Cole: Background and Issues for Congress," *CRS Report for Congress*, January 20, 2001.
184. David Brown, "A wellspring of war-fighting ideas; Secret 'Deep Blue' think tank putting theory into action," *Marine Corps Times*, September 2, 2002.
185. David Brown, "Deployment dominoes; When deployment plans change for one carrier group, the impact reaches far and can affect thousands of lives," *Navy Times*, November 26, 2001.
186. Geoff Fein, "Deep Blue Gives Way to Bolstered Director Navy Staff Office," *Defense Daily*, May 7, 2008.
187. "The Role of Naval Forces in the Global War on Terror," Committee on the Role of Naval Forces in the Global War on Terror, Naval Studies Board, 2007; Ronald

O'Rourke, "Navy Role in Global War on Terrorism," *CRS Report for Congress*, March 1, 2008; John B. Hattendorf, "Seventeenth International Seapower Symposium," Report of the Proceedings, September 19–23, 2005, "US Naval War College," http://www.nwc.navy.mil/cnws/marstrat/docs/library/ISS17web.pdf.
188. James A. Russell, "Transformation into What and against Whom? The United States Navy and the 2006 Quadrennial Defense Review," *World Defence Systems* 9.1 (March 2006).
189. Jason Sherman, "Navy Staff Prioritizing Capabilities, Missions for Global War on Terror," *Inside the Pentagon*, May 12, 2005; Jason Sherman, "Navy to Establish Ground Combat Units, River Force for Terror War," *Inside the Navy*, July 11, 2005.
190. Naval Studies Board 2007.
191. "Rotational Opportunities: U.S. Department of Defense—Chief of Naval Operations, N5 War on Terror," Office of Personnel Management, accessed July 10, 2012, https://www.pmf.opm.gov/RotationsDetail.aspx?num=1499.
192. Geoff Fein, "Navy Needs Combat Force Capability to Take on GWOT, Official Says," *Defense Daily*, July 15, 2005.
193. Johnson, "Navy Establishes Cell."
194. Guidance cited in Rati Bishnoi, "Navy Establishes Combat Readiness Center to Support Terror War," *Inside the Pentagon*, November 16, 2006.
195. O'Rourke, "Navy Role in Global War on Terrorism," 2008.
196. Bruce A. Ellemann, "Waves of Hope: The U.S. Navy's Response to the Tsunami in Northern Indonesia," Newport Paper #28 (2007), Naval War College, Newport, RI.
197. Fein, "Navy Needs Combat Force Capability to Take on GWOT"; Geoff Fein, "Naval Expeditionary Combat Command Aligns Forces for GWOT," *Defense Daily*, November 16, 2005.
198. Sherman, "Navy to Establish Ground Combat Units."
199. Christian Lowe, "Sailors Go Grunt? Navy May Train Infantry Unit to Handle Corps-Style Missions," *Army Times*, August 1, 2005; Jason Ma, "Mullen: Goal Is Not Naval Infantry, but 'Maritime Security Force,'" *Inside the Navy*, October 31, 2005.
200. Commander Glen Leverette cited in Tyler Jones, "NECC Establishes Riverine Squadron 2," Fleet Public Affairs Center Atlantic, February 4, 2007.
201. Commander William J. Guarini cited in Mandy McLaurin, "Navy Establishes First Riverine Group," Fleet Public Affairs Center Atlantic, May 26, 2006.
202. Daniel A. Hancock, "The Navy's Not Serious about Riverine Warfare," *Proceedings* 134 (2008): 14–19
203. Cited in Chris Johnson, "Analysts Discuss Maritime Implications of China's Energy Strategy," *Inside the Navy*, December 18, 2006.
204. Johnson, "Navy Establishes Cell."
205. David Kelly, "Submarine Requirements for the Global War on Terrorism," *RUSI Defence Systems*, Autumn 2006.
206. Kenny cited in Emelie Rutherford, "Irregular Warfare Official: SSGN Subs are Navy's Premier Counter-terrorism Tool," *Defense Daily*, October 27, 2008.

207. Ronald O'Rourke, "Navy Irregular Warfare and Counter-terrorism Operations: Background and Issues for Congress," *CRS Report for Congress*, May 28, 2010.
208. Philip A. Greene, "Irregular Agenda," *Defense News*, February 15, 2010.
209. Ronald O'Rourke, "Navy Irregular Warfare and Counter-terrorism Operations: Background and Issues for Congress," *CRS Report for Congress*, April 6, 2012; "Report Says Role of Aid in Navy's Plan for Irregular Threats Unclear," *Inside the Navy*, November 8, 2010; "Navy Putting Into Practice Plan for Meeting Irregular Threats," *Inside the Navy*, November 1, 2010.
210. Gates cited in Jim Garamone, "Gates: Sea Services Must Question Embedded Thinking," *Armed Forces Press Service*, May 3, 2010.
211. Christopher J. Castelli, "Navy Raises 313-Ship Goal to 324, Boosts Focus on Missile Defense," *Inside the Pentagon*, December 10, 2009.
212. For a discussion of Navy attitudes regarding the Chinese naval threat, see Ronald O'Rourke, "China Naval Modernization: Implications for Congress," *CRS Report for Congress*, August 10, 2012.
213. "Quadrennial Defense Review Report," US Department of Defense, February 2010, 24.
214. Department of the Navy, Chief of Naval Operations, *The U.S. Navy's Vision for Confronting Irregular Challenges*, January 2010.
215. David Axe, "War Is Boring: US Navy Awakens to Irregular Warfare," *World Politics Review*, February 24, 2010; Christopher P. Cavas, "US Navy Asking for $161 Billion," *Defense News*, February 8, 2010.
216. Rebekah Gordon, "Mcullough: Current Fleet Meets Many Irregular Warfare Missions," *Inside the Navy*, June 1, 2009.
217. Dan Taylor, "Kenny: Large-Diameter UUVs Already Making Their Way to the Fleet," *Inside the Navy*, February 9, 2009.
218. Andrew Scutro, "Converted Missile Subs Thrive in Multiple Roles," *Defense News*, October 27, 2008.
219. Henry J. Hendrix, "Buy Fords, Not Ferraris," *Proceedings* 135 (2009).
220. Alain C. Enthoven and K. Wayne Smith, *How Much Is Enough? Shaping the Defense Program 1961–1969* (New York: Harper and Row, 1971), 1.
221. Eisenhower cited in Charles J. Hitch and Roland N. McKean, *The Economics of Defense in the Nuclear Age* (Cambridge, MA: Harvard University Press, 1963), 48.
222. Ian S. Lustick, *Trapped in the War on Terror* (Philadelphia: University of Pennsylvania Press, 2006); John Mueller, *Overblown: How Politicians and the Terrorism Industry Inflate National Security Threats and Why We Believe Them* (New York: Free Press, 2006); Edward Luttwak, "Transcript: Are We Trapped in the War on Terror? Middle East Policy Council," *Federal News Service*, November 3, 2006.
223. For examples of this specific criticism, see Gordon Adams, "The Cost of War: Hidden from Purview," *The National Interest*, October 4, 2006; US Congress. House of Representatives. Subcommittee on National Security, Emerging Threats, and International Relations, "Issues in Estimating the Cost of Operations in Iraq and the War on Terrorism, Congressional Budget Office Testimony of Donald B. Marron," July 18, 2006; US Congress. House of Representatives. Committee on the Budget, "Issues in Budgeting for Operations in Iraq and the War on Terrorism, Congressional Budget Office Testimony of Robert A. Sunshine," January 18, 2007;

Fred Kaplan, "This Is Not an Emergency: Supplemental War Funds are a Backdoor Way to Boost the Defense Budget," *Salon*, February 20, 2008, http://www.slate.com/articles/news_and_politics/war_stories/2008/02/this_is_not_an_emergency.html; US Congress. House of Representatives. Committee on the Budget, "The Cost and Funding of the Global War on Terror (GWOT), Testimony of Steven M. Kosiak," January 18, 2007; "Global War on Terrorism: DoD Needs to Improve the Reliability of Cost Data and Provide Additional Guidance to Control Costs," US General Accountability Office-GAO-05-882, September 2005.
224. US Congress. House of Representatives. Committee on the Budget, "The Cost and Funding of the Global War on Terror (GWOT), Testimony of Steven M. Kosiak," January 18, 2007.
225. David C. Gompert, "G-What? A Review of Defense Department Spending on Counter-Terrorism," in "Working Group Papers Prepared for the National Policy Forum on Terrorism, Security and America's Purpose," ed. New America Foundation (Washington, DC: New America Foundation, 2005), 32–41, http://www.americaspurpose.org/downloads/working_group_papers.pdf.
226. Aaron L. Martin, "Paying for War: Funding US Military Operations Since 2001," (diss., Pardee RAND Graduate School, Santa Monica, CA, 2011).
227. Kosiak, "The Cost and Funding of the Global War on Terror."
228. Gordon England, "Memorandum for Secretaries of the Military Departments—Ground Rules and Process for FY'07 Spring Supplemental," October 25, 2006.
229. Memo cited in Kaplan, "This Is Not an Emergency."
230. Ibid.
231. Adams, "The Cost of War"; Kaplan, "This Is Not an Emergency," http://www.slate.com/articles/news_and_politics/war_stories/2008/02/this_is_not_an_emergency.html.
232. Kosiak, "The Cost and Funding of the Global War on Terror."
233. Stephen Daggett, Amy Belasco, Pat Towell, Susan B. Epstein, Connie Veilette, Curt Tarnoff, and Rhoda Margesson, "FY2007 Supplemental Appropriations for Defense, Foreign Affairs, and Other Purposes," *CRS Reports to Congress*, July 2, 2007.
234. Kaplan, "This Is Not an Emergency."
235. Donna Miles, "Terror War Needs Funded in Proposed 2005 Defense Budget," *American Forces Press Service*, February 2, 2004.
236. Al Kamen, "Pencil in that End of War Date," *The Washington Post*, February 28, 2007.
237. Bradley Graham, "Pentagon Can Now Fund Foreign Militaries," *The Washington Post*, January 29, 2006; Stewart Patrick and Kaysie Brow, "The Pentagon and Global Development: Making Sense of the DoD's Expanding Role," Working Paper Number 131, *Center for Global Development*, November 2007; Corine Hegland, "Pentagon, State struggle to define nation-building roles," *The National Journal*, April 30, 2007.
238. Jim Garamone, "Rumsfeld Says Best Way to Thank Troops Is to Fund Budget," *American Forces Press Service*, February 14, 2002; Gopal Ratnam and William Matthews, "DoD Loosens Supplemental Rules; 'Emergency Funds' No Longer Need Pay for Combat Ops," *Defense News*, November 6, 2006.

239. Scott Wilson and Al Kamen, "Global War on Terror Is Given New Name," *Washington Post*, March 25, 2009.
240. Kate Brannen, "OMB Asks Defense to Shift Programs Out of War Bill," *Federal Times*, December 7, 2011; Tyrone C. Marshall Jr., "Vice Chiefs Testify on Readiness, Contingency Funding," *American Forces Press Service*, May 10, 2012.
241. Otto Kreisher, "The Years of Noble Eagle," *Air Force Magazine* 90.6 (June 2007).
242. "DoD Needs to Assess the Structure of U.S. Forces for Domestic Military Missions, Report to the Chairman, Subcommittee on National Security, Emerging Threats, and International Relations, Committee on Government Reform, House of Representatives," General Accounting Office, July 2003; US Congress. House of Representatives. Armed Services Committee. Special Oversight Panel on Terrorism, "Statement of Lieutenant General David D. Mckiernan, Deputy Chief of Staff (G-3), United States Army," July 11, 2002.
243. Malina Brown, "Navy Decides against Decommissioning 13 Cyclone Patrol Craft," *Inside the Navy*, February 10, 2003; Ronald O'Rourke, "Homeland Security: Navy Operations—Background and Issues for Congress," *CRS Reports for Congress*, May 17, 2004; David Castellon, "Changing of the Guard?; With Noble Eagle Taking a Toll on Aircraft and Airmen, Some Worry Guard and Reserve Units Will Be Assigned Permanently to Homeland Defense," *Air Force Times*, February 4, 2002; Esther Schrader, "A Changed America: Military Fuses Old, New to Create a Lethal Force," *Los Angeles Times*, February 10, 2002; Bill Courtney, "Homeland Role Challenges Army Strategy," *Defense News*, May 20, 2002.
244. Ian Roxborough, "The Hart-Rudman Commission and the Homeland Defense," *Strategic Studies Institute*, September 2001; Antulio J. Echevarria II, "The Army and Homeland Security: A Strategic Perspective," *Strategic Studies Institute*, March 2001; Richard Brennan, "Protecting the Homeland: Insights from Army Wargames," *RAND*, January 1, 2002; Eric V. Larson and John E. Peters, "Preparing the US Army for Homeland Security: Concepts, Issues, and Options," Monograph, *RAND*, 2001.
245. Patrick Kelly, "Defining Homeland Security," *Military Intelligence Professional Bulletin*, July 1, 2002; Larson and Peters, "Preparing the US Army for Homeland Security."
246. Adrian A. Erckenbrack and Aaron Scholer, "The DoD Role in Homeland Security," *Joint Forces Quarterly* 1 (2006): 34–41.
247. William Safire, "The Way We Live Now: 9-30-01: On Language; Words at War," *The New York Times*, September 30, 2001.
248. "Quadrennial Defense Review Report," US Department of Defense, September 30, 2001, http://www.defenselink.mil/pubs/pdfs/qdr2001.pdf.
249. Christopher Bolkcom, Lloyd DeSerisy, Lawrence Kapp, "Homeland Security: Establishment and Implementation of Northern Command," *CRS Reports for Congress*, May 14, 2003.
250. W. Spencer Johnson, "New Challenges for the Unified Command Plan," *Joint Forces Quarterly*, Summer 2002, 62–70; Thomas E. Ricks, "Military Overhaul Considered; Rumsfeld Eyes Global Command for Terrorism Fight," *The Washington Post*, October 11, 2001; McMichael, William H. "Is Atlantic Command Outdated? Military Leaders Look to Reorganise with Eye on Future." *Daily Press*

(Newport News, VA), March 8, 1998; Bryan Bender, "Panel Urges Pentagon to Scale Back Cold War Weapons," *Defense Daily*, December 2, 1997; Carol Rosenberg, "Southcom to Yield Cuba Role to New Command; Other Latin Functions Will Stay," *The Miami Herald*, April 24, 2002.

251. David Phinney and Warren Zinn, "Pentagon Refines Homeland Defense Role," *Federal Times*, September 29, 2003.
252. Jeremy Feiler, "McHale Sorting Priorities for New Pentagon Homeland Defense Office," *Inside Missile Defense*, June 11, 2003.
253. Amy Butler, "Director Hopes to Form Accord for USAF Domestic Security Approach," *Inside the Air Force*, June 28, 2002; Jefferson Morris, "Clary: Central Command Will Serve as Model for NORTHCOM," *Aerospace Daily*, August 14, 2002.
254. US Congress. House of Representatives. Government Reform Committee. Subcommittee on National Security, Emerging Threats, and International Relations, "Testimony of Dr. James J. Carafano, Senior Fellow, Center for Strategic and Budgetary Assessments," April 29, 2003.
255. Katherine M. Peters, "Troops on the Beat: The Military's Role in Homeland Security Is Growing," *Government Executive*, April 2003.
256. Briefing to the president by Ryan Henry titled "Gaps and Seams in Protecting the US Homeland," August 11, 2005, accessed at http://www.rumsfeld.com.
257. Bill Gertz and Rowan Scarborough, "Inside the Ring," *The Washington Times*, March 29, 2002.
258. Jason Sherman, "England Approves New Pentagon Homeland Defense Strategy," *Inside the Army*, July 4, 2005.
259. Thomas Duffy, "New Strategy Gives Cruise Missile Defense Significant Attention," *Inside Missile Defense*, July 6, 2005.
260. Bradley Graham, "War Plans Drafted to Counter Terror Attacks in US; Domestic Effort Is Big Shift for Military," *The Washington Post*, August 8, 2005.
261. Joe Pappalardo, "US-Mexico: Rapport Transformed by Terrorist Threat," *National Defense*, August 1, 2004.
262. Harold Kennedy, "At War, Navy Finds New Uses for Reserve forces; Navy Reserves," *National Defense*, September 1, 2004.
263. Dana Priest and William M. Arkin, "Top Secret America: A Hidden World, Growing beyond Control," *Washington Post*, July 19, 2010; Matthew Rothschild, "Rumsfeld Spies on Quakers and Grannies," *The Progressive*, December 16, 2005.
264. Adam J. Herbert, "Homeland Air Force," *Air Force Magazine* 87.1 (January 2004): 36–40; Butler, "Director Hopes to Form Accord"; Cynthia Di Pasquale, "USAF, DHS Writing MOU to Define Air Patrol's Role in Homeland Defense," *Inside the Air Force*, December 12, 2003.
265. "2003 Summer Study on DoD Roles and Missions in Homeland Security," Defense Science Board, Office of the Under Secretary of Defense for Acquisition, Technology and Logistics, September 2004, http://www.acq.osd.mil/dsb/reports/2004-09-VOL_II.final_Part_B.pdf; James Pelkofski, "Defeat Al Qaeda on the Waterfront," *Proceedings*, June 2004.
266. Duffy, "New Strategy Gives Cruise Missile Defense Significant Attention"; Jason Sherman, "Military Set to Exercise Mobile Air Defense Package for US Skies,"

Homeland Defense Watch, June 19, 2006; James B. Brindle, "Deployable Homeland Anti-Cruise Missile Defense," *Air Defense Artillery*, October–December 2006; US Congress. Senate. Armed Services Committee, "Statement of Admiral Timothy J. Keating, Commander United States Northern Command and North American Aerospace Command," March 14, 2006.

267. Cindy Williams, "Paying for the War on Terrorism," Economists for Peace and Security, March 2004, http://www.epsusa.org/publications/newsletter/2004/mar2004/williams.pdf.
268. James Gerstenzang, "Response to Terror: Bush Hints at Broadening War," *Los Angeles Times*, December 5, 2001; Nicholas Wapshott, "US Ready to Strike at Global Terror Links," *The Times (London)*, December 3, 2001; John Barry, "After Afghanistan, What Next?" *Newsweek*, January 29, 2002; Ann Scott Tyson, "US Weighs Options beyond Afghanistan," *The Christian Science Monitor*, December 7, 2001; Damian Whitworth, "US Names the 'Rogue States,'" *The Times (London)*, November 20, 2001; Christopher A. Parrinello, "Operation Enduring Freedom, Phase II the Philippines, Islamic Insurgency, and Abu Sayyaf," *Military Intelligence Professional Bulletin*, April–June, 2002.
269. Gregory Wilson, "Anatomy of a Successful COIN Operations: OEF-Philippines and the Indirect Approach," *Military Review*, November–December 2006.
270. Stephen Collinson, "Ahead of Bush talks, Philippine President pledges full support for US war on terror," *Agence France Presse*, November 20, 2001.
271. John Gershman, "Is South East Asia the Second Front?" *Foreign Affairs* 81 (2002): 60–74.
272. Rommel C. Banlaoi, "The War on Terrorism in Southeast Asia" (Strategic and Integrative Studies Center, 2003).
273. Michael V. Bhatia, "Fighting Words: Naming Terrorists, Bandits, Rebels and Other Violent Actors," *Third World Quarterly* 26 (2005): 8; Robert F. Trager and Dessislava P. Zagrcheva, "Deterring Terrorism: It Can Be Done," *International Security* 30 (2005–6): 87–123; Steven Rogers, "Beyond the Abu Sayef," *Foreign Affairs*, January–February 2004, 15–20; Philip Bowring, "Stretching the War on Terror," *International Herald Tribune*, August 14, 2002; US Congress. House of Representatives. International Relations Committee. Subcommittee on Asia and Pacific, "US Security Policy in Asia and the Pacific: Restructuring America's Forward Deployment, Statement of Admiral Thomas B. Fargo Commander, US Pacific Command," June 26, 2003; US Congress. House of Representatives. International Relations Committee, "Statement of Admiral Thomas B. Fargo Commander, US Pacific Command," March 8, 2005; Phil Zabriskie, "Picking a Fight; The U.S. Takes Its War on Terrorism to the Philippines. But Is It Taking on the Right Bad Guys?" *Time International*, February 25, 2002; US Congress. House of Representatives. Armed Services Committee. Subcommittee on Terrorism, Unconventional Threats, and Capabilities, "FY 2004 Defense Authorization, Statement of Marshall Billingslea, Principal Deputy Assistant Secretary of Defense Special Operations/Low Intensity Conflict," April 1, 2003; Jim Gomez, "Muslim Separatist Rebels May Have Stronger al-Qaeda Links Than Group Targeted by US Troops," *The Associated Press*, March 15, 2002.

274. Eric Schmitt, "Hurdle Leapt, US Will Help Philippines Battle Rebels," *The New York Times*, January 30, 2002.
275. Andrew Feickert, "US Military Operations in the Global War on Terrorism: Afghanistan, Africa, the Philippines, and Colombia," *CRS Report for Congress*, January 20, 2006, 18.
276. Rumsfeld cited in Whitworth, "US Names the 'Rogue States.'"
277. Blair cited in Schmitt, "Hurdle Leapt."
278. Bowring, "Stretching the War on Terror."
279. Bhatia, "Fighting Words," 8.
280. Oliver Teves, "Philippine Court OKs US Exercise," *The Associated Press Online*, April 11, 2002; Oliver Teves, "Hundreds of US Construction Troops Land in Philippines to Aid Offensive against Extremists," *The Associated Press*, April 20, 2002; Peter Brookes, "No Bungle in the Jungle: Operation Enduring Freedom-Philippines Is Getting Results," *Armed Forces Journal*, September 2007; Bill Nichols, "Widening US Battle Stirs Unease," *USA Today*, January 17, 2002.
281. Ruffy L. Villanueva, "RP, US Scale Down Military Exercise Due to May Polls," *Business World*, April 27, 2001; John Baughman, "Exercise Balikatan," *Army Reserve Magazine*, Summer 2001; Rowan Scarborough, "What's Next: Anti-Terror War's Expanded Scope Touches 8 Nations," *The Washington Times*, April 7, 2002; Conrad Crane, "Final Report: The US Army's Initial Impressions of Operations Enduring Freedom and Noble Eagle," US Army War College, September 2002.
282. Banlaoi, "The War on Terrorism in Southeast Asia"; Tim Dyhouse, "Shoulder-to-shoulder: Combating terrorists in the Philippines: more than 600 U.S. troops are training Filipinos to eradicate Muslim extremists on Basilan Island," *Veterans of Foreign Wars Magazine*, May 1, 2002.
283. Rumsfeld cited in Bill Gertz and Rowan Scarborough "Philippine Confusion," *The Washington Times*, February 8, 2002.
284. Myers cited in ibid.
285. Schmitt, "Hurdle Leapt, US Will Help Philippines Battle Rebels."
286. Mark Lander, "Philippines Offers US its Troops and Bases," *The New York Times*, October 2, 2001; Dan Murphy, "Long-Term US Strategy Emerges Out of Philippines," *The Christian Science Monitor*, July 3, 2002; Paul Wiseman, "In Philippines, US Making Progress in War on Terror," *USA Today*, February 13, 2007; Larry Niksch, "Abu Sayyaf: Target of Philippine-US Anti-Terrorism Cooperation," *Congressional Research Service*, January 25, 2002.
287. Gertz and Scarborough, "Philippine Confusion."
288. Simon Montlake, "Where US Is Helping to Make Gains against Terrorism," *The Christian Science Monitor*, February 15, 2007; Eliza Griswold, "Waging Peace in the Philippines: With Innovative Tactics, US Makes Headway in War on Terror," *Smithsonian*, December 2006.
289. David S. Maxwell, "Operation Enduring Freedom-Philippines: What Would Sun Tzu Say?" *Military Review*, May–June 2004, 20–24.
290. "Statement of Admiral Thomas B. Fargo," March 2005.

291. US Congress. Senate. Armed Services Committee, "Military Strategy and Operations Requirements in the FY2007 Defense Budget, Testimony of Admiral William Fallon," March 7, 2006.
292. "Statement of Admiral Thomas B. Fargo," March 2005.
293. Wilson, "Anatomy of a Successful COIN Operations."
294. Wiseman, "In Philippines."
295. Haider cited in Linda Robinson, "Men on a Mission: US Special Forces Are Retooling for the War on Terror. Here's Their Plan," *US News & World Report*, September 11, 2006.
296. Armed Services Committee, "Testimony of Admiral William Fallon," March 7, 2006.
297. Feickert, "US Military Operations in the Global War on Terrorism."
298. Carlo Munoz, "US Boosts Military Support to Philippines," *The Hill*, May 3, 2012.
299. Feickert, "US Military Operations in the Global War on Terrorism," 20–21; Neil Renwick, "Southeast Asia and the Global 'War on Terror' Discourse," *Cambridge Review of International Affairs* 20 (2007): 249–65.
300. Carina I. Roncesvalles, "US Military Exec in the Country for Balikatan Preparation," *Business World*, June 5, 2003; Brett M. Decker, "A Fair Fight in the Philippines?" *The New York Times*, October 18, 2003.
301. Floyd Whaley, "Philippines Role May Expand as US Adjusts Asia Strategy," *The New York Times*, April 30, 2012; Dan Lamothe, "US, Philippines Discuss Tightening Military Bonds," *Navy Times*, February 6, 2012; Jonathan Manthorpe, "Southeast Asia Remains Major Terrorist Battlefield," *The Vancouver Sun*, February 3, 2012.
302. Greg Simons, "The Use of Rhetoric and the Mass Media in Russia's War on Terror," *Demokratizatsiya* 14 (2006): 579–600; Julian Borger, "Pentagon Outlines Plans to Take War on Terror to Georgia," *The Guardian*, February 28, 2002; Fred Weir, "A New Terror-Front War: The Caucasus," *The Christian Science Monitor*, February 26, 2002; Fred Weir, "US Antiterrorist Aid to Tbilisi Rankles Russians," *The Christian Science Monitor*, March 4, 2002; "Operation Enduring Freedom: One Year of Accomplishments," White House Press Release, October 7, 2002.
303. Stephen Blank, "American Grand Strategy and the Transcaspian Region," *World Affairs* 163 (2000): 65–79.
304. Interview with midlevel EUCOM official, December 10, 2007.
305. Henry Plater-Zyberk and Anne Aldis, "Russia's Reaction to the American Tragedy," *Conflict Studies Research Centre*, September 20, 2001; Mark A. Smith, "Russian Perspectives on Terrorism," *Conflict Studies Research Centre*, January 2004; John Russell, "Terrorists, Bandits, Spooks and Thieves: Russian Demonization of the Chechens before and since 9/11," *Third World Quarterly* 26 (2005): 101–16.
306. US Congress. House of Representatives. Armed Services Committee, "FY03 Defense Budget Request, Testimony of USAF General Joseph Ralston, Commander, US European Command," March 20, 2002; "News Transcript: Deputy Secretary Wolfowitz Media Availability with President of Georgia, Office of the Assistant Secretary of Defense (Public Affairs)," October 5, 2001.
307. Sally Buzbee, "Rumsfeld Offers Closer Military Ties to Former Soviet Republics in Exchange for Help in War against Terrorism," *The Associated Press*, December 16,

2001; Jim Mannion, "Rumsfeld Seeks Closer Military Ties in Caucasus," *Agence France Presse*, December 15, 2001; "DoD News Transcript—Secretary Donald Rumsfeld Joint Press Conference with President of Georgia Eduard Shevardnadze," December 15, 2001.
308. Charles W. Blandy, "Pankisskoye Gorge: Residents, Refugees and Fighters," *Conflict Studies Research Center*, March 2002; Ian Traynor, "US Targets al-Qaida Hideout in Georgia," *The Guardian*, February 15, 2002.
309. Irakly G. Areshidze, "Helping Georgia?" *Perspective*, 12.4 (March–April 2002).
310. "DoD News Briefing—Secretary of Defense Donald Rumsfeld and Georgian Defense Minister General Lieutenant David Tevzadze," May 7, 2002.
311. US Congress. House of Representatives. Armed Services Committee, "FY03 Defense Budget Request, Testimony of USAF General Joseph Ralston, Commander, US European Command," March 20, 2002.
312. Victoria Clarke and General Peter Pace, "DoD News Briefing—ASD PA Clarke and Gen. Pace," February 27, 2002.
313. "Phone Interview with the Commander of the Georgia Train and Equip Program, Lieutenant Colonel Robert M. Waltemeyer," *Federal News Service*, May 30, 2002, http://www.fas.org/terrorism/at/docs/2002/Georgia_Waltemeyer.htm.
314. "Georgia Train and Equip Program Begins," Department of Defense News Release, April 29, 2002, http://www.defenselink.mil/releases/release.aspx?releaseid=3326.
315. Richard A. Clarke, "Memo to Condoleeza Rice: Presidential Policy Initiative/Review—The Al Qida Network," January 25, 2001, http://www.gwu.edu/~nsarchiv/NSAEBB/NSAEBB147/index.htm.
316. US Congress. House of Representatives. International Relations Committee, "Testimony of Rear Admiral Hamlin B. Tallent, Director of Operations, US European Command," March 10, 2005.
317. Interview with US Special Forces senior officer previously stationed in Georgia, June 22, 2009.
318. Kurtis Wheeler and Kris Stillings, "In the Republic of Georgia," *Marines Corps Gazette*, October 2006; Jonathan C. Moor, "Republic of Georgia Puts Her Best into Iraq Fight," *US Marines Corps News*, August 30, 2005.
319. US Congress. Senate. Armed Services Committee, "Fiscal 2007 Budget: Department of Defense, Statement of General James L. Jones—Commander, US European Command," March 7, 2006.
320. Dan Lamothe, "Marines to Extend Georgia Training Mission," *Marine Corps Times*, April 6, 2011.
321. Carla Anne Robbins, "Post-War Afghanistan War on Terror Seen as Taking Shape," *The Wall Street Journal*, November 29, 2001.
322. Woodward, *Bush at War*, 87.
323. Douglas J. Feith, "A War Plan That Cast a Wide Net," *The Washington Post*, August 7, 2004.
324. "FY 2005 Budget Defense Programs, Testimony of General Peter Pace, Capitol Hill Hearing," February 4, 2004.
325. General Bantz Craddock, "Posture Statement of General Bantz J. Craddock, Commander, United States Southern Command before the 109th Congress, Senate Armed Services Committee," *States News Service*, March 15, 2005.

326. "DoD News Briefing—Secretary Rumsfeld and Gen. Abizaid," August 21, 2003.
327. "The National Security Strategy of the United States of America," White House, September 2002, http://merln.ndu.edu/whitepapers/USnss2002.pdf.
328. Gregory Weeks, "Fighting Terrorism While Promoting Democracy: Competing Priorities in US Defense Policy toward Latin America," *Journal of Third World Studies* 23 (2006): 64–65.
329. Tim Johnson, "SOUTHCOM's Future Role Is Blurred by War on Terror," *The Miami Herald*, November 25, 2001; Paul Richter, "Military Is Easing Its War on Drugs: The Pentagon Wants to Scale Back the $1 Billion Program and Focus More on Combating Terrorism," *Los Angeles Times*, October 20, 2002.
330. Sig Christenson, "The Promise of Army South: Move to Fort Sam Houston Next Year Comes Amid High Expectations," *San Antonio Express-News*, September 23, 2002; Linda Robinson, "Next Stop, Colombia," *US News and World Report*, February 25, 2002; Major General Alfred A. Valenzuela, "US Army South: The Component of Choice in US Southern Command's AOR," *Army*, October 2002.
331. Richter, "Military Is Easing Its War on Drugs."
332. Linda Robinson, "Warrior Class: Why Special Forces Are America's Tool of Choice in Colombia and Around the Globe," *US News and World Report*, February 10, 2003.
333. Pauline Jelinek, "Pentagon Says US Cost of War So Far Is about $20 Billion," *The Associated Press*, April 16, 2003.
334. "Defense Department Special Briefing, Dov Zakheim: FY2003 Budget Supplemental," April 16, 2003.
335. Kuster cited in Erin Winograd, "Pentagon Spending Counter-Narcotics Money to Fight War on Terror," *Inside the Army*, February 17, 2003.
336. Ibid.
337. Emma Björnehed, "Narco-Terrorism: The Merger of the War on Drugs and the War on Terror," *Global Crime* 6 (2004): 305–24.
338. US Congress. House of Representatives. Committee on House Appropriations. Subcommittee on Defense, "Statement of General Richard B. Myers, Chairman of the Joint Chiefs of Staff," February 12, 2004.
339. US Congress. House of Representatives. Armed Services Committee, "Testimony of General James T. Hill, US Army Commander, US Southern Command," March 24, 2004.
340. "DoD News Briefing—Joint Press Conference in Bogota, Colombia, Donald H. Rumsfeld and Colombian Minister of Defense Marta Lucia Ramirez," August 19, 2003.
341. Weeks, "Fighting Terrorism While Promoting Democracy."
342. "Testimony of General James T. Hill," March 24, 2004.
343. Ibid.
344. Scott Huddleston, "Talks Tackle All Kinds of Terrorism," *San Antonio Express-News*, August 10, 2005.
345. Weeks, "Fighting Terrorism While Promoting Democracy."
346. General Peter Pace, "FY 2005 Budget Defense Programs, Capitol Hill Hearing Testimony," February 4, 2004.

347. Steven L. Taylor, "When Wars Collide: The War on Drugs and the Global War on Terror," *Strategic Insights* 4 (2005).
348. Stavridis cited in David Morgan, "US Says Iran Increasing Activity in Latin America," *Reuters*, March 17, 2009.
349. Panetta and Fraser cited in Cheryl Pellerin, "Panetta: Violent Extremism Threatens Latin America," *Armed Forces Press Service*, April 24, 2012.
350. Toby Archer and Tihomir Popovic, "The Trans-Saharan Counter-Terrorism Initiative: The US War on Terrorism in North Africa," Finnish Institute of International Affairs, 2007.
351. *9/11 Commission Report*, 336.
352. Scarborough, "What's Next."
353. Timothy Ghormley, "Briefing with Marine Corps Major General Timothy Ghormley, Commander, Combined Joint Task Force—Horn of Africa," September 21, 2005.
354. Beth Potter, "War on Terrorism's African Front," *United Press International*, November 29, 2002.
355. For a broader discussion of these activities, see Robert G. Berschinski, "AFRICOM's Dilemma: The 'Global War on Terrorism,' 'Capacity Building,' Humanitarianism, and the Future of US Security Policy in Africa," *Strategic Studies Institute*, November 21, 2007, 43; Shashank Bengali, "Humane Mission Grows out of Hunt for al Qaeda; A Little-Known Chapter of the War on Terrorism Is Playing Out in East Africa," *The Miami Herald*, February 5, 2006.
356. Ghormley cited in Bengali, "Humane Mission Grows."
357. Sean D. Naylor, "Building Intel from Scratch," *Marine Corps Times*, December 5, 2011.
358. "Briefing with Commander of the Combined Joint Task Force—Horn of Africa, Major General Samuel Helland," Office of the Assistant Secretary of Defense (Public Affairs), March 23, 2005.
359. US Congress. Senate. Armed Services Committee, "FY 2007 Budget—Department of Defense, Statement of General John P. Abizaid—Commander, US Central Command," March 16, 2006.
360. Helland cited in Mike Pflanz, "US Troops Keep Watch along Kenya's Coast," *The Christian Science Monitor*, August 9, 2005.
361. Bengali, "Humane Mission Grows."
362. Helland, "Briefing with Commander."
363. Peter Kagwanja, "Africa: Draining the Swamps of 'Homegrown Terrorism,'" *Africa News*, September 15, 2006.
364. Interview with midlevel EUCOM official, December 10, 2007.
365. Chris Tomlinson, "US Executives Tour the Horn of Africa, Learn of the Terrorist Threats Ahead," *The Associated Press*, December 13, 2006.
366. Thom Shanker, "In Horn of Africa, a Glimpse of American 'Soft Power,'" *International Herald Tribune*, December 4, 2007; James Brandon, "To Fight Al Qaeda, US Troops in Africa Build Schools Instead," *The Christian Science Monitor*, January 9, 2006.

367. US Congress. House of Representatives. International Relations Committee, "Testimony of Rear Admiral Hamlin B. Tallent, Director of Operations, US European Command," March 10, 2005.
368. EUCOM spokesman cited in Stewart M. Powell, "Swamp of Terror in the Sahara," *Air Force Magazine* 87.11 (November 2004): 50–54.
369. Raffi Khatchadourian, "Pursuing Terrorists in the Great Desert," *The Village Voice (New York)*, January 31, 2006; Raffi Khatchadourian, "Arming the 'Camel Corps,'" *The Village Voice (New York)*, February 7, 2006.
370. "Quadrennial Defense Review Report," US Department of Defense, February 6, 2006, http://www.defense.gov/pubs/pdfs/QDR20060203.pdf.
371. Cliff Gyves and Chris Wyckoff, "Algerian Groupe Salafiste de la Predication et le Combat (GSPC): An Operational Analysis," Naval Postgraduate School's *Strategic Insights* 5 (2006).
372. Michael Moss, "A Ragtag Insurgency Gains a Qaeda Lifeline," *The New York Times*, July 1, 2008.
373. Jason Motlagh, "US Seeks to Secure Sahara Desert; Terror Potential Cited in Lawless, Struggling Area," *The Washington Times*, November 17, 2005.
374. Todd Pitman, "Africa Terrorism," *The Associated Press*, June 19, 2005.
375. Khatchadourian, "Pursuing Terrorists."
376. Archer and Popovic, "The Trans-Saharan Counter-Terrorism Initiative," 42–43.
377. Nelson cited in ibid., 44.
378. Jim Fisher-Thompson, "US-African Partnership Helps Counter Terrorists in Sahel Region," United States Department of State, March 23, 2004.
379. Khatchadourian, "Arming the 'Camel Corps.'"
380. Gregory Sieminski, "The Art of Naming Operations," *Parameters* 25 (1995): 81–98.
381. Vince Crawley and Gordon Lubold, "African deployments would enhance training, Jones says; US forces could help local armies fight terrorism," *Navy Times*, May 3, 2004.
382. Stew Magnuson, "Battleground Africa: U.S. Military Seeks to Quash Terrorism before It Takes Root," *National Defense*, March 1, 2007.
383. Thomas Dempsey, "Counter-terrorism in African Failed States: Challenges and Potential Solutions," *Strategic Studies Institute*, April 2006; J. Peter Pham, "Next Front? Evolving United States–African Strategic Relations in the 'War on Terrorism' and Beyond," *Comparative Strategy* 26 (2007): 39–54.
384. Berschinski, "AFRICOM's Dilemma."
385. Motlagh, "US seeks to secure Sahara Desert"; Dempsey, "Counter-terrorism in African Failed States."
386. Khatchadourian, "Arming the 'Camel Corps.'"
387. Craig Whitlock, "Proxy Fight in Africa Heats Up," *The Washington Post*, November 25, 2011.
388. Thom Shanker and Eric Schmitt, "Three Terrorist Groups in Africa Pose Threat to US, American Commander Says," *The New York Times*, September 15, 2011; Thom Shanker, "Djibouti Outpost behind Somali Rescue Is Part of New Defense Strategy," *The New York Times*, January 26, 2012; Thom Shanker and Rick

Gladstone, "Armed US Advisers to Help Fight African Renegade Group," *The New York Times*, October 15, 2011.
389. "Sustaining Global Leadership: Priorities for the 21st Century Defense," Department of Defense, January 2012.

Chapter 3

1. John T. Correll, "What Happened to Shock and Awe?" *Air Force Magazine* 86. 11 (November 2003).
2. Harlan Ullman and James Wade Jr., *Shock and Awe: Achieving Rapid Dominance* (Washington, DC: National Defense University, 1996).
3. Harlan Ullman, "Slogan or Strategy?" *The National Interest* 84 (2006): 43–49.
4. Ullman and Wade, *Shock and Awe*, 113–14.
5. Harlan K. Ullman and James P. Wade Jr., "Rapid Dominance: A Force for All Season," RUSI Whitehall Paper Series, 1998, x.
6. Michael R. Gordon and Bernard E. Trainor, *Cobra II: The Inside Story of the Invasion and Occupation of Iraq* (New York: Pantheon Books, 2006), 90–91.
7. Correll, "What Happened to Shock and Awe?"; Ullman, "Slogan or Strategy?"
8. Ralph Peters, "A Grave New World: 10 Lessons from the War in Iraq," *San Diego Union-Tribune*, April 17, 2005.
9. Ullman and Wade, "Rapid Dominance," 5.
10. Harlan Ullman, "Shock and Awe Misunderstood," *USA Today*, April 7, 2003.
11. Harlan Ullman, *Unfinished Business: Afghanistan, the Middle East, and Beyond—Defusing the Dangers That Threaten America's Security* (Washington, DC: Kensington Publishing Corporation, 2002).
12. Ibid., 204.
13. Ullman and Wade cited in Forrest E. Morgan, "'Shock and Awe': Its Origins, Its Role in Operation Iraqi Freedom and Why It Did Not Work," unpublished paper, last modified February 2005.
14. Ullman and Wade, *Shock and Awe*, 13.
15. For a more comprehensive examination of employing a "strategy of shock" at Hiroshima and Nagasaki, see Lawrence Freedman, "The Strategy of Hiroshima," *Journal of Strategic Studies* 1 (1978): 76–97.
16. Interview with RAND Corporation analyst, December 19, 2005.
17. John Hillen, "Report on INSS 1998 Joint Operations Symposium—21st Century Warfighting," National Defense University, September 9–10, 1998.
18. Harlan K. Ullman and Mark J. Conversino, "Reply to Review. Shock and Awe," *Naval War College Review*, Spring 1999.
19. Interview with former official in the Office of Force Transformation, December 21, 2005.
20. US Congress. House of Representatives. National Security Committee. Military Procurement Subcommittee, "Testimony of General Charles Horner," September 12, 1996.
21. Tom Clancy and General Chuck Horner, *Every Man a Tiger* (London: Penguin Putnam Inc., 2000), 504–5.

22. Gary E. Luck Jr., "Inducing Operational Shock to Achieve Quick Decisive Victory: How Does the Airborne Division Contribute," Monograph, Army Command and General Staff College, May 27, 1999; Bud Edney, "Deterring Threats: Shock and Awe," *Surface Warfare* 24 (1999).
23. Mark J. Conversino, "Book Review of Shock and Awe: Achieving Rapid Dominance," *Naval War College Review*, Summer 1998.
24. Ullman and Conversino, "Reply to Review."
25. Morgan, "Shock and Awe."
26. Ibid.
27. Interview with RAND Corporation analyst, December 19, 2005.
28. Ullman, "Shock and Awe Misunderstood."
29. Andrew M. Dorman, "Transforming to Effects-Based Operations: Lessons from the United Kingdom Experience," *Strategic Studies Institute*, January 2008.
30. Ullman and Wade, "Rapid Dominance," 80–84.
31. Ibid., 52–60.
32. Ibid., x.
33. Interview with senior US defense official, January 19, 2006.
34. Ullman and Wade, "Rapid Dominance," x.
35. Interview with senior US defense official, January 19, 2006.
36. Ibid.
37. Defense Group Inc., "Rapid Dominance Strategy of War," http://www.defensegroupinc.com/war_rdpaper.cfm.
38. Interview with senior US defense official, January 19, 2006.
39. Fred Kaplan, "Why the Army Shouldn't Be So Surprised by Saddam's Moves," *Slate*, March 28, 2003.
40. Thomas Barnett, "Donald Rumsfeld: Old Man in a Hurry," *Esquire*, July 1, 2005.
41. Interview with senior US defense official, January 19, 2006.
42. Ullman cited in Correll "What Happened to Shock and Awe?"
43. Rumsfeld cited in William Safire, "Shock and Awe: A Tactic, Not a Law Firm," *The New York Times*, March 30, 2003.
44. Joel Achenbach, "Victory That Defies Logic; Military Strategists Maintain the War Was Lost, in Theory," *The Washington Post*, June 12, 1999.
45. Interview with senior US defense official, January 19, 2006.
46. Scott Peterson, "US Mulls Air Strategies in Iraq," *The Christian Science Monitor*, January 30, 2003.
47. Letter extract cited in Correll, "What Happened to Shock and Awe?"
48. Ibid.
49. Interview with senior US defense official, January 19, 2006.
50. Memo, "Meeting with Secretary Bill Cohen and Don Rumsfeld—January 2001," June 21, 2001.
51. Ullman, *Unfinished Business*, 136.
52. Fred Kaplan, "Rumsfeld's Man: Why Generals Will Fight the New Secretary for the Army," *Slate*, May 6, 2003.
53. Ullman, *Unfinished Business*, 136.
54. Ben Rooney, "Bomb Blitz will 'Shock and Awe' the Taliban," *The Daily Telegraph*, September 27, 2001.

55. Robert A. Pape, "The True Worth of Air Power," *Foreign Affairs* 83 (2004): 116–30.
56. "Fletcher Conference. Remarks Prepared for Delivery by Deputy Secretary of Defense Paul Wolfowitz," Ronald Reagan Building and International Trade Center, Washington, DC, November 14, 2001; Kagan, *Finding the Target*, 327–28.
57. Gordon and Trainor, *Cobra II*, 21–22.
58. J. R. McKay, "Mythology and the Air Campaign in the Liberation of Iraq," *Journal of Military and Strategic Studies* 7 (2005): 1–17.
59. Joyce Battle and Thomas Blanton, eds., "CentCom PowerPoint Slides Briefed to White House and Rumsfeld in 2002," National Security Archive Electronic Briefing Book No. 214, February 14, 2007.
60. Gregory Hooker, *Shaping the Plan for Operation Iraqi Freedom: The Role of Military Intelligence Assessments* (Washington, DC: The Washington Institute for Near East Policy, 2005), 105.
61. Ibid., 26.
62. Gordon and Trainor, *Cobra II*, 35, 318.
63. Ibid., 35–36, 517.
64. Ibid., 517.
65. Williamson Murray and Robert H. Scales Jr., *The Iraq War: A Military History* (Cambridge, MA: Harvard University Press, 2003), 92–93; Tommy Franks, *American Soldier* (New York: Harper Collins Publishers, 2004), 294.
66. Bob Woodward, *Plan of Attack* (London: Simon and Schuster, 2004), 82.
67. Seymour M. Hersh, *Chain of Command: The Road from 9/11 to Abu Ghraib* (New York: Harper Collins Publishers, 2005), 172–73; Thomas E. Ricks, *Fiasco: The American Military Adventure in Iraq* (New York: Penguin Press, 2006), 23; Gordon and Trainor, *Cobra II*, 12.
68. Hersh, *Chain of Command*, 173.
69. Woodward, *Plan of Attack*, 102.
70. Gordon and Trainor, *Cobra II*, 44.
71. Interview with midlevel US Air Force officer previously stationed at CENTCOM HQ, December 8, 2005.
72. Hooker, *Shaping the Plan for Operation Iraqi Freedom*, 44.
73. Ibid., 30. The Iraq war plans were OPLAN 1003-98, produced on the normal two-year planning cycle beginning in 1998 and ending in 2000; OPLAN 1003V Generated Start, produced in an abbreviated planning process, with primary work conducted between December 2001 and March 2002; OPLAN 1003V Running Start, produced in abbreviated planning between March and July 2002; OPLAN 1003V Hybrid, produced in abbreviated planning from July to October 2002; and Operational Concept "Velocity," conceived in October 2002 but never fully developed into a formal Operational Plan.[1]
74. Stephen T. Hosmer, "Why the Iraqi Resistance to the Coalition Invasion Was So Weak," Monograph, *RAND*, 2007.
75. Hooker, *Shaping the Plan for Operation Iraqi Freedom*, 22; Gordon and Trainor, *Cobra II*, 106–8; Feith, *War and Decision*, 382–85; Linda Robinson and Kevin Whitelaw, "Deploying the 'Free Iraqi Forces': What Role for the Arriving Anti-Saddam Iraqi Fighters?" *US News and World Report*, April 7, 2003.

76. Hooker, *Shaping the Plan for Operation Iraqi Freedom*, 22.
77. Ricks, *Fiasco*, 42.
78. Hooker, *Shaping the Plan for Operation Iraqi Freedom*, 30.
79. Ibid., 25.
80. Nicholas E. Reynolds, *Basrah, Baghdad, and Beyond: The US Marine Corps in the Second Iraq War* (Annapolis, MD: US Naval Institute Press, 2005), 17.
81. William M. Arkin, "Planning an Iraqi War but Not an Outcome," *Los Angeles Times*, May 5, 2002.
82. Gordon and Trainor, *Cobra II*, 44–45.
83. Arkin, "Planning an Iraqi War."
84. Ibid.; Battle and Blanton, "CentCom PowerPoint Slides."
85. Hooker, *Shaping the Plan for Operation Iraqi Freedom*, 22–24.
86. Clayton Dennison, "Operation Iraqi Freedom: What Went Wrong? A Clausewitzian Analysis," *Journal of Military and Strategic Studies* 9 (2006–7): 1–33.
87. Bradley Graham, "After 9/11, US Planes Began Softening Iraqi Defenses," *The Boston Globe*, July 20, 2003.
88. McKay, "Mythology and the Air Campaign."
89. Kevin M. Woods, Michael R. Pease, and Mark E. Stout, *The Iraqi Perspectives Report: Saddam's Senior Leadership on Operation Iraqi Freedom* (Annapolis: US Naval Institute Press, 2006), 34; Clifford Beal, "Military Lessons from Iraq: After the War, the Struggle Over Strategy Goes On," *International Herald Tribune*, April 30, 2003.
90. Hooker, *Shaping the Plan for Operation Iraqi Freedom*, 24.
91. Murray and Scales, *The Iraq War*, 75.
92. Hooker, *Shaping the Plan for Operation Iraqi Freedom*, 24.
93. Ibid., 25.
94. Rowan Scarborough, "Sparing Targets Softens Effect of 'Shock and Awe,'" *The Washington Times*, March 31, 2003.
95. Romesh Ratnesar, "Awestruck," *Time Magazine*, March 31, 2003.
96. Cited in Bradley Graham and Vernon Loeb, "An Air War of Might, Coordination and Risks," *The Washington Post*, April 27, 2003.
97. Peter J. Boyer, "The New War Machine: How General Tommy Franks Joined Donald Rumsfeld in the Fight to Transform the Military," *The New Yorker*, June 30, 2003.
98. Dennison, "Operation Iraqi Freedom."
99. Murray and Scales, *The Iraq War*, 167.
100. Gordon and Trainor, *Cobra II*, 210.
101. Sophy Gardner, "Operation Iraqi Freedom: Coalition Operations," *Air and Space Power Journal* 18 (2004): 87–99; Air Marshall Brian Burridge, "House of Commons Select Committee on Defence—Examination of Witness," June 11, 2003, http://www.publications.parliament.uk/pa/cm200304/cmselect/cmdfence/57/3061104.htm.
102. David Charter and Michael Evans, "Britain Reined in US Military's Shock and Awe Strategy," *The Times*, May 2, 2003.
103. Burridge, "House of Commons Select Committee on Defence."

104. Burridge cited in Charter and Evans, "Britain Reined in US Military's Shock and Awe Strategy"; Mark Mazzetti; Julian E. Barnes; Kit R. Roane; and Joellen Perry, "Battle Ready," *US News and World Report*, March 24, 2003.
105. Boyer, "The New War Machine."
106. McKay, "Mythology and the Air Campaign in the Liberation of Iraq."
107. Arkin, "Planning an Iraqi War."
108. Ibid.
109. Correll, "What Happened to Shock and Awe?"
110. Interview with RAND Corporation analyst, December 19, 2005.
111. Col. Gary L. Crowder, "Effects Based Operations Briefing," US Department of Defense News Transcript, March 19, 2003.
112. Ibid.
113. Interview with RAND Corporation analyst, December 19, 2005.
114. Correll, "What Happened to Shock and Awe?"
115. James R. Compton, "Shocked and Awed: The Convergence of Military and Media Discourse," *Global Politics in the Information Age*, ed. in Peter Wilkin and Mark Lacy (Manchester: Manchester University Press, 2006).
116. Ullman cited in Correll, "What Happened to Shock and Awe?"
117. Ullman cited in Peterson, "US Mulls Air Strategies in Iraq."
118. Correll, "What Happened to Shock and Awe?"
119. Myers cited in ibid.
120. Ibid.
121. Bruce Rolfsen, "DoD Favors 'Shock and Awe' Strategy: Desert Storm Leaders Shy Away from Drawn-Out Ground War," *Air Force Times*, March 17, 2003.
122. Sarah Chartrand, "Patents; Before Shock and Awe Can Go from Battlefield to Lunch Box, There Is a stop at the Trademark Office," *The New York Times*, April 21, 2003.
123. Boyer, "The New War Machine."
124. Rumsfeld cited in Correll, "What Happened to Shock and Awe?"
125. Franks cited in Gardner, "Operation Iraqi Freedom."
126. Ibid.
127. Achenbach, "Victory that Defies Logic."
128. Ullman, "Shock and Awe Misunderstood."
129. Ullman cited in Oliver Burkeman, "Shock Tactics," *The Guardian*, March 25, 2003.
130. Stephen Budiansky, *Air Power: From Kitty Hawk to Gulf War II: A History of the People, Ideas, and Machines That Transformed War in the Century of Flight* (London: Penguin Books, 2003), 437.
131. Murray and Scales, *The Iraq War*, 166.
132. Mark D. Faram, "We've Got Your Back: Navy Air Units Clear Way for Ground Troops En Route to Baghdad," *Navy Times*, April 7, 2003; Peter Smolowitz, "Lack of Iraq Resistance Surprises F-16CJ Pilots," *Charlotte Observer (North Carolina)*, March 24, 2003.
133. Budiansky, *Air Power*, 434–41; McKay, "Mythology and the Air Campaign in the Liberation of Iraq."
134. Murray and Scales, *The Iraq War*, 173.

135. Pape, "The True Worth of Air Power"; McKay, "Mythology and the Air Campaign in the Liberation of Iraq."
136. Gray cited in Smolowitz, "Lack of Iraq Resistance Surprises F-16CJ Pilots."
137. Hosmer, "Why the Iraqi Resistance."
138. Woods, Pease and Stout, *The Iraqi Perspectives Report.*
139. Morgan, "Shock and Awe."
140. Woods, Pease and Stout, *The Iraqi Perspectives Report*, 51–55, 118; Reynolds, *Basrah, Baghdad, and Beyond.*
141. Dennison, "Operation Iraqi Freedom"; Woods, Pease, Stout, *The Iraqi Perspectives Report.*
142. US Congress. House of Representatives. Committee on Armed Services, "On Operation Iraqi Freedom: Outside Perspectives, Statement by Dr. Stephen Biddle," October 21, 2003.
143. Morgan, "Shock and Awe"; Gordon and Trainor, *Cobra II*, 313.
144. Woods, Pease and Stout, *The Iraqi Perspectives Report.*
145. Stephen Biddle, "Speed Kills? Reassessing the Role of Speed, Precision, and Situation Awareness in the Fall of Saddam," *Journal of Strategic Studies* 30 (2007): 3–46.
146. Morgan, "Shock and Awe."
147. Burkeman, "Shock Tactics."
148. Safire, "Shock and Awe."
149. Seth Stern, "From Paper to the Battlefield," *The Christian Science Monitor*, March 20, 2003.
150. Manny Fernandez and Justin Blum, "Antiwar Protesters Spar with Police," *Washington Post*, March 22, 2003; Jenna Russell, "Tens of Thousands Rally in Boston for Peace," *The Boston Globe*, March 30, 2003; Jefferson Morley, "World Media Recoil from 'Shock and Awe,'" *The Washington Post*, March 20, 2003.
151. Fernandez and Blum, "Antiwar Protesters Spar with Police."
152. Morley, "World Media Recoil."
153. Vernon Loeb and Thomas E. Ricks, "Questions Raised about Invasion Force: Some Ex-Gulf War Commanders Say U.S. Needs More Troops, Another Armored Division." *The Washington Post*, March 25, 2003; Borger, "Knives Come Out for Rumsfeld as the Generals Fight Back: Interfering Style Blamed for Army Setbacks," *The Guardian*, March 31, 2003; Michael R. Gordon, "A Nation at War: Strategy; A New Doctrine's Test," *The New York Times*, April 1, 2003.
154. Stern, "From Paper to the Battlefield"; Loeb and Ricks, "Questions Raised about Invasion Force."
155. Barry McCaffrey, "Gaining Victory in Iraq," *U.S. News and World Report*, April 7, 2003.
156. Ibid.
157. Loeb and Ricks, "Questions Raised about Invasion Force."
158. Ralph Peters, "Shock, Awe and Overconfidence," *The Washington Post*, March 25, 2003.
159. Ibid.
160. Scarborough, "Sparing Targets."
161. DeLong, *Inside CENTCOM*, 105–6.
162. Max Boot, "The New American Way of War," *Foreign Affairs* 82 (2003): 41–48.

163. Ibid.
164. Harlan K. Ullman, "Shock and Awe Revisited," *RUSI Journal* 148.3 (2003).
165. Rachel Smolkin, "Media Mood Swings," *American Journalism Review*, June–July 2003; Boyer, "The New War Machine."
166. Rumsfeld cited in Correll "What Happened to Shock and Awe?"
167. Wolfowitz cited in ibid.
168. Moseley cited in ibid.
169. "Interview with General Richard Myers," *Fox News*, April 3, 2003.
170. John Keegan, *The Iraq War: The 21-Day Conflict and Its Aftermath* (London: Pimlico, 2005), 248.
171. Ann Scott Tyson, "Gates Criticizes Conventional Focus at Start of Iraq War," *The Washington Post*, September 30, 2008.
172. Lieutenant General James N. Mattis, "Memorandum for US Joint Forces Command-Subject: Assessment of Effects Based Operations," August 14, 2008, http://smallwarsjournal.com/documents/usjfcomebomemo.pdf.
173. Ibid.
174. Antulio J. Echevarria II, "Toward an American Way of War," *Strategic Studies Institute*, March 2004.
175. Christopher Coker, *War in an Age of Risk* (Cambridge, MA: Polity Press, 2009), 122.
176. Ibid., 111.
177. Interview with senior US defense official, January 19, 2006.

Chapter 4

1. Lawrence Freedman, "Know, Rather Than Imagine, Your Enemy," *The Financial Times*, May 12, 2008.
2. Memo from Rumsfeld to Wolfowitz, "Terminology," January 7, 2004.
3. James Risen, "CIA Warned Pentagon of Guerrilla Tactics," *The New York Times*, March 28, 2003; Johanna McGeary, "3 Flawed Assumptions," *Time*, April 7, 2003.
4. Stephen Biddle, "Speed Kills?"
5. Kevin M. Woods, Michael R. Pease, and Mark E. Stout, *The Iraqi Perspectives Report: Saddam's Senior Leadership on Operation Iraqi Freedom* (Annapolis, MD: US Naval Institute Press, 2006).
6. Wallace cited in Jim Dwyer, "A Gulf Commander Sees a Longer Road," *The New York Times*, March 28, 2003.
7. Michael R. Gordon and Bernard E. Trainor, "As War Began, U.S. Generals Feuded," *The New York Times*, March 13, 2006.
8. Pauline Jelinek, "Thugs, Terrorists, Death Squads—By Any Name, Pentagon Hates Iraqi Militias," *The Associated Press*, March 27, 2003.
9. Rumsfeld cited in ibid.
10. Myers cited in James Rosen, "Iraqi Paramilitary Group Hampers Allied Advance: Ruthless Vigilantes Basically Unheard of during War's Lead-Up," *Modesto Bee*, March 30, 2003.

11. Myers cited in Vince Crawley, "Outing Saddam: Troops Find Task Will Be No Walk in the Park," *Air Force Times*, April 7, 2003.
12. See for example Brigadier General Vincent Brooks, "Central Command Briefing," March 31, 2003; Brigadier General Vince Brooks, "US Central Command Daily Operational Update Briefing, Doha, Qatar," April 1, 2003; Brigadier General Vince Brooks, "US Central Command Daily Operational Update Briefing, Doha, Qatar," April 8, 2003; Brigadier General Vince Brooks, "US Central Command Daily Operational Update Briefing, Doha, Qatar," April 9, 2003.
13. Brooks, "Central Command Briefing," March 31, 2003.
14. Ibid.
15. Ibid.
16. Renuart cited in Anne Barnard, "US Uses Alternative Terms for Fedayeen—US Reluctant to Give Credence to Hussein Unit," *The Boston Globe*, April 2, 2003.
17. Reynolds, *Basrah, Baghdad, and Beyond*.
18. Michael R. Gordon and Bernard E. Trainor, *Cobra II: The Inside Story of the Invasion and Occupation of Iraq* (New York: Pantheon Books, 2006), 258.
19. Reynolds, *Basrah, Baghdad, and Beyond*.
20. Rajiv Chandrasekaran and Peter Baker, "Allies Struggle for Supply Lines; Massive Air Strikes Hit Baghdad; Iraq Says Market Explosion Kills 58," *The Washington Post*, March 30, 2003; Elaine M. Grossman, "US Military Watches Chalabi, Gives Forces Largely Symbolic Role," *Inside the Pentagon*, May 1, 2003.
21. Elaine M. Grossman, "Key Generals: Response to Fedayeen a Vital Milestone in Iraq War," *Inside the Pentagon*, May 8, 2003.
22. Gregory Fontenot, E. J. Degen, and David Tohn (2005), *On Point: The United States Army in Operation Iraqi Freedom* (Annapolis, Md.: Naval Institute Press, 2005).
23. Nathaniel Harrison, "Official US Rhetoric Links Iraqi Resistance to 'Terrorists,'" *Agence France Presse*, March 30, 2003.
24. Gordon and Trainor, *Cobra II*, 258.
25. Gordon and Trainor, "As War Began."
26. Michael Eisenstadt and Jeffrey White, "Assessing Iraq's Sunni Arab Insurgency," *Military Review*, May–June 2006; Donald P. Wright and Timothy R. Reese, *On Point II: Transition to the New Campaign: The United States Army in Operation IRAQI FREEDOM, May 2003–January 2005* (Defense Dept., US Army Combined Arms Center, Combat Studies Institute, 2008), 87–129; Ahmed S. Hashim, *Insurgency and Counter-Insurgency in Iraq* (New York: Cornell University Press, 2006).
27. Wright and Reese, *On Point II*, 162.
28. Jim Garamone, "Operation Desert Scorpion Continues Throughout Iraq," *Armed Forces Press Service*, July 17, 2003; Wright and Reese, *On Point II*, 121–22.
29. Wright and Reese, *On Point II*, 37.
30. Patricia Slayden Hollis, "Second Battle of Fallujah-Urban Operations in a New Kind of War," *Field Artillery Journal* 11 (2006).
31. Rumsfeld cited in William Safire, "Fruitcake," *The New York Times*, August 10, 2003.

32. Email correspondence with former senior defense intelligence officer attached to the Joint Staff, November 23, 2008.
33. McCain cited in Walter Pincus, "CIA Studies Provide Glimpse of Insurgents in Iraq," *The Washington Post*, February 6, 2005.
34. Wright and Reese, *On Point II*, 114; Interview with midlevel US Army officer, October 28, 2006.
35. Safire, "Fruitcake." According to Rumsfeld, "the use of the phrase 'former regime loyalist' is unfortunate in that 'loyalist' has a positive connotation." See Memo from Rumsfeld to Wolfowitz, "Terminology," January 7, 2004.
36. "National Strategy for Victory in Iraq: Helping the Iraqi People Defeat the Terrorists and Build an Inclusive Democratic State," National Security Council, November 2005, http://www.washingtonpost.com/wp-srv/nation/documents/Iraqnationalstrategy11-30-05.pdf.
37. Odum cited in Wright and Reese, *On Point II*, 115.
38. Steven K. O'Hern, *The Intelligence Wars: Lessons from Baghdad* (Amherst, NY: Prometheus Books, 2008), 43.
39. DIA report cited in Edward T. Pound, "Seeds of Chaos," *US News and World Report*, December 20, 2004.
40. Ibid.
41. Wright and Reese, *On Point II*, 125.
42. Hashim, *Insurgency and Counter-Insurgency in Iraq*, 59–124; William R. Hawkins, "Iraq: Heavy Forces and Decisive Warfare," *Parameters* 33 (2003): 61–67; Wright and Reese, *On Point II*, 87–129.
43. Seymour M. Hersh, *Chain of Command: The Road from 9/11 to Abu Ghraib* (New York: Harper Collins, 2005), 281.
44. Wright and Reese, *On Point II*, 87–129.
45. Bob Woodward, *The War Within: A Secret White House History 2006–2008* (New York: Simon and Schuster, 2008), 23
46. Ibid., 18, 23–24.
47. Gareth Porter, "US/Iraq: General Reveals Rift with Rumsfeld on Insurgents," *IPS*, April 15, 2006.
48. Ibid.
49. "National Strategy for Victory in Iraq."
50. Donald H. Rumsfeld, "Defense Department News Briefing," April 20, 2004.
51. Brigadier General Mark Kimmitt, "Coalition Provisional Authority News Briefing," April 24, 2004.
52. Richard Whittle, "Does Iraq Look a Lot Like Germany? Post-War Comparisons are Many and Inevitable—and Sometimes They're Accurate," *Dallas Morning News*, October 12, 2003.
53. Hashim, *Insurgency and Counter-Insurgency in Iraq*, 46–47.
54. Jeffrey Record, "The Use and Abuse of History: Munich, Vietnam and Iraq," *Survival* 49 (2007), 163–80.
55. Daniel Benjamin, "Reinventing History: The US Is Wrong to Compare Post-War Iraq with Germany after the Defeat of the Nazis," *Slate*, September 5, 2003; Whittle, "Does Iraq Look a Lot Like Germany?"; Tom Blackburn, "Werewolves? Must Be a Full Moon," *Palm Beach Post*, September 1, 2003.

56. Rumsfeld cited in Benjamin, "Reinventing History."
57. Ibid.
58. Rice cited in Blackburn, "Werewolves?"
59. Interview with senior US Army officer, January 10, 2008.
60. Paul Wolfowitz, "Remarks with King County Journal Editorial Board in Tacoma, WA," Department of Defense Transcripts, Department of Defense Transcripts, July 24, 2004.
61. Ibid.
62. Hersh, *Chain of Command*, 281.
63. Ricks, *Fiasco*, 386.
64. Wolfowitz cited in ibid., 412.
65. Paul Wolfowitz, Joshua Bolten, and General John Keane, "Testimony as Delivered by Deputy Secretary of Defense Paul Wolfowitz, and Director, Office of Management and Budget Joshua Bolten and Acting Chief of staff, US Army, General John Keane," US Department of Defense Speeches, July 29, 2003.
66. Donald H. Rumsfeld, "What We've Gained in Three Years in Iraq," *The Washington Post*, March 19, 2006.
67. L. Paul Bremer III, *My Year in Iraq: The Struggle to Build a Future of Hope* (New York: Simon and Schuster, 2006), 126–27.
68. Ibid., 127.
69. Wolfowitz cited in Alex Belida, "Wolfowitz Blames Former Iraqi Intelligence Agents for Role in Insurgency," *Voice of America News*, April 21, 2004.
70. Ibid.
71. Radek Sikorski, "Interview: Paul Wolfowitz," *Prospect*, November 18, 2004.
72. Paul Wolfowitz, "Remarks at the National Press Club," December 7, 2005.
73. Conway cited in Eamon Javers, "Spinning Fallujah," *Slate Magazine*, May 5, 2004.
74. Ibid.
75. Hartsell cited in ibid.
76. Ibid.
77. Wright and Reese, *On Point II*, 351.
78. Ibid., 524.
79. The Wikileaks war logs can be found at http://www.wikileaks.org.
80. Colby Buzzell, *My War: Killing Time in Iraq* (New York: G. P. Putnam's Sons, 2005).
81. For example, "CENTAF releases airpower summary," CENTAF, June 30, 2006; "CENTAF releases airpower summary," CENTAF, October 10, 2006.
82. John Mueller, "Simplicity and Spook: Terrorism and the Dynamics of Threat Exaggeration," *International Studies Perspectives* 6 (2005): 208–34; Lawrence Freedman, "War in Iraq: Selling the Threat," *Survival* 46 (2004): 7–49; Ronald R. Krebs and Jennifer Lobasz, "Fixing the Meaning of 9/11: Hegemony, Coercion, and the Road to War in Iraq," *Security Studies* 16 (2007): 409–45; Jeffrey Record, "Threat Confusion and Its Penalties," *Survival* 46 (2004): 51–72.
83. Paul Wolfowitz, "Iraq at the Center of the War on Terrorism," *The Wall Street Journal*, September 2, 2003; Seymour M. Hersh, "The Gray Zone: How a Secret Pentagon Program Came to Abu Ghraib," *The New Yorker*, May 24, 2004.

84. Thomas E. Ricks, *Fiasco: The American Military Adventure in Iraq* (New York: Penguin Press, 2006), 392–93; Bob Woodward, *State of Denial: Bush at War Part III* (New York: Simon and Schuster, 2006), 427.
85. Donald H. Rumsfeld, "Secretary Rumsfeld and Ambassador Bremer," *DoD News Briefing Transcript*, July 24, 2003.
86. Wolfowitz cited in Rowan Scarborough, "Pro-Saddam Guerrillas Turn to Terrorist Tactics," *The Washington Times*, August 6, 2003.
87. Email correspondence with former senior defense intelligence officer attached to the Joint Staff, November 23, 2008.
88. Woodward, *State of Denial*, 246–47.
89. Scott Shane, "Bush's Speech on Iraq Echoes Analyst's Voice," *The New York Times*, December 4, 2005; Christopher Gelpi, Peter D. Feaver and Jason Reifler, "Success Matters: Casualty Sensitivity and the War in Iraq," *International Security* 30 (2005–6): 7–46.
90. Interview with former DIA official, previously stationed in Iraq, March 2, 2008.
91. Grant, "Iraqi Insurgents Prove Resilient."
92. Andrew Tilghman, "The Myth of AQI," *The Washington Monthly*, October 2007.
93. Interview with midlevel US European Command counterterrorism official, December 10, 2007.
94. Ricks, *Fiasco*, 283–84.
95. Jackson, *Writing the War on Terrorism*, 5.
96. Ricks, *Fiasco*, 274.
97. Major General Antonio M. Taguba, "Article 15-6 Investigation of the 800th Military Police Brigade," http://www.npr.org/iraq/2004/prison_abuse_report.pdf; Errol Morris and Philip Gourevitch, *Standard Operating Procedure* (New York: Penguin Press, 2008); Scott Higham, Josh White, and Christian Davenport, "A Prison on the Brink: Usual Military Checks and Balances Went Missing," *The Washington Post*, May 9, 2004; Scott Wilson and Sewell Chan, "As Insurgency Grew, So Did Prison Abuse: Needing Intelligence, US Pressed Detainees," *The Washington Post*, May 10, 2004.
98. Jerome Bernard, "US plays up Zarqawi role in Iraq," *Agence France Presse*, June 8, 2006.
99. Thomas E. Ricks, "Military Plays Up Role of Zarqawi: Jordanian Painted as Foreign Threat to Iraq's Stability," *The Washington Post*, April 10, 2006.
100. O'Hern, *The Intelligence Wars*, 44.
101. Carol Williams, "Increasingly, the Bombers Are Iraqis instead of Foreign Infiltrators. Civilians and Police, Not GIs, are the Prime Targets," *Los Angeles Times*, June 2, 2005; Dexter Filkins, "Profusion of Rebel Groups Helps Them Survive in Iraq," *The New York Times*, December 2, 2005.
102. Cordesman cited in Jonathan Finer, "Among Insurgents in Iraq, Few Foreigners are Found," *The Washington Post*, November 17, 2005.
103. Jim Krane, "Iraqi Insurgency Led by Angry Sunnis, Believed Larger than Once Thought," *The Associated Press*, July 9, 2004.
104. John Mueller, *Overblown: How Politicians and the Terrorism Industry Inflate National Security Threats and Why We Believe Them* (New York: Free Press, 2006), 187–88; Joshua Alexander Geltzer, "Al-Qaeda as Audience: Signalling in American

Counter-Terrorist Policy and the Al-Qaeda World-View," PhD Diss. submitted to the Department of War Studies, King's College London, 2008, 41–42, 256.
105. Memo from Rumsfeld to Hadley, "Reward for Zarqawi," May 16, 2006.
106. A. J. Rossmiller, *Still Broken: A Recruit's Inside Account of Intelligence Failures, from Baghdad to the Pentagon* (New York: Ballantine Books, 2008), 31.
107. Hashim, *Insurgency and Counter-Insurgency in Iraq*, 13.
108. Ibid., 141–42, 147.
109. Eric Schmitt and Thom Shanker, "Estimates by US See More Rebels with More Funds," *The New York Times*, October 22, 2004; Richard Beeston and James Hider, "Following the Trail of Death: How Foreigners Flock to Join the Holy War," *The Times (London)*, June 25, 2005.
110. Abizaid cited in Wright and Reese, *On Point II*, 110.
111. Bill Gertz and Rowan Scarborough, "Inside the Ring," *The Washington Times*, November 12, 2004.
112. See, for instance, Embassy Baghdad, "1st Marine Expeditionary Force Discusses Situation in AL Anbar Province," July 23, 2004. Accessed via Wikileaks.
113. Evan Thomas, John Barry, and Christian Caryl, "A War in the Dark," *Newsweek*, November 10, 2003.
114. Raymond Bonner and Joel Brinkley, "Latest Attacks Underscore Differing Intelligence Estimates of Strength of Foreign Guerrillas," *The New York Times*, October 28, 2003; Greg Grant, "Iraqi Insurgents Prove Resilient," *Army Times*, March 6, 2006.
115. Bradley Graham, "US Officers in Iraq Put Priority on Extremists; Hussein Loyalists Not Seen as Greatest Threat," *The Washington Post*, May 9, 2005; O'Hern, *The Intelligence Wars*, 48.
116. Joseph Felter and Brian Fishman, "Al-Qai'da's Foreign Fighters in Iraq: A First Look at the Sinjar Records," Monograph, Combating Terrorism Center, US Military Academy, 2007.
117. Graham, "U.S. Officers in Iraq Put Priority on Extremists."
118. Krane, "Iraqi Insurgency Led by Angry Sunnis."
119. "Measuring Stability and Security in Iraq: Report to Congress—May 2006," US Department of Defense, http://www.defenselink.mil/home/features/Iraq_Reports.
120. "Measuring Stability and Security in Iraq," March 2007.
121. Sam Dagher, "Across Iraq, Battles Erupt with Mahdi Army," *The Christian Science Monitor*, March 26, 2008.
122. "Petraeus's Remarks during the House Committee on Armed Services Hearings on Iraq," *CQ Transcripts Wire*, April 9, 2008.
123. Barbara Starr, "Iran Is the Biggest Threat to Iraq's Security Says Pentagon Official," CNN, August 16, 2011.
124. "Measuring Stability and Security in Iraq," April 2010.
125. Michael S. Schmidt and Eric Schmitt, "Leaving Iraq, US Fears New Surge of Qaeda Terror," *The New York Times*, November 6, 2011; Liz Sly, "US General Predicts Unrest in Iraq," *The Washington Post*, November 22, 2011; Rowan Scarborough, "Al Qaeda in Iraq Mounts Comeback," *The Washington Times*, March 5, 2012; Greg Jaffe, "Specter of Al Qaeda Looms in Iraq," *The Washington Post*, July 24, 2012.

126. "National Strategy for Victory in Iraq."
127. "Endgame: *Frontline* Interview with Colonel William Hix, Chief Strategist, Multinational Task Force—Iraq 2004–2005," PBS, 2007, http://www.pbs.org/wgbh/pages/frontline/endgame/interviews/hix.html.
128. Jonathan Finer, "Threat of Shiite Militias Now Seen as Iraq's Most Critical Challenge," *The Washington Post*, April 8, 2006; James Baker and Lee H. Hamilton, *The Iraq Study Group Report* (New York: Vintage, 2006), 11; Nora Bensahel, "Preventing Insurgencies after Major Combat Operations," *Defence Studies* 6 (2006): 278.
129. "National Strategy for Victory in Iraq." See also "Measuring Stability and Security in Iraq" reports from 2005 to 2006.
130. O'Hern, *The Intelligence Wars*, 29.
131. Bremer III, *My Year in Iraq*, 190–91.
132. Hashim, *Insurgency and Counter-Insurgency in Iraq*, 256.
133. Andrew Hubbard, "Plague and Paradox: Militias in Iraq," *Small Wars and Insurgencies* 18 (2007): 345–62; Jill Carroll, "Sadr Militia's New Muscle in South," *The Christian Science Monitor*, September 21, 2005; Steven Vincent, "Switched Off in Basra," *The New York Times*, July 31, 2005; Anna Mulrine, "The Violent Consequences of a Pullout," *US News and World Report*, September 10, 2007.
134. See, for instance, Embassy Baghdad, "MCNS Discusses Militia Death Squads, Recent Military Operations," March 25, 2006. Accessed via Wikileaks.
135. Woodward, *The War Within*, 112, 215, 217.
136. Interview with midlevel US Army officer, October 28, 2006.
137. Interview with former DIA official, previously stationed in Iraq, March 2, 2008.
138. David W. Pendall, "Military Epistemologies in Conflict," *Military Intelligence Professional Bulletin*, July 1, 2005.
139. Rowan Scarborough, "Shiite Iraqi Militia Regroups into 'Gang of Thugs,'" *The Washington Times*, June 28, 2006.
140. Solomon Moore, "Iraqi Militias Seen as Spinning Out of Control," *Los Angeles Times*, September 12, 2006.
141. Hubbard, "Plague and Paradox"; Anthony J. Schwarz, "Iraq's Militias: The True Threat to Coalition Success in Iraq," *Parameters* 37 (2007): 55–71.
142. Gartenstein-Ross, Daveed, and Bill Roggio, "Sadr's Special Groups; Moktada al-Sadr Influences the Mahdi Army's 'Special Groups' More Than the Military Will Admit," *The Daily Standard*, June 9, 2008.
143. Michael R. Gordon, "US Says Iran-Supplied Bomb Kills More Troops," *The New York Times*, August 8, 2007.
144. See, for instance, "Measuring Stability and Security in Iraq," August 2010.
145. Michael S. Schmidt and Jack Healy, "Iraqi Shiite Militias Again Pose a Threat as US Forces Leave," *The New York Times*, May 27, 2011.
146. Ed O'Keefe and Tim Craig, "US Suspects Iran behind Increase in Troop Deaths in Iraq," *The Boston Globe*, July 1, 2011.
147. Feith, *War and Decision*, 284–86, 414–16.
148. Report extract cited in Ricks, *Fiasco*, 151.
149. Phillip Deery, "The Terminology of Terrorism: Malaya, 1948–1952," *Journal of Southeast Asian Studies* 34 (2003): 231–47.

150. Department of Defense Dictionary of Military and Associated Terms, http://www.dtic.mil/doctrine/dod_dictionary.
151. CIA definition cited in Hashim, *Insurgency and Counter-Insurgency in Iraq*, xviii; Joe Klein, "Saddam's Revenge," *Time*, September 26, 2005.
152. Wright and Reese, *On Point II*, 89.
153. Isaiah Wilson III, "What Kind of War?" February 4, 2005, http://thinkbeyondwar.com/Documents/What_Kind_of_War.pdf.
154. Interview with US contractor formerly attached to the Combined Intelligence Operations Center-Baghdad, April 4, 2007; Elaine M. Grossman, "Until Last Month, Iraq Campaign Plan Lacked Specific Benchmarks," *Inside the Pentagon*, March 31, 2005.
155. Peter J. Boyer, "Downfall: How Donald Rumsfeld Reformed the Army and Lost Iraq," *The New Yorker*, November 20, 2006.
156. Ibid.
157. Email correspondence with former senior defense intelligence officer attached to the Joint Staff, November 23, 2008.
158. Hammes cited in Tom Gjelten, "Military Planners Scrambling to Prepare for New Counterinsurgency Challenges Being Faced in the 21st Century," National Public Radio, November 5, 2004.
159. Ibid.
160. US officer cited in George Packer, "The Lesson of Tal Afar: Is It Too Late for the Administration to Correct Its Course in Iraq?" *The New Yorker*, April 10, 2006.
161. Rumsfeld cited in ibid.
162. McMaster cited in ibid.
163. Memo from Cambone to Rumsfeld, July 10, 2003.
164. Memo from Rumsfeld to Col. Bucci, "DoD Dictionary," July 23, 2003.
165. Ron Suskind, *The Way of the World: A Story of Truth and Hope in an Age of Extremism* (New York: HarperCollins, 2008), 372.
166. Woodward, *State of Denial*, 265–66; Tenet, *At the Center of the Storm*, 437–38.
167. Woodward, *State of Denial*, 265–66.
168. Ibid., 266.
169. Ibid.
170. Memo from Abizaid to Rumsfeld, November 11, 2003.
171. Interview with senior US Army officer, January 18, 2008.
172. Memo from Rumsfeld to Di Rita, "History of Insurgency," November 12, 2003.
173. Memo from Rumsfeld to Abizaid, "Counterinsurgency," January 2, 2004.
174. George Packer, *Assassin's Gate: America in Iraq* (London: Farrar, Straus and Giroux, 2006), 305.
175. Interview with US contractor formerly attached to the Combined Intelligence Operations Center-Baghdad, April 4, 2007.
176. Email correspondence with former senior defense intelligence officer attached to the Joint Staff, November 23, 2008.
177. "Interview with Deputy Secretary of Defense Paul Wolfowitz," June 24, 2004.
178. "Wolfowitz Remarks with King County Journal Editorial Board in Tacoma, WA," July 24, 2004.
179. Ibid.

180. Wolfowitz cited in Demetri Sevastopulo, "There Is No Nationalist Insurgency in Iraq, Wolfowitz Tells Congress," *The Financial Times*, February 4, 2005.
181. Rumsfeld cited in Paul Richter, "Rumsfeld Hasn't Hit a Dead End in Forging Terms for Foe in Iraq; The Defense Chief's Lexicon on the Topic Keeps Changing. Now 'Insurgents' Is Out," *Los Angeles Times*, November 30, 2005.
182. Ibid. See also memo from Rumsfeld to Bush, "Progress in Iraq," November 29, 2005.
183. Lawrence Freedman, "The Transformation of Strategic Affairs," Adelphi Paper #379, International Institute for Strategic Studies, London, 2006, 59; John Nagl, *Learning to Eat Soup with a Knife: Counterinsurgency Lessons from Malaya and Vietnam* (Chicago: University of Chicago Press, 2005), 205–8; Linn, *The Echo of Battle*, 193–232.
184. Ricks, *Fiasco*, 264; James S. Corum, "Rethinking US Army Counter-Insurgency Doctrine," *Contemporary Security Policy* 28 (2007): 127–42; Brian Burton and John Nagl, "Learning as We Go: The US Army Adapts to Counterinsurgency in Iraq, July 2004–December 2006," *Small Wars and Insurgencies* 19 (2008): 303–27.
185. Interview with midlevel US Army officer, November 9, 2006; Douglas Jehl and Thom Shanker, "Rewriting the Book on Guerrilla War," *The New York Times*, November 15, 2004.
186. Keith J. Costa, "Army Crafting Field Manual for Counterinsurgency Operations," *Inside the Army*, August 30, 2004.
187. Wright and Reese, *On Point II*, 125–26.
188. Ibid., 125.
189. "Endgame: *Frontline* Interview with Colonel Kalev Sepp (Rtd), Adviser to General George Casey, 2004–2005," PBS, 2007, http://www.pbs.org/wgbh/pages/frontline/endgame/interviews/sepp.html.
190. Anthony James Joes, "Recapturing the Essentials of Counterinsurgency," *Foreign Policy Research Institute*, June 2, 2006.
191. James D. Kiras, "Terrorism and Irregular Warfare," in *Strategy in the Contemporary World: An Introduction to Strategic Studies*, ed. John Baylis, James Wirtz, Eliot Cohen, Colin S. Gray (Oxford: Oxford University Press, 2002), 165.
192. Memo from Rumsfeld to Wolfowitz, "Terminology," January 7, 2004.
193. Wolfowtz cited in Ricks, *Fiasco*, 170.
194. Odeirno cited in ibid., 170–71.
195. Odierno cited in ibid.
196. Ibid.
197. Donald H. Rumsfeld, "Defense Department News Briefing," June 30, 2003.
198. Ibid.
199. General John Abizaid and Lawrence Di Rita, "DoD News Briefing," July 16, 2003.
200. Ibid.
201. Ibid.
202. Boyer, "Downfall"; Gordon and Trainor, *Cobra II*, 489.
203. Donald H. Rumsfeld, "Secretary Rumsfeld and Ambassador Bremer," *DoD News Briefing Transcript*, July 24, 2003.
204. Ibid.

205. Farah Stockman, "US Intelligence Assessment on Iraq in Line with Global Reports," *The Boston Globe*, September 17, 2004; Ken Silverstein, "Sources: Negroponte Blocks CIA Analysis of Iraq 'Civil War,'" *Harper's Magazine*, July 21, 2006.
206. Richard Morin, "Majority in US Fears Iraq Civil War Poll Also Finds Growing Doubt about Bush," *The Washington Post*, March 7, 2006.
207. Bradley Graham, "Little Change in Troop Levels Expected Soon," *The Washington Post*, June 22, 2005.
208. Chiarelli cited in Julian E. Barnes, "General Explains Baghdad Buildup," *Los Angeles Times*, July 27, 2006.
209. David A. Patten, "Is Iraq in a Civil War?" *Middle East Quarterly* 14 (2007): 27–32; James D. Fearon, "Iraq's Civil War," *Foreign Affairs* 86 (2007): 2–16.
210. Memo from Rumsfeld to Bush, "Iraq: Illustrative Courses of Action," November 6, 2006.
211. Edward Wong, "A Matter of Definition: What Makes a Civil War, and Who Declares It So?" *The New York Times*, November 26, 2006; Bartle Bull and John Keegan, "The Definition of 'Civil War' Is Critical to Iraq's Future," *The Financial Times*, November 20, 2006; Errol A. Henderson and David J. Singer, "Civil War in the Post-Colonial World, 1946–1992," *Journal of Peace Research* 37 (2000): 275–99.
212. Finer, "Threat of Shiite Militias Now Seen as Iraq's Most Critical Challenge."
213. Maples cited in Margaret Besheer, "Top US Intelligence Officials Concerned with Latest Iraq Violence," *Voice of America*, February 28, 2006.
214. Abizaid cited in Dana Milbank, "The Waging of the 'Civil' Tongues," *The Washington Post*, August 22, 2006.
215. Pace cited in Dana Priest and Mary Jordan, "Iraq at Risk of Civil War, Top Generals Tell Senators," *The Washington Post*, August 4, 2006.
216. Allawi cited in Patten, "Is Iraq in a Civil War," 29.
217. Bush cited in Juan Cole, "Civil War? What Civil War?" *Salon*, March 23, 2006.
218. "Press Briefing by Tony Snow," White House Conference Center Briefing Room, August 16, 2006.
219. Rice cited in Milbank "The Waging of the 'Civil' Tongues."
220. William Safire, "Sectarian Violence or Civil War?" *Pittsburgh Post-Gazette*, April 9, 2006; Fearon "Iraq's Civil War"; Sheryl Gay Stolberg, "Bush Declines to Call Situation in Iraq Civil War," *The New York Times*, November 29, 2006.
221. Reid cited in Safire, "Sectarian Violence or Civil War."
222. Biden cited in Wong, "A Matter of Definition."
223. Milbank "The Waging of the 'Civil' Tongues."
224. Wong "A Matter of Definition"; Fearon "Iraq's Civil War."
225. Ben Macintyre, "The Brutal Truth: It's Civil War," *The Times*, March 10, 2006.
226. "DoD News Briefing with Secretary of Defense Rumsfeld and Chairman of the Joint Chiefs of Staff General Peter Pace," *DoD News Briefing Transcript*, August 2, 2006.
227. Cordesman cited in Jake Tapper, "Expert on Iraq: We're in a Civil War," *ABC News*, March 5, 2005.
228. Silverstein, "Sources: Negroponte Blocks CIA Analysis of Iraq 'Civil War.'"

229. Email correspondence with former senior defense intelligence officer attached to the Joint Staff, November 23, 2008.
230. Emma Sky, "Transcript: Testimony to Iraq Inquiry," January 14, 2011, 49–50, http://www.iraqinquiry.org.uk/media/52057/Sky-2011-01-14-S1-declassified.pdf.
231. Ibid., 35.
232. Woodward, *The War Within*, 200–201.
233. Rossmiller, *Still Broken*, 184, 187.
234. Nash cited in Tapper, "Expert on Iraq: We're in a Civil War."
235. Bruce J. Reider, "Strategic Realignment: Ends, Ways, and Means in Iraq," *Parameters* 37 (2007): 46–57.
236. Damien Cave and Edward Wong, "Radical Militia and Iraqi Army in Fierce Battle," *The New York Times*, August 29, 2006; Scarborough, "Shiite Iraqi Militia Regroups"; Moore, "Iraqi Militias"; Jim Michaels, "US-Iraqi Offensive Tries to Steer Clear of Shiite Militia," *USA Today*, August 15, 2006; Barnes, "General Explains."
237. "Measuring Stability and Security in Iraq," May 2006.
238. "Measuring Stability and Security in Iraq," August 2006.
239. Donald H. Rumsfeld, "Speech to World Affairs Council," May 25, 2005.
240. For instance, see memo from Myers to Rumsfeld, "Ideas from Senator Alexander," November 17, 2003; Attachment to Memo from Ryan Henry to Rumsfeld, "Metrics for Iraq Weekly Update," July 12, 2004.
241. Rowan Scarborough, "Metrics Help Guide Pentagon," *The Washington Times*, April 5, 2005.
242. Dana Priest and Joshua White, "War Helps Recruit Terrorists, Hill Told: Intelligence Officials Talk of Growing Insurgency," *The Washington Post*, February 17, 2005; Memo from Rumsfeld to Cambone "Size of the Insurgency," February 7, 2005.
243. Sandra Erwin, "Defense Department Rhetoric Reflects War Frustrations," *National Defense*, September 1, 2005.
244. Di Rita cited in ibid.
245. Email correspondence with former senior defense intelligence officer attached to the Joint Staff, November 23, 2008.
246. Headline cited in Woodward, *State of Denial*, 483; Bradley Graham, "Enemy Body Counts Revived: US Is Citing Tolls to Show Success in Iraq," *The Washington Post*, October 24, 2005.
247. Brigadier General Donald Alston, "Defense Department Briefing," *Federal News Service*, January 12, 2006.
248. Joseph L. Galloway, "The Numbers Games: Use of Enemy Body Counts Doesn't Add Up," *Army Times*, November 7, 2005.
249. Woodward, *State of Denial*, 319.
250. Woodward, *The War Within*, 482–83.
251. Jeffrey White, "Assessing the Iraqi Insurgency (Part 1): Problems and Approaches," *The Washington Institute for Near East Policy*, March 24, 2005.
252. Ibid.
253. Michael Handel, "Leaders and Intelligence," *Intelligence and National Security* 3 (1988): 25.
254. Bruce R. Pirnie and Edward O'Connell, "Counterinsurgency in Iraq (2003–2006)," Monograph, *RAND*, 2008, 84.

255. Eisenstadt and White, "Assessing Iraq's Sunni Arab Insurgency."
256. T. E. Lawrence, *Seven Pillars of Wisdom* (New York: Doubleday, 1991), 381.
257. Joshua Green, "The Numbers War: In Washington Measuring the Changing Size of the Insurgency Has Become the Battle to Watch," *The Atlantic Monthly*, May 1, 2006, http://www.theatlantic.com/magazine/archive/2006/05/the-numbers-war/304778.
258. Cordesman cited in Krane, "Iraqi Insurgency Led by Angry Sunnis."
259. Schmitt and Shanker, "Estimates by US."
260. Ann Scott Tyson, "Iraqi Insurgency Is Weakening Abizaid Says," *The Washington Post*, March 2, 2005.
261. Eisenstadt and White, "Assessing Iraq's Sunni Arab Insurgency."
262. Senior US Military Intelligence Officer, "Background Briefing," The Combined Press Information Center, Baghdad, June 2, 2005.
263. Eisenstadt and White, "Assessing Iraq's Sunni Arab Insurgency."
264. Green, "The Numbers War."
265. Rowan Scarborough, "Sunni Insurgency Continues to Grow," *Washington Examiner*, March 21, 2007; Email correspondence with former senior defense intelligence officer attached to the Joint Staff, November 23, 2008.
266. Email correspondence with former senior defense intelligence officer attached to the Joint Staff, November 23, 2008.
267. "Senior US Commander in Iraq, General George Casey Discusses Progress of War in Iraq," *Meet the Press*, March 19, 2006.
268. Sky, "Transcript: Testimony to Iraq Inquiry," 41–42.
269. Wright and Reese, *On Point II*, 89.
270. For arguments that stress cultural reasons the US military was slow to adapt to counterinsurgency, see David Ucko, "Innovation or Inertia: The US Military and the Learning of Counterinsurgency," *Orbis* 52 (2008): 290–310; Burton and Nagl, "Learning as We Go."

Chapter 5

1. See, for instance, Attachment to Memo from Myers to Rumsfeld, "Iraqi Force Estimate," July 13, 2004, http://www.rumsfeld.com.
2. Memo from Rumsfeld to Bush, "Iraq—Illustrative New Courses of Action," November 6, 2006. The idea of a QRF seems to have been drawn from a memo prepared by Michael Vickers, who also presented the idea at a Camp David meeting in the summer 2006. See memo from Vickers to Rumsfeld, "Transitioning to an Indirect Approach in Iraq," June 12, 2006.
3. Memo from Rumsfeld to Bush, "Iraq Policy: Proposal for the New Phase," December 8, 2006.
4. Michael Hirsh, "All the Troops in the World Won't Make Any Difference," *Newsweek*, January 8, 2007.
5. James Baker and Lee H. Hamilton, *The Iraq Study Group Report* (New York: Vintage, 2006).
6. Ibid.

7. See, for instance, Woodward, *The War Within*; Thomas Ricks, *The Gamble: General Petraeus and the Untold Story of the American Surge in Iraq* (London: Penguin, 2009); Peter D. Feaver, "The Right to be Right: Civil-Military Relations and the Iraq Surge Decision," *International Security* 35 (2011): 87–125.
8. General David H. Petraeus, "The Surge of Ideas: COINdinistas and Change in the US Army in 2006," Speech delivered at the American Enterprise Institute, May 6, 2010, http://www.aei.org/article/foreign-and-defense-policy/regional/middle-east-and-north-africa/the-surge-of-ideas.
9. Frederick W. Kagan, "We Can Put More Forces in Iraq," *The Weekly Standard*, December 4, 2006.
10. Tom Vanden Brook and Jim Michaels, "Questions Fill the Air as Bush Speaks on Iraq," *USA Today*, January 10, 2007.
11. As of June 2010, the United States maintained 88,000 troops in Iraq, and on June 30, all US combat troops were withdrawn to bases outside Iraqi cities. The remaining troops were withdrawn by December 31, 2011. See "Timeline: Invasion, Surge, Withdrawal; US forces in Iraq," *Reuters*, December 15, 2011.
12. For text of Bush's speech, see http://www.washingtonpost.com/wp-dyn/content/article/2007/01/10/AR2007011002208.html.
13. Ibid.
14. Bryan Bender, "General Seeks Another Brigade in Iraq," *The Boston Globe*, March 16, 2007; Charles M. Sennott, "The Petraeus Doctrine," *The Boston Globe*, January 28, 2007.
15. Ann Scott Tyson, "Commanders in Iraq See 'Surge' into '08: Pentagon to Deploy 35,000 Replacement Troops," *The Washington Post*, May 9, 2007; John J. Kruzel, "Elements of Final 'Surge' Brigade Begin Arriving in Iraq," *American Forces Press Service*, May 30, 2007.
16. Jim Rutenberg, "The Struggle for Iraq; Democrats Rush to Frame Political Debate Over Troops," *The New York Times*, January 10, 2007.
17. Figures cited in Stephen Biddle, Jeffrey A. Friedman, and Jacob N. Shapiro, "Testing the Surge: Why Violence Declined in Iraq in 2007," *International Security* 37 (2012): 1.
18. Among the mainstream and official narratives, see Kimberly Kagan, *The Surge: A Military History* (New York: Encounter Books, 2009); James R. Crider, "A View from Inside the Surge," *Military Review* 89 (March/April 2009): 81–88; Dale Andrade, *Surging South of Baghdad: The 3d Infantry Division and Task Force Marne in Iraq, 2007–2008* (Washington, DC: U.S. Army Center of Military History, 2010).
19. Charles J. Hanley, "Air Force Quietly Builds Iraq Presence," *The Associated Press*, July 14, 2007.
20. Charles J. Dunlap Jr., "Making Revolutionary Change: Airpower in COIN Today," *Parameters* 38 (2008): 52–66; Craig A. Collier, "Now That We're Leaving Iraq, What Did We Learn?" *Military Review* 90 (September–October 2010): 88–93.
21. Andrew J. Bacevich, "The Petraeus Doctrine," *The Atlantic*, October 2008.
22. Peter Baker, "General Is Front Man for Bush's Iraq Plan: Petraeus Making Hard Sell to Congress," *Washington Post*, February 7, 2007; Thomas E. Ricks, "Bush

Leans on Petraeus as War Dissent Deepens," *The New York Times*, July 15, 2007; Julian E. Barnes, "A Soldier, a Scholar and Also a Politician," *Los Angeles Times*, September 9, 2007; Thomas E. Ricks and Peter Baker, "Petraeus Returns to War That Is Now His Own," *Washington Post*, September 13, 2007.
23. "Report to Congress on the Situation in Iraq, General David H. Petraeus, Commander Multi-National Force—Iraq," September 10–11, 2007, http://www.defense link.mil/pubs/pdfs/Petraeus-Testimony20070910.pdf.
24. Biddle, Friedman and Shapiro, "Testing the Surge," 2.
25. Thomas E. Ricks, "The Dissenter Who Changed the War," *The Washington Post*, February 8, 2009.
26. Nathan Freier, Maren Leed, and Rick Nelson, "Iraq versus Afghanistan: A Surge Is Not a Surge Is Not a Surge," Center for Strategic and International Studies, Washington, DC, October 23, 2009.
27. Steven Metz, "Decision-Making in Operation Iraqi Freedom: The Strategic Shift of 2007," Operation IRAQI FREEDOM Key Decisions Monograph Series, *Strategic Studies Institute*, May 2010.
28. Daniel Davis, "Dereliction of Duty II: Senior Military Leaders' Loss of Integrity Wounds Afghan War Effort," Draft document, January 27, 2012, 63–64, http://www1.rollingstone.com/extras/RS_REPORT.pdf; Sky, "Transcript: Testimony to Iraq Inquiry."
29. Rajiv Chandrasekaran, *Little America: The War Within the War for Afghanistan* (London: Bloomsbury, 2012), 117–18.
30. Gian P. Gentile, "Mired in 'Surge' Dogma," *The New York Times*, November 4, 2008.
31. Jeffrey Michaels and Matthew Ford, "Bandwagonistas: Rhetorical Redescription, Strategic Choice, and the Politics of Counterinsurgency," *Small Wars and Insurgencies* 22 (2011): 352–84.
32. Jon Mikolashek and Sean N. Kalic, "Deciphering Shades of Gray: Understanding Counterinsurgency," *Small Wars Journal*, May 9, 2011.
33. Ibid.
34. Gian P. Gentile, "Counterinsurgency Cookie Cutter Doesn't Fit Afghanistan," USNEWS.com, October 27, 2009. For a similar complaint, see Charles D. Allen, "The Danger of Déjà Vu: Why the Iraq Surge Is Not a Lesson for Afghanistan," *Armed Forces Journal*, December 2009/January 2010, 30.
35. John A. Nagl, "We Can't Win These Wars on Our Own," *Washington Post*, March 9, 2008.
36. Anna Mulrine, "Gates Wants to Send More US Troops to Afghanistan, but How Many?" USNEWS.com, December 11, 2008.
37. Peter Spiegel, "Why Afghan 'Surge' Isn't in the Works; Rugged Terrain and a Lack of Troops Lead the Pentagon to Consider Special Ops Teams to Zero In on Insurgents," *Los Angeles Times*, October 26, 2008.
38. William H. McMichael, "DoD Official Sets Afghanistan Agenda for Obama," *Air Force Times*, November 24, 2008.
39. Tom Vanden Brook, "A 'Tough Fight' Seen for Afghan War in '09; Twice as Many Troops Needed up to 4 Years," *USA Today*, December 8, 2008.

40. Ann Scott Tyson, "Commander in Afghanistan Wants More Troops," *Washington Post*, October 2, 2008.
41. Department of Defense News Briefing with Pentagon Press Secretary Geoff Morrell, *Federal News Service*, January 29, 2009.
42. "Petraeus: Iraq-Style Surge Wouldn't Work in Afghanistan," FoxNews, March 13, 2009, http://www.foxnews.com/politics/2009/03/13/petraeus-iraq-style-surge-wouldnt-work-afghanistan.
43. James Mann, *The Obamians: The Struggle inside the White House to Redefine American Power* (New York: Viking, 2012), 126.
44. "COMISAF's Initial Assessment," August 30, 2009, available at http://media.washingtonpost.com/wp-srv/politics/documents/Assessment_Redacted_092109.pdf.
45. Joe Klein, "Why Did the Iraq Surge Work?" *Time*, November 11, 2009.
46. Cited in Jonathan Alter, "Secrets from Inside the Obama War Room," *Newsweek*, May 14, 2010.
47. Helene Cooper, David E. Sanger and Thom Shanker, "Once Wary, Obama Relies on Petraeus," *The New York Times*, September 16, 2010.
48. Walter Alarkon, "Petraeus Says Obama Told Him Iraq Surge Was a Success," *The Hill*, December 6, 2009.
49. Cited in Klein, "Why Did the Iraq Surge Work?"
50. Anna Mulrine, "Obama Weighs Troop Increase in Afghánistan," USNEWS.com, November 20, 2009; Michael R. Gordon, "Afghanistan a Vexing Test for Obama and Advisers," *The New York Times*, December 3, 2008.
51. Alter, "Secrets from Inside."
52. Gerry Gilmore, "Petraeus: Afghan 'Surge' Will Target Terror Leaders," *American Forces Press Service*, December 2, 2009.
53. Rajiv Chandrasekaran, "In Kandahar, US tries the lessons of Baghdad," *Washington Post*, August 3, 2011.
54. Doyle McManus, "The Kandahar Gambit," *Los Angeles Times*, April 4, 2010.
55. Chandrasekaran, *Little America*, 73.
56. Kimberly Dozier, "Petraeus Fights Time, Enemy in Afghanistan," *The Washington Times*, September 29, 2010.
57. "Lessons in Iraq Applied to Afghanistan, Robert Siegel Speaks with Ryan Crocker," NPR, July 16, 2010.
58. Chandrasekaran, *Little America*, 221–22.
59. Email correspondence with midlevel US Army Reserve intelligence officer, July 2012.
60. H. D. S. Greenway, "General Petraeus's 'Anaconda Plan,'" *The Boston Globe*, April 28, 2009.
61. John Wendle, "The Limits of the Surge: Petraeus' Legacy in Afghanistan," *Time*, August 8, 2011.
62. Chandrasekaran, *Little America*, 234–35.
63. Alissa J. Rubin, "Afghan Program Adds Local Units to Resist Taliban," *The New York Times*, July 15, 2010.
64. Alex Rodriguez, "Anti-Taliban Tribal Militias Come with Baggage," *Los Angeles Times*, June 19, 2010.

65. "Report on Progress toward Security and Stability in Afghanistan and United States Plan for Sustaining the Afghan National Security Forces," Department of Defense, April 2011, http://www.humansecuritygateway.com/documents/DoD-ReportOn ProgressinAfghanistan-SustainingANSF.pdf.
66. Chandrasekaran, *Little America*, 327–28.
67. Ken Dilanian, "Petraeus cites successes in Afghanistan," *Los Angeles Times*, March 16, 2011.
68. Ken Dilanian and David S. Cloud, "US Intelligence Reports Cast Doubt on War Progress in Afghanistan," *Los Angeles Times*, December 15, 2010; Steve Coll, "Let's Hear from the Spies," *The New Yorker*, November 24, 2011, http://www.newyorker.com/online/blogs/comment/2011/11/steve-coll-afghanistan-national-intelligence-estimate.html.
69. David S. Cloud and Christi Parsons, "Obama orders rapid drawdown of US troops from Afghanistan," *Los Angeles Times*, June 23, 2011. For a transcript of Obama's speech, see http://articles.cnn.com/2011-06-22/politics/obama.afghanistan.transcript_1_al-qaeda-network-bin-afghanistan?_s=PM:POLITICS.
70. Mark Landler and Helene Cooper, "Obama to Announce Plans for Afghan Surge Pullout," *The New York Times*, June 20, 2011.
71. Chandrasekaran, *Little America*, 327–28.
72. Thom Shanker, "Warning against Wars Like Iraq and Afghanistan," *The New York Times*, February 25, 2011.

Conclusion

1. "US Looks to Vietnam for Afghan Tips," *The Associated Press*, August 6, 2009; Tom Bowman, "Is Afghan Conflict Akin to Vietnam," NPR, October 1, 2009.
2. Rajiv Chandrasekaran, *Little America: The War within the War for Afghanistan* (London: Bloomsbury, 2012), 230.
3. Obama cited in John Harwood, "Obama Rejects Afghanistan-Vietnam Comparison," *The New York Times*, September 15, 2009; James Mann, *The Obamians: The Struggle inside the White House to Redefine American Power* (New York: Viking, 2012), 13–14, 131.
4. Jason Burke, "Bin Laden Wanted to Change Al-Qaida's Bloody Name," *The Guardian*, June 24, 2011; Jason Burke, "Osama bin Laden Considered Rebranding Al-Qaida, Documents Reveal," *The Guardian*, May 3, 2012.
5. Phillip Deery, "The Terminology of Terrorism: Malaya, 1948–1952," *Journal of Southeast Asian Studies* 34 (2003): 231–47.
6. Antulio J. Echevarria II, "Challenging Transformation's Clichés," *Strategic Studies Institute*, December 2006, 1.

Bibliography

Primary Sources

"2003 Summer Study on DoD Roles and Missions in Homeland Security," Defense Science Board, Office of the Under Secretary of Defense for Acquisition, Technology and Logistics, September 2004.

Action memorandum from Assistant Secretary of State for African Affairs George E. Moose; Assistant Secretary of State for Democracy, Human Rights, and Labor John Shattuck; and Assistant Secretary of State, "Has Genocide Occurred in Rwanda?" May 21, 1994. Secret. http://www.gwu.edu/~nsarchiv/NSAEBB/NSAEBB53/index.html.

"Admiral Fargo Speaks at SOCPAC Change of Command," States News Service, January 7, 2004.

"Background Briefing—Senior US Military Intelligence Officer," The Combined Press Information Center, Baghdad, June 2, 2005.

"Briefing with Commander of the Combined Joint Task Force—Horn of Africa, Major General Samuel Helland," Office of the Assistant Secretary of Defense (Public Affairs), March 23, 2005.

"Briefing with Marine Corps Major General Timothy Ghormley, Commander, Combined Joint Task Force—Horn of Africa," September 21, 2005.

"CENTAF releases airpower summary," CENTAF, June 30, 2006.

"CENTAF releases airpower summary," CENTAF, October 10, 2006.

"Defense Department Special Briefing, Dov Zakheim: FY2003 Budget Supplemental," April 16, 2003.

Defense Group Inc., "Rapid Dominance Strategy of War." http://www.defensegroupinc.com/war_rdpaper.cfm.

"Department of Defense News Briefing with Pentagon Press Secretary Geoff Morrell," January 29, 2009.

Department of the Navy, Chief of Naval Operations, *The U.S. Navy's Vision for Confronting Irregular Challenges*, January 2010.

"DoD Capstone Capabilities Briefing: Quadrennial Defense Review Results," February 3, 2006. http://www.defenselink.mil/qdr/report/Pressbriefing3FebFINAL2.ppt.

"DoD Needs to Assess the Structure of U.S. Forces for Domestic Military Missions, Report to the Chairman, Subcommittee on National Security, Emerging Threats, and International Relations, Committee on Government Reform, House of Representatives," General Accounting Office, July 2003.

222 • Bibliography

"DoD News Briefing—Assistant Secretary of Defense for Public Affairs Victoria Clarke and Vice Chairman of the Joint Chiefs of Staff, General Peter Pace," February 27, 2002.

"DoD News Briefing—Joint Press Conference in Bogota, Colombia, Donald H. Rumsfeld and Colombian Minister of Defense Marta Lucia Ramirez," August 19, 2003.

"DoD News Briefing—Secretary Donald H. Rumsfeld and General John Abizaid," August 21, 2003.

"DoD News Briefing—Secretary of Defense Donald Rumsfeld and Georgian Defense Minister General Lieutenant David Tevzadze," May 7, 2002.

"DoD News Briefing with Secretary of Defense Rumsfeld and Chairman of the Joint Chiefs of Staff General Peter Pace," *DoD News Briefing Transcript*, August 2, 2006.

"DoD News Transcript—Secretary Donald Rumsfeld Joint Press Conference with President of Georgia Eduard Shevardnadze," December 15, 2001.

"Endgame: *Frontline* Interview with Colonel Kalev Sepp (Rtd), Adviser to General George Casey, 2004–2005," PBS, 2007.

"Endgame: *Frontline* Interview with Colonel William Hix, Chief Strategist, Multinational Task Force—Iraq 2004–2005," PBS, 2007.

"Fletcher Conference. Remarks Prepared for Delivery by Deputy Secretary of Defense Paul Wolfowitz," Ronald Reagan Building and International Trade Center, Washington, DC, November 14, 2001.

"FY 2005 Budget Defense Programs, Testimony of General Peter Pace, Capitol Hill Hearing," February 4, 2004.

"Georgia Train and Equip Program Begins," Department of Defense News Release, April 29, 2002. http://www.defenselink.mil/releases/release.aspx?releaseid=3326.

"Global War on Terrorism: DoD Needs to Improve the Reliability of Cost Data and Provide Additional Guidance to Control Costs," US General Accountability Office-GAO-05-882, September 2005.

"UK House of Commons Select Committee on Defence—Examination of Witness Air Marshall Brian Burridge," June 11, 2003. http://www.publications.parliament.uk/pa/cm200304/cmselect/cmdfence/57/3061104.htm.

"Interview with General Richard Myers," *Fox News*, April 3, 2003.

"Interview with Defense Secretary Donald Rumsfeld and Cal Thomas of Fox News Watch," News Transcript, Office of the Assistant Secretary of Defense (Public Affairs), December 7, 2006.

"Measuring Stability and Security in Iraq: Report to Congress," US Department of Defense. All the reports in this series can be found at: http://www.defenselink.mil/home/features/Iraq_Reports.

"Military Operations Research Society Workshop Report—The Global War on Terrorism: Analytical Support, Tools, and Metrics of Assessment 30 November–2 December," US Naval War College, August 11, 2005.

"National Military Strategic Plan for the War on Terrorism," Department of Defense, 2006. http://www.strategicstudiesinstitute.army.mil/pdffiles/gwot.pdf.

"National Strategy for Victory in Iraq: Helping the Iraqi People Defeat the Terrorists and Build an Inclusive Democratic State," National Security Council, November 2005.

http://www.washingtonpost.com/wp-srv/nation/documents/Iraqnationalstrategy 11-30-05.pdf.

"News Transcript: Deputy Secretary Wolfowitz Media Availability with President of Georgia, Office of the Assistant Secretary of Defense (Public Affairs)," October 5, 2001.

"Operation Enduring Freedom: One Year of Accomplishments," White House Press Release, October 7, 2002.

"Petraeus's Remarks during the House Committee on Armed Services Hearings on Iraq," *CQ Transcripts Wire*, April 9, 2008.

"Phone Interview with the Commander of the Georgia Train and Equip Program, Lieutenant Colonel Robert M. Waltemeyer," *Federal News Service*, May 30, 2002.

"Posture Statement of General Bantz J. Craddock, Commander, US Southern Command before the 109th Congress, Senate Armed Services Committee," *States News Service*, March 15, 2005.

"Press Briefing by Tony Snow," White House Conference Center Briefing Room, August 16, 2006.

"Quadrennial Defense Review Report," US Department of Defense, September 30, 2001. http://www.defenselink.mil/pubs/pdfs/qdr2001.pdf.

"Quadrennial Defense Review Report," US Department of Defense, February 6, 2006. http://www.defense.gov/pubs/pdfs/QDR20060203.pdf.

"Quadrennial Defense Review Report," US Department of Defense, February 2010. http://www.defense.gov/qdr/qdr%20as%20of%2029jan10%201600.PDF.

"Report on Progress toward Security and Stability in Afghanistan and United States Plan for Sustaining the Afghan National Security Forces," Department of Defense, April 2011. http://www.humansecuritygateway.com/documents/DoD-ReportOnProgressin Afghanistan-SustainingANSF.pdf.

"Report to Congress on the Situation in Iraq, General David H. Petraeus, Commander Multi-National Force—Iraq," September 10–11, 2007. http://www.defenselink.mil/pubs/pdfs/Petraeus-Testimony20070910.pdf.

"Senate Report 108-046—National Defense Authorization Act for Fiscal Year 2004 Report, Committee Reports for the 108th Congress," Senate Armed Services Committee, May 12, 2003.

"Senior US Commander in Iraq, General George Casey Discusses Progress of War in Iraq," *Meet the Press*, March 19, 2006.

"State of the Union Address by President George W. Bush," January 31, 2006.

"Sustaining Global Leadership: Priorities for the 21st Century Defense," Department of Defense, January 2012.

"Terrorism and the Modern World," Transcript of Secretary of State George P. Shultz's Address, Department of State Bulletin, December 1, 1984.

"Testimony as Delivered by Deputy Secretary of Defense Paul Wolfowitz, Director, Office of Management and Budget Joshua Bolten, and Acting Chief of Staff, US Army, General John Keane," US Department of Defense Speeches, July 29, 2003

"The National Security Strategy of the United States of America," White House, September 2002. http://merln.ndu.edu/whitepapers/USnss2002.pdf.

"The Role and Status of DoD Red Teaming Activities," Defense Science Board Task Force, Office of the Under Secretary of Defense for Acquisition, Technology, and Logistics, September 2003. http://www.acq.osd.mil/dsb/reports/redteam.pdf.

"The Role of Naval Forces in the Global War on Terror," Committee on the Role of Naval Forces in the Global War on Terror, Naval Studies Board, 2007.

"The Triumph of Evil: Transcript of Frontline Interview with Deputy Assistant Secretary for African Affairs James Woods at the Department of Defense from 1986–1994," PBS, January 26, 1999.

"The Triumph of Evil: Transcript of Frontline Interview with Tony Marley, Political-Military Advisor for the US State Department from 1992–95," PBS, January 26, 1999.

"The US Navy's Vision for Confronting Irregular Challenges," US Navy, January 2010.

"Transcript: Emma Sky Testimony to UK Iraq Inquiry," January 14, 2011.

US Congress. Senate. Armed Services Committee. "Fiscal 2007 Budget: Department of Defense, Statement of General James L. Jones—Commander, US European Command," March 7, 2006.

US Congress. House of Representatives. Armed Services Committee. Subcommittee on Terrorism, Unconventional Threats, and Capabilities. "FY 2004 Defense Authorization, Statement of Marshall Billingslea, Principal Deputy Assistant Secretary of Defense Special Operations/Low Intensity Conflict," April 1, 2003.

US Congress. Senate. Armed Services Committee. "FY 2007 Budget—Department of Defense, Statement of General John P. Abizaid—Commander, US Central Command," March 16, 2006.

US Congress. House of Representatives. Armed Services Committee. "FY03 Defense Budget Request, Testimony of USAF General Joseph Ralston, Commander, US European Command," March 20, 2002.

US Congress. House of Representatives. Committee on the Budget. "Issues in Budgeting for Operations in Iraq and the War on Terrorism, Congressional Budget Office Testimony of Robert A. Sunshine," January 18, 2007.

US Congress. House of Representatives. Subcommittee on National Security, Emerging Threats, and International Relations. "Issues in Estimating the Cost of Operations in Iraq and the War on Terrorism, Congressional Budget Office Testimony of Donald B. Marron," July 18, 2006.

US Congress. Senate. Armed Services Committee. "Military Strategy and Operations Requirements in the FY2007 Defense Budget, Testimony of Admiral William Fallon," March 7, 2006.

US Congress. House of Representatives. Committee on Armed Services. "On Operation Iraqi Freedom: Outside Perspectives, Statement by Dr. Stephen Biddle," October 21, 2003.

US Congress. House of Representatives. Armed Services Committee. Subcommittee on Terrorism, Unconventional Threats, and Capabilities, "SOCOM's Missions And Roles—Testimony of Michael G. Vickers," June 29, 2006.

US Congress. House of Representatives. International Relations Committee. "Statement of Admiral Thomas B. Fargo Commander, US Pacific Command," March 8, 2005.

US Congress. House of Representatives. Committee on House Appropriations. Subcommittee on Defense. "Statement of General Richard B. Myers, Chairman of the Joint Chiefs of Staff," February 12, 2004.

US Congress. House of Representatives. Armed Services Committee. Special Oversight Panel on Terrorism. "Statement of Lieutenant General David D. Mckiernan, Deputy Chief of Staff (G-3), United States Army," July 11, 2002.

US Congress. Senate. Armed Services Committee. "Statement of Admiral Timothy J. Keating, Commander United States Northern Command and North American Aerospace Command," March 14, 2006.

US Congress. House of Representatives. Government Reform Committee. Subcommittee on National Security, Emerging Threats, and International Relations. "Testimony of Dr. James J. Carafano, Senior Fellow, Center for Strategic and Budgetary Assessments," April 29, 2003.

US Congress. House of Representatives. National Security Committee. Military Procurement Subcommittee. "Testimony of General Charles Horner," September 12, 1996.

US Congress. House of Representatives. Armed Services Committee. "Testimony of General James T. Hill, US Army Commander, US Southern Command," March 24, 2004.

US Congress. House of Representatives. International Relations Committee. "Testimony of Rear Admiral Hamlin B. Tallent, Director of Operations, US European Command," March 10, 2005.

US Congress. House of Representatives. Committee on the Budget. "The Cost and Funding of the Global War on Terror (GWOT), Testimony of Steven M. Kosiak," January 18, 2007.

US Congress. Senate. Committee on the Budget. "The Global War on Terror (GWOT): Costs, Cost Growth, and Estimating Funding Requirements, Testimony of Steven M. Kosiak," February 6, 2007.

US Congress. House of Representatives. International Relations Committee. Subcommittee on Asia and Pacific. "US Security Policy in Asia and the Pacific: Restructuring America's Forward Deployment, Statement of Admiral Thomas B. Fargo Commander, US Pacific Command," June 26, 2003.

"US Joint Chiefs of Staff, Joint Publication 3–26, Counter-Terrorism I-2," November 13, 2009.

Abizaid, and Lawrence Di Rita, "DoD News Briefing," July 16, 2003.

Alston, Brigadier General Donald. "Defense Department Briefing." *Federal News Service*, January 12, 2006.

Brooks, Brigadier General Vince. "US Central Command Daily Operational Update Briefing, Doha, Qatar," April 1, 2003.

Brooks, Brigadier General Vince. "US Central Command Daily Operational Update Briefing, Doha, Qatar," April 8, 2003.

Brooks, Brigadier General Vince. "US Central Command Daily Operational Update Briefing, Doha, Qatar," April 9, 2003.

Brooks, Brigadier General Vince. "Central Command Briefing," March 31, 2003.

Bush, George W. "Address before a Joint Session of the Congress on the United States Response to the Terrorist Attacks of September 11," September 20, 2001, Weekly Compilation of Presidential Documents. http://www.gpo.gov/fdsys/pkg/WCPD-2001-09-24/pdf/WCPD-2001-09-24-Pg1347.pdf.

Crowder, Colonel Gary L. "Effects Based Operations Briefing." US Department of Defense News Transcript, March 19, 2003.

Fisher-Thompson, Jim. "US-African Partnership Helps Counter Terrorists in Sahel Region." US Department of State, March 23, 2004.

Kimmitt, Brigadier General Mark. "Coalition Provisional Authority News Briefing," April 24, 2004.

Mattis, Lieutenant General James N. "Memorandum for US Joint Forces Command—Subject: Assessment of Effects Based Operations," August 14, 2008. http://smallwarsjournal.com/documents/usjfcomebomemo.pdf.

Petraeus, General David H. "The Surge of Ideas: COINdinistas and Change in the US Army in 2006." Speech delivered at the American Enterprise Institute, May 6, 2010. http://www.aei.org/article/foreign-and-defense-policy/regional/middle-east-and-north-africa/the-surge-of-ideas.

Rumsfeld, Donald H. "Air Force War College." US Department of Defense Speeches, October 18, 2006

Rumsfeld, Donald H. "Defense Department News Briefing," April 20, 2004.

Rumsfeld, Donald H. "Defense Department News Briefing," October 16, 2003.

Rumsfeld, Donald H. "Defense Department News Briefing," June 30, 2003.

Rumsfeld, Donald H. "Defense Department News Briefing," September 20, 2001. http://www.defenselink.mil/transcripts/transcript.aspx?transcriptid=1901.

Rumsfeld, Donald H. "Landon Lecture," November 9, 2006. http://www.k-state.edu/media/newsreleases/landonlect/rumsfeldtext1106.html.

Rumsfeld, Donald H. "Secretary Rumsfeld and Ambassador Bremer." DoD News Briefing Transcript, July 24, 2003.

Rumsfeld, Donald H. "Speech Delivered at Council on Foreign Relations." News Transcript, Office of the Assistant Secretary of Defense for Public Affairs, October 4, 2004.

Rumsfeld, Donald H. "Speech to World Affairs Council," May 25, 2005.

Schissler, Brigadier General Mark. "Joint Staff Briefing," 2006. http://www.dtic.mil/ndia/2006psa_psts/schiss.pdf.

Sky, Emma. "Transcript: Testimony to Iraq Inquiry," January 14, 2011, 49–50. http://www.iraqinquiry.org.uk/media/52057/Sky-2011-01-14-S1-declassified.pdf.

Taguba, Major General Antonio M. "Article 15-6 Investigation of the 800th Military Police Brigade," Undated. http://www.npr.org/iraq/2004/prison_abuse_report.pdf.

Wolfowitz, Paul. "Interview with Deputy Secretary of Defense." Department of Defense Transcripts, June 24, 2004.

Wolfowitz, Paul. "Remarks at the National Press Club," December 7, 2005.

Wolfowitz, Paul. "Remarks with King County Journal Editorial Board in Tacoma, WA." Department of Defense Transcripts, July 24, 2004.

Secondary Sources

Achenbach, Joel. "Victory That Defies Logic; Military Strategists Maintain the War Was Lost, in Theory." *The Washington Post*, June 12, 1999.
Adams, Gordon. "The Cost of War: Hidden from Purview." *The National Interest*, October 4, 2006.
Adams, Sam. *War of Numbers: An Intelligence Memoir*. South Royalton, VT: Steerforth Press, 1994.
Ahrari, Ehsan M. "Why the Long War Can and Cannot Be Compared to the Cold War." *Comparative Strategy* 26 (2007): 275–84.
Alarkon, Walter. "Petraeus Says Obama Told Him Iraq Surge Was a Success." *The Hill*, December 6, 2009.
Allen, Charles D. "The Danger of Déjà Vu: Why the Iraq Surge Is Not a Lesson for Afghanistan." *Armed Forces Journal*, December 2009/January 2010.
Alter, Jonathan. "Secrets from Inside the Obama War Room." *Newsweek*, May 14, 2010.
Andrade, Dale. *Surging South of Baghdad: The 3d Infantry Division and Task Force Marne in Iraq, 2007–2008*. Washington, DC: U.S. Army Center of Military History, 2010.
Archer, Toby, and Tihomir Popovic. "The Trans-Saharan Counter-Terrorism Initiative: The US War on Terrorism in North Africa." Finnish Institute of International Affairs, Helsinki, 2007.
Arendt, Hannah. *Crises of the Republic*. San Diego, CA: Harcourt Brace and Co., 1972.
Areshidze, Irakly G. "Helping Georgia?" *Perspective* 12, no. 4 (March–April 2002). http://www.bu.edu/iscip/vol12/areshidze.html.
Arkin, William M. "Planning an Iraqi War but Not an Outcome." *Los Angeles Times*, May 5, 2002.
Arkin, William M. "Rumsfeld's New War Plan." *The Washington Post*, January 25, 2006.
Axe, David. "War Is Boring: US Navy Awakens to Irregular Warfare." *World Politics Review*, February 24, 2010.
Bacevich, Andrew J. "The Petraeus Doctrine." *The Atlantic*, October 2008.
Badey, Thomas J. "US Counterterrorism: Change in Approach, Continuity in Policy." *Contemporary Security Strategy* 27 (2006): 308–24.
Baker, James, and Lee H. Hamilton. *The Iraq Study Group Report*. New York: Vintage, 2006.
Baker, Peter. "General Is Front Man for Bush's Iraq Plan: Petraeus Making Hard Sell to Congress." *The Washington Post*, February 7, 2007.
Banlaoi, Rommel C. "The War on Terrorism in Southeast Asia." Strategic and Integrative Studies Center, Quezon City, Philippines, 2003.
Barnard, Anne. "US Uses Alternative Terms for Fedayeen—US Reluctant to Give Credence to Hussein Unit." *The Boston Globe*, April 2, 2003.
Barnes, Julian E. "A Soldier, a Scholar and Also a Politician." *Los Angeles Times*, September 9, 2007.
Barnes, Julian E. "General Explains Baghdad Buildup." *Los Angeles Times*, July 27, 2006.
Barnett, Thomas P. *The Pentagon's New Map: War and Peace in the 21st Century*. New York: Berkley Books, 2004.
Barnett, Thomas P. "Donald Rumsfeld: Old Man in a Hurry." *Esquire*, July 1, 2005.

Barnett, Thomas P. "The Man between War and Peace." *Esquire*, April 1, 2008.
Barry, John. "After Afghanistan, What Next?" *Newsweek*, January 29, 2002.
Battle, Joyce, and Thomas Blanton, eds. "CentCom PowerPoint Slides Briefed to White House and Rumsfeld in 2002." National Security Archive Electronic Briefing Book No. 214, February 14, 2007.
Baughman, John. "Exercise Balikatan." *Army Reserve Magazine*, Summer 2001.
Beal, Clifford. "Military Lessons from Iraq: After the War, the Struggle over Strategy Goes On." *International Herald Tribune*, April 30, 2003.
Beeston, Richard, and James Hider. "Following the Trail of Death: How Foreigners Flock to Join the Holy War." *The Times (London)*, June 25, 2005.
Belida, Alex. "Wolfowitz Blames Former Iraqi Intelligence Agents for Role in Insurgency." *Voice of America News*, April 21, 2004.
Bender, Bryan. "General Seeks Another Brigade in Iraq." *The Boston Globe*, March 16, 2007.
Bender, Bryan. "Panel Urges Pentagon to Scale Back Cold War Weapons." *Defense Daily*, December 2, 1997.
Bengali, Shashank. "Humane Mission Grows out of Hunt for al Qaeda; A Little-Known Chapter of the War on Terrorism Is Playing Out in East Africa." *The Miami Herald*, February 5, 2006.
Benjamin, Daniel. "Reinventing History: The US Is Wrong to Compare Postwar Iraq with Germany after the Defeat of the Nazis." *Slate*, September 5, 2003.
Bennet, James. "Mission Improbable: War against Terrorism." *The Washington Monthly* 22 (1990): 22–32.
Bensahel, Nora. "Preventing Insurgencies after Major Combat Operations." *Defence Studies* 6 (2006): 278–91.
Berger, Mark T., and Douglas A. Borer. "The Long War: Insurgency, Counterinsurgency, and Collapsing States." *Third World Quarterly* 28 (2007): 197–215.
Berke, Richard L. "Political Memo; A High-Profile Speech Poses Knotty Challenges." *The New York Times*, January 28, 2002.
Berke, Richard L., and Thom Shanker. "As Guns Still Blaze, Bush Aides Debate Shifting Focus to Butter." *The New York Times*, December 2, 2001.
Bernard, Jerome. "US Plays Up Zarqawi Role in Iraq." *Agence France Presse*, June 8, 2006.
Berschinski, Robert G. "AFRICOM's Dilemma: The 'Global War on Terrorism,' 'Capacity Building,' Humanitarianism, and the Future of US Security Policy in Africa." Strategic Studies Institute, November 21, 2007.
Besheer, Margaret. "Top US Intelligence Officials Concerned with Latest Iraq Violence." *Voice of America*, February 28, 2006.
Bhatia, Michael V. "Fighting Words: Naming Terrorists, Bandits, Rebels and Other Violent Actors." *Third World Quarterly* 26 (2005): 5–22.
Biddle, Stephen. "Speed Kills? Reassessing the Role of Speed, Precision, and Situation Awareness in the Fall of Saddam." *Journal of Strategic Studies* 30 (2007): 3–46.
Biddle, Stephen, Jeffrey A. Friedman, and Jacob N. Shapiro. "Testing the Surge: Why Violence Declined in Iraq in 2007." *International Security* 37 (2012): 1–34.

Bishnoi, Rati. "Navy Establishes Combat Readiness Center to Support Terror War." *Inside the Pentagon*, November 16, 2006.

Björnehed, Emma. "Narco-Terrorism: The Merger of the War on Drugs and the War on Terror." *Global Crime* 6 (2004): 305–24.

Blackburn, Tom. "Werewolves? Must Be a Full Moon." *Palm Beach Post*, September 1, 2003.

Blandy, Charles W. "Pankisskoye Gorge: Residents, Refugees and Fighters." Conflict Studies Research Centre, March 2002.

Blank, Stephen. "American Grand Strategy and the Transcaspian Region." *World Affairs* 163 (2000): 65–79.

Bolkcom, Christopher, Lloyd DeSerisy, and Lawrence Kapp. "Homeland Security: Establishment and Implementation of Northern Command." *CRS Reports for Congress*, May 14, 2003.

Bonner, Raymond, and Joel Brinkley. "Latest Attacks Underscore Differing Intelligence Estimates of Strength of Foreign Guerrillas." *The New York Times*, October 28, 2003.

Boot, Max. "The New American Way of War." *Foreign Affairs* 82 (2003): 41–48.

Borger, Julian. "Knives Come Out for Rumsfeld as the Generals Fight Back: Interfering Style Blamed for Army Setbacks." *The Guardian*, March 31, 2003.

Borger, Julian. "Pentagon Outlines Plans to Take War on Terror to Georgia." *The Guardian*, February 28, 2002.

Bowman, Tom, "Is Afghan Conflict Akin to Vietnam," NPR, October 1, 2009.

Bowring, Philip. "Stretching the War on Terror." *International Herald Tribune*, August 14, 2002.

Boyer, Peter J. "Downfall: How Donald Rumsfeld Reformed the Army and Lost Iraq." *The New Yorker*, November 20, 2006.

Boyer, Peter J. "The New War Machine: How General Tommy Franks Joined Donald Rumsfeld in the Fight to Transform the Military." *The New Yorker*, June 30, 2003.

Brandon, James. "To Fight Al Qaeda, US Troops in Africa Build Schools Instead." *The Christian Science Monitor*, January 9, 2006.

Brannen, Kate. "OMB Asks Defense to Shift Programs Out of War Bill." *Federal Times*, December 7, 2011.

Bremer, L. Paul, III. *My Year in Iraq: The Struggle to Build a Future of Hope*. New York: Simon and Schuster, 2006.

Brennan, Richard. "Protecting the Homeland: Insights from Army Wargames." RAND, January 1, 2002.

Brindle, James B. "Deployable Homeland Anti-Cruise Missile Defense." *Air Defense Artillery*, October–December 2006.

Brooke, Micool. "US Navy Ready if Taiwan Crisis Explodes, Admiral Says," *The Associated Press*, August 13, 1999.

Brookes, Peter. "No Bungle in the Jungle: Operation Enduring Freedom-Philippines is Getting Results." *Armed Forces Journal*, September 2007.

Brown, David. "A Wellspring of War-Fighting Ideas; Secret 'Deep Blue' Think Tank Putting Theory into Action." *Marine Corps Times*, September 2, 2002.

Brown, David. "Deployment Dominoes; When Deployment Plans Change for One Carrier Group, the Impact Reaches Far and Can Affect Thousands of Lives." *Navy Times*, November 26, 2001.

Brown, Malina. "Navy Decides against Decommissioning 13 Cyclone Patrol Craft." *Inside the Navy*, February 10, 2003.

Brumley, Bryan. "Weinberger: Force Remains an Option to Fight Terrorism." *The Associated Press*, January 21, 1987.

Budiansky, Stephen. *Air Power: From Kitty Hawk to Gulf War II: A History of the People, Ideas, and Machines that Transformed War in the Century of Flight*. London: Penguin Books, 2003.

Bull, Bartle, and John Keegan. "The Definition of 'Civil War' is Critical to Iraq's Future." *The Financial Times*, November 20, 2006.

Burke, Jason. "Bin Laden Wanted to Change Al-Qaida's Bloody Name." *The Guardian*, June 24, 2011.

Burke, Jason. "Osama bin Laden Considered Rebranding Al-Qaida, Documents Reveal." *The Guardian*, May 3, 2012.

Burkeman, Oliver. "Shock Tactics." *The Guardian*, March 25, 2003.

Burton, Brian, and John Nagl. "Learning As We Go: The US Army Adapts to Counterinsurgency in Iraq, July 2004–December 2006." *Small Wars and Insurgencies* 19 (2008): 303–27.

Butler, Amy. "Director Hopes to Form Accord for USAF Domestic Security Approach." *Inside the Air Force*, June 28, 2002.

Buzbee, Sally. "Rumsfeld Offers Closer Military Ties to Former Soviet Republics in Exchange for Help in War against Terrorism." *The Associated Press*, December 16, 2001.

Buzzell, Colby. *My War: Killing Time in Iraq*. New York: G. P. Putnam's Sons, 2005.

Byman, Daniel. "Scoring the War on Terrorism." *The National Interest* 72 (2003): 75–85.

Cable, Larry. *Unholy Grail: The US and the Wars in Vietnam 1965–1968*. London: Routledge, 1991.

Cameron, Gavin. "Weapons of Mass Destruction Terrorism Research: Past and Future." In *Research on Terrorism: Trends, Achievements and Failures*, ed. Andrew Silke, 72–90. New York: Frank Cass, 2004.

Cannon, Lou, and David Hoffman. "US Officials Claim Unrest in Libya; Targets Said Chosen to Raise Discontent." *The Washington Post*, April 17, 1986.

Carroll, Jill. "Sadr Militia's New Muscle in South." *The Christian Science Monitor*, September 21, 2005.

Castelli, Christopher J. "Navy Raises 313-Ship Goal to 324, Boosts Focus on Missile Defense." *Inside the Pentagon*, December 10, 2009.

Castellon, David. "Changing of the Guard? With Noble Eagle Taking a Toll on Aircraft and Airmen, Some Worry Guard and Reserve Units Will Be Assigned Permanently to Homeland Defense." *Air Force Times*, February 4, 2002.

Cavas, Christopher P. "US Navy Asking for $161 Billion." *Defense News*, February 8, 2010.

Cave, Damien, and Edward Wong. "Radical Militia and Iraqi Army in Fierce Battle." *The New York Times*, August 29, 2006.
Chandrasekaran, Rajiv. "In Kandahar, US Tries the Lessons of Baghdad." *The Washington Post*, August 3, 2011.
Chandrasekaran, Rajiv. *Little America: The War within the War for Afghanistan*. London: Bloomsbury, 2012.
Chandrasekaran, Rajiv, and Peter Baker. "Allies Struggle for Supply Lines; Massive Air Strikes Hit Baghdad; Iraq Says Market Explosion Kills 58." *The Washington Post*, March 30, 2003.
Charter, David, and Michael Evans. "Britain Reined in US Military's Shock and Awe Strategy." *The Times*, May 2, 2003.
Chartrand, Sarah. "Patents; Before Shock and Awe Can Go from Battlefield to Lunch Box, There Is a Stop at the Trademark Office." *The New York Times*, April 21, 2003.
Christenson, Sig. "The Promise of Army South: Move to Fort Sam Houston Next Year Comes amid High Expectations." *San Antonio Express-News*, September 23, 2002.
Clancy, Tom, and General Chuck Horner. *Every Man a Tiger*. London: Penguin Putnam Inc., 2000.
Clarke, Richard A. *Against All Enemies: Inside America's War on Terror*. Sydney: Free Press, 2004.
Cloud, David S., and Christi Parsons. "Obama Orders Rapid Drawdown of US Troops from Afghanistan." *Los Angeles Times*, June 23, 2011.
Coker, Christopher. *War in an Age of Risk*. Cambridge, UK: Polity Press, 2009.
Cole, Juan. "Civil War? What Civil War?" *Salon*, March 23, 2006.
Coll, Steve. "Let's Hear from the Spies." *The New Yorker*, November 24, 2011. http://www.newyorker.com/online/blogs/comment/2011/11/steve-coll-afghanistan-national-intelligence-estimate.html.
Collier, Craig A. "Now That We're Leaving Iraq, What Did We Learn?" *Military Review* 90 (September–October 2010): 88–93.
Collinson, Stephen. "Ahead of Bush talks, Philippine President Pledges Full Support for US War on Terror." *Agence France Presse*, November 20, 2001.
Compton, James R. "Shocked and Awed: The Convergence of Military and Media Discourse." In *Global Politics in the Information Age*, edited by Peter Wilkin and Mark Lacy, 39–62. Manchester: Manchester University Press, 2006.
Conversino, Mark J. "Book Review of Shock and Awe: Achieving Rapid Dominance." *Naval War College Review*, Summer 1998.
Cooper, Helene, David E. Sanger, and Thom Shanker. "Once Wary, Obama Relies on Petraeus." *The New York Times*, September 16, 2010.
Correll, John T. "What Happened to Shock and Awe?" *Air Force Magazine* 86, no. 11 (November 2003): 52–57
Correll, John T. "Verbatim." *Air Force Magazine* 89, no. 2 (February 2006): 10.
Cortell Andrew P., and James W. Davis Jr. "Understanding the Domestic Impact of International Norms: A Research Agenda." *International Studies Review* 2 (2000): 65–87.

Corum, James S. "Rethinking US Army Counterinsurgency Doctrine." *Contemporary Security Policy* 28 (2007): 127–42.

Costa, Keith J. "Army Crafting Field Manual for Counterinsurgency Operations." *Inside the Army*, August 30, 2004.

Courtney, Bill. "Homeland Role Challenges Army Strategy." *Defense News*, May 20, 2002.

Cox, Michael. "From the Cold War to the War on Terror." In *The Globalization of World Politics: An Introduction to International Relations*, edited by John Baylis and Steve Smith, 150–67. Oxford: Oxford University Press, 2005.

Crane, Conrad. "Facing the Hydra: Maintaining Strategic Balance While Pursuing a Global War against Terrorism." Monograph, *Strategic Studies Institute*, May 2002.

Crane, Conrad. "Final Report: The US Army's Initial Impressions of Operations Enduring Freedom and Noble Eagle." US Army War College, Carlisle, PA, September 2002.

Crawley, Vince. "Outing Saddam: Troops Find Task Will Be No Walk in the Park," *Air Force Times*, April 7, 2003.

Crawley, Vince, and Gordon Lubold. "African Deployments Would Enhance Training, Jones Says; US Forces Could Help Local Armies Fight Terrorism." *Navy Times*, May 3, 2004.

Creveld, Martin Van. *Command in War*. Cambridge, MA: Harvard University Press, 1985.

Crider, James R. "A View from Inside the Surge." *Military Review* 89 (March/April 2009): 81–88.

Daggett, Stephen, Amy Belasco, Pat Towell, Susan B. Epstein, Connie Veilette, Curt Tarnoff, and Rhoda Margesson. "FY2007 Supplemental Appropriations for Defense, Foreign Affairs, and Other Purposes." *CRS Reports to Congress*, July 2, 2007.

Dagher, Sam. "Across Iraq, Battles Erupt with Mahdi Army." *The Christian Science Monitor*, March 26, 2008.

David, Matthew. "New Name for War on Terror." BBC, July 27, 2005.

Davis, Daniel. "Dereliction of Duty II: Senior Military Leaders' Loss of Integrity Wounds Afghan War Effort." Draft document, last modified January 27, 2012. http://www1.rollingstone.com/extras/RS_REPORT.pdf; Sky, "Transcript: Testimony to Iraq Inquiry.

Decker, Brett M. "A Fair Fight in the Philippines?" *The New York Times*, October 18, 2003.

Deery, Phillip. "The Terminology of Terrorism: Malaya, 1948–1952." *Journal of Southeast Asian Studies* 34 (2003): 231–47.

DeLong, Michael. *Inside CENTCOM: The Unvarnished Truth about the Wars in Afghanistan and Iraq*. Washington, DC: Regency Publishing, 2004.

Deming, Angus. "How to Strike Back?" *Newsweek*, November 7, 1983.

Dempsey, Thomas. "Counterterrorism in African Failed States: Challenges and Potential Solutions." *Strategic Studies Institute*, April 2006.

Dennison, Clayton. "Operation Iraqi Freedom: What Went Wrong? A Clausewitzian Analysis." *Journal of Military and Strategic Studies* 9 (2006–7): 1–33.

Di Pasquale, Cynthia. "USAF, DHS Writing MOU to Define Air Patrol's Role in Homeland Defense." *Inside the Air Force*, December 12, 2003.

Dilanian, Ken, and David S. Cloud. "US Intelligence Reports Cast Doubt on War Progress in Afghanistan." *Los Angeles Times*, December 15, 2010.

Dilanian, Ken. "Petraeus Cites Successes in Afghanistan." *Los Angeles Times*, March 16, 2011.

Dorman, Andrew M. "Transforming to Effects-Based Operations: Lessons from the United Kingdom Experience." *Strategic Studies Institute*, January 2008.

Dorr, Robert F. "GWOT or Not? The Term Isn't Important, but the Facts Are." *Army Times*, October 29, 2007.

Dozier, Kimberly. "Petraeus Fights Time, Enemy in Afghanistan." *The Washington Times*, September 29, 2010.

Drehle, David von. "Rumsfeld's Transformation: There's Been a Small Change in Plan." *The Washington Post*, February 12, 2006.

Duffy, Brian, Richard J. Newman, David E. Kaplan, and Thomas Omestad. "The Price of Payback." *US News and World Report*, September 7, 1998.

Duffy, Thomas. "New Strategy Gives Cruise Missile Defense Significant Attention." *Inside Missile Defense*, July 6, 2005.

Dunlap, Charles J., Jr. "Making Revolutionary Change: Airpower in COIN Today." *Parameters* 38 (2008): 52–66.

Duyvesteyn, Isabelle. "How New is the New Terrorism." *Studies in Conflict and Terrorism* 27 (2004): 439–54.

Dwyer, Jim. "A Gulf Commander Sees a Longer Road." *The New York Times*, March 28, 2003.

Dyhouse, Tim. "Shoulder-to-Shoulder: Combating Terrorists in the Philippines: More Than 600 U.S. Troops Are Training Filipinos to Eradicate Muslim Extremists on Basilan Island." *Veterans of Foreign Wars Magazine*, May 1, 2002.

Echevarria, Antulio J., II. "Challenging Transformation's Clichés." *Strategic Studies Institute*, December 2006.

Echevarria, Antulio J., II. "The Army and Homeland Security: A Strategic Perspective." *Strategic Studies Institute*, March 2001.

Echevarria, Antulio J., II. "Toward an American Way of War." *Strategic Studies Institute*, March 2004.

Edney, Bud. "Deterring Threats: Shock and Awe." *Surface Warfare* 24 (1999): 23–27.

Edsall, Thomas B. "GOP Touts War as Campaign Issue; Bush Adviser Infuriates Democrats with Strategy Outlined at RNC Meeting." *The Washington Post*, January 19, 2002.

Eisenstadt, Michael, and Jeffrey White. "Assessing Iraq's Sunni Arab Insurgency." *Military Review*, May–June 2006.

Ellemann, Bruce A. "Waves of Hope: The U.S. Navy's Response to the Tsunami in Northern Indonesia." Newport Paper #28 (2007). Naval War College, Newport, RI.

Emerson, Steven. "Bush's Toothless War against Terrorism." *US News and World Report*, October 31, 1988.

Emerson, Steven. "Stymied Warriors." *The New York Times*, November 13, 1988.

Engelberg, Stephen. "Washington Talk: The Bureaucracy; Tug and Pull over a Vacant Chart." *The New York Times*, December 31, 1987.

Enthoven, Alain C., and K. Wayne Smith. *How Much Is Enough? Shaping the Defense Program 1961–1969*. New York: Harper and Row, 1971.

Erckenbrack, Adrian A., and Aaron Scholer. "The DoD Role in Homeland Security." *Joint Forces Quarterly* 1 (2006): 34–41.

Erwin, Sandra. "Defense Department Rhetoric Reflects War Frustrations." *National Defense*, September 1, 2005.

Faram, Mark D. "We've Got Your Back: Navy Air Units Clear Way for Ground Troops En Route to Baghdad." *Navy Times*, April 7, 2003.

Fearon, James D. "Iraq's Civil War." *Foreign Affairs* 86 (2007): 2–16.

Feaver, Peter D. "The Right to be Right: Civil-Military Relations and the Iraq Surge Decision." *International Security* 35 (2011): 87–125.

Feickert, Andrew. "US Military Operations in the Global War on Terrorism: Afghanistan, Africa, the Philippines, and Colombia." *CRS Report for Congress*, January 20, 2006.

Feiler, Jeremy. "McHale Sorting Priorities for New Pentagon Homeland Defense Office." *Inside Missile Defense*, June 11, 2003.

Fein, Geoff. "Deep Blue Gives Way to Bolstered Director Navy Staff Office." *Defense Daily*, May 7, 2008.

Fein, Geoff. "Naval Expeditionary Combat Command Aligns Forces for GWOT." *Defense Daily*, November 16, 2005.

Fein, Geoff. "Navy Needs Combat Force Capability to Take on GWOT, Official Says." *Defense Daily*, July 15, 2005.

Feith, Douglas J. "A War Plan That Cast a Wide Net." *The Washington Post*, August 7, 2004.

Feith, Douglas J. *War and Decision: Inside the Pentagon at the Dawn of the War on Terrorism*. New York: Harper Collins, 2008.

Felter, Joseph, and Brian Fishman. "Al-Qai'da's Foreign Fighters in Iraq: A First Look at the Sinjar Records." Monograph, Combating Terrorism Center, US Military Academy, 2007.

Fernandez, Manny, and Justin Blum. "Antiwar Protesters Spar with Police." *The Washington Post*, March 22, 2003.

Filkins, Dexter. "Profusion of Rebel Groups Helps Them Survive in Iraq." *The New York Times*, December 2, 2005.

Finer, Jonathan. "Among Insurgents in Iraq, Few Foreigners are Found." *The Washington Post*, November 17, 2005.

Finer, Jonathan. "Threat of Shiite Militias Now Seen as Iraq's Most Critical Challenge." *The Washington Post*, April 8, 2006.

Fontenot, Gregory, E. J. Degen, and David Tohn. *On Point: The United States Army in Operation Iraqi Freedom*. Annapolis, MD: Naval Institute Press, 2005.

Ford, Harold P. "Unpopular Pessimism: Why CIA Analysts Were So Doubtful about Vietnam." *Studies in Intelligence* 1 (1997): 85–95.

Ford, Harold P. *CIA and the Vietnam Policymakers: Three Episodes 1962–1968*. Washington, DC: CIA Center for the Study of Intelligence, 1998.
Franks, Tommy. *American Soldier*. New York: Harper Collins, 2004.
Freedman, Lawrence. "Know, Rather Than Imagine, Your Enemy." *The Financial Times*, May 12, 2008.
Freedman, Lawrence. "Prevention, Not Preemption." *The Washington Quarterly* 26 (2003): 105–14.
Freedman, Lawrence. "The Strategy of Hiroshima." *Journal of Strategic Studies* 1 (1978): 76–97.
Freedman, Lawrence. "The Transformation of Strategic Affairs." Adelphi Paper #379, International Institute for Strategic Studies, London, 2006.
Freedman, Lawrence. "War in Iraq: Selling the Threat." *Survival* 46 (2004): 7–49.
Freedman, Lawrence. *A Choice of Enemies: America Confronts the Middle East*. New York, NY: Public Affairs, 2008.
Freier, Nathan, Maren Leed, Rick Nelson. "Iraq versus Afghanistan: A Surge is Not a Surge is Not a Surge." Center for Strategic and International Studies, Washington, DC, October 23, 2009.
Galloway, Joseph L. "The Numbers Games: Use of Enemy Body Counts Doesn't Add Up." *Army Times*, November 7, 2005.
Ganor, Boaz. *The Counterterrorism Puzzle: A Guide for Decision-Makers*. London: Transaction, 2007.
Garamone, Jim. "Americans Must Understand US Is at War, General Says." *American Forces Press Service*, January 18, 2006.
Garamone, Jim. "Gates: Sea Services Must Question Embedded Thinking." *Armed Forces Press Service*, May 3, 2010.
Garamone, Jim. "Life is Not Predictable, Rumsfeld Tells New Army Officers." *American Forces Press Service*, May 29, 2004.
Garamone, Jim. "Military Culture Must Change to Fight 'Long War.'" *American Forces Press Service*, January 23, 2006.
Garamone, Jim. "Operation Desert Scorpion Continues throughout Iraq." *Armed Forces Press Service*, July 17, 2003.
Garamone, Jim. "Rumsfeld Says Best Way to Thank Troops is to Fund Budget." *American Forces Press Service*, February 14, 2002.
Gardner, Sophy. "Operation Iraqi Freedom: Coalition Operations." *Air and Space Power Journal* 18 (2004): 87–99.
Gartenstein-Ross, Daveed, and Bill Roggio. "Sadr's Special Groups; Moktada al-Sadr Influences the Mahdi Army's 'Special Groups' More Than the Military Will Admit." *The Daily Standard*, June 9, 2008.
Gelb, Leslie H., and Richard K. Betts. *The Irony of Vietnam: The System Worked*. Washington, DC: Brookings Institution, 1979.
Gelpi, Christopher, Peter D. Feaver, and Jason Reifler. "Success Matters: Casualty Sensitivity and the War in Iraq." *International Security* 30 (2005–6): 7–46.

Geltzer, Joshua Alexander. "Al-Qaeda as Audience: Signalling in American Counter-Terrorist Policy and the Al-Qaeda World-View." PhD Diss., Department of War Studies, King's College London, 2008.

Gentile, Gian P. "Counterinsurgency Cookie Cutter Doesn't Fit Afghanistan." USNEWS.com, October 27, 2009.

Gentile, Gian P. "Mired in 'Surge' Dogma." *The New York Times*, November 4, 2008.

Gershman, John. "Is South East Asia the Second Front?" *Foreign Affairs* 81 (2002): 60–74.

Gerstenzang, James. "Response to Terror: Bush Hints at Broadening War." *Los Angeles Times*, December 5, 2001.

Gertz, Bill, and Rowan Scarborough. "Inside the Ring." *The Washington Times*, March 29, 2002.

Gertz, Bill, and Rowan Scarborough. "Inside the Ring." *The Washington Times*, November 12, 2004.

Gertz, Bill, and Rowan Scarborough. "Philippine Confusion." *The Washington Times*, February 8, 2002.

Getler, Michael. "Soviets and Terrorist Activity: World of Shadow and Shading." *The Washington Post*, February 7, 1981.

Gilmore, Gerry. "Petraeus: Afghan 'Surge' Will Target Terror Leaders." *American Forces Press Service*, December 2, 2009.

Gjelten, Tom. "Military Planners Scrambling to Prepare for New Counterinsurgency Challenges Being Faced in the 21st Century." National Public Radio, November 5, 2004.

Glasser, Susan B. "Review May Shift Terror Policies: US is Expected to Look beyond Al Qaida." *The Washington Post*, May 29, 2005.

Gold, Philip. *The Coming Draft: The Crisis in Our Military and Why Selective Service is Wrong for America*. New York: Balantine Books, 2006.

Gomez, Jim. "Muslim Separatist Rebels May Have Stronger al-Qaeda Links Than Group Targeted by US Troops." *The Associated Press*, March 15, 2002.

Gompert, David C. "G-What? A Review of Defense Department Spending on Counter-Terrorism." In *Working Group Papers Prepared for the National Policy Forum on Terrorism, Security and America's Purpose*, edited by New America Foundation, 32–41. Washington, DC: New America Foundation, 2005.

Gordon, Michael R. "A Nation at War: Strategy; A New Doctrine's Test." *The New York Times*, April 1, 2003.

Gordon, Michael R. "Afghanistan a Vexing Test for Obama and Advisers." *The New York Times*, December 3, 2008.

Gordon, Michael R. "US Says Iran-Supplied Bomb Kills More Troops." *The New York Times*, August 8, 2007.

Gordon, Michael R., and Bernard E. Trainor. "As War Began, U.S. Generals Feuded." *The New York Times*, March 13, 2006.

Gordon, Michael R., and Bernard E. Trainor. *Cobra II: The Inside Story of the Invasion and Occupation of Iraq*. New York: Pantheon Books, 2006.

Gordon, Philip H. "Can the War on Terror Be Won?" *Foreign Affairs* 86 (2007): 53–66.

Gordon, Rebekah. "McCullough: Current Fleet Meets Many Irregular Warfare Missions." *Inside the Navy*, June 1, 2009.

Graham, Bradley, and Josh White. "Abizaid Credited with Popularizing the Term 'Long War.'" *The Washington Post*, February 3, 2006.

Graham, Bradley, and Vernon Loeb. "An Air War of Might, Coordination and Risks." *The Washington Post*, April 27, 2003.

Graham, Bradley. "After 9/11, US Planes Began Softening Iraqi Defenses." *The Boston Globe*, July 20, 2003.

Graham, Bradley. "Enemy Body Counts Revived: US is Citing Tolls to Show Success in Iraq." *The Washington Post*, October 24, 2005.

Graham, Bradley. "Little Change in Troop Levels Expected Soon." *The Washington Post*, June 22, 2005.

Graham, Bradley. "Pentagon Can Now Fund Foreign Militaries." *The Washington Post*, January 29, 2006.

Graham, Bradley. "US Officers in Iraq Put Priority on Extremists; Hussein Loyalists Not Seen as Greatest Threat." *The Washington Post*, May 9, 2005.

Graham, Bradley. "War Plans Drafted to Counter Terror Attacks in US; Domestic Effort Is Big Shift for Military." *The Washington Post*, August 8, 2005.

Grant, Greg. "Iraqi Insurgents Prove Resilient." *Army Times*, March 6, 2006.

Green, Joshua. "The Numbers War: In Washington Measuring the Changing Size of the Insurgency Has Become the Battle to Watch." *The Atlantic Monthly*, May 1, 2006. http://www.theatlantic.com/magazine/archive/2006/05/the-numbers-war/304778.

Greene, Philip A. "Irregular Agenda." *Defense News*, February 15, 2010.

Greenway, H. D. S. "General Petraeus's 'Anaconda Plan.'" *The Boston Globe*, April 28, 2009.

Griswold, Eliza. "Waging Peace in the Philippines: With Innovative Tactics, US Makes Headway in War on Terror." *Smithsonian*, December 2006.

Gross, Richard C. "Weinberger on US Military Might against Adversaries." *United Press International*, January 14, 1986.

Grossman, Elaine M. "Key Generals: Response to Fedayeen a Vital Milestone in Iraq War." *Inside the Pentagon*, May 8, 2003.

Grossman, Elaine M. "Until Last Month, Iraq Campaign Plan Lacked Specific Benchmarks." *Inside the Pentagon*, March 31, 2005.

Grossman, Elaine M. "US Military Watches Chalabi, Gives Forces Largely Symbolic Role." *Inside the Pentagon*, May 1, 2003.

Gyves, Cliff, and Chris Wyckoff. "Algerian Groupe Salafiste de la Predication et le Combat (GSPC): An Operational Analysis." *Strategic Insights* 5 (2006). http://www.isn.ethz.ch/isn/Digital-Library/Publications/Detail/?ots591=0c54e3b3-1e9c-be1e-2c24-a6a8c7060233&lng=en&id=32150.

Halloran, Richard. "Swift US Retribution for Terrorists Called Doubtful." *The New York Times*, February 3, 1981.

Hancock, Daniel A. "The Navy's Not Serious about Riverine Warfare." *Proceedings* 134 (2008): 14–19.

Handel, Michael. "Leaders and Intelligence." *Intelligence and National Security* 3 (1988): 3–39.

Hanley, Charles J. "Air Force Quietly Builds Iraq Presence." *The Associated Press*, July 14, 2007.

Harrison, Nathaniel. "Official US Rhetoric Links Iraqi Resistance to 'Terrorists.'" *Agence France Presse*, March 30, 2003.

Harwood, John. "Obama Rejects Afghanistan-Vietnam Comparison." *The New York Times*, September 15, 2009.

Hashim, Ahmed S. "Iraqi Insurgency is no Monolith." *Pacific News Service*, July 29, 2003.

Hashim, Ahmed S. *Insurgency and Counter-Insurgency in Iraq*. New York: Cornell University Press, 2006.

Hattendorf, John B. "Seventeenth International Seapower Symposium, Report of the Proceedings, 19–23 September 2005." Naval War College, Newport, RI. 2006. http://www.usnwc.edu/getattachment/a56bf61f-f637-4391-a9d1-7e261146b3ed/ROP-17th.

Hattendorf, John B. "US Naval Strategy in the 1990s—Selected Documents." Newport Papers #27 (September 2006). Naval War College, Newport, RI. http://www.ibiblio.org/anrs/docs/V/1103%20US%20Naval%20Strategy%20in%20the%201990s.pdf.

Hawkins, William R. "Iraq: Heavy Forces and Decisive Warfare," *Parameters* 33 (2003): 61–67.

Hegland, Corine. "Pentagon, State Struggle to Define Nation-Building Roles." *The National Journal*, April 30, 2007.

Heinze, Eric. A. "The Rhetoric of Genocide in U.S. Foreign Policy: Rwanda and Darfur Compared." *Political Science Quarterly* 122 (2007): 359–84.

Henderson, Errol A., and David J. Singer. "Civil War in the Post-Colonial World, 1946–1992." *Journal of Peace Research* 37 (2000): 275–99.

Hendrix, Henry J. "Buy Fords, Not Ferraris." *Proceedings* 135 (2009).

Heng, Yee-Kuang. *War as Risk Management: Strategy and Conflict in an Age of Globalised Risks*. London: Routledge, Taylor and Francis Group, 2006.

Herbert, Adam J. "Homeland Air Force." *Air Force Magazine* 87, no. 1 (January 2004): 36–40.

Hersh, Seymour M. "The Gray Zone: How a Secret Pentagon Program Came to Abu Ghraib." *The New Yorker*, May 24, 2004.

Hersh, Seymour M. *Chain of Command: The Road from 9/11 to Abu Ghraib*. New York: Harper Collins, 2005.

Hess, Pamela. "Terror War May Need Name Change." *United Press International*, September 5, 2006.

Higham, Scott, Josh White, and Christian Davenport. "A Prison on the Brink: Usual Military Checks and Balances Went Missing." *The Washington Post*, May 9, 2004.

Highland, Grant R. "New Century, Old Problems: The Global Insurgency within Islam and the Nature of the War on Terror." Naval War College, Newport, RI. February 3, 2003.

Hillen, John. "Report on INSS 1998 Joint Operations Symposium—21st Century Warfighting." National Defense University, September 9–10, 1998. http://www.ndu.edu/inss/symposia/jointops98/summary.html.

Hirsh, Michael. "All the Troops in the World Won't Make Any Difference." *Newsweek*, January 8, 2007.

Hitch, Charles J., and Roland N. McKean. *The Economics of Defense in the Nuclear Age*. Cambridge, MA: Harvard University Press, 1963.

Hollis, Patricia Slayden. "Second Battle of Fallujah—Urban Operations in a New Kind of War." *Field Artillery Journal* 11 (2006).

Holsti, Ole R. *Public Opinion and American Foreign Policy*. Ann Arbor: University of Michigan Press, 2007.

Hooker, Gregory. *Shaping the Plan for Operation Iraqi Freedom: The Role of Military Intelligence Assessments*. Washington, DC: The Washington Institute for Near East Policy, 2005.

Hosmer, Stephen T. "Why the Iraqi Resistance to the Coalition Invasion Was So Weak." Monograph, *RAND*, 2007.

Howard, Michael, and Peter Paret, trans. *On War*. Norwalk, CT: Easton Press, 1991.

Hoyt, Timothy D. "Operational Limitations of Military Force in the Global War on Terrorism." Paper Prepared for the Annual Meeting of the American Political Science Association, Hilton Chicago and the Palmer House Hilton, Chicago, IL, September 2, 2004.

Hsu, Emily. "Lawmakers Reject Proposal to Cut US Military Aid to Colombia." *Inside the Army*, July 28, 2003.

Hubbard, Andrew. "Plague and Paradox: Militias in Iraq." *Small Wars and Insurgencies* 18 (2007): 345–62.

Huddleston, Scott. "Talks Tackle All Kinds of Terrorism." *San Antonio Express-News*, August 10, 2005.

Hulse, Carl. "Threats and Responses: Plans and Criticisms; Pentagon Prepares A Futures Market on Terror Attacks." *The New York Times*, July 29, 2003.

Jackson, Richard. *Writing the War on Terrorism: Language, Politics, and Counter-Terrorism*. Manchester, UK: Manchester University Press, 2005.

Jacobs, Seth. *Cold War Mandarin: Ngo Dinh Diem and the Origins of America's War in Vietnam 1950–1963*. New York: Rowman and Littlefield, 2006.

Jaffe, Greg. "Specter of Al Qaeda Looms in Iraq." *The Washington Post*, July 24, 2012.

Javers, Eamon. "Spinning Fallujah." *Slate Magazine*, May 5, 2004.

Jehl, Douglas, and Thom Shanker. "Rewriting the Book on Guerrilla War." *The New York Times*, November 15, 2004.

Jelinek, Pauline. "Pentagon Says US Cost of War So Far is about $20 Billion." *The Associated Press*, April 16, 2003.

Jelinek, Pauline. "Thugs, Terrorists, Death Squads—By Any Name, Pentagon Hates Iraqi Militias." *The Associated Press*, March 27, 2003.

Jennings, Diane. "In Global Fight, Defining Enemies Not So Simple." *Dallas Morning News*, September 23, 2001.

Jervis, Robert. *Perception and Misperception in International Politics*. Princeton, NJ: Princeton University Press, 1976.
Joes, Anthony James. "Recapturing the Essentials of Counterinsurgency." *Foreign Policy Research Institute*, June 2, 2006.
Johnson, Chris. "Analysts Discuss Maritime Implications of China's Energy Strategy." *Inside the Navy*, December 18, 2006.
Johnson, Chris. "Navy Establishes Cell for Submarine Counterterrorism Operations." *Inside the Navy*, April 3, 2006.
Johnson, Matthew. "The Growing Relevance of Special Operations Forces in US Military Strategy." *Comparative Strategy* 25 (2006): 273–96.
Johnson, Robert H. "Exaggerating America's Stakes in Third World Conflicts." *International Security* 10 (1985): 32–68.
Johnson, Robert H. "Misguided Morality: Ethics and the Reagan Doctrine." *Political Science Quarterly* 103 (1988): 509–29.
Johnson, Thomas H., and James A. Russell. "A Hard Day's Night? The United States and the Global War on Terrorism." *Comparative Strategy* 24 (2005): 127–51.
Johnson, Tim. "SOUTHCOM's Future Role is Blurred by War on Terror." *The Miami Herald*, November 25, 2001.
Johnson, W. Spencer. "New Challenges for the Unified Command Plan." *Joint Forces Quarterly*, Summer 2002, 62–70.
Jones, Tyler. "NECC Establishes Riverine Squadron 2." Fleet Public Affairs Center Atlantic, February 4, 2007. http://www.navy.mil/submit/display.asp?story_id=27601.
Kagan, Frederick W. "We Can Put More Forces in Iraq." *The Weekly Standard*, December 4, 2006.
Kagan, Frederick W. *Finding the Target: The Transformation of American Military Policy*. New York: Encounter Books, 2006.
Kagan, Kimberly. *The Surge: A Military History*. New York: Encounter Books, 2009.
Kagwanja, Peter. "Africa: Draining the Swamps of 'Homegrown Terrorism.'" *Africa News*, September 15, 2006.
Kamen, Al. "Pencil in that End of War Date." *The Washington Post*, February 28, 2007.
Kanwisher, Nancy. "Cognitive Heuristics and American Security Policy." *Journal of Conflict Resolution* 33 (1989): 652–75.
Kaplan, Fred. "Rumsfeld's Man: Why Generals Will Fight the New Secretary for the Army." *Slate*, May 6, 2003.
Kaplan, Fred. "This Is Not an Emergency: Supplemental War Funds Are a Backdoor Way to Boost the Defense Budget." *Salon*, February 20, 2008.
Kaplan, Fred. "Why the Army Shouldn't Be So Surprised by Saddam's Moves." *Slate*, March 28, 2003.
Katzenstein, Peter J. ed. *The Culture of National Security: Norms and Identity in World Politics*. New York: Columbia University Press, 1996.
Keegan, John. *The Iraq War: The 21-Day Conflict and Its Aftermath*. London: Pimlico, 2005.
Kelly, David. "Submarine Requirements for the Global War on Terrorism." *RUSI Defence Systems*, Autumn 2006.

Kelly, Patrick. "Defining Homeland Security." *Military Intelligence Professional Bulletin*, July 1, 2002.

Kennedy, Harold. "At War, Navy Finds New Uses for Reserve Forces; Navy Reserves." *National Defense*, September 1, 2004.

Kennedy, Harold. "SOCOM Creates New Hub for Fighting War on Terror." *National Defense*, February 1, 2004.

Khatchadourian, Raffi. "Arming the 'Camel Corps.'" *The Village Voice (New York)*, February 7, 2006.

Khatchadourian, Raffi. "Pursuing Terrorists in the Great Desert." *The Village Voice (New York)*, January 31, 2006.

Khong, Yuen Foong. *Analogies at War: Korea, Munich, Dien Bien Phu and the Vietnam Decisions of 1965*. Princeton, NJ: Princeton University Press, 1992.

Kilcullen, David. "Countering Global Insurgency." *Journal of Strategic Studies* 28 (2005): 597–617.

Kiras, James D. "Terrorism and Irregular Warfare." In *Strategy in the Contemporary World: An Introduction to Strategic Studies*, edited by John Baylis, James Wirtz, Eliot Cohen, and Colin S. Gray, 208–34. Oxford: Oxford University Press, 2002.

Klein, Joe. "Saddam's Revenge," *Time*, September 26, 2005.

Klein, Joe. "Why Did the Iraq Surge Work?" *Time*, November 11, 2009.

Knickerbocker, Brad. "A Cautious Battle against Terrorism." *The Christian Science Monitor*, December 12, 1984.

Krane, Jim. "Iraqi Insurgency Led by Angry Sunnis, Believed Larger Than Once Thought." *The Associated Press*, July 9, 2004.

Krause, Keith, and Michael C. Williams. "Broadening the Agenda of Security Studies: Politics and Methods." *Mershon International Studies Review* 40 (1996): 229–54.

Krebs, Ronald R., and Jennifer Lobasz. "Fixing the Meaning of 9/11: Hegemony, Coercion, and the Road to War in Iraq." *Security Studies* 16 (2007): 409–45.

Kreisher, Otto. "The Years of Noble Eagle." *Air Force Magazine*, 90, no. 6 (June 2007): 50–53.

Kruzel, John J. "Elements of Final 'Surge' Brigade Begin Arriving in Iraq." *American Forces Press Service*, May 30, 2007.

Kuusisto, Riikka. "Framing the Wars in the Gulf and in Bosnia: The Rhetorical Definitions of the Western Leaders in Action." *Journal of Peace Research* 35 (1998): 603–20.

Lamothe, Dan. "Marines to Extend Georgia Training Mission." *Marine Corps Times*, April 6, 2011.

Lamothe, Dan. "US, Philippines Discuss Tightening Military Bonds." *Navy Times*, February 6, 2012.

Lander, Mark. "Philippines Offers US its Troops and Bases." *The New York Times*, October 2, 2001.

Landler, Mark, and Helene Cooper. "Obama to Announce Plans for Afghan Surge Pullout." *The New York Times*, June 20, 2011.

Larson, Eric V., and John E. Peters. "Preparing the US Army for Homeland Security: Concepts, Issues, and Options." Monograph, *RAND*, 2001.

Lawrence, T. E. *Seven Pillars of Wisdom*. New York: Doubleday, 1991.

"Lessons in Iraq Applied to Afghanistan, Robert Siegel Speaks with Ryan Crocker." NPR, July 16, 2010. http://www.npr.org/templates/story/story.php?storyId=128571997.

Lichfield, John. "US Gives Freedom Fighters a Bad Name." *The Independent*, January 14, 1989.

Linn, Brian McAllister. *The Echo of Battle: The Army's Way of War*. Cambridge, MA: Harvard University Press, 2007.

Loeb, Vernon, and Thomas E. Ricks. "Questions Raised about Invasion Force: Some Ex-Gulf War Commanders Say U.S. Needs More Troops, Another Armored Division." *The Washington Post*, March 25, 2003.

Lowe, Christian. "Department of Measures: The Pentagon Tries to Come Up with a Metric for Success in the War on Terror." *The Daily Standard*, August 23, 2005.

Lowe, Christian. "Sailors Go Grunt? Navy May Train Infantry Unit to Handle Corps-Style Missions." *Army Times*, August 1, 2005.

Luck, Gary E, Jr. "Inducing Operational Shock to Achieve Quick Decisive Victory: How Does the Airborne Division Contribute." Monograph, Army Command and General Staff College, Fort Leavenworth, KS, May 27, 1999.

Lum, Thomas, and Larry A. Niksch. "The Republic of the Philippines: Background and US Relations." *CRS Report for Congress*, January 10, 2006.

Lustick, Ian S. *Trapped in the War on Terror*. Philadelphia: University of Pennsylvania Press, 2006.

Luttwak, Edward. "Transcript: Are We Trapped in the War on Terror? Middle East Policy Council." *Federal News Service*, November 3, 2006.

Ma, Jason. "Mullen: Goal is Not Naval Infantry, but 'Maritime Security Force.'" *Inside the Navy*, October 31, 2005.

Macintyre, Ben. "The Brutal Truth: It's Civil War." *The Times*, March 10, 2006.

Magnuson, Stew. "Battleground Africa: U.S. Military Seeks to Quash Terrorism before It Takes Root." *National Defense*, March 1, 2007.

Malvesti, Michele L. "Explaining the United States' Decision to Strike Back at Terrorists." *Terrorism and Political Violence* 13 (2001): 85–100.

Mann, James. *The Obamians: The Struggle inside the White House to Redefine American Power*. New York: Viking, 2012.

Mannion, Jim. "Rumsfeld Seeks Closer Military Ties in Caucasus." *Agence France Presse*, December 15, 2001.

Manthorpe, Jonathan. "Southeast Asia Remains Major Terrorist Battlefield." *The Vancouver Sun*, February 3, 2012.

Marshall, Tyrone C, Jr. "Vice Chiefs Testify on Readiness, Contingency Funding." *American Forces Press Service*, May 10, 2012.

Martin, Aaron L. "Paying for War: Funding US Military Operations since 2001." Diss., Pardee RAND Graduate School, Santa Monica, CA, 2011.

Martin, David C., and John Walcott. *Best Laid Plans: The Inside Story of America's War against Terrorism*. New York: Harper and Row, 1988.

Martin, Zachary D. "By Other Means." *Marine Corps Gazette*, September 2005.

Maxwell, David S. "Operation Enduring Freedom-Philippines: What Would Sun Tzu Say?" *Military Review*, May–June 2004, 20–24.

Mazzetti, Mark, Julian E. Barnes, Kit R. Roane, and Joellen Perry. "Battle Ready." *US News and World Report*, March 24, 2003.
McCaffrey, Barry. "Gaining Victory in Iraq." *U.S. News and World Report*, April 7, 2003.
McGeary, Johanna. "3 Flawed Assumptions." *Time*, April 7, 2003.
McKay, J. R. "Mythology and the Air Campaign in the Liberation of Iraq." *Journal of Military and Strategic Studies* 7 (2005): 1–17.
McLaurin, Mandy. "Navy Establishes First Riverine Group." Fleet Public Affairs Center Atlantic, May 26, 2006. http://www.navy.mil/submit/display.asp?story_id=23854.
McMahon, Robert J. "Eisenhower and Third World Nationalism: A Critique of the Revisionists." *Political Science Quarterly* 101 (1986): 453–73.
McManus, Doyle. "The Kandahar Gambit." *Los Angeles Times*, April 4, 2010.
McMichael, William H. "DoD Official Sets Afghanistan Agenda for Obama." *Air Force Times*, November 24, 2008.
McMichael, William H. "Is Atlantic Command Outdated? Military Leaders Look to Reorganise with Eye on Future." *Daily Press (Newport News, VA)*, March 8, 1998.
Merton, Robert K. "The Unanticipated Consequences of Purposive Social Action." *American Sociological Review* 1 (1936): 894–904.
Metz, Steven. "Decision-Making in Operation Iraqi Freedom: The Strategic Shift of 2007." Operation IRAQI FREEDOM Key Decisions Monograph Series, *Strategic Studies Institute*, Carlisle, PA, May 2010.
Michaels, Jim. "US-Iraqi Offensive Tries to Steer Clear of Shiite Militia." *USA Today*, August 15, 2006.
Michaels, Jeffrey, and Matthew Ford. "Bandwagonistas: Rhetorical Redescription, Strategic Choice, and the Politics of Counterinsurgency." *Small Wars and Insurgencies* 22 (2011): 352–84.
Mickolus, Edward. "How Do We Know We're Winning the War against Terrorists? Issues in Measurement." *Studies in Conflict and Terrorism* 25 (2002): 151–60.
Mikolashek, Jon, and Sean N. Kalic. "Deciphering Shades of Gray: Understanding Counterinsurgency." *Small Wars Journal*, May 9, 2011.
Milbank, Dana. "The Waging of the 'Civil' Tongues." *The Washington Post*, August 22, 2006.
Miles, Donna. "Terror War Needs Funded in Proposed 2005 Defense Budget." *American Forces Press Service*, February 2, 2004.
Miles, Donna. "Terror War Strategy Goes beyond Iraq and Afghanistan." *American Forces Press Service*, November 29, 2005.
Mills, Sara. *Michel Foucault*. London: Routledge, 2003.
Mockaitis, Thomas R. *The "New" Terrorism: Myths and Realities*. Stanford, CA: Stanford Security Studies, 2008.
Montlake, Simon. "Where US Is Helping to Make Gains against Terrorism." *The Christian Science Monitor*, February 15, 2007.
Moor, Jonathan C. "Republic of Georgia Puts Her Best into Iraq Fight." *US Marines Corps News*, August 30, 2005.
Moore, Molly. "Pentagon Publishes Profiles of International Terrorists; 'Know the Enemy,' Carlucci Says in Guide's Preface." *The Washington Post*, January 11, 1989.

Moore, Solomon. "Iraqi Militias Seen as Spinning Out of Control." *The Los Angeles Times*, September 12, 2006.

Morgan, David. "US Says Iran Increasing Activity in Latin America." *Reuters*, March 17, 2009.

Morgan, Forrest E. "'Shock and Awe': Its Origins, Its Role in Operation Iraqi Freedom and Why It Did Not Work." Draft paper, prepared for the International Studies Association Annual Convention in Honolulu, Hawaii, March 1–5, 2005.

Morgan, Joseph G. *The Vietnam Lobby: The American Friends of Vietnam 1955–1975*. Chapel Hill: University of North Carolina Press, 1997.

Morgan, Matthew J. *The American Military after 9/11: Society, State and Empire*. New York: Palgrave Macmillan, 2008.

Morgenthau, Hans. "We Are Deluding Ourselves in Vietnam." *The New York Times Magazine*, April 18, 1965.

Morin, Richard. "Majority in US Fears Iraq Civil War Poll Also Finds Growing Doubt about Bush." *The Washington Post*, March 7, 2006.

Morley, Jefferson. "World Media Recoil from 'Shock and Awe.'" *The Washington Post*, March 20, 2003.

Morris, Errol, and Philip Gourevitch. *Standard Operating Procedure*. New York: Penguin Press, 2008.

Morris, Jefferson. "Clary: Central Command Will Serve As Model for NORTHCOM." *Aerospace Daily*, August 14, 2002.

Morrison, David C. "The 'Shadow War': The Air Attack on Libya." *The National Journal* 18 (1986): 1100–5.

Moss, Michael. "A Ragtag Insurgency Gains a Qaeda Lifeline." *The New York Times*, July 1, 2008.

Motlagh, Jason. "US Seeks to Secure Sahara Desert; Terror Potential Cited in Lawless, Struggling Area." *The Washington Times*, November 17, 2005.

Mueller, John. "Simplicity and Spook: Terrorism and the Dynamics of Threat Exaggeration." *International Studies Perspectives* 6 (2005): 208–34.

Mueller, John. *Overblown: How Politicians and the Terrorism Industry Inflate National Security Threats and Why We Believe Them*. New York: Free Press, 2006.

Mulrine, Anna. "Gates Wants to Send More US Troops to Afghanistan, but How Many?" USNEWS.com, December 11, 2008. http://www.usnews.com/news/iraq/articles/2008/12/11/gates-wants-to-send-more-us-troops-to-afghanistan-but-how-many.

Mulrine, Anna. "Obama Weighs Troop Increase in Afghanistan." USNEWS.com, November 20, 2009.

Mulrine, Anna. "The Violent Consequences of a Pullout." *US News and World Report*, September 10, 2007.

Munoz, Carlo. "US Boosts Military Support to Philippines." *The Hill*, May 3, 2012.

Murphy, Dan. "Long-Term US Strategy Emerges out of Philippines." *The Christian Science Monitor*, July 3, 2002.

Murray, Williamson, and Robert H. Scales Jr. *The Iraq War: A Military History*. Cambridge, MA: Harvard University Press, 2003.

Naftali, Tim. *Blind Spot: The Secret History of American Counterterrorism*. New York: Basic Books, 2005.

Nagl, John A. "We Can't Win These Wars on Our Own." *The Washington Post*, March 9, 2008.

Nagl, John. *Learning to Eat Soup with a Knife: Counterinsurgency Lessons from Malaya and Vietnam*. Chicago: University of Chicago Press, 2005.

Nashel, Jonathan. *Edward Lansdale's Cold War*. Boston: University of Massachusetts Press, 2005.

National Commission on Terrorist Attacks upon the United States. *The 9/11 Commission Report, Final Report of the National Commission on Terrorist Attacks upon the United States*. New York: W. W. Norton, 2004.

Naylor, Sean D. "Building Intel from Scratch." *Marine Corps Times*, December 5, 2011.

Naylor, Sean D. "More Than Door-Kickers; Special Ops Forces Are Misused As Man-Hunters, Critics Say." *Armed Forces Journal*, March 1, 2006.

Neumann, Peter R., and M. L. R. Smith. "Missing the Plot? Intelligence and Discourse Failure." *Orbis* 49 (2005): 95–107.

Nichols, Bill. "Widening US Battle Stirs Unease." *USA Today*, January 17, 2002.

Niksch, Larry. "Abu Sayyaf: Target of Philippine-US Anti-Terrorism Cooperation." *Congressional Research Service*, January 25, 2002.

O'Hern, Steven K. *The Intelligence Wars: Lessons from Baghdad*. Amherst, NY: Prometheus Books, 2008.

O'Keefe, Ed, and Tim Craig. "US Suspects Iran behind Increase in Troop Deaths in Iraq." *The Boston Globe*, July 1, 2011.

O'Rourke, Ronald. "China Naval Modernization: Implications for Congress." *CRS Report for Congress*, August 10, 2012.

O'Rourke, Ronald. "Homeland Security: Navy Operations—Background and Issues for Congress." *CRS Reports for Congress*, May 17, 2004.

O'Rourke, Ronald. "Navy Irregular Warfare and Counterterrorism Operations: Background and Issues for Congress." *CRS Report for Congress*, April 6, 2012.

O'Rourke, Ronald. "Navy Irregular Warfare and Counterterrorism Operations: Background and Issues for Congress." *CRS Report for Congress*, May 28, 2010.

O'Rourke, Ronald. "Navy Role in Global War on Terrorism." *CRS Report for Congress*, March 1, 2008.

Packer, George. "Knowing the Enemy: Can Social Scientists Redefine the War on Terror." *The New Yorker*, December 18, 2006.

Packer, George. "The Lesson of Tal Afar: Is It Too Late for the Administration to Correct Its Course in Iraq?" *The New Yorker*, April 10, 2006.

Packer, George. *Assassin's Gate: America in Iraq*. London: Farrar, Straus and Giroux, 2006.

Page, Caroline. *US Official Propaganda during the Vietnam War, 1965–1973: The Limits of Persuasion*. London: Leicester University Press, 1996.

Pape, Robert A. "The True Worth of Air Power." *Foreign Affairs* 83 (2004): 116–30.

Pappalardo, Joe. "US-Mexico: Rapport Transformed by Terrorist Threat." *National Defense*, August 1, 2004.

Parrinello, Christopher A. "Operation Enduring Freedom, Phase II the Philippines, Islamic Insurgency, and Abu Sayyaf." *Military Intelligence Professional Bulletin*, April–June 2002.

Patrick, Stewart, and Kaysie Brow. "The Pentagon and Global Development: Making Sense of the DoD's Expanding Role." Working Paper Number 131, Center for Global Development, November 2007.

Patten, David A. "Is Iraq in a Civil War?" *Middle East Quarterly* 14 (2007): 27–32.

Pelkofski, James. "Defeat Al Qaeda on the Waterfront." *Proceedings* 130 (2004): 32–35.

Pellerin, Cheryl. "Panetta: Violent Extremism Threatens Latin America." *Armed Forces Press Service*, April 24, 2012.

Pendall, David W. "Military Epistemologies in Conflict." *Military Intelligence Professional Bulletin*, July 1, 2005.

Perl, Raphael, and Ronald O'Rourke. "Terrorist Attack on USS Cole: Background and Issues for Congress." *CRS Report for Congress*, January 20, 2001.

Perl, Raphael. "Combating Terrorism: The Challenge of Measuring Effectiveness." *CRS Report for Congress*, March 12, 2007.

Peters, Katherine M. "Troops on the Beat: The Military's Role in Homeland Security is Growing." *Government Executive*, April 2003.

Peters, Ralph. "A Grave New World: 10 Lessons from the War in Iraq." *San Diego Union-Tribune*, April 17, 2005.

Peters, Ralph. "Shock, Awe and Overconfidence." *The Washington Post*, March 25, 2003.

Peterson, Scott. "US Mulls Air Strategies in Iraq." *The Christian Science Monitor*, January 30, 2003.

"Petraeus: Iraq-Style Surge Wouldn't Work in Afghanistan." Fox News, March 13, 2009. http://www.foxnews.com/politics/2009/03/13/petraeus-iraq-style-surge-wouldnt-work-afghanistan.

Pflanz, Mike. "US Troops Keep Watch along Kenya's Coast." *The Christian Science Monitor*, August 9, 2005.

Pham, J. Peter. "Next Front? Evolving United States–African Strategic Relations in the 'War on Terrorism' and Beyond." *Comparative Strategy* 26 (2007): 39–54.

Phinney, David, and Warren Zinn. "Pentagon Refines Homeland Defense Role." *Federal Times*, September 29, 2003.

Pincus, Walter. "CIA Studies Provide Glimpse of Insurgents in Iraq." *The Washington Post*, February 6, 2005.

Pincus, Walter. "Elite Secret US Unit Trains to Foil Terror." *The Washington Post*, February 7, 1982.

Pine, Art. "A Navy in Search of a Course." *The National Journal*, December 2, 2006.

Pirnie, Bruce R., and Edward O'Connell. "Counterinsurgency in Iraq (2003–2006)." Monograph, *RAND*, 2008.

Pitman, Todd. "Africa Terrorism." *The Associated Press*, June 19, 2005.

Plater-Zyberk, Henry, and Anne Aldis. "Russia's Reaction to the American Tragedy." *Conflict Studies Research Centre*, September 20, 2001.

Porter, Gareth. "Document Recently Published about the Iraq War Decisions; Pentagon Targeted Iran for Regime Change after 9/11." *IPS*, May 6, 2008.

Porter, Gareth. "US/Iraq: General Reveals Rift with Rumsfeld on Insurgents." *IPS*, April 15, 2006.

Potter, Beth. "War on Terrorism's African Front." *United Press International*, November 29, 2002.

Pound, Edward T. "Seeds of Chaos." *US News and World Report*, December 20, 2004.

Powell, Stewart M. "Swamp of Terror in the Sahara." *Air Force Magazine* 87, no. 11 (November 2004): 50–54.

Priest, Dana, and Joshua White. "War Helps Recruit Terrorists, Hill Told: Intelligence Officials Talk of Growing Insurgency." *The Washington Post*, February 17, 2005.

Priest, Dana, and Mary Jordan. "Iraq at Risk of Civil War, Top Generals Tell Senators." *The Washington Post*, August 4, 2006.

Priest, Dana, and William M. Arkin. "Top Secret America: A Hidden World, Growing beyond Control." *The Washington Post*, July 19, 2010.

Quigley, Samantha. "War in Iraq Moving in the Right Direction, Says CENTCOM Leader." *American Forces Press Service*, September 26, 2004.

"Quotes from AP Interview with Abizaid." *USA Today*, September 11, 2007.

Ratnam, Gopal, and William Matthews. "DoD Loosens Supplemental Rules; 'Emergency Funds' No Longer Need Pay for Combat Ops." *Defense News*, November 6, 2006.

Ratnesar, Romesh. "Awestruck." *Time Magazine*, March 31, 2003.

Raven, Francis, and Carolyn Kousky. "Name Game; Defense Department Renames Total Information Awareness, Does Little Else." *In These Times*, July 8, 2003.

Record, Jeffrey. "The Use and Abuse of History: Munich, Vietnam and Iraq." *Survival* 49 (2007): 163–80.

Record, Jeffrey. "Threat Confusion and Its Penalties." *Survival* 46 (2004): 51–72.

Record, Jeffrey. *The Wrong War: Why We Lost In Vietnam*. Annapolis, MD: Naval Institute Press, 1998.

Reider, Bruce J. "Strategic Realignment: Ends, Ways, and Means in Iraq." *Parameters* 37 (2007): 46–57.

Renwick, Neil. "Southeast Asia and the Global 'War on Terror' Discourse." *Cambridge Review of International Affairs* 20 (2007): 249–65.

"Report Says Role of Aid in Navy's Plan for Irregular Threats Unclear." *Inside the Navy*, November 8, 2010.

Reynolds, Maura. "Bush to Seek $87 Billion for Effort in Iraq." *Los Angeles Times*, September 8, 2003.

Reynolds, Nicholas E. *Basrah, Baghdad, and Beyond: The US Marine Corps in the Second Iraq War*. Annapolis, MD: US Naval Institute Press, 2005.

Richter, Paul. "Military Is Easing Its War on Drugs: The Pentagon Wants to Scale Back the $1 Billion Program and Focus More on Combating Terrorism." *Los Angeles Times*, October 20, 2002.

Richter, Paul. "Rumsfeld Hasn't Hit a Dead End in Forging Terms for Foe in Iraq; The Defense Chief's Lexicon on the Topic Keeps Changing. Now 'Insurgents' Is Out." *Los Angeles Times*, November 30, 2005.

Ricks, Thomas E. "Bush Leans on Petraeus as War Dissent Deepens." *The New York Times*, July 15, 2007.

Ricks, Thomas E. "For Pentagon, Asia Moving to Forefront: Shift Has Implications for Strategy, Forces, Weapons." *The Washington Post*, May 26, 2000.Ricks, Thomas E. "Military Overhaul Considered; Rumsfeld Eyes Global Command for Terrorism Fight." *The Washington Post*, October 11, 2001.

Ricks, Thomas E. "Military Plays Up Role of Zarqawi: Jordanian Painted as Foreign Threat to Iraq's Stability." *The Washington Post*, April 10, 2006.

Ricks, Thomas E. "The Dissenter Who Changed the War." *The Washington Post*, February 8, 2009.Ricks, Thomas E., and Peter Baker. "Petraeus Returns to War That Is Now His Own." *The Washington Post*, September 13, 2007.

Ricks, Thomas E. *Fiasco: The American Military Adventure in Iraq*. New York: Penguin Press, 2006.

Ricks, Thomas. *The Gamble: General Petraeus and the Untold Story of the American Surge in Iraq*. London: Penguin, 2009.

Risen, James. "CIA Warned Pentagon of Guerrilla Tactics." *The New York Times*, March 28, 2003.

Robbins, Carla Anne. "Post-War Afghanistan War on Terror Seen as Taking Shape." *The Wall Street Journal*, November 29, 2001.

Robinson, Linda, and Kevin Whitelaw. "Deploying the 'Free Iraqi Forces': What Role for the Arriving Anti-Saddam Iraqi Fighters?" *US News and World Report*, April 7, 2003.

Robinson, Linda. "Men on a Mission: US Special Forces Are Retooling for the War on Terror. Here's Their Plan." *US News and World Report*, September 11, 2006.

Robinson, Linda. "Next Stop, Colombia." *US News and World Report*, February 25, 2002.

Robinson, Linda. "Plan of Attack." *US News and World Report*, August 1, 2005.

Robinson, Linda. "Warrior Class: Why Special Forces Are America's Tool of Choice in Colombia and around the Globe." *US News and World Report*, February 10, 2003.

Rodriguez, Alex. "Anti-Taliban Tribal Militias Come with Baggage." *Los Angeles Times*, June 19, 2010.

Rogers, Steven. "Beyond the Abu Sayef." *Foreign Affairs*, January–February 2004, 15–20.

Rolfsen, Bruce. "DoD Favors 'Shock and Awe' Strategy: Desert Storm Leaders Shy Away from Drawn-Out Ground War." *Air Force Times*, March 17, 2003.

Roncesvalles, Carina I. "US Military Exec in the Country for Balikatan Preparation." *Business World*, June 5, 2003.

Rooney, Ben. "Bomb Blitz will 'Shock and Awe' the Taliban." *The Daily Telegraph*, September 27, 2001.

Rosen, James. "Iraqi Paramilitary Group Hampers Allied Advance: Ruthless Vigilantes Basically Unheard Of during War's Lead-Up." *Modesto Bee*, March 30, 2003.

Rosenberg, Carol. "Southcom to Yield Cuba Role to New Command; Other Latin Functions Will Stay." *The Miami Herald*, April 24, 2002.

Ross, Andrew L., Michele A. Flournoy, Cindy Williams, and David Mosher. "What Do We Mean by 'Transformation?'" *Naval War College Review* 55 (2002): 27–42.

Rossmiller, A. J. *Still Broken: A Recruit's Inside Account of Intelligence Failures, from Baghdad to the Pentagon.* New York: Ballantine Books, 2008.

Rothschild, Matthew. "Rumsfeld Spies on Quakers and Grannies." *The Progressive*, December 16, 2005.

Roxborough, Ian. "Globalization, Unreason and the Dilemmas of American Military Strategy." *International Sociology* 17 (2002): 339–59.

Roxborough, Ian. "The Hart-Rudman Commission and the Homeland Defense." *Strategic Studies Institute*, September 2001.

Rubin, Alissa J. "Afghan Program Adds Local Units to Resist Taliban." *The New York Times*, July 15, 2010.

Rumsfeld, Donald H. "What We've Gained in Three Years in Iraq." *The Washington Post*, March 19, 2006.

Russell, James A. "Transformation into What and against Whom? The United States Navy and the 2006 Quadrennial Defense Review." *World Defence Systems*, 9.1 (March 2006). http://www.comw.org/qdr/fulltext/0603russell.pdf.

Russell, Jenna. "Tens of Thousands Rally in Boston for Peace." *The Boston Globe*, March 30, 2003.

Russell, John. "Terrorists, Bandits, Spooks and Thieves: Russian Demonization of the Chechens before and since 9/11." *Third World Quarterly* 26 (2005): 101–16.

Rutenberg, Jim. "The Struggle for Iraq; Democrats Rush to Frame Political Debate over Troops." *The New York Times*, January 10, 2007.

Rutherford, Emelie. "Irregular Warfare Official: SSGN Subs are Navy's Premier Counterterrorism Tool." *Defense Daily*, October 27, 2008.

Safire, William. "Fruitcake." *The New York Times*, August 10, 2003.

Safire, William. "Sectarian Violence or Civil War?" *Pittsburgh Post-Gazette*, April 9, 2006.

Safire, William. "Shock and Awe: A Tactic, Not A Law Firm." *The New York Times*, March 30, 2003.

Safire, William. "The Way We Live Now: 9-30-01: On Language; Words At War." *The New York Times*, September 30, 2001.

Sandler, Norman D. "Reagan: Terrorist 'Murder Inc.' at War against US." *United Press International*, July 8, 1985.

Sarbin, Theodore R. "The Metaphor-to-Myth Transformation with Special Reference to the 'War on Terrorism,' Peace and Conflict." *Journal of Peace Psychology* 9 (2003): 149–57.

Scarborough, Rowan. "Al Qaeda in Iraq Mounts Comeback." *The Washington Times*, March 5, 2012.

Scarborough, Rowan. "Decisive Force Now Measured By Speed." *The Washington Times*, May 7, 2003.

Scarborough, Rowan. "Metrics Help Guide Pentagon." *The Washington Times*, April 5, 2005.

Scarborough, Rowan. "Pro-Saddam Guerrillas Turn to Terrorist Tactics." *The Washington Times*, August 6, 2003.

Scarborough, Rowan. "Shiite Iraqi Militia Regroups into 'Gang of Thugs.'" *The Washington Times*, June 28, 2006.

Scarborough, Rowan. "Sparing Targets Softens Effect of 'Shock and Awe.'" *The Washington Times*, March 31, 2003.

Scarborough, Rowan. "Sunni Insurgency Continues to Grow." *Washington Examiner*, March 21, 2007.

Scarborough, Rowan. "What's Next: Anti-Terror War's Expanded Scope Touches 8 Nations." *The Washington Times*, April 7, 2002.

Schlesinger, Mark, and Richard R. Lau. "The Meaning and Measure of Policy Metaphors." *American Political Science Review* 3 (2000): 611–26.

Schmidt, Michael S., and Eric Schmitt. "Leaving Iraq, US Fears New Surge of Qaeda Terror." *The New York Times*, November 6, 2011.

Schmidt, Michael S., and Jack Healy. "Iraqi Shiite Militias Again Pose a Threat as US forces Leave." *The New York Times*, May 27, 2011.

Schmitt, Eric, and Thom Shanker. "Estimates by US See More Rebels with More Funds." *The New York Times*, October 22, 2004.

Schmitt, Eric, and Thom Shanker. "Washington Recasts Terror War As 'Struggle.'" *International Herald Tribune*, July 27, 2005.

Schmitt, Eric. "Hurdle Leapt, US Will Help Philippines Battle Rebels." *The New York Times*, January 30, 2002.

Schmitt, Eric. "In Iraq, US Officials Cite Obstacles to Victory." *The New York Times*, October 31, 2004.

Schmitt, Eric. "Pentagon Draws Up a 20-to-30-Year Anti-Terror Plan." *The New York Times*, January 17, 2003.

Schrader, Esther. "A Changed America: Military Fuses Old, New to Create a Lethal Force." *Los Angeles Times*, February 10, 2002.

Schultz, Richard. "Global Insurgency and Counterinsurgency: United States Plans and Strategy for the 'Long War.'" Fletcher School, Tufts University, Boston, 2007.

Schwarz, Anthony J. "Iraq's Militias: The True Threat to Coalition Success in Iraq." *Parameters* 37 (2007): 55–71.

Scutro, Andrew. "Converted Missile Subs Thrive in Multiple Roles." *Defense News*, October 27, 2008.

Sennott, Charles M. "The Petraeus Doctrine." *The Boston Globe*, January 28, 2007.

Sevastopulo, Demetri. "Security Chief Decries 'War on Terror.'" *The Financial Times*, May 29, 2008.

Sevastopulo, Demetri. "There Is No Nationalist Insurgency in Iraq, Wolfowitz Tells Congress." *The Financial Times*, February 4, 2005.

Shafer, D. Michael. "The Unlearned Lessons of Counter-Insurgency." *Political Science Quarterly* 103 (1988): 57–80.

Shane, Scott. "Bush's Speech on Iraq Echoes Analyst's Voice." *The New York Times*, December 4, 2005.

Shane, Scott, Mark Mazzetti, and Robert F. Worth. "A Secret Assault on Terror Widens on Two Continents." *The New York Times*, August 15, 2010, A1.

Shanker, Thom, and Eric Schmitt. "Three Terrorist Groups in Africa Pose Threat to US, American Commander Says." *The New York Times*, September 15, 2011.

Shanker, Thom, and Rick Gladstone. "Armed US Advisers to Help Fight African Renegade Group." *The New York Times*, October 15, 2011.

Shanker, Thom. "All Quiet on the Home Front, and Some Soldiers Are Asking Why." *The New York Times*, July 24, 2005.

Shanker, Thom. "Djibouti Outpost behind Somali Rescue is Part of New Defense Strategy." *The New York Times*, January 26, 2012.

Shanker, Thom. "In Horn of Africa, a Glimpse of American 'Soft Power.'" *International Herald Tribune*, December 4, 2007.

Shanker, Thom. "Warning against Wars Like Iraq and Afghanistan." *The New York Times*, February 25, 2011.

Sherman, Jason. "Abizaid Key in Persuading Senior Leaders to Adopt 'Long War' Label." *Inside the Pentagon*, February 2, 2006.

Sherman, Jason. "England Approves New Pentagon Homeland Defense Strategy." *Inside the Army*, July 4, 2005.

Sherman, Jason. "Military Set to Exercise Mobile Air Defense Package for US Skies." *Homeland Defense Watch*, June 19, 2006.

Sherman, Jason. "Navy Staff Prioritizing Capabilities, Missions for Global War on Terror." *Inside the Pentagon*, May 12, 2005.

Sherman, Jason. "Navy to Establish Ground Combat Units, River Force for Terror War." *Inside the Navy*, July 11, 2005.

Sherman, Jason. "President Issues 'War on Terror' Directive to Improve Government Coordination." *Inside Defense*, March 13, 2006.

Shy, John, and Thomas W. Collier. "Revolutionary War." In *Makers of Modern Strategy from Machiavelli to the Nuclear Age*, edited by Peter Paret, Gordon A. Craig, and Felix Gilber, 815–62. Oxford: Clarendon Press, 1991.

Sieminski, Gregory. "The Art of Naming Operations." *Parameters* 25 (1995): 81–98.

Sikorski, Radek. "Interview: Paul Wolfowitz." *Prospect*, November 18, 2004.

Silverstein, Ken. "Sources: Negroponte Blocks CIA Analysis of Iraq 'Civil War.'" *Harper's Magazine*, July 21, 2006.

Simons, Greg. "The Use of Rhetoric and the Mass Media in Russia's War on Terror." *Demokratizatsiya* 14 (2006): 579–600.

Singer, Peter W. "The War on Terrorism: The Big Picture." *Parameters* 34 (2004): 141–48.

Sirak, Michael. "Meeting Demands of GWOT Still a Challenge, SOF Official Says." *C4I News*, July 6, 2006.

Slater, Jerome. "Dominos in Central America: Will They Fall? Does It Matter?" *International Security* 12 (1987): 105–34.

Sly, Liz. "US General Predicts Unrest in Iraq." *The Washington Post*, November 22, 2011.

Smith, Mark A. "Russian Perspectives on Terrorism." *Conflict Studies Research Centre*, January 2004.

Smith, Steven D. "Chairman Cites Continued Progress in Afghanistan, Iraq." *American Forces Press Service*, February 17, 2006.

Smolkin, Rachel. "Media Mood Swings." *American Journalism Review*, June–July 2003.

Smolowitz, Peter. "Lack of Iraq Resistance Surprises F-16CJ Pilots." *Charlotte Observer (North Carolina)*, March 24, 2003.

Snyder, Jack. *Myths of Empire: Domestic Politics and International Ambition*. Ithaca, NY: Cornell University Press, Ithaca, 1991.

Spiegel, Peter. "All Agree Insurgents are Overwhelmingly Domestic, Sunni and Nationalist." *The Financial Times*, January 29, 2005.

Spiegel, Peter. "Why Afghan 'Surge' Isn't in the Works; Rugged Terrain and a Lack of Troops Lead the Pentagon to Consider Special Ops Teams to Zero in on Insurgents." *Los Angeles Times*, October 26, 2008.

Sprenger, Sebastian. "Edelman Sets Up Advisory Panel to Foster OSD-Joint Staff Cooperation." *Inside the Army*, November 21, 2005.

Starr, Barbara. "Iran Is the Biggest Threat to Iraq's Security Says Pentagon Official." CNN, August 16, 2011.

Stern, Seth. "From Paper to the Battlefield." *The Christian Science Monitor*, March 20, 2003.

Stevenson, Richard W. "President Makes It Clear: Phrase Is 'War on Terror.'" *The New York Times*, August 4, 2005.

Stockman, Farah. "US Intelligence Assessment on Iraq in Line with Global Reports." *The Boston Globe*, September 17, 2004.

Stolberg, Sheryl Gay. "Bush Declines to Call Situation in Iraq Civil War." *The New York Times*, November 29, 2006.

Suskind, Ron. *The Way of the World: A Story of Truth and Hope in an Age of Extremism*. New York: HarperCollins, 2008.

Swartz, Peter. "US Navy Capstone Strategies and Concepts (1970–2007) with Insights for the U.S. Navy of 2008 and Beyond." Center for Naval Analyses, 2007. http://www.jhuapl.edu/maritimestrategy/historic/swartz/Swartz_8-23-07.pdf.

Tapper, Jake. "Expert on Iraq: We're in a Civil War." ABC News, March 5, 2005.

Taylor, Stuart, Jr. "Reagan Sends Congress Four Bills Aimed at International Terrorism." *The New York Times*, April 27, 1984.

Taylor, Dan. "Kenny: Large-Diameter UUVs Already Making Their Way to the Fleet." *Inside the Navy*, February 9, 2009.

Taylor, Steven L. "When Wars Collide: The War on Drugs and the Global War on Terror." *Strategic Insights* 4 (2005). http://www.isn.ethz.ch/isn/Digital-Library/Publications/Detail/?ots591=0c54e3b3-1e9c-be1e-2c24-a6a8c7060233&lng=en&id=32276.

Tenet, George. *At the Center of the Storm: My Years at the CIA*. New York: Harper Collins, 2007.

Teves, Oliver. "Hundreds of US Construction Troops Land in Philippines to Aid Offensive against Extremists." *The Associated Press*, April 20, 2002.

Teves, Oliver. "Philippine Court OKs US Exercise." *The Associated Press Online*, April 11, 2002.

Thomas, Evan, John Barry, and Christian Caryl. "A War in the Dark." *Newsweek*, November 10, 2003.

Thomas, William I. *The Child in America*. New York: Alfred A. Knopf, 1928.

Tilghman, Andrew. "The Myth of AQI." *The Washington Monthly*, October 2007.
"Timeline: Invasion, Surge, Withdrawal; US Forces in Iraq." *Reuters*, December 15, 2011.
Tiron, Roxana. "Irregular Warfare: Counterinsurgency in Iraq Provides Template for Fighting Terrorism." *National Defense*, April 2005.
Tisdall, Simon, and Ewen MacAskill. "America's Long War." *The Guardian*, February 15, 2006.
Tomlinson, Chris. "US Executives Tour the Horn of Africa, Learn of the Terrorist Threats Ahead." *The Associated Press*, December 13, 2006.
Trager, Robert F., and Dessislava P. Zagrcheva. "Deterring Terrorism: It Can Be Done." *International Security* 30 (2005–6): 87–123.
Traynor, Ian. "US Targets al-Qaida Hideout in Georgia." *The Guardian*, February 15, 2002.
Trewhitt, Henry. "A New War—And New Risks." *US News and World Report*, April 28, 1986.
Trout, Thomas. "Rhetoric Revisited: Political Legitimation and the Cold War." *International Studies Quarterly* 19 (1975): 251–84.
Tyson, Ann Scott. "Commander in Afghanistan Wants More Troops." *The Washington Post*, October 2, 2008.
Tyson, Ann Scott. "Commanders in Iraq See 'Surge' into '08: Pentagon to Deploy 35,000 Replacement Troops." *The Washington Post*, May 9, 2007.
Tyson, Ann Scott. "Gates Criticizes Conventional Focus at Start of Iraq War." *The Washington Post*, September 30, 2008.
Tyson, Ann Scott. "Iraqi Insurgency Is Weakening Abizaid Says." *The Washington Post*, March 2, 2005.
Tyson, Ann Scott. "Rumsfeld OKs Expansive Plans for Terror Fight." *The Washington Post*, April 23, 2006.
Tyson, Ann Scott. "US Weighs Options beyond Afghanistan." *The Christian Science Monitor*, December 7, 2001.
Ucko, David. "Innovation or Inertia: The US Military and the Learning of Counterinsurgency." *Orbis* 52 (2008): 290–310.
Ullman, Harlan K., and James Wade Jr. *Shock and Awe: Achieving Rapid Dominance*. Washington, DC: National Defense University, 1996.
Ullman, Harlan K., and James P. Wade Jr. "Rapid Dominance: A Force for All Season." RUSI Whitehall Paper Series, 1998.
Ullman, Harlan K., and Mark J. Conversino. "Reply to Review. Shock and Awe." *Naval War College Review*, Spring 1999.
Ullman, Harlan K. "Shock and Awe Misunderstood." *USA Today*, April 7, 2003.
Ullman, Harlan K. "Shock and Awe Revisited," *RUSI Journal* 148, no. 3 (2003).
Ullman, Harlan K. "Slogan or Strategy?" *The National Interest* 84 (2006): 43–49.
Ullman, Harlan K. *Unfinished Business: Afghanistan, the Middle East, and Beyond—Defusing the Dangers That Threaten America's Security*. Washington, DC: Kensington Publishing Corporation, 2002.
"US Looks to Vietnam for Afghan Tips." *The Associated Press*, August 6, 2009.

Valceanu, John. "Abizaid: War on Terror Requires Patience, Perseverance." *American Forces Press Service*, February 17, 2005.

Valenzuela, Major General Alfred A. "US Army South: The Component of Choice in US Southern Command's AOR." *Army*, October 2002.

Vanden Brook, Tom, and Jim Michaels. "Questions Fill the Air As Bush Speaks on Iraq." *USA Today*, January 10, 2007.

Vanden Brook, Tom. "A 'Tough Fight' Seen for Afghan War in '09; Twice as Many Troops Needed up to 4 Years." *USA Today*, December 8, 2008.

Villanueva, Ruffy L. "RP, US Scale Down Military Exercise Due to May Polls." *Business World*, April 27, 2001.

Vincent, Steven. "Switched Off in Basra." *The New York Times*, July 31, 2005.

Vlahos, Michael. "The Long War: A Self-Fulfilling Prophecy of Protracted Conflict and Defeat." *The National Interest*, September 5, 2006.

Vogel, Steve. "Troops Parachute in to Open a New Front." *The Washington Post*, March 26, 2003.

Waller, Douglas. "Counter-Terrorism: Victim of Success?" *Newsweek*, July 5, 1993.

Wapshott, Nicholas. "US Ready to Strike at Global Terror Links." *The Times (London)*, December 3, 2001.

Weeks, Gregory. "Fighting Terrorism While Promoting Democracy: Competing Priorities in US Defense Policy toward Latin America." *Journal of Third World Studies* 23 (2006): 59–77.

Weinberg, Leonard, Ami Pedahzur, and Sivan Hirsch-Hoefler. "The Challenges of Conceptualizing Terrorism." *Terrorism and Political Violence* 16 (2004): 777–94.

Weir, Fred. "A New Terror-Front War: The Caucasus." *The Christian Science Monitor*, February 26, 2002.

Weir, Fred. "US Antiterrorist Aid to Tbilisi Rankles Russians." *The Christian Science Monitor*, March 4, 2002.

Wendle, John. "The Limits of the Surge: Petraeus' Legacy in Afghanistan." *Time*, August 8, 2011.

West, Paul. "Keeping Focus on Fighting Terror; President Warns against Letdown amid Successes." *The Baltimore Sun*, January 30, 2002.

Whaley, Floyd. "Philippines Role May Expand as US Adjusts Asia Strategy." *The New York Times*, April 30, 2012.

Wheeler, Kurtis, and Kris Stillings. "In the Republic of Georgia." *Marines Corps Gazette*, October 2006.

White, Jeffrey. "Assessing the Iraqi Insurgency (Part 1): Problems and Approaches." *The Washington Institute for Near East Policy*, March 24, 2005.

White, Josh, and Ann Scott Tyson. "Rumsfeld Offers Strategies for Current War: Pentagon to Release 20-Year Plan Today." *The Washington Post*, February 3, 2006.

Whitlock, Craig. "Proxy Fight in Africa Heats Up." *The Washington Post*, November 25, 2011.

Whittle, Richard. "Does Iraq Look a Lot Like Germany? Postwar Comparisons Are Many and Inevitable—and Sometimes They're Accurate." *Dallas Morning News*, October 12, 2003.

Whitworth, Damian. "US Names the 'Rogue States.'" *The Times (London)*, November 20, 2001.
Williams, Carol. "Increasingly, the Bombers Are Iraqis Instead of Foreign Infiltrators. Civilians and Police, Not GIs, Are the Prime Targets." *Los Angeles Times*, June 2, 2005.
Wills, David C. *The First War on Terrorism: Counter-Terrorism Policy during the Reagan Administration*. Lanham, MD: Rowman and Littlefield, 2003.
Wilson, Isaiah, III. "What Kind of War?" February 4, 2005. http://thinkbeyondwar.com/Documents/What_Kind_of_War.pdf.
Wilson, Gregory. "Anatomy of a Successful COIN Operation: OEF-Philippines and the Indirect Approach." *Military Review*, November–December 2006.
Wilson, Scott, and Al Kamen. "Global War on Terror Is Given New Name." *The Washington Post*, March 25, 2009.
Wilson, Scott, and Sewell Chan. "As Insurgency Grew, So Did Prison Abuse: Needing Intelligence, US Pressed Detainees." *The Washington Post*, May 10, 2004.
Winograd, Erin. "Pentagon Spending Counter-Narcotics Money to Fight War on Terror." *Inside the Army*, February 17, 2003.
Wiseman, Paul. "In Philippines, US Making Progress in War on Terror." *USA Today*, February 13, 2007.
Wolfowitz, Paul. "Iraq at the Center of the War on Terrorism." *The Wall Street Journal*, September 2, 2003.
Wong, Edward. "A Matter of Definition: What Makes a Civil War, and Who Declares It So?" *The New York Times*, November 26, 2006.
Woods, Kevin M., Michael R. Pease, Mark E. Stout. *The Iraqi Perspectives Report: Saddam's Senior Leadership on Operation Iraqi Freedom*. Annapolis: US Naval Institute Press, 2006.
Woodward, Bob. *Bush at War*. New York: Simon and Schuster, 2002.
Woodward, Bob. *Plan of Attack*. London: Simon and Schuster, 2004.
Woodward, Bob. *State of Denial: Bush at War Part III*. New York: Simon and Schuster, 2006.
Woodward, Bob. *The War Within: A Secret White House History 2006–2008*. New York: Simon and Schuster, 2008.
Woodward, Bob. *Veil: The Secret Wars of the CIA 1981–1987*. New York: Simon and Schuster, 1990.
Wright, Donald P., and Timothy R. Reese. *On Point II: Transition to the New Campaign: The United States Army in Operation IRAQI FREEDOM, May 2003–January 2005*. Defense Department, US Army Combined Arms Center, Combat Studies Institute, Ft. Leavenworth, KS, 2008.
Wright, Ronald. "From the Desk of Donald Rumsfeld," *Washington Post*, November 1, 2007.
Zabriskie, Phil. "Picking a Fight; The U.S. Takes Its War on Terrorism to the Philippines. But Is It Taking on the Right Bad Guys?" *Time International*, February 25, 2002.
Žižek, Slavoj. "What Rumsfeld Doesn't Know That He Knows about Abu Ghraib." *In These Times*, May 21, 2004.1.

Index

Abizaid, John, 32–34, 38–39, 73–74, 115, 122–23, 131, 134, 136, 140, 142, 145, 182n124
Abrams, Creighton, 14–11
Abu Ghraib, 120–21
Abu Nidal Organization, 27
Abu Sayyaf Group (ASG), 62–65
"the adversary," and Iraq, 107–28, 144
   and anti-Iraqi forces, 117–18
   and dead-enders, 111–17
   and death squads, 108–11
   and foreign fighters, 119–24
   and former regime elements, 111–17
   and liberation versus occupation, 127–28
   and Shiite militias, 124–27
   and terrorists, 119–24
adversary characterizations, 107, 144
Afghanistan war (2001–present), 18, 20–22, 28–29, 32–36, 38, 40–49, 52, 54–57, 60–63, 65, 67–69, 72–78, 88–89, 120, 147–48, 151–65, 167–68, 171–73, 180n74
   See Afghan surge
Afghan surge, 154–60
   criticism of, 156–58
   proponents of, 158–60
   and the success narrative, 154–56
AFP. *See* Armed Forces of the Philippines
Africa, 28, 40, 46–47, 51, 68, 72–77, 120, 165
Africa Command (AFRICOM), 77
AFRICOM. *See* Africa Command
Ahl al-Haq, 127
Al Askari Mosque (Samarra) (2006), 135–37
al-Dulaymi, Al-Halbusi, 116
Algeria, 72, 75–76
Algerian Salafist Group for Prayer and Combat (GSPC), 75, 77

Allawi, Iyad, 136
al-Qaeda, 4, 17, 19, 21, 28–29, 31–36, 38, 41, 43, 45, 58, 61–62, 65–69, 72–75, 77, 88, 108, 119–21, 123, 126, 138, 158–59, 168–69
al-Qaeda al-Jihad, 168
Al-Qaeda Associated Movement (AQAM), 45–46
Al-Qaeda in the Arabian Peninsula (AQAP), 77
Al-Qaeda in the Islamic Maghreb (AQIM), 77
al-Qaida in Iraq (AQI), 121–24, 127, 145, 154, 164
al-Sadr, Moqtadr, 125–26
al Shabaab, 77
Alston, Donald, 140
al-Zarqawi, Abu Mussab, 121–22, 145
American Enterprise Institute (AEI), 150
Amos, Jim T., 110
Anaconda strategy, 162
Anbar Awakening, 152
Anbar Province, 117, 150–52
Ansar al-Islam, 46
anticoalition forces, 117–18
anti-Iraqi forces, 108, 117–18, 138, 144
AQAM. *See* Al-Qaeda Associated Movement
AQAP. *See* Al-Qaeda in the Arabian Peninsula
AQI. *See* al-Qaida in Iraq
AQIM. *See* Al-Qaeda in the Islamic Maghreb
Arendt, Hannah, 15
Argentina, 69, 71
Armed Forces of the Philippines (AFP), 62, 64
Arroyo, Gloria, 62–64

ASG. *See* Abu Sayyaf Group
Axis of Evil, 170

Ba'ath party, 94, 100–101, 111–13
Baghdad's fall, 82, 105, 110, 115,
    119–20, 143–45
Balikatan (shoulder-to-shoulder), 63
bandits, 128
bandwagoning, 10
Basilan Island, 64
Basra, 125
Betts, Richard K., 12
Biddle, Stephen, 101
Biden, Joseph, 136–37, 157, 164–65
Bin Laden, Osama, 28–29, 67, 121, 165, 168
Blair, Dennis, 62–63
Block III Tomahawk Land Attack Cruise Missile, 94
blowback, 9–10
Blue Sky paper, 29
body counts, 14, 140–41
Boko Haram, 77
Boot, Max, 103
Boyd, John, 95
Boykin, William, 22
Brazil, 69, 71
Bremer, Paul, 116, 132
Brooks, Vincent, 109–10
Brown, Harold, 87
brown-water capabilities, 50
Buchanan, Jeffrey, 124, 127
Buddhist crisis (1963), 13
Burkina Faso, 77
Burridge, Brian, 95–96
Bush, George H. W., 27–28, 35
Bush, George W., 18, 20, 23–24, 31–33,
    35–39, 41, 44, 52, 54, 58, 62–63,
    65, 67, 70–71, 88, 91–92, 111,
    113, 119–20, 128, 131, 135–37,
    140–41, 143, 148–52, 157–58, 164
Bush Doctrine, 62

Cable, Larry, 14
Cambone, Steve, 37, 139–40
Carlucci, Frank C., 87
Carter, Jimmy, 25
Casey, George, 126, 133, 143, 148–49,
    152–53

Cebrowski, Arthur K., 84
Cell for Submarine Counterterrorism
    Operations, 40–41, 50
CENTAF. *See* Central Command Air
    Force component
CENTCOM. *See* Central Command
Center for Expeditionary
    Counterterrorism Operations, 51
Center for Special Operations, 46
Central African Republic, 77
Central Command (CENTCOM),
    28–29, 36, 38–39, 41, 46, 66, 70,
    72–74, 76–77, 82, 84, 88–97, 103,
    109–10, 113–15, 118, 120, 123
Central Command Air Force component
    (CENTAF), 118
Central Intelligence Agency (CIA), 12,
    14–15, 27, 29, 32–33, 116, 120,
    129–31, 140–41
CIA Near East Division, 131
Chad, 75
Chalabi, Ahmad, 92
characterizing the Iraq war
    and the adversary (*see* "the adversary," and Iraq)
    and the conflict (*see* "the conflict," and Iraq)
Chechens, 67
"Checkmate" (US Air Force), 48
Cheek, Gary, 23
Chiarelli, Peter, 135
Chief of Naval Operations (CNO),
    48–49, 53
"China threat," 17, 47, 50, 66, 173
Church III, Albert, 49
Churchill, Winston, 13
Civil Operations and Rural Development
    Support program, 15
civil unrest, 132
civil war, 107, 128, 135–38, 145
CJTF-HOA. *See* Combined Joint Task
    Force—Horn of Africa
Clancy, Tom, 84
Clark, Vern, 48
Clarke, Richard, 29
Clarke, Victoria, 109
classic guerrilla war, 145
Clausewitz, Carl von, 8, 16
Clinton, William Jefferson, 8, 27–28, 30–31

CNN, 87
CNO. *See* Chief of Naval Operations
Coalition Provisional Authority (CPA), 111, 132
Cohen, William, 28–29, 87–88
COINdinistas, 155
Coker, Christopher, 106
Cold War, 7, 11–12, 21, 25, 37, 47–48, 50–51, 53–54, 78, 128, 171
Coleman, John, 118
Colombia, 34, 45, 61, 69–72, 74, 78, 110
Combined Air Operations Center at Prince Sultan Air Base (Saudi Arabia), 95
Combined Joint Task Force—Horn of Africa (CJTF-HOA), 73–76
communist terrorists, 128, 171
Comoros, 74
Concept of Operations Plan (CONPLAN)
 "0500," 59
 "2002," 59
 "7500," 46
Concerned Local Citizens, 152
 See Sons of Iraq
"the conflict," and Iraq, 128–38
 and civil war, 135–38
 and "conflict," 128
 and guerrilla war, 129–34
 and insurgency, 129–34
 and sectarian violence, 135–38
CONPLAN. *See* Concept of Operations Plan
constituted government, 129–30
constructing the Global War on Terrorism (GWOT), 60–79
 and Africa, 72–77
 and Georgia, 66–68
 and the Philippines, 61–66
 and South America, 68–72
Conversino, Mark, 85
Conway, James T., 38, 118
Cordesman, Anthony, 121, 137, 142
Council of Colonels, 40, 137
counterinsurgency (COIN), 3, 14, 17, 22–23, 51, 62, 64, 104, 121, 129–33, 135, 138, 143, 145–46, 147–48, 151–56, 158–59, 162, 165

counternarcotics, 70
Cox, Michael, 31
CPA. *See* Coalition Provisional Authority
Crane, Conrad, 20
Crocker, Ryan, 161
Crowder, Gary, 96–97
Csrnko, Thomas, 75
Cuba, 21–22

Dailey, Dell, 46
DART. *See* Defense Adaptive Red Team
dead-enders, 108, 111–17, 143–44
death squads, 108–11, 126, 135–36, 138
Deep Blue, 48–49
Defense Adaptive Red Team (DART), 45
Defense Advanced Research Projects Agency, 41
Defense Group Inc. (DGI), 82
Defense Intelligence Agency (DIA), 27, 41, 113, 116–17, 120, 126, 136–37, 140–41
Defreitas, John, 125
DeLong, Michael, 103
Delta Force (US Army), 25
"democracy," 12–13, 40
Dempsey, Martin, 118
Department of Defense Global War on Terrorism Campaign Plan, 46
 See "7500": Concept of Operations Plan (CONPLAN)
Department of Homeland Security, 57–60
DGI. *See* Defense Group Inc.
Dictionary of Military and Associated Terms, 129, 134
Diem, Ngo Dinh, 13
Di Rita, Lawrence, 38, 140
discourse and the Global War on Terrorism (GWOT), 24–41
 and the first war on terrorism, 25–27
 and general observations of pre-9/11 wars on terrorism, 30–31
 from GWOT to Long War, 36–41
 and limiting the GWOT, 35–36
 and the second war on terrorism, 27–29
 and the third war on terrorism, 31–35

discourse trap, 1–16, 18, 23, 36, 42, 81, 119, 145, 163, 168–74
 and bandwagoning, 10
 and blowback, 9–10
 and entrapment, 11–15
 and historical precedents, 11–15
 and marginalization, 10–11
 types of, 9–11, 170
Djibouti, 45, 73, 77
domino theory, 5
Dora Farms complex, 99
drawdown discourse, 148–50
DUSD-ASC. *See* Office of the Deputy Undersecretary of Defense for Advanced Systems and Concepts

Echevarria, Antulio J., 172–73
Edelman, Eric, 157
Edney, Leon, 82, 84–85
Effects Based Operations (EBO), 81–82, 85–86, 89, 95–97, 104, 171
Egyptian Islamic Jihad, 31–32, 46
Eisenhower, Dwight D., 54
El Salvador, 110
emergency funds, 54–56
"enemies of the legitimate Iraqi government," 132
England, Gordon, 55
Eritrea, 73–74
escalation (1965), 168
Ethiopia, 72–73, 77
EUCOM. *See* US European Command
EUCOM AOR, 66
Every Man a Tiger (Clancy), 84
extremism, 74
extremists, 122–23

Fallujah, battle for (2004), 114, 118, 122, 140, 143
FARC. *See* Fuerzas Armadas Revolucionarias de Colombia
Fedayeen Saddam, 100, 108–10, 112–13
Feith, Douglas, 4, 21–22, 32–33, 44, 69, 127
First Gulf War, 82–84, 100, 102
First Marine Expeditionary Force (I MEF), 100, 117–18
FM. *See* US Army-Marine Corps Counterinsurgency Field Manual (FM)

foreign fighters, 119–24
former regime elements (FRE), 108, 111–17, 122–23, 144
former regime loyalists, 112
Foster, John, 86
Franks, Fred, 82
Franks, Tommy, 73, 82–83, 88–89, 91–93, 96, 98
FRE. *See* former regime elements
Freedman, Lawrence, 108
Fuerzas Armadas Revolucionarias de Colombia (FARC), 45, 69–72, 74, 78

Gates, Robert, 51–52, 104, 106, 149, 157, 165
Gelb, Leslie, 12
genocide, 8
Gentile, Gian, 155–56
Georgia, 36, 40, 66–68, 72
Georgia Deployment Program (EUCOM), 68
Georgia Sustainment and Stability Operations Program, 68
Georgia Train and Equip (GTEP), 66–68
Ghormley, Timothy, 73
Gingrich, Newt, 87
global counterinsurgency, 17, 22–23
global insurgency, 22–23, 45–46, 178
Global Struggle against Violent Extremism (GSAVE), 37–38, 40, 79
Global War on Terrorism (GWOT), 2, 17–79
 and Africa, 72–77
 constructing the (*see* constructing the GWOT)
 criticism of, 19–24
 and discourse (*see* discourse and the GWOT)
 institutionalizing (*see* institutionalizing the GWOT)
 limiting the, 35–36
 and the Long War, 36–41
 and the US Navy, 47–53
Goldwater-Nichols Act (1986), 47
Greene, Philip, 51
green-water capabilities, 50
Greenwood, Thomas, 137
GSAVE. *See* Global Struggle against Violent Extremism

GSPC. *See* Algerian Salafist Group for Prayer and Combat
GTEP. *See* Georgia Train and Equip
Guantanamo Bay, 69, 70, 121
Guernica (Picasso), 102
guerrilla war, 107, 129–35
Guevara, Che, 131
GWOT. *See* Global War on Terrorism

Hadley, Stephen, 40
Haiti, 40
Hamas, 34, 69–71
Hammes, Thomas X., 130
Hamre, John, 58
Harvey, Derek, 113
Hashim, Ahmed, 111–12
Hathaway, David, 95
"hearts and minds," 49, 63, 73, 152, 154
Helland, Samuel, 74
Henry, Ryan, 39, 45–46
Hezbollah, 34, 69–72
High Collateral Damage, 95
Hill, James T., 69–71
Hiroshima, 83, 97, 105
Hix, William, 125, 133
Holbrooke, Richard C., 167
Holsti, Ole, 5
homeland defense, 58
homeland security, 58–59
Homeland Security Directorate, 59
Horner, Charles ("Chuck"), 82–85, 91
Horn of Africa, 40, 51, 72–74
hostage rescue, 25
"How and Where to Apply Shock and Awe" (Horner), 91
Howe, Jonathan, 82
Hoyt, Timothy, 24
humanitarian assistance, 19
Hurricane Katrina, 40
Hussein, Qusay, 111
Hussein, Saddam, 89–90, 92, 95, 99–101, 108–17, 119, 126
Hussein, Uday, 111

ICBMs. *See* Intercontinental Ballistic Missiles
ideology, 6
Indonesia, 46, 61

Infinite Reach. *See* Operation Infinite Reach
Infinite Resolve. *See* Operation Infinite Resolve
information warfare, 17
institutionalizing the Global War on Terrorism (GWOT), 41–60
  and defending the homeland, 57–60
  and the defense budget, 53–56
  and the US Navy, 47–53
insurgency, 107, 113–14, 128–34, 139–45, 148–49
insurgency metrics, 139–43
insurgents, 132, 136
Intercontinental Ballistic Missiles (ICBMs), 60
Iran, 22, 39–40, 72, 124–27, 171
Iranian Revolutionary Guard Corps (IRGC), 72
Iraq, bombing of (1993), 27–28
Iraqi Intelligence Service (Mukhabarat), 113, 116
Iraqi National Congress, 92
Iraq Room, 139
"Iraq Status Brief," 139
Iraq Study Group, 149
Iraq War (2003–2011)
  characterizing (*see* characterizing the Iraq War)
  and conventional phase of operations, 104, 132
  See Shock and Awe; "the surge"
"Iraq War Logs" (Wikileaks), 118
"Iraq Weekly Update," 139
IRGC. *See* Iranian Revolutionary Guard Corps
"Irregular Adversary in Iraq," 2, 107–46
  and characterizing the adversary, 108–28
  and characterizing the conflict, 128–38
  and insurgency metrics, 139–43
irregular warfare, 50–53, 104
Irregular Warfare Office on the Navy Staff, 51
Islamic extremism, 22, 39
Islamic Movement of Uzbekistan, 31
Islamist ideology, 22, 38–39, 60, 69, 72, 74, 76, 123
Islamiyya al Gammat, 69

Jackson, Richard, 24, 120–21
Jama'at al-Tawhid w'al-Jihad (Unity and Jihad Group) (TWJ), 121, 169
Jama'at I'Adat al-Khilafat al-Rashida (Restoration of the Caliphate Group), 168
JCS dictionary (Joint Publication–1), 130–31
Jemaah Islamiya (JI), 46, 62–63
JFCOM. *See* US Joint Forces Command
JI. *See* Jemaah Islamiyah
jihadist, 121–22
Johnson, Lyndon, 12–14, 167–68
Joint Intelligence Task Force-Counterterrorism (Defense Intelligence Agency), 41
Joint Interagency Task Force-Former Regime Elements, 113
Joint Operational Concept for Defeating Terrorist Organizations, 23, 46
Joint Special Operations Command, 26
Joint Special Operations Task Force-Philippines (JSOTF-P), 64–66
Joint Staff (J-5), 32, 34–35, 38, 41, 43, 59, 178n29
Joint Staff Director of Operations (J-3), 38
Joint Task Force–510, 64
Joint Task Force-6, 59
Joint Task Force for Civil Support, 59
Jones, James, 74
Journal of Strategic Studies, 22
JSOTF-P. *See* Joint Special Operations Task Force-Philippines
Jumper, John, 59

Kabul, fall of (2001), 20
Karbala gap, 100
Karnow, Stanley, 167
Kataib Hezbollah, 127
Keane, Jack, 130
Keegan, John, 103–4
Kelly, David, 50–51
Kenny, Mark, 51
Kenya, 73, 77
Khan, Genghis, 91
Khobar Towers attack (1996), 27
Khong, Yuen Foong, 5–6
Kilcullen, David, 22
Kimmitt, Mark, 114, 117

Komer, Robert, 15
Kosiak, Stephen, 54
Kosovo war, 87
Kurds, 90, 93
Kuster, Tom, 70
Kuusisto, Riikka, 8
Kuwait, 83

"language of power," 170
Lawrence, T. E., 141
Lebanon, 34, 104
Lebanon war (2006), 104
liberation versus occupation, 127–28
Liberia, 40
Libya, 21–22, 26–28
  and 1986 attack, 27–28
Linn, Brian M., 36
Long War, 23, 36–41
Lord's Resistance Army (LRA), 74, 77
loyalist, 112
LRA. *See* Lord's Resistance Army
Luck, Gary, 82, 84–85, 91
Lute, Douglas, 39, 159
Luti, William, 33

M-14, 116–17
Maguire, John, 131
Mahdi Army, 125–26, 138, 144
Mahon, Michael, 49
Makers of Modern Strategy (Shy and Collier), 1
Malaya, 128, 171
Malaysia, 131
Mali, 72, 75
Maples, Michael, 136
marginalization, 10–11
Marshall, Andrew, 86
Martin, David, 97
Marxist-Leninist ideology, 69
Mattis, J. N., 104, 110
Mauritania, 75, 77
McCaffrey, Barry, 102
McCain, John, 112
McChrystal, Stanley, 151, 159–61, 167
McCullough, Barry, 53
McKiernan, David, 109, 157–59
McMaster, H. R., 130
Merton, Robert K., 2
Metz, Steven, 153–54

Mikolashek, Paul, 93
MILF. *See* Moro Islamic Liberation Front
Military Assistance Command-Vietnam (MACV), 14
militias, 126
Milosevic, Slobodan, 87
MNC-I. *See* Multinational Corps-Iraq
MNF-I. *See* Multinational Forces-Iraq
Morgan, Tom, 82
Morgenthau, Hans, 13
Morocco, 75–76
Moro Islamic Liberation Front (MILF), 62–63
Morrell, Geoff, 157–58
Moseley, Michael, 103
Mukhabarat. *See* Iraqi Intelligence Service
Mullen, Mike, 49, 161
Multinational Corps-Iraq (MNC-I), 114
Multinational Forces-Iraq (MNF-I), 113, 121–26, 132–33, 140–41, 148–49
Multinational Forces-Iraq Combined Intelligence Operations Center, 132
Munns, Chuck, 50
Myers, Richard, 21, 37–38, 43, 59, 63, 97–98, 103, 105, 109, 130

N5–War on Terrorism (N5WoT) (US Navy), 41–42, 49
N5WoT. *See* N5–War on Terrorism
Nagasaki, 83, 105, 198n15
Nagl, John, 156
Najaf, 101, 125
narco-terrorism, 70
Nash, William L., 102, 138
Nasiriyah, 101
National Capital Region, 57
National Defense University (NDU), 82–86
National Military Strategic Plan for the War on Terrorism (NMSP-WOT), 35, 40, 42–47
National Press Club, 39
National Security Council (NSC), 33, 43–44, 68–69, 92, 119, 131, 140, 149–50, 162
National Security Presidential Directive-18, 70
National Security Presidential Directive-46/Homeland Security Presidential Directive-15, 44

National Strategy for Victory in Iraq (NSV-I) (2005), 112, 114, 119–20, 125
National War College, 87
NATO. *See* North Atlantic Treaty Organization
Natonski, Richard, 118
Naval Operations Group. *See* Deep Blue
Naval War College Review, 85
Navy Expeditionary Combat Command (NECC), 49–50, 52–53
Navy War College, 84
Nazi dead-enders, 115–16
NDU. *See* National Defense University
NECC. *See* Navy Expeditionary Combat Command
Nelson, Victor, 76
network-centric warfare, 17, 89
Neumann, Peter, 4
New People's Army, 62–63, 65
Nicaragua, 110
Niger, 75
Nigeria, 76
9/11. *See* September 11, 2011
NMSP-WOT. *See* National Military Strategic Plan for the War on Terrorism
North Atlantic Treaty Organization (NATO), 66–67, 156
NORTHCOM. *See* US Northern Command
Northern Alliance, 29, 88
North Korea, 21–22, 170
NSV-I. *See* National Strategy for Victory in Iraq

Obama, Barack, 18, 23–24, 41, 51–52, 56, 61, 66, 72, 77, 79, 124, 156–61, 163–64, 167–68
occupation versus liberation, 127–28
OCO. *See* Overseas Contingency Operations
Odierno, Raymond, 39, 120, 126, 134, 137, 153
Odum, Wesley, 112
OEF. *See* Operation Enduring Freedom
OEF-TS. *See* Operation Enduring Freedom-Trans Sahara
Office of the Deputy Undersecretary of Defense for Advanced Systems and Concepts (DUSD-ASC), 44–45

Index

Office of Force Transformation, 84
Office of Homeland Defense, 59
Office of Management and Budget, 56
Office of Net Assessment (ONA), 86
Office of Strategic Influence, 45
Omar, Mullah, 88, 112
Operation Active Endeavour, 48
Operational Concept "Velocity," 92–93
Operation Desert Fox, 94
Operation Desert Scorpion, 111
Operation Desert Storm, 83, 93, 105
Operation El Dorado Canyon, 26, 30
Operation Enduring Freedom (OEF), 54–55, 57, 63–64, 73, 76
  OEF-Afghanistan, 63
  OEF-Philippines, 63–64, 76
  OEF-Trans Sahara, 76
Operation Infinite Reach, 28, 30
Operation Infinite Resolve, 28–29
Operation Iraqi Freedom, 54, 91, 106, 120
Operation Iron Sabre, 118
Operation Noble Eagle, 54, 57
Operation Peninsula Strike, 111
Operation Rolling Thunder III, 85
Operation Southern Focus, 94
Operation Southern Watch, 94
Operation Together Forward, 126
OPLAN 1003–98, 91
OPLAN 1003V ("Generated Start"), 90–92
O'Rourke, Ronald, 50
Overseas Contingency Operations (OCO), 18, 41, 54, 56, 79, 165
overstretch, 20

Pace, Peter, 39, 71, 136, 140
PACOM. *See* US Pacific Command
Pakistan, 21–22, 61, 74, 76, 124, 158–59, 167
Panetta, Leon, 72
Pankisi Gorge, Georgia, 66–68
Pan-Sahel Initiative (PSI), 40, 72–73, 75–76
Pape, Robert, 88
Paraguay, 69, 71
Peters, Ralph, 102
Petraeus, David, 124, 150–64
  the Petraeus Doctrine. *See* US Army-Marine Corps Counterinsurgency Field Manual (FM) 3–24

"Petraeus Report," 152
Philippines, 34, 36, 40, 45, 47, 61–66, 72, 76, 131
Policy Counterterrorism Evaluation Group (Office of the Secretary of Defense), 41, 69
population-centric tactics, 152–55, 161
Powell, Colin, 68–69
Predator, 94
preemption, 19
prevention, 19
Proceedings (US Navy publication), 50

QDR. *See* Quadrennial Defense Review
QJBR. *See* Tanzim Qa'idat Al-Jihad in Bilad al-Rafidayn Organization
Quadrennial Defense Review (QDR), 39–40, 49, 51–52, 58, 74, 87–88

radical Islam, 22
Ralston, Joseph, 67
Ramstein Airbase, 92
Rapid Dominance, 82–88, 91, 99
"Rapid Dominance: A Force for all Seasons" (book), 86
"Rapid Dominance: A Strategic Roadmap for Fielding and Testing an Experimental Rapid Dominance Force" (report), 86
Reagan, Ronald, 18, 24–27, 30
Record, Jeffrey, 13–14
regime death squads, 110
Regional Defense Counterterrorism Fellowship Program (DoD), 71
Reid, Harry, 136
Reider, Bruce, 138
Renuart, Gene, 110
"republican," 110
Republican Guard, 100
resistance movement, 132
Revolution in Military Affairs (RMA), 17, 81–82, 87, 92–93, 105–6, 171
Rhame, Thomas G., 102
Rice, Condoleeza, 115, 136
Rice, Wesley, 26
Richer, Rob, 131
Ricks, Thomas, 121
RMA. *See* Revolution in Military Affairs
Roberts, James, 22

Rodman, Peter, 32–33
rogue states, 17
Rostow, Walt, 14–15
Roughead, Gary, 52
Royal Navy, 33
Rumsfeld, Donald, 4, 19–22, 31–40,
　　42–47, 58–59, 62–63, 67, 69, 71,
　　73, 79, 82, 84, 87–89, 91–92, 94,
　　98, 102–03, 105, 108–09, 112–16,
　　119, 122, 129–35, 137, 139–40,
　　145, 149–50
RUSI Journal, 85–86
Russia-Georgia war (2008), 68
Rwanda (1994), 8

Saharan Africa, 46, 75
Sahel, 75–76
Salafist Group for Preaching and Combat
　　in Saharan Africa, 46
Sattler, John, 118
Saudi Arabia, 21–22, 95
Schlesinger, James R., 87
School of Advanced Air and Space
　　Studies, 85
Schoomaker, Peter, 40
Schultz, George, 26
"Sea Power 21" (Navy 2020 vision
　　statement), 48–49
sectarian violence, 107, 128, 135–38
self-fulfilling prophecy, 1–2
Sepp, Kalev, 123, 133
Seychelles, 74, 77
shamal, 99–100
Shelton, Hugh, 28
Shevardnadze, Eduard, 67
Shiite Al Askari Mosque (Samarra),
　　135–36
Shiites, 45, 108–13, 123–27, 136, 138,
　　141, 143–44, 153, 150, 153–54
Shock and Awe, 2, 81–106
　　creation and dissemination of, 82–89
　　targets, 100
　　and war and aftermath, 98–104
　　and war planning, 89–98
"Shock and Awe: Achieving Rapid
　　Dominance" (NDU publication), 82
Sky, Emma, 137, 144
Slocombe, Walter, 28–29
Smith, Greg, 124

Smith, Leighton, 87
Smith, M. L. R., 4
Snow, Tony, 136
Snyder, Jack, 12
SOCEUR. *See* Special Operations
　　Command-Europe
SOCOM. *See* Special Operations
　　Command
Somalia, 34, 61, 73–74, 77
"Some Thoughts for CINCs as They
　　Prepare Plans" (Rumsfeld), 33–34
Sons of Iraq, 123–24, 152, 157, 162
South America, 68–72
SOUTHCOM. *See* US Southern
　　Command
Special National Intelligence Estimate
　　11/2-81, 27
Special Operations Command
　　(SOCOM), 46
Special Operations Command-Europe
　　(SOCEUR), 75–76
Special Republican Guards, 101, 113
Special Security Organization, 113
stability operations, 19
State Department, 27, 33, 56, 75
Stavridis, James, 72
Steiner, Rick, 23
"Strategic Guidance for the Campaign
　　against Terrorism" (document), 35
"Strategic Thoughts" (document), 34
"Strategy for Homeland Defense and
　　Civil Support" (June 2005), 59
success narrative, 154–56
Sudan, 21–22, 28, 34, 48, 61, 73
Sunni Arab rejectionist, 114, 125, 141, 144
Sunni Awakening, 162
Sunni insurgency, 123–26, 141–44, 154
Sunni-Islamic extremism, 39
Sunni Triangle, 113
"Supporting Homeland Defense" (White
　　Paper), 58
"the surge," 2, 138, 147–66
　　and the Afghan surge, 154–63
　　and drawdown, 148–50
　　overview of, 147–48
　　and success, 150–54
　　and the success narrative, 154–56
surge brigades, 151–52
Syria, 21–22, 85, 123–24

Taifat al-Tawheed Wal-Jihad (Monotheism and Jihad Group), 168
Tal Afar operation (2005), 140
Taliban, 29, 33, 35, 88, 112, 157, 161–63
Tallent, Hamlin, 74–75
Tanzania, 74
Tanzim Qa'idat Al-Jihad in Bilad al-Rafidayn (Organization of Jihad's Base in the Country of the Two Rivers) (QJBR), 121
Tarnak Farms, 28
Task Force Tarawa, 110
terrorism, 27, 37, 67, 74, 119–24
Terrorism Information Awareness (Defense Advanced Research Projects Agency), 41
Tet Offensive (1968), 15
Thomas, William Isaac, 7
Total Information Awareness (Defense Advanced Research Projects Agency), 41
"Toward a More Aggressive Counterterrorism Posture" (memo), 29
transformation, 20
Trans-Sahara Counter Terrorism Program (TSCTP), 76
Tunisia, 75–76
"Twenty-first Century Warfighting" (symposium) (1998), 84
TWJ. *See* Jamaat al-Tawhid w'al-Jihad

UAV. *See* Unmanned Aerial Vehicles
Uganda, 74, 77
Ullman, Harlan K., 82–88, 97, 99–100, 102–3
unconventional war, 134
Unmanned Aerial Vehicles (UAV), 60
uprising, 132
US Air Force, 48, 55–59, 81–82, 84–85, 92, 96, 98, 118
  F-22 air-to-air fighter, 55
  School of Advanced Airpower Studies, 85
US Army, 15, 20, 23, 25, 36, 40, 47, 50–51, 55–60, 70, 82, 87–88, 93, 99–102, 109–10, 116–17, 120, 123, 129–35, 138, 140, 152, 155, 165

82nd Airborne Division, 117
902nd Military Intelligence Group, 60
Comanche helicopter, 55
F-35 Joint Strike Fighter, 55
Stryker combat vehicle, 55
Training and Doctrine Command, 58
V Corps, 100–101, 109, 112
VII Corps, 82
US Army-Marine Corps Counterinsurgency Field Manual (FM), 3–24, 152–55, 161
US Army South, 70
US Army Special Forces, 132
US Army War College, 101
US Civil War, 137
US Congress, 20, 31, 53–54, 56, 59, 64, 67, 70–71, 101, 112, 116–17, 123, 137, 152, 171
US embassy bombings (1998), 28
US European Command (EUCOM), 66–68, 72–76
US House Armed Services Committee, 139–40
US Joint Forces Command (JFCOM), 59, 96, 104
US Marine Corps, 26, 47–48, 50–51, 55, 82, 93, 99–100, 110, 117–18, 140, 152, 156
  Counterinsurgency Field Manual (FM) 3–24, 152
  V-22 tilt-rotor aircraft, 55
US National Guard, 57
US Naval Forces Europe, 82
US Navy, 33, 41–42, 47–53, 55, 57–58, 60, 82, 84
  and the GWOT, 47–53
  See N5–War on Terrorism
"The US Navy's Vision for Confronting Irregular Challenges" (document), 52
US Northern Command (NORTHCOM), 58–59
US Pacific Command (PACOM), 61–62, 64–66
US presidential election (2008), 156
USS Cole, 29–30
USS Mount Whitney, 73
US Southern Command (SOUTHCOM), 59, 69–70

US Special Forces, 23, 27, 30–32, 41, 46, 53, 61, 63, 73, 77, 90, 92, 132, 151–54, 159, 165–66, 180n74
US Special Operations Command, 23
USSR, 47

VC/NVA. *See* Viet Cong/North Vietnamese Army
Venezuelan Margarita Island, 69–70
Vessey, John, 26
Viet Cong insurgency, 13–15
Viet Cong/North Vietnamese Army (VC/NVA), 15
Viet Cong order of battle (O/B), 14–15
Viet Cong Self-Defense Forces, 14
Vietnam, 5, 11–15, 25–26, 130, 132, 139–40, 143, 151, 167–68
Vines, John, 114
violent extremism, 37
violent extremists, 21, 40

Wade, James P., Jr., 82–86, 91, 99–100
Wald, Charles F., 74
Wallace, William, 109–10, 132–33
"war," 21
Warden, John, 95–96
war of choice, 42
War on Drugs, 27, 68–70, 78

war on terror, 19–27, 31, 36, 38, 64, 73–74, 78, 119, 158, 165, 171–73
war on terrorism, 24, 27, 33, 41–52, 58, 70–71, 75–77, 119, 121, 158
War Studies, 1–2, 16, 169–74
weapons of mass destruction (WMD), 31
Weinberger, Caspar, 25–26
Werewolf analogy, 115
"What Are We Fighting? Is It a Global War on Terror?" (Rumsfeld), 37
"What Will Be the Military Role in the War on Terrorism?" (Rumsfeld), 32
Whelan, Theresa, 73
Whitehall paper series (RUSI), 128
Wikileaks, 118
Wilson III, Isaiah, 129–30
WMD. *See* weapons of mass destruction
Wolfowitz, Paul, 3, 4, 33, 67, 70, 84, 89, 91–92, 103–05, 108, 115–17, 119, 132–33
World Trade Center bombing (1993), 27
World War II, 11, 21, 54, 115

Yemen, 29, 61, 73, 124

Zakheim, Dov, 33, 70
Zarqawi, Abu Mussab al-, 121–22, 145
Zinni, Anthony, 28–29
Žižek, Slavoj, 6

Printed in the United States of America